weird sex & snowshoes

weird sex &
snowshoes

and other Canadian film phenomena

Katherine Monk

RAINCOAST BOOKS
www.raincoast.com

First published in 2001 by

Raincoast Books
9050 Shaughnessy Street
Vancouver, B.C.
CANADA
V6P 6E5

www.raincoast.com

1 2 3 4 5 6 7 8 9 10

NATIONAL LIBRARY OF CANADA CATALOGUING IN PUBLICATION DATA

Monk, Katherine, 1965–
Weird sex & snowshoes

Includes bibliographical references and index.
ISBN 1-55192-474-9

1. Motion pictures–Canada. I. Title.
PN1993.5.C3M66 2001   791.43'0971   C2001-910861-3

THE CANADA COUNCIL | LE CONSEIL DES ARTS
FOR THE ARTS | DU CANADA
SINCE 1957 | DEPUIS 1957

Raincoast Books gratefully acknowledges the support of the Government of Canada, through the Book Publishing Industry Development Program, the Canada Council for the Arts and the Department of Canadian Heritage. We also acknowledge the assistance of the Province of British Columbia, through the British Columbia Arts Council.

Printed and bound in Canada

For Nash, my rooster muse — keep on pluckin'.

Contents

Foreword

At a garden party last summer, I was asked to give a short speech to a gathering of cinephiles, patrons, and filmmakers. It was a fund-raising event, and the assembly was there to hear the good news — our national film culture was in great shape. Canadian films were regularly selling out at festivals, cinémathèque screenings were well attended, and there seemed to be vital interest — even passion — about the films we were making and showing.

As I was about to speak to this crowd, I noticed that I was in the presence of two extraordinary film artists who, for very different reasons, had helped shape my decision to become a director. As I looked upon Norman Jewison and Michael Snow, I realized that while one couldn't imagine two more contrasting practices, both these Canadians had given me a tremendous sense of national pride at the beginning of my career. Snow's *Wavelength* and *Jesus Christ Superstar* are hugely important works for me. While both these films were shot outside Canada (one in a loft in New York, the other in the deserts of Israel), I choose to identify them as Canadian because of what I projected into the makers.

On reflection, I wonder how much of what I projected into these films — and the people who made them — was based on my own early ideas that to become successful, one had to leave home. In the roughly thirty years since the films were made, a radical shift has taken place in our self-perception. While Michael Snow may have had to go to New York to secure his reputation, and Norman Jewison

certainly had to go to Hollywood, I didn't have to go anywhere. Neither did Patricia Rozema, Peter Mettler, John Greyson, Ron Mann, Anne Wheeler, Mina Shum, Bruce McDonald, Bruce Sweeney, Bruce LaBruce (is that three or four Bruces?), Guy Maddin, Lynne Stopkewich, Andy Jones, Jeremy Podeswa, Gary Burns, everyone at Rhombus Media, every great filmmaker working out of Quebec (they never dreamt of leaving anyway), and David Cronenberg (who sort of started the whole shift in thinking).

All of us (and if I forgot to mention one of your favourite filmmakers, I'll always blame the editor for demanding that I make this shorter) have had the luxury of knowing that we had a chance to do something special — the opportunity to build an indigenous film culture on our own terms. Though we started quietly — applying to arts councils, borrowing Bolexes, asking friends for favours — we are now making films that have secured an international reputation for quality and originality. Maybe the simple explanation for the rapid growth of such a persistently, even stubbornly independent cinema is that it's virtually impossible to "sell out" in the Canadian film industry. You really have to go south for that.

While it may sound perverse, we benefit from not having a strong internal market. We don't compete with each other over box-office share, gigantic fees or star treatment, because it's simply not an issue. This is both a blessing and a curse. As artists, it means that our survival is not set by public taste, but by the opinion of our peers — festival programmers (the most influential is actually called Piers!), arts council juries, and even Telefilm, which labels itself a "cultural investor" (try using that term in Hollywood!). We can't permit ourselves to rest on our laurels (since they are not lucrative enough), and consequently we have to keep working in order to survive. Since we're not seduced or deformed by market pressures, we continue to make our films in a highly idiosyncratic and distinct way.

We experiment with form, tell unconventional stories, use brilliant actors who aren't "stars" (though really are), and are generally free of the test screenings, market research, and all the other industrial processes that have homogenized film culture. If this has made our films less "commercial," this has been the result of getting away with making our films less commercially. This is something we cherish. We started making our films outside the "system" and — if I can be so presumptuous to speak for any group — we'd prefer to go back to the margins than run the risk of becoming banal. Stated bluntly, if we act like we've been spoiled, it's because we've taken full advantage of a culturally subsidized environment. Great art needs patrons. It always has, and it always will. In return for this support, we have brought honour and glory to our national film culture.

Okay, I'm getting a little carried away. We're not rock stars or athletic champions. What we have done, however, in a brief amount of time is stayed at home and created a body of work that has been noticed all over the world and is now being celebrated in the book you're about to read. Enjoy.

Atom Egoyan
Victoria, 2001

Introduction

"The problem with Canadian film is ..." Fill in the blank with anything from Telefilm policy to regional funding formulas to the lack of private investment or Canadian theatre chains — it doesn't matter. That's generally the way any conversation about Canadian film begins, because when we compare our small, young, hand-crafted industry to the glitzy assembly line productions being pumped out of Hollywood, we assume there's something broken. It's absurd to think Canada should be turning out multi-million-dollar blockbusters, but somewhere in the depths of the colonized Canadian psyche — colonized not by our European ancestors, but by American popular culture — we've come to believe we don't measure up to the American watermark.

Film is not the only Canadian cultural industry asphyxiated by bloated expectations. Bashing Canadian culture has become a sort of cottage industry in this country, spawning pamphlets about the perceived waste of taxpayer dollars to a chorus of rent-a-quote pop-up talking heads, who appear on the face of national newscasts like pesky cold sores, spewing blistering critiques for the pus-filled purpose of self-promotion.

I see it all the time. Whether it's a nimrod politico trying to score points by bashing the tax system, a media mogul regurgitating a thesaurus in the name of free markets or a Hollywood wannabe dumping on publicly funded productions because they aren't commercial enough — Canadians have grown to respect the rhetoric of self-loathing more than the language of self-love.

It's tragic — but true, and nothing illustrates this better than the way we've tended to view Canadian film as some poor, maladjusted backwoods cousin to Chiclet-toothed Tinseltown.

"Our movies are too depressing," we sigh. "They're all about smoking pot and sleeping with your mother," we groan. "They're boring," we collectively lament. Over the course of my professional career as a pop culture critic in this country, I've heard all those whines and more — lots more. I've heard directors excuse their own shortcomings by blaming bureaucrats. I've read books on Canadian cinema that began with apologies for an entire era of filmmaking, and I've watched countless Canadian journalists symbolically lick the shoes of third-rate, self-absorbed and only marginally intelligent American stars.

I've never truly understood why, but I guess part of it has to do with self-preservation: If you slag yourself first, it disarms others who will then take pity on you. The rest of it is either plain ignorance, or perpetually low self-esteem — and personally speaking, I never bought into the latter. We may well respect the rhetoric of self-loathing when we talk about our cultural industries, but when it comes to Canada vs. the World, we're a quietly confident nation. In fact, I believe most of us look down our nose at our unsophisticated neighbours to the south with a vague sense of superiority. Not that we'd ever say anything out loud! Heaven forbid! We're far too polite. So we keep quiet, and we keep to ourselves, hoping no one notices our high standard of living, our rich resources, our unmatched scenic beauty and our nearly non-existent department of national defense.

That said, if we love Canada — and we love being Canadian, which I believe almost every Canadian does — why, then, do we spend more time trashing Canadian music, and Canadian television, and Canadian radio, and Canadian theatre, and Canadian literature and Canadian film than we do celebrating it?

Well, I never said we were well adjusted. To be blunt: We're absolutely batty. We're all children of a dysfunctional family. Born together in the wilderness when two European cultures squatted in dense underbrush and gave birth to fledgling colonies on the shores of the St. Lawrence, Canada's twin identities have been at each other since the day they were born. For more than 200 years, they've been threatening to break up — not realizing that while you can leave the house, change your name and cut off all ties, you can never escape your own twin. He's always there — an amniotic consciousness to remind us of our other half. No wonder we're a bit screwed up. We deny we're even related. Neglect begets neglect. Abuse breeds abuse. Ignorance spawns ignorance and so we have developed this bizarre love-hate relationship with our own reflection as it's communicated through our cultural industries.

In decades past, this bipolar condition was called "the Canadian identity crisis." Today, it's called everything from "the unity question" to "Western alienation" to "The Ministry of Canadian Heritage." No matter what you call it, the underlying message remains the same: we are broken; we need to be fixed. Or, "The problem with Canadian film is..."

For years, Canada — like most other countries in the world — has tried to come up with a workable film policy that would keep some percentage of Canadian box-office receipts in this country to support homegrown film. Since 1923, when the Allen Theatres chain was bought out by Famous Players, Hollywood has controlled Canadian theatres. For a brief period in the 1980s, thanks to Technicolor dreamer Garth Drabinsky, Canada was home to Cineplex, one of the largest theatre chains in North America. But that didn't last long. Cineplex was eventually swallowed by American interests until just recently, when it was acquired by Winnipeg-born financier Gerry Schwartz of Onex Corporation. The ownership title has changed, but the forces of the marketplace have not. More Canadians spend money on American entertainment product than anything homegrown, and Canadian box-office figures are still included as part of the American domestic market, which means the majority of cash we spend on movie entertainment in this country goes back into U.S. bank accounts. At least three separate attempts were made to bring in legislation to protect Canadian film — and to encourage reinvestment — but every one of them died on the table because the United States will stop at nothing to protect its number one export.

That's right. Entertainment is the "driving wheel" of the U.S. economy[1] — not cars, not trees, not even pharmaceuticals, petroleum or genetically modified food products are worth more to the American economy than movies, music and computer entertainment software which pump more than $480 billion U.S. into the American economy a year.

The way Jack Valenti, president of the Motion Picture Association of America, sees it: The more people in the world who are exposed to American values, the safer it is for everyone. After all, if we all believe in the American dream as it is packaged and sold by Hollywood, then we're all on the same side.

No wars. No nasty ethnic conflicts. Just lots of *Premiere Magazine* subscriptions and a bigger worldwide audience share (and higher ad rates) for next year's Academy Awards (trademark, registered). It may not be good, but Valenti is right.

If you really want to look at the forces that led to the dismantling of the Berlin Wall, forget politics, comrade. Look at the flood of western TV signals that spread across the east side of the city with images of *Baywatch* and *Dynasty*. The imagination is the fertile ground from which entire civilizations spring, and Hollywood is expropriating territory after territory.

While it may seem daunting, we have to remember the battle against American monoculture and the forces of globalization is not futile. A recent study showed Canadians are spending more on domestic entertainment than they have in the past — thanks to the likes of Alanis Morissette, Celine Dion, Deborah Cox, Nelly Furtado and others — but we're still in the hole, culturally speaking, especially when it comes to movies.

That said, I'd like to appeal to your growing sense of Canadian pride in the name of Canadian film. Let's think about ourselves for a change. Watching a Canadian movie is like looking in the mirror. It tells us who we are — and shows us things about ourselves we may never have noticed. If you want to support Canadian culture, support Canadian cultural industries. If you're tired of watching mind-numbing formula films flushed out of Hollywood, watch a Canadian movie. Even if it sucks — and chances are it won't — you'll at least see something unique and human and reflective of your own self. Canadians — and the rest of the world — happily spend money on bad Hollywood films all the time, but get despondent after seeing a mediocre home-grown effort. Why are we happier throwing money at *The Phantom Menace* than the work of our own countrymen and women?

Culture is a habit and sadly, few Canadians ever got in the habit of gobbling up CanCon. It felt like a duty: the cod liver oil of the entertainment world. No, we don't make sugar-coated serials. We make challenging, cerebral, ambiguous and decidedly offbeat films. True, they are more difficult to swallow than some of the processed schlock that comes from Hollywood. Yes, a lot of them are depressing and cold. Some of them are funny and warm. Some are good. Some are bad. The point is, they reflect who *we* are, not someone else's bogus myth. If we spent a quarter of what we spend on Hollywood entertainment, and put it back into Canadian film, we would have a viable — if not thriving — industry tomorrow. So what's the problem with Canadian film? We are. We don't watch them. We don't respect them. We don't know how to love them.

That's the purpose of this book. We need a little mental re-jigging — a crash course in deprogramming — a little chicken soup for our neglected Canadian psyche. At the risk of sounding like a complete beaver-tail flapping bonehead with a bad case of boosterism, I love Canadian film. I really, really do. I love it because it speaks to me. It reflects my reality, shows my currency, speaks my languages, shows me where I live, tells the stories of my peers, shares my sense of humour and makes me believe I'm not alone.

Granted, Canadian films are often mind-altering, sometimes harrowing descents into personal hells. They resist closure, revel in ambiguity and tend to defy every rule in the genre handbook. As a result, they hang around in your imagination long after the final credits roll and burrow into your subconscious as you search for answers, or some sense of closure that never comes. They can make you crazy. So indulge wisely. Appreciate it in moderation, but most of all, understand how it works.

Over the course of this book, we'll look at more than 100 Canadian films and hear from a variety of Canadian filmmakers in the hopes of capturing the essence of the Canadian film experience. This book is not an encyclopedia of Canadian cinema — nor is it exhaustive nor all-inclusive. It is intended to be a primer that communicates years of critical theory on Canadian cinema to the masses. There is nothing all that original about the book, except its mere existence. Not since Martin Knelman's *This is Where We Came In*, which was printed in 1977, has one author attempted to decrypt Canadian film for a popular audience. As a Canadian film critic, I always wondered why there was no one, single-voiced book on the subject of contemporary Canadian cinema. Now that I've written one, I know why I was the only one foolish enough to make the attempt: Canadian film defies easy categorization. It is not uniform, nor does it follow any one formulaic pattern. It metamorphoses and mutates generation by generation, and speaks in many tongues. Diversity of approach, individual voice and ambiguity are what unite Canadian cinema as a whole — which makes a linear study almost impossible. For this reason, this book has attempted to emulate the structure of its subject. Not only is it nonlinear and reliant on repeated themes, but I've also tried to follow the overall evolution of Canadian film from an external, realist tradition toward an increasingly idiosyncratic, and imaginative, investigation of the internal landscape — with the camera itself taking on the role of mediator between both worlds.

Chapter by chapter, we'll move from the outside in. We'll delve into the guts of our cinematic tradition, where it came from, where it's going, what it looks like and what's going on beneath the surface of the frame and why. We'll pull it apart at the splice marks, rip open its subtext, probe the soundtracks and expose not just the beating blood-pump of one very plucky cinematic species — but the hidden soul of a nation that has never been given the tools to truly love itself.

So let's forget the whining and get on with it.

A Note on How to Use This Book

This book consists of three different elements: 10 thematically driven chapters, 20 expanded biographical profiles of key Canadian film figures, and 100 reviews of significant Canadian films.

The different elements are geared to work together, but they were written to make sense in isolation in the hopes of providing as many doors to the text as possible. The profiles were placed at the end of relevant chapters to provide a deeper understanding of the people behind the camera. The reviews are placed together at the end of the book and arranged alphabetically.

Despite the heft, there's a lot missing. I wish I could have included everyone and everything, but that's not only unrealistic — it would have turned this book into an intimidating text book that's too cumbersome to use. My goal is to turn people on to Canadian film, not bore them to tears, and so I had to make some difficult choices along the way about what to include and what to cut.

Selecting the people to profile was no easier. There are many young, talented Canadian filmmakers just beginning to emerge on the Canadian film horizon. I would have loved to include them all, but again, more isn't necessarily better. The profiles were decided by "body of work." In my mind, one amazing feature and one mediocre movie do not a "body of work" make. Sadly, because most indigenous film activity takes place in central Canada and because demographics dictate funding, that means the East and the West are under-represented — as per usual. I thought

about bending the criteria to make it more representative, but in the end I decided that would have bent the frame and been counterproductive. This book is supposed to be a reflection of what our movies and our industry look like. I have no intention of creating institutional propaganda to make the country look more balanced than it really is — that's the kind of thinking that put us in this self-loathing hole in the first place.

In the thematic chapters, I looked for the most obvious examples to illustrate a given point — or the ones that seemed most appropriate in my mind. Because all the films share certain themes, I could have selected from any number of examples — so I just went with my gut and hoped an alert reader would bring his or her own examples to the fore to either argue for or against a given thesis. Remember, these are just ideas. I don't think I'm saying anything all that new, nor do I believe there's only one way to interpret Canadian film. There is no right way, and no wrong way to read a movie. Movies are open texts that mean different things to the people who watch them. This book echoes some long-standing academic theories on Canadian film, and introduces a few of my own, but this is just the door. My only hope is that I am articulate enough, and passionate enough, to coax every reader past the threshold to discover his or her own ideas about Canadian cinema. If that happens, then the real dialogue can begin as we move away from the American mirror and look into the eyes of our own forgotten soul.

CHAPTER ONE

Rooted in Realism

WHERE IS HERE?

Canadians have never been accused of being big dreamers. While other nations spend billions developing giant rocket ships and space stations, we build practical, lower-profile appendages such as space arms. We are the peacekeepers who mop up after wars, the wheat farmers who put food on the table and the ones who always say "please" and "thank you." We are grounded realists and non threatening world citizens, which is why most of the globe likes us, even though historically we have a hard time loving ourselves. As far back as childhood, I can remember hearing about the so-called "Canadian identity crisis." I've been told how Canadians are a self-loathing lot who revel in dysfunction and immerse themselves in self-effacing bath salts. As a proud Canadian, I've always had a hard time buying into the rhetoric, but it clearly exists. Whether it's real or perceived doesn't matter — "the Canadian identity crisis" has a life unto itself — to the point where it's an inextricable part of our cultural luggage, along with hockey and Tim Horton's.

The goal of this book is to check some of those chronic preoccupations and explore the roots, as well as the modern blooms, of the Canadian cultural landscape. We'll look at photographic, written and visual art, but because film is a true *métissage* of art forms — combining drama, landscape, music and philosophy into one alluring pop culture package — it provides us with an excellent medium to access the Canadian subconscious. Making the trip even richer is the drastic shift that's taken place on the Canadian film hori-

zon over the past ten years. From a country recognized in film circles for a strong documentary tradition, and little else, Canadian films began to crawl out of the amniotic celluloid soup in the late 1980s — when Denys Arcand's *Le Déclin de l'empire Américain* was celebrated around the world, picking up the FIPRESCI Award at Cannes, a wheelbarrow full of Genies and an Oscar nomination for Best Foreign Film in 1987. These days, we have even more to celebrate now that English-language Canadian film has caught up to its Quebec counterpart. We're doing well, but with only two percent of Canadian screen time, there's plenty of room for improvement. I have no doubt we have it in us to take that Via railcar to film Nirvana, but we can't get there from here. In order to understand the Canadian condition and how it's reflected onscreen, we have to go back to the beginning and see where Canadian film came from, how it evolved, and what was framed through the lens and why.

In this chapter, we'll look at the foundation of the Canadian film industry and the emergence of "Canadian film." We'll take a trip back in time to the early days of the National Film Board and time-warp forward into the sixth dimension of Canadian Feature Film Policy. Expect to feel a little nauseous. It's gonna be a bumpy ride on the backroads of our old cottage industry, but think of it as cultural regression therapy. By the end of the exercise, you'll hopefully have a better awareness of Canadian film and how it reflects the Canadian self.

Getting Real

As Piers Handling, former film professor and current director of the Toronto International Film Festival, wrote in 1984: "The overwhelming artistic tradition within which the Canadian artist functions is realist. Realism has informed our literature, our painting, our theatre, our television and our filmmaking. Cinema in this country is virtually synonymous in many people's minds with documentary film. Even our fictive creations are born out of this soil. It is a heritage that has an extensive history, and it stretches back through most of our filmmaking endeavours ..." Even if you've never studied art history or sat in on a university film theory class, you probably know exactly what Handling is talking about. You know that we are regarded as world leaders in news and broadcast journalism. We watch a lot of non-fiction television like *Hockey Night in Canada*. We like to analyze and discuss issues. We are pragmatic and realistic, and chances are, most of us check the weather forecast before we get dressed for the day. Realism is at the root of the Canadian psyche, and so it is that Canadian film began in a documentary tradition and continues as a world leader in a variety of non-fiction formats. Independent feature film production was certainly around in the early days of the industry: for a brief time, Canada was even a world industry leader. Not only did the Ottawa-born Andrew Holland open the first Kinetoscope parlour (an early predecessor to the movie theatre that showed looped shorts) in Manhattan and become the first entrepreneur to ever turn a profit showing filmed entertainment on April 14, 1894, but Leo-Ernest Ouimet opened the first luxury movie palace in North America built exclusively for film (The Ouimetoscope in Montreal) in 1907. Canada was also the first home of such Hollywood titans as Louis B. Mayer, Sidney Olcott, Mack Sennett, Mary Pickford and Florence Lawrence ("the first Hollywood star"). Later on, there were success stories like F. R. "Budge" Crawley, whose Crawley Films produced several award-winning features, including *The Loon's Necklace* (which featured images of West Coast aboriginal masks and a voice-over recounting First Nations' legends), *Newfoundland Scene* (a 1952 travelogue of Canada's newest province) and *The Man Who Skied Down Everest*, which won Canada its first Documentary Feature Oscar in 1976.

For all the successes of early Canadian film pioneers, their achievements never fully registered in the minds of the Canadian people because — just as it is today — when people went out to the picture shows, it was to indulge in escapist entertainment, not to view a documentary on everyday life in another part of the country. People wanted to see a mainstream Hollywood movie or some chic European art film playing at the diminutive — and usually ratty — art house theatre in the beatnik part of town. Nonetheless, Canadian documentary films were everywhere. They were squished between regular CBC programming when the hockey game ended earlier than the broadcaster anticipated. They were in our classrooms. They were on the opening reel of mainstream movies — trailers before the big feature — like some quickie reminder that we were Canadian and not in any way related to the glossy mythmakers who lived down south, whose movies we had just paid big bucks to see. Given a choice of watching something like "How to Build an Igloo" or "Hinterland Who's Who" as opposed to the sci-fi adventures of "Booster Rocketman," the preference was clear: Give me the eye candy. Pretty please. No wonder a lot of people still, to this day, see Canadian film as little more than a bad, scholastic flashback with an earnest voice-over by Lorne Greene. No wonder there are a lot of cynics out there when it comes to Canadian art: it's always been sold as something that's good for us, something we should do as good Canadians ... like paying our taxes and swimming in cold lakes. It may not be all that much fun, but it's important. Given all that, our hesitation about Canadian cinema isn't hard to understand. But it's not altogether fair.

Without the National Film Board, chances are we wouldn't have much of an industry at all. Moreover, the films the NFB produced have been some of the best features (narrative, animated and non-fiction) this country has ever seen. Claude Jutra's *Mon Oncle Antoine* (1971), Terri Nash's *If You Love This Planet* (1982) and Denys Arcand's *Le Déclin de l'empire Américain* (1986) are just a few obvious examples, but there are many more — and we'll talk about a lot of them as we venture ever further into the dark heart of the Canadian film experience.

When I lived in Montreal as a kid, my sister and I would actually head down to the NFB's head office in St. Laurent and watch movies on three-quarter-inch tapes — as many as we could in one sitting. I remember watching the hand-scratched films of legendary Canadian animator Norman McLaren for an entire afternoon, and at other times heading over to do research for a school project on a famous Canadian. Not only was it completely free (as long as you said it was for school), but it beat going to the library. The best part was we were pretty much the only ones there. Walking into the beige lobby was plainly magical. They even had Oscar statuettes from their winning films in a display case, making it by far the most glamorous government building I have ever

set foot in. There is something decidedly absurd about Oscar statues in government buildings. They are manifestations of two completely different realities: one is a symbol of the American entrepreneurial spirit and dramatic self-creation; the other is a symbol of Canadian socialism. Understanding the relationship between the two is key to understanding Canadian film in general.

The Board is Born

When the National Film Board was created in 1939, it was a formal rebirth of something called the Canadian Government Motion Picture Bureau, which had been making films since 1923. The films the bureau churned out were mostly how-to exercises for federal departments. There wasn't much glamour to them, let alone a pressing need for them to be seen by anyone but bureaucrats and government technicians. But in 1939, the bureau was reborn with the arrival of an outgoing Scot named John Grierson.

Already widely known as "the father of documentary" from his work in Britain, where he attracted swarms of eager filmmakers, Grierson was committed to film not just as a means of nuts and bolts communication, but as an agent for social change. With this in mind, he lobbied the Canadian government to create a special film office to that end.

By 1941, after convincing the government to transfer the Motion Picture Bureau from the Department of Trade and Commerce to his Ottawa offices, Grierson was forming the building blocks of what would become the National Film Board.

In 1949, it was official. After the Massey Commission concluded "arts and letters lie at the roots of our life as a nation," there was a government desire to get behind Grierson's vision, and the National Film Board was born.

"The Father of Documentary Film": John Grierson. Born in Scotland in 1889, Grierson founded the National Film Board of Canada as a way of "bringing Canada alive to itself and the rest of the world." An unapologetic socialist, he fled his new home of Canada, and later the U.S., in the midst of Cold War paranoia. After a brief return to Montreal, where he taught classes at McGill University, he died in England in 1972.
PHOTO LIBRARY OF THE NATIONAL FILM BOARD OF CANADA

more concerned — and more intrusive in board affairs. After all, they didn't trust those film types: people at the NFB were creative and eccentric. According to author Gary Evans, who wrote a readable history of the board (and one I highly recommend to those aching to learn more about the NFB) titled *In the National Interest*, the people at the film board were not trusted by the government's grey-flannel-suit brigade because they wore purple pants. As a result, the establishment regularly hurled ignorant insults at the board and its projects, and in 1948 enemies of the NFB pushed the *Globe and Mail* to write a series of stories on the board's "wasteful" productions. An accompanying illustration was a picture of a kid brushing his teeth under the headline "$40,000?" Similar tactics were used by the former Reform Party of Canada in the 1990s, when it hurled insults at the funding agencies that supported Cynthia Roberts' *Bubbles Galore* (1997), a pro-feminist look at the pornography industry. *Plus ça change, plus c'est la même chose.*

After the end of the Second World War, Grierson headed to the United States for several reasons. First, the Ottawa bureaucrats figured a film board in peacetime was a frivolous expense. Second, he was catching flak from Hollywood studio types who didn't like his idea of "Canadian reinvestment" that would see 30 to 40 percent of Tinseltown profits in Canada (about $17 million annually at the time) appropriated in the name of the national interest. And third, because he feared he might become a victim of Cold War paranoia when the Conservative opposition of the day called the NFB a "commie hangout" and hinted that Grierson was involved in the Gouzenko spy scandal (because of his pronounced socialist values and "damn the capitalist torpedoes" rhetoric). Grierson was often

In 1956, they moved offices to brand new digs in Montreal. (The same building that later housed the Oscar statuettes I marvelled at as a kid, and which still stands today, despite massive cutbacks over the past ten years and a reduction of staff by nearly half.)

During his time as chief film commissioner for the board (1939–1945), Grierson recruited others who believed in film's public duty to his cause, and he lobbied hard to ensure the board had as much autonomy as possible. His motto was widely known to be "Keep one inch to the left of the party in power," but that only made his bosses in office

quoted as saying, "Peace must be made more exciting than war."[1]

For Grierson, a man who had selflessly dedicated his time at the NFB in the name of all that was righteous, moral, socially just and Canadian, becoming a political shuttlecock was a betrayal. "The Film Board was a deliberate creation to do a deliberate work," he said in a 1970 television interview. "It was there to bring Canada alive to itself and to the rest of the world. It was there to declare the excellences of Canada to Canadians and the rest of the world. It was there to invoke the strength of Canadians and the imagination of Canadians in respect of creating their present and their future."[2] In case you failed to notice, he never once mentions money. Film was a pretty serious vocation for Grierson. Filmmakers working at the board were expected to be part artist, part pastor preaching moral values to the masses, and part cheerleader — showing Canadians how good, how big, how successful and how selfless they are. In this Scotsman's mind, film was not — in any way, shape or form — supposed to be a vehicle for mindless entertainment aimed at making oodles of box-office cash or building a completely bogus national identity. Therein lies the seminal difference between Canadian and American film: Canada's tradition grew out of an institution and a socialist-minded idea of showing Canadians honest reflections of themselves. The American, or Hollywood, film tradition began as a collective dream in the minds of several Jewish immigrants who were possessed by a desire to create pure fantasy and to reinvent the American Dream as an accessible, if entirely ethereal, ideal.

Everyone is Everyman

Despite regular upheavals, constant interference and more than one internal uprising, the NFB survived into the sixties, when — thanks to the invention of smaller, portable cameras and sound recording equipment — it became a hotbed of creative cinematic invention. On the English side, the most exciting things were happening in something called Unit B, headed up by Tom Daly. As Gary Evans writes in *In the National Interest,* Daly was a "self-described rational idealist whose roots stemmed from two major, if contrasting influences: the esoteric philosophy of Gurdieff and the commitment to public duty enunciated by John Grierson. The two threads combined to create a recognizably Canadian form of self-abnegation, where 'ego' was downplayed because it cut people off from each other, and consciousness was pursued for its power to create a universal quality of humanness."[3]

Some of the key filmmakers in Unit B were animator Norman McLaren; Wolf Koenig; Colin Low (a pioneer animator who made the film *Universe*, which inspired images in Stanley Kubrick's *2001: A Space Odyssey*); Roman Kroitor (who would later develop the Canadian IMAX technology with Graeme Ferguson and Robert Kerr), and Stanley Jackson, a former schoolteacher who became known as "the voice of the NFB."

Kroitor and Jackson were responsible for creating the revolutionary series *The Candid Eye* — a documentary television series that was born from a near fanatical appreciation for the work of French photographer and writer Henri Cartier-Bresson. Kroitor saw Bresson's book *The Decisive Moment* as the foundation for the modern philosophy of the "photographic document": a physical bridge between art and life — a real moment frozen in time through the photographic process. *The Candid Eye* endeavoured to show people as they really were by catching them in the midst of their everyday routines. For instance, in the classic film *Lonely Boy* — which clearly inspired and remains far superior to Madonna's concert film, *Truth or Dare* — we see a young Paul Anka in his dressing room. Though primped and preened, the young man looks perfectly ordinary as he smiles in the mirror and talks to his entourage, but in the background you can hear hysterical teenage girls screaming his name. A similar refusal to bow at the feet of celebrity can be seen in *Glenn Gould: On the Record*, where we see the world famous pianist drinking coffee and reading the newspaper like any old Joe (or CBC tech).

These classics from Unit B articulated a whole new approach to making documentary that has been described as "innocent"[4] and as "self-abandonment in the face of reality … a reflection of life as seen by the colonized artist."[5] Regardless of the adjectives, these

A positive pioneer, Norman McLaren (1914–1986) is a veritable legend. An animator who often interacted directly with the film stock to create moving pictures without a camera, McLaren set up the animation studio at the NFB at the bidding of his good friend, fellow Scotsman and mentor, John Grierson. McLaren's prestigious filmography includes *Spheres* (seen in *Thirty Two Short Films About Glenn Gould*). PHOTO LIBRARY OF THE NATIONAL FILM BOARD OF CANADA

films were designed to reaffirm the human-to-human relationship between the viewer and the celebrity, not to stimulate a sense of untouchability or awe. In this way, the Canadian film experience is closely tied to the Canadian identity bugbear. As Evans says: "The productions confirmed one quality that characterizes how English Canada has long identified itself: denying the thread of a central nexus while persistently avoiding conflict and confrontation ... Some think of this as the art of accommodation, compromise or concession; it is also the art of national self-effacement ... The aphorism that art is a mirror of society presents a challenge for Canadians: to paraphrase Margaret Atwood, if they look in a mirror, they see either another's face or no face at all. Historically, this has been the way Canada has avoided absorption by the United States, which remains disinterested in the faceless Canadian social realities, except to complain of them when they affect business."[6]

We'll question the "negative" implications of Evans' statement later on, but for now, we can isolate a clear preference for realism and realistic depictions of people, as a opposed to Hollywood artifice. While both the English and French units were building on the documentary tradition that defined early Canadian film, there was a critical difference between the two tangents that deserves mention because what were at first little more than cerebral, esthetic differences eventually turned into two entirely separate schools that, in turn, reflected two entirely different political realities.

The Direct Approach

The main schism occurred in the late fifties and early sixties, just as Jean Lesage rose to power in Quebec, beginning what would become known as the Quiet Revolution. After centuries of real and perceived oppression at

Gilles Groulx (1931–1994): Seminal Quebecois director who said, "A film is a critique of daily life."
PHOTO LIBRARY OF THE NATIONAL FILM BOARD OF CANADA

the hands of the English establishment — compounded by decades of being patronized by the Duplessis regime — the French-Canadian people were beginning to resist. They needed to define themselves. They needed to resurrect their past, their heroes and their unique sense of self — and they did so by defining themselves in opposition to everything else around them. Feeling like they were on the verge of a whole new era that offered a chance at nationhood, the young, aspiring and (it should be noted) bourgeois Québécois members of *l'équipe française* began documenting their own culture as it was expressed in everyday ritual. They made movies about urban life (*A Saint-Henri, le 5 septembre*), lumberjacks (*Bucherons de la Manouane*), wrestling (*La Lutte*) and snowshoeing (*Les Raquetteurs*).

Les Raquetteurs — made by Michel Brault and Gilles Groulx — is considered the seminal film in the Quebec tradition because it shows not only the seriousness of a snowshoers' convention in Sherbrooke (complete with heartfelt discussions about technique and an announcer berating kids who aren't paying attention), but it does so with the informal,

Les Raquetteurs (1958): Once destined for stock-shot slaughter when it was deemed too unorthodox by the board executive, this movie about a snowshoeing convention in Sherbrooke, Quebec may be considered "a caricature" by its co-director Michel Brault, but it was the first films to capture "the people" with intimacy and awareness.
PHOTO LIBRARY OF THE NATIONAL FILM BOARD OF CANADA

casual tone of a home movie. The movie offered something that all Québécois could understand and identify with: images of their reality. Here was something distinct, largely unrecognized by the mainstream, and funny in that zany, fun-loving way that English Canada is only now beginning to understand. Now we can see the humour in the shots of snowshoers racing on cleared pavement (instead of on the abundant surrounding snow), and a wandering camera capturing the sight of kids jeering the "snowshoe Queen," or the mayor of Sherbrooke paying tribute to a blank-faced American, but back then, it presented a conflict in our earnest souls. Not surprisingly, the English heads of the NFB were not amused. They had given Brault (who worked

as a camera operator on the English side) $6,000 to make a three-minute short for the newsmagazine, *Temps present*. It was supposed to be a throwaway vignette — not a high-concept, 12-minute trek through the surreal world of serious snowshoers. After the head of the board threatened to dissect the movie into stock shots without a soul, Daly intervened on Groulx and Brault's behalf. Groulx called the finished film a "documentary of the social behaviour of man,"[7] and the great minds of the day agreed. Here was a movie that showed people as they really were. Moreover, here was a movie that showed a slice of undeniably "tribal" life via a technologically advanced medium.

Things were changing in Quebec, and

even though *Les Raquetteurs* focused on an ancient ambulatory tradition, the minds behind the camera saw more than a group of people with wood and leather strapped to their feet. They saw an image of *Les Québécois* — The People — and in the mere act of capturing those faces and that event on film, Brault and Groulx assumed the roles of socio-anthropologists, bringing a long-buried people back into the light.

Encouraged by the success of *Les Raquetteurs*, *l'équipe française* continued in the same vein, incorporating the theories of the rising French New Wave — a film movement that formally appeared in France in 1959 with the emergence of Francois Truffaut, Alain Resnais and Jean-Luc Godard — into their "cinéma direct" movement. Emphasis was on the personal, not the communal, placing them in stark contrast to the socialist-minded work of Grierson. Even though the subjects — such as they were — had a socialist edge (the workers in Saint-Henri, for example), there was something highly individualistic about the films that resisted the idea of the detached filmmaker who refuses to make judgements. These young radicals were eager to make statements through their work, and usually those statements echoed the rising nationalist feelings of the Québécois people.

The first feature film to emerge from the cinema direct tradition was *Pour la suite du monde* (1964) — a movie about a beluga whale hunt on the St. Lawrence — which actually garnered the attention of New Wave director and critic Jean Rouch. Comparing it to the work of *Man with a Movie Camera*'s Dziga Vertov, Rouch said *Pour la suite du monde* was a complete success: "as if Vertov had used Cartier-Bresson's camera, or if Robert Flaherty had shot *Man of Aran* in sound. Brault's camera had captured a fantastic people in an unmediated fashion." Once again, two key words reappear: "people" and "unmediated." For the politically charged filmmakers at the NFB like Brault and Jutra, the value of film as a revolutionary tool became obvious, and with the validation of big-time Europeans like Rouch behind them, *l'équipe française* soon gained the mindset and cohesive ideology of a political movement. Everything was new and exciting and positively brimming with potential. In an interview with Brault, I asked him about those early days at the board and his voice accelerated with adrenalin as his mind fell back on the first encounter with Rouch. Having already met Claude Jutra on an anthropological expedition in Africa, where Rouch was experimenting with cinema direct, Rouch invited Jutra and Brault to Paris, where the team would essentially develop the foundation for the entire French New Wave. According to Brault, Jutra and Rouch had a great understanding of one another and that mutual support let them take more risks: "Claude was a real lover of cinema. He wasn't just committed to documentary or direct, he was also a big devotee of the work of Norman McLaren. He loved to experiment with the form, and so did Rouch. The whole *Nouvelle Vague* was started by this re-examination of the form. It told people to take liberties with the medium and create a dialectical model for film. It was not about what you call entertainment ... For us, it really felt like we were on the verge of discovering a whole new art form ... a whole new way of seeing the world."[8]

"When we [Jutra and I] returned to Quebec," says Brault, "we continued in the same vein at the ONF [NFB] in Montreal. It became a powerful force, at least on the French side. We had so many powerful hopes of what film could be. Thanks to the ONF, we could get our hands on cameras, and Claude got his hands on a Bolex. The first duty of a filmmaker is to make films, and that's what we did ... with Gilles Carle and others."

In Peter Wintonick's excellent film about this particular chapter in Canadian film history, *Cinéma Vérité: Defining the Moment* (1999), you can see the shots that Rouch fell in love with, particularly a shot of a woman walking down a street on cobblestones as the camera drifts away from her. To Rouch, this communicated the emotional state of the subject with a simple, unscripted camera move. To Rouch, it was nothing less than genius – and it set the tone for the New Wave about to break on international shores.

"There was something so emancipating for those first filmmakers experimenting with all this new, lightweight equipment. Not only were the French Québécois filmmakers feeling a whole new sense of self about who they were as a culture, they were able to articulate those feelings through their films. They were finally able to show themselves to the world without an outside hand guiding the action," said Wintonick in an interview after the film's Vancouver premiere. "It was more than a film movement; it was a cultural expression."

Given that the rest of the country was just beginning to grapple with the idea of an independent Canadian nation, set apart from the British crown in the late sixties, this idea of self-knowledge put the Québécois far ahead of the rest of the country in its pursuit of identity — and, not surprisingly, the race for a viable, self-sustaining narrative film tradition. For all the desire to be distinct and different from the English establishment and the avid desire to leave the patronizing institution represented by the federally supported film board, the French and English documentary traditions were still children of a common mother. The values were essentially the same, but the con-

tent and the ideology behind the camera were necessarily different. In the anthology *Take Two*, contributor David Clandfield explains it this way:

Both movements [the French and the English units at the NFB] had much in common; shooting without a script or conscious staging; use of light-weight equipment, a search for the real which deliberately shunned the dramatic or the heroic ... For the [English unit] Candid Eye filmmakers, the starting point was a social or human event — ephemeral, inscribed in an ephemeral world — the form and meaning of which require the mediation of the filmic process to become evident. The function of the filmic process, then, was not to mould but to reveal form, and with it, meaning ... For the cinema direct [French unit] filmmaker, the point of departure is the filmmaking process in which the filmmaker is deeply implicated as a consciousness, individual or collective. It is this process — this consciousness — which will give form and meaning to an amorphous objective reality. Instead of effacing his presence, the filmmaker will affirm it. Instead of rendering the technical process transparent (supposedly), he will emphasize its materiality.[9]

In other words, while the English documentary filmmakers at the NFB believed the outside world, the external reality, was the most important thing, the French filmmakers next door figured the outside world was just a backdrop, subject to the imaginative powers of the filmmaker him or herself. Put more simply, the French imagination was free to subjectively take part in the creative process of filmmaking, while the typically uptight

Mon Oncle Antoine (1971): There is nothing faux — especially not the fur — about Claude Jutra's classic about a kid coming of age in a Quebec asbestos town. Photographed almost entirely in natural light by Michel Brault, the movie marks the next rung in the auteurial ladder from documentary to narrative fiction. Here, Antoine (Jean Duceppe) and Benoit (Jacques Gagnon) have a family moment in the sleigh before picking up the body of a dead boy.
PHOTO LIBRARY OF THE NATIONAL FILM BOARD OF CANADA

English documentary movement recoiled at the very idea of conscious interference and maintained the objective stance.

Regardless of whether the work was created by the French or the English side of the NFB, there's no doubt the board facilitated the Canadian film imagination and set the course that generations of filmmakers would follow as they attempted to show Canadians who and what they were. As Evans notes, if Northrop Frye had even bothered to look at the list of films coming out of the NFB, he probably never would have asked his famous question: "Where is here?"[10]

Here and Now

With our feet firmly planted on the ground and our eyes drawn to unmediated images of the people, our initial steps toward narrative fiction were, quite logically, steeped in documentary technique. Eschewing the entire Hollywood system with its inherent worship of commercial interests over social values, the NFB encouraged filmmaking on a human — not grandiose — scale. One need only look at Claude Jutra's seminal Canadian feature, *Mon Oncle Antoine*, to see how similar it is in look and feel to straight documentary — about the only thing missing is talking heads. Shooting on location without cranes, dolly tracks or klieg lights, Jutra wanted to capture the essence of life in industrial, small-town

Quebec in a very real, unmediated way. As a result, few of the scenes were tightly scripted, the film is grainy and several scenes are so dark — particularly the night scene in the sleigh — that you can barely make out the figures on the screen.

The same sensibilities can be seen on the English side in Don Shebib's Canuck classic, *Goin' Down the Road*. Grainy and packed with unflattering images of the pasty-faced lead actors, artifice is hard to find in this seminal Canadian road movie — which explains why a lot of early Canadian features left audiences with a bit of a hangover and no buzz. They didn't have all the high-key lighting, slick camera moves, special effects and casts of thousands of Hollywood movies.

Things have changed considerably since the early 1970s. Canadians have learned the slick tricks of the trade thanks to our wealth of experience crewing on American movies over the past 10 years, but we haven't forgotten our roots. We are still realists at heart, and documentary film remains a Canadian specialty. Filmmakers like Nettie Wild (*A Rustling of Leaves, A Place Called Chiapas, Blockade*), Simcha Jacobovici (*Hollywoodism, Peacekeeper at War*), Mark Achbar (*Two Brides and a Scalpel*), Alanis Obomsawin (*Kanehsatake: 270 Years of Resistance*) and Catherine Annau (*Just Watch Me*) are just a few of the talents dedicated to exploring pressing social issues through a documentary lens. In addition to the talent, we also have an infrastructure — thanks to the film board — of small independent production houses making non-fiction programming for specialty channels and festivals such as HotDocs — one of the largest international documentary film festivals in the world that unfurls every spring in Toronto. And yet, while there is now a vast network of organizations and events outside the "institution" — i.e., the

federally sponsored National Film Board — Canadian film, and Canadian filmmakers, remain burdened by the remnants of our "institutional mentality." It's not always easy to spot the symptoms, especially in the French stream, where the whole notion of institutionalism was synonymous with the patronizing federal government or the equally oppressive Catholic Church. The Québécois rebelled against this institutionalism, and in doing so, became the first to make real progress outside the documentary box. But as we will see later, they are still grappling with the psychic aftershocks of their institutional and colonial formative years — just like the rest of us.

The Importance of Being Earnest

In the fall of 2000, the depth of our institutional mentality hit home. Federal Heritage Minister Sheila Copps travelled to Vancouver to unveil her office's long-awaited feature film policy. The presentation took place at the Vogue Theatre, an old Granville Mall movie house that was reclaimed as a live music venue and special event movie theatre. Copps' announcement began with a short film presentation that "celebrated" the contributions of Canadian film around the world, complete with a woefully earnest narrator who spoke in reverent tones. "Now that we've built an industry, it's time to build an audience," he said as images of natural wonders and hard-working film professionals unravelled on the video projector. After the presentation was over and Copps had read her equally cheery prepared speech that essentially guaranteed more money to market Canadian film to Canadians, a few of the directors in attendance walked away stifling giggles. They weren't laughing over the plan to get more Canadians into movie houses — which is a perfectly wizard idea, if you ask me — they were laughing at the presentation. A collection of overly earnest vignettes, the short film that Heritage produced to announce its new strategy was the embodiment of the industry's lingering battle in balancing sincerity with patronizing kitsch. I know from first-hand experience that for a long time many Canadians believed English-Canadian film was hokey, cheesy, amateurish and plain dull — and here was a government-produced short that reaffirmed every one of these suspicions.

Of course, things have changed recently in the wake of success stories like *The Sweet Hereafter, Cube, waydowntown* and *New Waterford Girl*, but the Copps presentation was so drenched in that oh-so-drab variety of institutional sincerity that it was altogether off-putting.

I spotted filmmaker Anne Wheeler in the crowd and asked her for a quote. The first thing out of her mouth was: "They need to get new people to produce their presentations." The second thing out of her mouth was equally symbolic. "At least they didn't refer to us as a region. They called us a community — an industry," said Wheeler, who is one of many West Coast filmmakers with persistent doubts about the West getting its fair share of the film funding pie — or any pie, for that matter. This brings up another sizeable obstacle to Canadian psychic emancipation that bears mention before we forge ahead any further: We are hampered by a lack of goodwill toward our fellow creators. Forced to compete for pieces of the government-funding pie provided by public agencies like Telefilm, the film industry in Canada has all the same institutional luggage as a prison or an orphanage or a school. People feel there is only so much money — or attention or gold stars — to go around. As a result, the community is divided in two: those who get what they want, and those who don't. Those who don't

get what they want are generally a little bitter about the process, and will often have negative things to say both about those who did receive the appropriate strokes and the institutions themselves.

Over the years, through my capacity as a journalist, I have heard more than one filmmaker cry in his beer about not being in the right clique or knowing "the right people." I hate hearing these stories because no culture can get ahead by "eating its own," but I've heard them often enough to be sympathetic. I also believe that like all institutions, agencies like Telefilm come with a prefab set of values, and either you ascribe to that value system, or you don't. Those who do will generally receive preferential treatment while the rest are frozen out, giving rise to all the bad blood that sits just beneath the tender skin of our young industry. We don't like to talk about the festering underbelly of the system, but I could feel it at Copps' press conference as I watched people smile at those they'd backstabbed just days before. Such things happen all the time in the high-profile, big-ego entertainment industry — especially in the United States, where getting the shiv is almost a part of the movie-making myth itself. But I always have a hard time dealing with the same game in socialist-minded Canada — where we generally resist the sycophantic reflex, at least toward our own. (God knows one too many metro Canadian daily newspaper prostrates itself at the feet of American celebrities for no good reason, but the Canadian media's hero-worship of all things American is a whole different book.) The Copps press conference was clearly intended as a celebration of Canada's filmmaking accomplishments, but optics and intent can often work against each other — and this was a prime example. By the end of the event, three of the main challenges presenting Canadian film came home loud and clear:

1. The Canadian film industry began as a socialist experiment under John Grierson. It was a government-sponsored project and continues to be one. For this reason, Canadian film will always be subject to the same endemic diseases that infect any institution, such as an overabundance of paperwork, preferential treatment toward those who agree with the executive position and "fit in," and a rigid mandate. For example, within the institution of Telefilm, there are strict Canadian content regulations that must be followed. Moreover, almost every artistic project funded by the Canadian government demands a positive "national unity" message, which can only harm the creative process — which is all about exploring problems, not packaging pre-fab solutions.

2. Appealing to a government-funded agency for creative support can often put the artist in a vulnerable position because it can erode the artist's self-esteem. For instance, when Guy Maddin was turned down for funding on one of his movies, he says he took it personally. "I was superenraged and indignant and then I got kind of depressed. It just hurts your feelings when they say no because you think it's a reflection of how they feel about you," says Maddin. The vulnerability can extend past creative angst and interfere with the artist's concept of home, since the funding formulas dictate where and how much money is spent in each region. People in British Columbia, for example, always feel shortchanged by the feds because the lion's share of funding is usually spent in Ontario and Quebec —

and for obvious reasons: it's where the majority of the voting population lives.

3. The short Heritage vignette clinched it: Canada is still recovering from an overdose of earnest messages. Anyone old enough to remember the Centennial song, "Ca-na-da, We Love You," is only too well aware of how lame and embarassingly cheesy we can look when the federal government gets involved. If you're too young to remember, then check out Robert Lepage's Nô, and listen to the main character, Sophie, utter the word "Tabernacle" fast and furious as she gets ready to act the idiot in the Canadian pavilion's production of a Feydeau farce. Not only does she look stupid, but the play, written by a Frenchman (from France), bears no resemblance to the Canadian political reality of the day (an irony Lepage pushes by setting the movie against the backdrop of the 1970 October Crisis).

To Lepage, our reliance on institutions is a side-effect of our colonial roots. "We are an incredibly colonized people," he said in an interview following Nô's screening at the Vancouver International Film Festival. "Only recently can you talk to a Canadian cultural attaché who doesn't have a British accent. I mean, why would the Canadian pavilion present an outdated Feydeau play as a representation of this country at the World's Fair, which they did? It makes no sense. That's why I say [the national approach to institutions and art] is just a little surreal."

Things have improved only marginally since the days when 1880s-era French farces represented Canadian culture, says Lepage, pointing to the "national unity" mandate embedded within the arts councils' funding formulas. "When Sheila Copps says all artists who receive funding must promote Canadian unity, she's making a huge mistake — because she's not allowing an honest reflection of ideas to travel past the borders. Not only is she eliminating most of the excellent work coming out of Quebec, she's exporting a false image of Canada and Canadian art — which, to me, is wrong."

In the end, it's a bit of a love-hate relationship, which, as it turns out, is perfectly Canadian. For all the challenges, there's no doubt the institutions are worth the effort. Without strong federal and provincial support, Canada and Canadian culture would have been colonized by the United States long ago. In the absence of a strong private sector willing to invest significant dollars in Canadian film, we need strong and well-financed agencies like Telefilm and institutions like the NFB to reflect Canada back to Canadians and promote a sense of self-awareness. I've heard people say we should attempt to build an industry like the one in the United States, and I always ask why. Why would we want to make mindless commercial dreck when we have a system that promotes individuality and art for art's sake? The answer is usually "Because it makes money and the taxpayer doesn't have to pay for someone else's self-indulgent, crappy art."

This is the type of thinking that nearly destroyed the Film Board in 1982, when the Applebaum-Hébert Federal Policy Review Committee issued a report that declared too much money was wasted in the making of movies. They urged legislators to dismantle the board piece by piece and put a halt to

things like the research and development of cutting-edge computer animation equipment — which the board did, selling the patents to a New York firm that would later cash in big on the Canadian innovations. Personally, I think no one makes vacuous eye candy quite as well as those aspiring Spielbergs in the U.S. of A., so why compete at a game they've already won? We don't have a big enough population to support even a $10-million picture domestically, let alone a $100-million epic like *Titanic*. Besides, the last time I visited the Sundance Film Festival in Park City, Utah, every independent producer I spoke to was envious of the Canadian funding system. They have nothing that even comes close, which means if you want to make movies in the United States, you either surrender your personal vision and buy into the bogus Los Angeles reality hoping to cash in big — or you lie, cheat, steal and cajole cash out of the pockets of the private sector to make a movie that has personal meaning. Given the harsh reality of making movies elsewhere in the world, Canada is clearly one of the lucky countries to support filmmaking as an art and as a psychic mirror to the soul. In other words, without our institutions, it's doubtful if we'd even have a "here" to recognize as our own. Moreover, the self-contained love-hate relationship we've developed with those institutions, and their inherent earnestness, has only strengthened our identity as a culture built on paradox, internal tension and the subtle subversion of all things stuffy.

CHAPTER TWO

Survivors & Surviving

THE GUILT TRIP BEGINS

I had one of those magic moments of pre-sleep enlightenment when I was watching the TV broadcast of the Hollywood shake 'n' bake volcano movie, *Dante's Peak*. The final line — "Make room, there are survivors here ..." — filtered into that last strained moment of genuine consciousness before I reached slumberland. I pulled my head off the pillow to look at the silhouettes of Linda Hamilton and two kids emerging from a cave entombed in lava, and then I started crying. It's not a proud moment. But I was struck by the word "survivor." It resonated.

People who survive disaster — the ones who emerge from the smoking skeleton of a train wreck with that hollow glare of shock at being alive — and being alive to meet the next absurd moment before the vacuum gaze of a news camera — are transformed creatures.

We naturally empathize with them. Not only because we are a species genetically engineered for survival, but because from a purely spiritual perspective, those who survive represent something miraculous in the mere mortal. For whatever reason, the survivor is someone who has managed to beat the odds — or perhaps even an act of God — and lived to tell the tale. They are changed people, and as such, they are outsiders unable to see the world as it once was.

Survival. It's a powerful concept, and it's the central core of what has been loosely pieced together as the Canadian identity ever since Margaret Atwood wrote her aptly titled thematic dissection of Canadian literature, *Survival*, more than 30 years ago. After spot-ting the repeated motif of frozen corpses, drowned bodies and accidental tragedies, Atwood maintained the Canadian literary tradition could be defined by a variety of basic victim positions.

The first and most primitive position is to deny that you are a victim, as in: "I made it, therefore it's obvious that we aren't victims. The rest are just lazy ..." The second position is to acknowledge victimhood, but "explain this as an act of Fate, the Will of God, the dictates of Biology ... or any other large general powerful idea." The third victim position is the self-affirming victim, the one who takes no responsibility for his or her victimhood, as in: "My mother died when I was young — it's not my fault." The fourth victim position in Atwood's *Survival* is the "creative non-victim." This is the person who is a former victim; a person who, for some reason or other, managed to take responsibility, overcome the odds, and survive. Anyone who had the power to create anything — whether it be a crop of wheat or a romantic novel — was in position four because their creative energies were no longer being suppressed or mischannelled into a victim stance. In the United States, they call these people "winners." We call them "creative non-victims." This, in a nutshell, describes the essential difference between our two nations.

In this chapter, we'll begin to pull apart the nuts and bolts of the Canadian identity and explore survival as a central concept in Canadian criticism. We'll look at how our survival mythology is different from that in the

United States and how those differences are translated onto film to form the fundamental themes of the Canadian cinematic experience.

Winners vs. Creative Non-victims

As we'll explore further in subsequent chapters, most American film is predicated on the concept of good and bad. In the standard Hollywood handbook, the good is generally represented by a white man with big muscles, a big gun and a big moral agenda. The bad is generally represented by a "foreigner" with a menacing accent. The good generally win. The bad absolutely, positively have to lose. (Studio audience tracking numbers guarantee it — justice must prevail in order to reach blockbuster status.) This black-and-white worldview is the foundation of the Hollywood mythology, just as it is the foundation of any organized value system — or religion — because it forces us to isolate the "outsider" as the potential enemy. In the days of the Crusades, any non-Christian was the heathen enemy and had to be destroyed. Likewise, in the days of Cold War American film, the enemy was any Soviet or Communist sympathizer. Belief systems need believers, and believers need to feel they are on the "right side." They need to feel they are "righteous" in order to gain meaning in the eyes of God. Hence, the creation of "winner" heroes: the backbone of the American Dream.

In Canada, things look entirely different. The foundation of our mythology is survival, as Atwood, Northrop Frye and others have made abundantly clear. Bordered by untamable elements on all sides except the south, where we face a different type of threat — the threat of assimilation from the most powerful nation on the planet — Canada is a nation that could never afford to buy into the artificial warrior-hero mythology. Overwhelmed by the vast landscape and humbled by the First Nations people's symbiotic relationship to the natural world, the Canadian knows the key to survival is to be aware of one's limitations. Ego is a sizable liability in the bush. Overconfidence can kill, but a quiet and humble approach can often save your life — as Winnipeg director Guy Maddin makes absolutely clear in his film *Careful*, where all the characters live in fear of triggering an avalanche. The only thing they can do to prevent the disaster is whisper at all times. The image proves we aren't so stupid to believe that you can ever truly tame the forces of nature.

If Canadians have a nice summer, they will automatically suspect winter will be twice as nasty. We believe in a natural sense of balance or magical retribution, which means if *Dante's Peak* had been a Canadian film, no townspeople would have waited for an evacuation order: people would have picked up sticks and hightailed it out of town at the mere mention of an eruption because as real survivors, we are naturally worst-case scenario thinkers. Those who were foolish enough to stay behind would surely pay the ultimate price for their stupidity. And yet, regardless of how well one prepares — or how wise one may be — survival is a commodity that is mostly out of our hands. As a result, the Canadian literary and film tradition is littered with corpses. Here, people freeze in the snow, drown in lakes and oceans, suffocate in avalanches, get lost in the woods and fall down craggy cliffs. But for every person who perishes, there are others who live to tell the tale — and it is through their eyes, the transformed eyes of the survivor, that the Canadian film experience is framed.

Surfacing vs. Deliverance

While I'm loath to open this discussion with a film as universally maligned as *Surfacing* (1980) — the Claude Jutra-directed adaptation of the Margaret Atwood novel — it's a logical place to start for several reasons. (Besides, by talking about it at length I can tell you why the film is important, without subjecting you to the actual experience of watching it.) Not only does it allow us to catch up with Claude Jutra and bring into crisp focus why so many Canadians developed a skepticism with regards to Canadian film, but from a thematic perspective, the characters in *Surfacing* are survivors — people who emerge fundamentally altered from their stay in the woods. They encounter almost every one of the afore-mentioned natural disasters — and more — as they head up to Ontario cottage country on a quest to find one character's missing father. (Note: this is not the first missing father in Canadian film, and it is definitely not going to be the last.)

Kate (Kathleen Beller), who is the first-person narrator in the book, is trying to locate her dad after she hears from her family that he's been declared missing. She can't believe her wonderful woodsman daddy figure could have succumbed to the elements. "It can't be true!" she protests. "He knows those woods better than anyone. He'll come back! I have to go there and try to find him!" Within a few scenes and some strung-together flashbacks, Kate, her boyfriend, Joe, and another couple are at the lake cabin, trying to piece together the events that led to Dad's disappearance. They find a collection of strange sketches on the table. They can't really figure out what they are, but there's something raw and oddly sexual about them. In fact, the two men pick out the elongated penis in the drawings almost immediately and begin to make off-colour remarks about what dear old Dad was really up to all those weeks by himself. Sex enters the frame at the same time as the missing father figure. This is important — as dads and sex are a recurring theme in Canadian film — but for now, let's simply assume the two are variables in the same equation. Father is missing, and now the default daddy figure (who takes the form of David, the college professor character played by R. H. Thompson) is assuming his place with a sexual swagger.

Because sex is procreative and therefore a symbolic challenge to the natural forces that continually take lives — another subject we'll explore in depth later — it doesn't take long for the professor to face a sizeable challenge to his own survival. It comes in the form of two hunters who stumble upon Kate and the professor after an aborted rape. The professor thinks Kate has been teasing him and makes his move to "conquer her" when the two of them are alone in the woods. Kate struggles, then submits. Her refusal to fight prompts the professor to lose his erection because now she is no longer a conquest and he can't satisfy himself in the knowledge that he is the conquering hero. He is merely a predator — a pathetic loser who preys on young innocents to build his self-esteem. Just as the professor skulks away, the hunters' rifles rip through the silence. They appear moments later, catching Kate and the professor in this most compromising and highly vulnerable pants-down position.

The scene bears a striking similarity to another survival-based film — one crafted in the American tradition: *Deliverance*. Hugely successful when it debuted in 1972 with a buff Burt Reynolds in leather pants, *Deliverance* is the ultimate American story of survival of the fittest. It deals with a group of men who venture into the woods for no other reason than manly boy-bonding adventure (not necessity or family ties). There are no women in *Deliverance*. There are only the men on the river, and the creepy, banjo-playing hillbillies who stalk them. The ingredients in both films are similar: We have a contrast between "civilized world citizens" and the wild landscape that threatens to destroy them. In *Deliverance*, we have the adventurers posed against the natural forces of the river and the inbred hillbillies. The split between man and nature is very clear, but in *Surfacing*, things are far more ambiguous — which a dissection of the "rape sequences" in each film makes abundantly clear.

In *Deliverance*, Bobby (Ned Beatty) is told to "squeal like a piggy" as he is about to be raped by the hillbillies, who represent the forces of nature gone wrong. This is the defining moment in the film because after all that macho interplay between the boys, Bobby is forced to realize his vulnerability, and so is his buddy Ed (Jon Voight), who is forced to watch passively with his neck strapped to a tree. In *Surfacing*, Kate — our central character and de facto protagonist — is first threatened by the most "civilized" character of all: the educated, intellectual professor who needs to feel in control now that he's been removed from the classroom and his adoring students. After she defuses his pantalooned missile by being completely submissive, the hunters appear, posing yet another threat to the group's survival. Here, the hunters are macho twits. They kill deer and destroy nature, which means if we were to draw a diagram of the forces working against Kate in her quest, they are symbols of civilization — not nature. Kate, in a perfectly Canadian twist, may look like the victim, but she actually turns out to be the one with the most control. She can distance the sex act from her own sense of self, unlike the men, who

base their entire masculine identity on their copulatory prowess. She is somehow in-tune with nature while the men are not.

In both cases, men are subjected to sexual humiliation. In *Deliverance*, Bobby is humiliated at gunpoint by hillbillies. In *Surfacing*, the professor is first humiliated at the hands of Kate, when she submits to his macho bid for sexual control and takes off her own pants; then, he is humiliated at gunpoint by the hunter. The professor pees his jeans when the hunter threatens to blow his head off. For the professor, the humiliation is just too much to bear, and after a scuffle that gives him control of the rifle, he starts to beat the hunter, screaming at him to "piss 'em" in a desperate bid to regain his manly composure. Unable to assert his sexual dominance, the professor begins taking out his frustration on the group, particularly his weak-minded girlfriend (Margaret Dragu), whom he humiliates several times over.

In both *Surfacing* and *Deliverance*, our supposed heroes survive canoe accidents, long tumbles down cliffs and sexual predation. Both are also stories focused on flooding bodies of water. But where *Deliverance* gives us a river — a long, flowing snake across the landscape, *Surfacing* gives us the lake — a stagnant body of water that is usually far more circular than any river, and therefore a far more "feminine" landscape.

In *Deliverance* there's a genuine sense of victory at the end of the film because Lewis, Bobby and Ed survive, but in *Surfacing* there's no euphoria at the end of the day at all. First, there is fear, then a huge sense of relief, a quiet sense of peace and understanding. We do see something similar in the final frames of *Deliverance*, as Ed and Bobby eat dinner together on their first night back in civilization, but it's far more celebratory than anything we see in *Surfacing*, which ends on an ambiguous note as the characters leave the frame, and we end up looking at a still life of the lake.

The difference in heroic stance can be seen in other details. For example, after Joe (Kate's boyfriend) stops the professor from blowing the hunter's head off, he takes the gun and throws it into the river shouting, "Goddamn guns!" There is certainly no such disdain of firearms in *Deliverance* — if anything, the primitive hunter re-emerges with bow and arrow in hand — nor, for that matter, was there any potential for women to emerge as bigger heroes than the men, since women are not part of this picture. After the hunter incident in *Surfacing*, Kate remarks to Joe: "He pees his pants and he's still a hero?" Kate questions the very notion of the hero mythology because it ignores the humiliating reality of a battle with death. Sure David — the professor — survives and beats the crap out of the hunter, but he's forced to wash his jeans in the river with a permanent pout on his lips. He then goes to great and perverse lengths to re-establish his macho superiority over the others when he makes the sexually humiliating film of his girlfriend dancing around the dead heron. Once again, however, Kate intercedes and unspools the film in daylight — essentially crippling the over-confident prof one more time, and, more importantly, removing his intellectual distance from the situation by exposing the negative. The movie camera objectifies the situation, but Kate reminds the prof that he is human, and no distancing device can make him otherwise. In short, no matter which way you look at it, the Canadian survival experience is far more humble and it could be argued, far more realistic in the way it positions man (and naturally, woman) in his environment.

Surfacing (1981): These lame survivors are Kate (Kathleen Beller) and Joe (Joseph Bottoms). Watch them help each other out of the bush. Notice who's carrying whom — as well as the questioning gaze of Kate. You won't find any buddy-bonding in this movie, as the woman turns out to be the one with all the heroic proportions. TORONTO FILM LIBRARY

Those who survive *Surfacing* (with the possible exclusion of the audience, which has the heaviest burden of all just watching this assemblage of nail-on-chalkboard scenes) emerge alive — and that's all. There is no ascension to the heavens. No ticker-tape parade. Not even a small child waving a flag. Rather, the only thing the characters emerge from the wilderness with is a greater understanding of self: that we are small, that we are fragile and that we are inextricably tied to the wild world beyond in ways that we can't necessarily predict or control.

What's better: to confidently move through the wilderness with an eye for adventure and conquest, or to humbly scramble across the rocks, constantly aware of your own mortality and your place in the universe? It's a complicated question, but we'll unravel our qualitative judgement about heroism by looking at how we react to the films from an entertainment perspective.

From an amusement standpoint, obviously, *Deliverance* is a far better movie than *Surfacing*, which has often been described as the worst film ever made in Canada. As film critic and writer Martin Knelman noted in a 1982 piece in *Toronto Life*: "[*Surfacing*] transformed Margaret Atwood's unfilmable quest allegory into a simple-minded feminist equivalent of a woodsy Boy's Own adventure story. Even if the script hadn't been impossible, the casting was lethal: the cow-eyed, tiresomely sincere Kathleen Beller as the searching heroine and the loutish jock-mannequin Joseph Bottoms as her boyfriend. Unlike many Canadian movies, *Surfacing* at least came out of honest intentions, yet the reputations of Jutra and Fox were seriously damaged by its deficiencies ..."[1] Note the words "sincere" and "deficiencies" in Knelman's critique. These words tend to find their way into a discussion of Canadian film, so let's deviate for a second to consider what they mean in context. Knelman says Kate's sincerity is tiresome, and he suggests it's one of the bigger problems in this already weak-scripted film. While I agree with Knelman that Beller's performance is weak and suffers from a soap-opera acting style, the word "sincerity" suggests that Knelman would have preferred a slightly more ersatz tone — an acting style that more closely matches Hollywood blood and guts action/adventure movies than an NFB documentary on backwoods survival.

Once again, on that score, I agree with Knelman that if *Surfacing* had been shot like an action movie instead of a serious drama, it would have been a far more entertaining experience, but that only signals to me just how powerful Hollywood formula is in shaping our expectations around motion pictures. Whether critics care to admit it or not, we're always comparing movies to our expectations of what they should be, and because most of us were brought up in TV households and weaned on American entertainment product, we're generally always comparing things to Hollywood. In that context, *Surfacing* surely stood no chance whatsoever for a charitable reading — especially not when *Deliverance* came out a decade before this film and featured big stars and included several high-octane stunt sequences. No wonder Knelman finds *Surfacing* so "deficient" — it has none of the above. However, it does have original music from Anne Mortifee, which more adequately illustrates the idea of "tiresome sincerity" than anything Beller does in the entire film.

When we compare *Surfacing* to *Deliverance*, we are comparing the Canadian experience to the American experience, and inevitably the American vision comes across much stronger. the American experience has been highly romanticized and commodified by an industry that gives us macho heroes like Burt Reynolds and Jon Voight instead of pee-pee pants professors like R. H. Thompson.

Exactly as Knelman says, the "sincerity" in *Surfacing* is its biggest liability. It is not romantic or idealized, it's just goofy and awkward and painfully embarrassing to watch — a description that could easily match our reactions to a variety of Canadian cultural efforts, from our attempts to duplicate American talk shows to any speech by Prime Minister Jean Chrétien. Again, it all comes down to this boxed institutional quality of cultural life in Canada. On one hand, we are overjoyed to have government-subsidized art. On the other, we distrust anything even remotely institutional because it smacks of nerdy earnestness.

But getting back to our question, "What's better?" I'd have to say that personally, I've grown to respect our national sincerity because it's far more human in scale than the incredulous heroics performed by Hollywood he-men. While there's no doubt that we human animals have demonstrated a remarkable craving for hero mythology — from Hercules to Russell Crowe in *Gladiator* — Canadian culture is one that steadfastly refuses to play the hero game. This may make us look like pansies to our American neighbours, but it means Canadians can look at the hero myth with a grain of salt and stand back to make up their own minds. We are allowed to have a humble approach to life instead of constantly feeling the need to assert ourselves in the world at large.

Survivor Guilt

With survival comes guilt. People who survive an ordeal, large or small, will often feel guilty at having emerged from the crisis alive — especially if others didn't. Often referred to in psychological circles as "post-traumatic stress disorder," specialists like Aphrodite Matsakis (*Survivor Guilt, Post-Traumatic Stress Disorder: A Complete Treatment Guide; Trust After Trauma: A Guide to Relationships for Survivors and Those Who Love Them; Vietnam Wives: Facing the Challenges of Life with Veterans Suffering Post-Traumatic Stress*) describe survivor guilt as intense depression, a sense of meaninglessness and an inability to function according to social expectations. For instance, people who survived the Oklahoma City bombing were unable to assume their regular workload even years after the incident. They had a hard time returning to work, parking cars in underground garages and walking into buildings of any kind. They were prone to spontaneous teary outbursts. Long-term effects included distraction, memory loss and loss of motor coordination and mental ability. The only thing that could help them was art therapy.

One may find the comparison between Canadians and survivors of the Oklahoma City blast a little far-fetched, but considering our close relationship with the survival experience, it deserves a little tangent. Survivor guilt can affect anyone. It can be as anonymous as witnessing a car crash or as personal as losing a loved one to disease. We feel guilty because death is arbitrary. There is no inherent meaning in the Grim Reaper's selection. Some go before others. That's all there is to it, leaving many of us to feel completely powerless in the face of our inevitable fate.

Since the concept of powerlessness is as foreign to the American psyche as "losing," it should come as no surprise that American film convention has generally tried to give death a good reason for appearing on screen. People who die in Hollywood formula films are generally evil-doers who deserve what they get. People who survive in Hollywood formula films are generally worthy and virtuous. The convention may be completely fictitious, but it's far more satisfying than the sadly arbitrary reality. It gives us a sense of meaning, and for that reason, the same techniques have been used in the inception of other belief systems, particularly religions, which almost universally see death as "the last judgement" in the eyes of God. All of which brings us back to guilt. In a religious context, guilt follows sin and a lack of faith. In the context of survival, guilt is simply part of living.

Canadian film is full of guilt. We are a nation of humble survivors who know just how difficult and unheroic survival really is, and we are probably one of the most guilt-laden nations in the world, considering we haven't carried out any premeditated programs of wholesale genocide or ethnic cleansing. In fact, almost every Canadian film I've ever seen — with the notable exceptions of films from First Nations peoples — are infused with tangible amounts of guilt and most of that guilt is the result of simply being alive. With that in mind, let's take a look at some of the central guilt stories in Canadian film — and see where the guilt trip takes us as we travel ever deeper into the heart of the Canadian psyche.

Not Wanted on the Voyage: The Sweet Hereafter

After subjecting you to a drawn-out discussion of *Surfacing* (which was a better book than a film, by far), it's only fair that I show you the other side of the spectrum. Without doubt the most important English-Canadian film to date (for various reasons), Atom Egoyan's *The Sweet Hereafter* is not only the most visible success in this new age of Canadian cinema, but its success signals a solid connection to the loose nerve bundle we probed in *Surfacing*. A series of inter-connected personal stories revolving around a tragic school bus crash in a small town, *The Sweet Hereafter* puts survivor guilt on the mental marquee. Guilt is the main driving force behind all the characters who are now left behind: it warps their worldviews and twists every relationship before the lens. For this reason, it is ripe for dissection in this chapter as it dredges the subtext of almost every Canadian movie that went before and places the tangled wreckage above the waterline — much like the film's central visual theme: the mangled bus.

When we first see the bus, it is through the eyes of the lawyer, Mitchell Stephens (Ian Holm). In the opening sequence of the film, Mitchell is sitting in the womblike comfort of his own car as it moves passively through a car wash. Isolated in this private, quiet place surrounded by warm streams of water and cleansing suds, Mitchell drifts far, far away before us. We don't really know where his mind is until the silence is invaded by the angst-prompting ring of a cell phone. It is Mitchell's daughter Zoe (Caerthan Banks, Russell Banks' daughter), calling her father from a pay phone. Immediately we know that Zoe and Mitchell live in two completely different realities. Mitchell's world is much like his luxury car: sheltered, lonely and comfortable. Zoe's world is the street: hostile, unforgiving and public. Mitchell clearly has a hard time reconciling this difference. He is impatient with Zoe because he can't control her. She is a drug addict and he feels guilty because he can't change the situation. Moments after this brief phone call, Mitchell is forced to get out of his car. The car wash belt is broken and his car sits idle, unable to move back or forth. Symbolically, Mitchell is also stuck: he is emotionally constipated. He can't move past his guilt, and as a result, the love within him grows harder — and more painful to express. As he says in one sequence, where he is speaking with his daughter's friend and his *de facto* confessor, Allison (Stephanie Morgenstern), "Enough rage and pain and your love turns to something else ... it turns to steaming piss."

The excretory metaphor is slightly different, but the emotional intent is the same: Mitchell is all tied up inside. To escape, he must leave the comfort of his car and experience the baptismal force of the autowash. When he does, Egoyan subtly changes locales and cuts to a scene of Mitchell walking into a gas station. At first we think it's the gas station attached to the car wash. But as he moves through several rooms, approaching the camera at each turn, we see bits and pieces of old cars — lifeless mechanical appendages and rusted parts. Mitchell has entered a type of limbo: the timeless world of a small town where this tragic crash took place. Egoyan's camera pulls back, giving us a point of view shot to reveal the mangled bus through the shop windows. Mitchell is a voyeur to the carnage, but something deep within him is clearly on that bus along with the ghosts of the town's children. The bus, then, becomes the vehicle capable of taking us to the other side. It is also the main repository of guilt in the community, and as such, becomes the centrepiece in Mitchell's class-action suit on behalf of the families. Mitchell wants someone to pay for the tragedy. He arrives on the scene as a soulless profiteer, playing a game of cards with the parents' burden of guilt. Mitchell promises to point a finger at the guilty party. He is all about alleviating pain through projection and twisting the facts in an attempt to alleviate his own guilt. He tries to project all that negative, accusatory energy at some faceless corporate entity, but we know — just from the way he looks at the bus in the opening sequence and gets trapped in the car wash (like the bus in the ice) — he's connected to the tragedy on more than a professional level. We just aren't sure how.

As the movie progresses and Egoyan's cool exteriors — shot in British Columbia's Nicola Valley between Merritt and Spence's Bridge — gradually move past the outside walls and into the grieving interior mind-

The Sweet Hereafter (1997): Mitchell (Ian Holm) and Nicole (Sarah Polley) share a moment of deep reflection about past events, and describe the shape, colour and dimensions of their lingering personal luggage. One opts to face the truth, the other tries to shape it for personal ends. Can you tell which is which? COURTESY OF JOHNNIE EISEN © EGO FILM ARTS scapes of the characters, we begin to form a psychic connection to Nicole (Sarah Polley) and Dolores (Gabrielle Rose), the two survivors of the crash. Dolores was behind the wheel of the bus when it veered off the road and skidded onto a frozen lake, where it broke through the ice and sank into the cold black water with all the children aboard. Dolores is clearly shattered. She deals with her guilt using denial and drugs, but she can't escape the horror of surviving when her precious children perished. Likewise, Nicole is awash in survivor guilt as the sole kid to emerge from the crash alive. Like the one lame child in the *Pied Piper* — another sympathetic motif that Egoyan uses to reinforce the ideas of death and guilt in this children's world — Nicole did not meet the same fate as the others. She ends up in a wheelchair, but is alive to witness the town unravel beneath the weight of its loss. Aided and abetted by Mitchell's greedy manipulations, the community cleaves. Nicole feels guilt about more than simply surviving. She feels guilty because she is no longer a complete innocent. A sexual relationship with her father (Tom McCamus) has pulled her away from the rest of the children, and now she is forever trapped somewhere between adulthood and innocence.

Much like the young Benoit (Jacques Gagnon) in *Mon Oncle Antoine* (1971), who picks up the body of a dead teenager with his uncle in a snowstorm, Nicole was forced to deal with death in her own image. Death isn't just something that takes away the old and tarnished, its bony fingers touch everyone — including the young and innocent — and that's what makes it so hard to reconcile. The people of this small town are destroyed because the innocent were victimized, which only exacerbates their feelings of guilt. After all, why should all these aging sinners be given the chance to live while the sinless, and clearly saintly, children were taken away? This is the question that eventually pushes Mitchell into a much-needed emotional catharsis. Confessing his sins to Allison, Zoe's childhood friend, Mitchell is able to relate a story about "the summer they almost lost her."

This is the coda to the opening frames of the film, where we see a simple shot of a family sleeping peacefully in the same bed. We learn this is Mitchell and his wife and daughter in happier times, before Mitchell sold his soul to the amoral world of the legal profession. From this blissful image, Mitchell tells the story of how Zoe almost died from a spider bite, and how he was ready to cut her throat open with a sharp pen knife should her throat close and she be unable to breathe. "I was ready to go all the way," he says, tearing up. The story, and particularly Egoyan's image (a close-up of the child's face and the glinting steel blade beside it) has clear Biblical connections as it harkens back to Abraham's near-sacrifice of Isaac. Mitchell says he was ready to "go all the way," just as Abraham was ready to go all the way and surrender unto God what was God's by taking a knife and cutting Isaac's throat. Neither Abraham nor Mitchell is forced to take the blade to his child's throat, but they were ready to do so.

In a Biblical context, Abraham's gesture was enough to appease God and prove his loyalty to the one and only Creator. In *The Sweet Hereafter*, the imagery is secularized and internalized into one system. Mitchell's readiness to cut his child's throat is a testament to his love for his own child. He loved her enough to risk killing her, and that commitment was enough to spare her life — at least as a child. Now that Zoe is all grown up, the dynamic is different — but the ingredients are the same. Zoe is an intravenous drug user who tells her father she tested positive for HIV. Once again, her life is at risk and Mitchell, who has tried everything from "tough love" to a string of treatment centres, is pushed into asking himself how much further he has to go. He was ready for the knife, but is he ready to be heartbroken by her addiction all over again? The answer is always the same: Yes, because he loves her. And that love is both his burden and his salvation. A step in the wrong direction and guilt will follow, hounding you until the end — eating you alive — until one dies, or finds forgiveness in the eyes of God (Abraham), one's peers (Dolores), or oneself (Mitchell, Nicole).

The secular bent of the film, the visual importance of the snow-covered landscape and the dominance of guilt imagery make *The Sweet Hereafter* a decidedly Canadian film. One might argue that because the book was written by American novelist Russell Banks, the film's Canadianess is compromised, but I disagree because it was brought to the screen by a Canadian director. This means that everything we see before us, from the snow-covered landscape to the wood-panelled interiors, was framed by someone who was framed by the Canadian experience. Moreover, because Egoyan wrote the screenplay, he was able to re-imagine the contents of the novel and incorporate his own imagery into the piece, making for an entirely new, and thoroughly Canadian, vision of the original source material.

Some of the elements were altered to meet Canadian-content funding guidelines, but other changes were purely for artistic reasons. For instance, Egoyan changed the locale from the Adirondacks to the Coastal mountains of British Columbia to place the film north of the 49th parallel, but the Pied Piper motif was an Egoyan invention. So was the character of the confessor, Allison. Other Canadianisms include

the Canadian Legion badge on the breast-pocket of Dolores' stroke-impaired spouse (another survivor motif: the war veteran), the vernacular language (several characters say "eh?"), the thoroughly Canadian soundtrack (the Tragically Hip to Jane Siberry), fragmentation of linear time, and the recurrent use of photography as a symbol of both emotional distance and loss (Mitchell videotapes the bus interior, while Egoyan shows us images of the dead child, Bear, in his parents' A-frame home). We'll explore this idea in greater depth later on, but it's worth mentioning here that the photographic process is often used as a symbol of distance, and emotional removal, in Canadian film. Egoyan has used photographic device in practically every film he's ever made, from *Speaking Parts* to *Felicia's Journey*, and to find it in *The Sweet Hereafter* only proves how much of an Egoyan — and hence, Canadian — film it really is.

Similarly, *The Sweet Hereafter*'s guilt trips also reflect back through Egoyan's oeuvre — proving how much of a continuation it is of his own artistic journey. We can see evidence of survivor guilt in several Egoyan efforts. In *Exotica*, Bruce Greenwood plays Francis, another grieving father/survivor. Francis survives two tragedies: his daughter's murder and his estranged wife's death in a car crash. Further eroding his sense of community, Francis has been cuckolded by his own brother, who survived the accident and is now confined to a wheelchair. Left alone, Francis tries to recreate the past in several ways: he asks his niece to "babysit" the house, and he makes regular visits to Exotica, a swanky peeler bar, where his late daughter's one-time babysitter works as a dancer.

In *Speaking Parts*, Clara (Gabrielle Rose) survives the death of her brother. Her guilt is compounded by the fact he died as a result of donating an organ to help her live. Now, awash in guilt, she tries to give him a tribute by writing a screenplay about his sacrifice — only to have money-grubbing studio executives change the details of the drama, eliminating her role in the saga altogether. Again, we have survivor guilt, photographic remnants of the survivors — here, in the form of a videotape mausoleum — but we also have the inclusion of another theme which we will bump into later on, and that's an attempt at healing through art. Clara tries to soothe the emptiness she feels inside by recreating her brother on the page, and hopefully on film. She isn't entirely successful, but the gesture is significant as it shows us a person in a clear "victim stance #4: Creative Non-Victim."

The Great Canadian Guilt Rush

Mon Oncle Antoine and Egoyan's catalogue are good places to find guilt, but there are a great many other stewpots simmering on the Canadian cinematic stove. David Cronenberg gave us a bunch of transformed, self-loathing survivors in *Crash*. Guy Maddin gives a Gothic take on the subject in *Careful*, replete with hauntings and acts of vengeance. Mort Ransen's film, *Margaret's Museum,* shows us another mining town full of surviving widows and women who have yet to become widows.

A brief survey of the landscape also reveals more than a few crosses in Quebec, thanks to the intense guilt training at the hands of the Catholic church. Denys Arcand and Robert Lepage have mined the guilt-edged mother lode more than once. Arcand's *Jesus of Montreal* plays out guilt on two levels: the guilt we carry for such everyday sins as adultery and money-worship, and how those surface transgressions resonate on a deeper spiritual level, to the point where our

actor/Jesus (Lothaire Bluteau) is sacrificed all over again. Guilt is an inherent part of the myth and ritual that binds our society together. Eve ate the fruit, we were cast from Eden, and now we are left to mourn the loss of perfection. The Christ myth is an attempt to regain paradise, and not surprisingly, most American films will often attempt to give us a happy ending where people attain some sense of salvation. But Canadian film does not. There is not much room for absolution at the hands of God in this country. Living here, on the edge of the great white tundra, we are far — very far — from Eden. The landscape is rich and rugged, but it is clearly not benevolent. Here, in Eden's polar opposite, we are reminded of our exile — and our fall from grace. However, where other traditions may try to deny this reality of the human condition, Canadian film loves to mirror it on the screen. When "Jesus" dies in Arcand's film, there is nothing artificial about it: He passes out in the Metro station and people walk right by, thinking he's just another crackhead or alcoholic taking a snooze on the sidewalk.

Another variation on guilt can be found in two seminal Robert Lepage films. *Le Polygraphe* screams "guilt theme here" thanks to the title. The basic premise mirrors elements in Egoyan's *Speaking Parts* as it focuses on the murder of a young woman and the back-story of an actress who will play her in the movie version. Even though the actress doesn't know the woman who was murdered, she is connected to her through a friend — a man who stands accused of the woman's murder. Lepage uses layered narrative to peel away the complex series of truths that eventually reveal the murderer, but the people who figure in the drama itself are all people undergoing various degrees of survivor guilt. One is the murderer, but everyone is guilty by nature or by association.

Le Confessionnal is another trip into self-created hell where people turn up dead and others are left to continue living in pain. The film opens with the death of a patriarch, but as the movie twists and turns back in time, we realize there was another death that left the family paralyzed and guilt-laden. A young mother takes her life when she realizes there is no escape from her sin, leaving her infant son screwed up for the rest of his days as he struggles to reconcile his life with his mother's death.

More guilt-spilling guts are visible in Denis Villeneuve's *Maelström,* which tells the story of a woman who has an abortion, gets behind the wheel of her car drunk, and, just to make the guilt cocktail complete, kills someone in a hit-and-run. Her actions cause incredible harm and she feels unfathomable remorse — to the point where she attempts suicide as a remedy for her survivor guilt — but there is no real escape. She tries to open up to her best friend, another confidante character played by Stephanie Morgenstern, who tells her that "every human act is a rebellion against death." Morgenstern, having played two characters at the receiving end of survivor guilt — in *Maelström* and *The Sweet Hereafter* — is well aware of the Canadian victim stance. When I spoke to her in the course of preparing this book, this near-ubiquitous Canadian actor, director, pop-epistemologist pointed out the differences between Canadian victims and the generic brand of American losers. "In the States, victimology is all about making the hero look good. In Canada, the victim is often the hero, which makes for a far more complex narrative. That's why I don't mind playing victims in Canadian movies," said Morgenstern (who appeared in the dramatized pulp elements in *Forbidden Love* as well as providing one of the voices in the kid's show *Sailor Moon*). "Canadian victims are usually really good parts. In *Maelström*, I don't play a victim: I play the best friend who can't get past her best friend's wall of guilt. She thinks her guilt is all about the abortion. She wants to help, but she has no idea what's really going on because Bibi has exiled herself."

Precisely. The guilt is now a part of Bibiane's life. All she can hope for is forgiveness from her victim's surviving relatives, which adds yet another layer to the whole shellac.

The guilt rush isn't limited to film. It's pervasive in our literature as well. I know it doesn't make a lot of sense considering we've been one of the most considerate, peace-oriented and charitable nations on Earth, but our heavy conscience is evident in everything from Robertson Davies' *Fifth Business* (in which a rock in a snowball leaves a legacy of guilt for several characters), to *The English Patient* (in which a pilot badly burned in a crash wrestles with the guilt of surviving the war, while the one woman he truly loved did not). Clearly, guilt is a fixture in the Canadian psyche. The only real question that remains is why? What type of guilt is it, really? We've made a strong case for survivor guilt, but there are other potential sources. As we noted in regard to Lepage and Arcand, in Quebec this lingering guilt is associated with the legacy of Catholic institutions. There is the foundation of Christian guilt as a result of Christ's sacrifice, but there is also guilt borne from a lack of faith in the wake of increased institutional secularism.

If we take a closer look at *Mon Oncle Antoine,* we can see the fault line of faith. In the opening sequence of the film, Benoit — the mischievous altar boy — can be seen stealing communion wafers and wine behind the priest's back. Meanwhile, the citizens of his

Maelström (2000): Bibiane Champagne (Marie Josée Croze) is ensnared in a weave of her own creation in this Denis Villeneuve drama about a woman, a Norweigian fisherman, a frogman and an ancient fish (who serves as the narrator). ODEON

small asbestos-mining town bitch and whine about their poor treatment at the hands of the company and the Anglos who run it. Both the church and the corporate establishment are therefore symbols of outdated institutionalism. Only in their subversion, or dissolution, will the people be freed from their slow, circular walk toward death and be given a chance to create something new for the next generation. After one monolith falls, and before another can take its place, however, a big hole is created within the fabric of the community and as is the case with all missing items, guilt will often seep into the waiting void as an emotional substitute.

The Story Behind the Skeletal Remains
We are clearly not created from the same stuff

as the American psyche. The very foundation of our film industry, as well as the themes we choose to explore, is the polar opposite to that found south of the 49th parallel. Margaret Atwood called us victims in *Survival*, her investigation into early Canadian literature, but we are clearly beyond the victim stage. In the context of Canadian film, we are in victim stance #4: We are creative non-victims, because film itself is a creative process. Sure, as every film we've looked at over the course of this chapter proves, we still see images of frozen corpses, drowning victims, car crash casualties and other accidental deaths, but we are no longer telling these stories from a first-person perspective. The film process demands a shift in perspective because the very act of picking up a movie camera is empowering —

as Brault and Jutra made clear in their subtle peek at the roots of the Quebec revolution in *Mon Oncle Antoine*. The camera pushes one into a state of heightened awareness because it removes the image from the viewer, and gives one a different take on the big picture.

Remember how Mitchell Stephens picks up the camcorder to peer around the wreckage of the school bus like some forensic surgeon? The camera gives him distance on the tragedy and greater power over the event and those affected by it, but also alienates him and places him outside the community. In short, the camera delineates the boundaries between self and other. Other is on the "other" side of the camera, while self is the mind that makes the pictures. In much the same way that survivors used art therapy as a way of moving past their own guilt, we appear to be using the artistic process of film to explore our hefty and long-lost emotional baggage proving that we are no longer "victims" but survivors — and survivors who may well be on the road to creative recovery thanks to our burgeoning film vision.

Gary Burns

Born 1960 — Calgary, Alberta

ODEON

A former construction/oil worker who turned to filmmaking at the age of 30, Burns is a lone wolf on the Alberta landscape howling at the moon. A guy who generally works alone and steers clear of the "film scene," Burns makes movies that appeal to his own personal brand of darkly comic wackiness. "I don't really know what's going on in Alberta from a film standpoint. I'm not a part of it. I'm not really part of anything. I don't crew. I don't work in the industry. My friends have nothing to do with the film business. I don't even go to see movies. I'm guess I'm just another alienated Canadian filmmaker," says the man who used to sandblast oil rig equipment.

A graduate of the University of Calgary's drama program, Burns decided to enroll in the film program at Concordia University in Montreal in the hopes of turning his passion for storytelling into a career. After graduating from Concordia in 1992, he began putting the pieces together for his first feature, *The Suburbanators*, a layered study of the generic strip mall universe where people seek comfort at the butt end of a big fatty — if they can get their hands on one, that is. Picked up by the people at Troma Entertainment (the ones who spotted the talents of *South Park* creators Matt Stone and Trey Parker), the film established Burns on the cult film circuit — but failed to make a dent in the mainstream. *Kitchen Party*, his second feature, was another look at the subtle dramas that unravel between the cracks of the social veneer as it contrasts one last blowout bash before Scott (Scott Speedman) goes to college with a somewhat tamer, but no less dramatic, party where his parents are spending the soirée. *Kitchen Party* fared somewhat better, earning Burns the title of best emerging western director at the 1997 Vancouver International Film Festival and a great review from the *New York Times* when it screened as part of the New Directors series put on by the Museum of Modern Art — but it tanked commercially. "My real problem is that I can make pretty much anything I want. I made two movies that no one saw ... Where else but Canada would I get a chance to make a third?"

With the 2000 release of *waydowntown*, Burns finally emerged from the primordial soup of the Canadian film scene with some legs to stand on. Winner of the CityTV award for best Canadian feature at the 2000 Toronto International Film Festival (which comes with a cheque for $25,000), the man from "Wild Rose Country" may finally be looking at a rosy future. Not that he's counting on it. He's learned enough about the Canadian film scene to know expectations are a bad thing, but *waydowntown* was clearly his most successful film to date with decent theatrical runs across the country and a respectable box-office tally that put the low-budget film in the proverbial black. The film was also picked up for an American release (by indie distributors Lot 47), which puts him in a rare Canadian category, indeed. "With *waydowntown*, I wanted to make a movie that people actually saw. It's one thing to go out there and sacrifice everything to make a movie, but it would be really nice to actually make a living at it ... Not that I'm complaining. I feel very lucky to be one of the few people in this country who is able to make the movies I want to make, but you go to so much effort to make them that you want other people to see them, too. But if it's a choice between making movies that I don't care about, or can't control creatively, then I'd rather do what I'm doing right now ... In that respect, the Canadian system is preferable to American one, but when you're told that your movie has a marketing problem because it's identifiably Canadian — which I was told with *waydowntown* — it's easy to get a little frustrated, because Canadians don't seem all that interested in seeing Canadian movies. Quebecers watch their own movies, but English Canada is so overwhelmed by American movies that have $20 million marketing budgets that it's hard to compete."

Marketing and money problems aside, Burns is a proud Canuck and his movies are steeped in Canadian sensibilities. From the hosers who tool around suburbia to his questioning of the superhero myth, Burns' characters will often knock the land down south with subtle jabs at the prevailing consumer ideology with comments such as "Is your car your penis?" Burns says that's just his own ideas coming to the fore more than any premeditated poke at the muscle-car mentality down south. Besides, most of his barbs are aimed at the metaphorical mirror. In *waydowntown*, for instance, Burns slams the plus-

15 skywalk system as he tells the story of a bunch of young office workers who make a bet as to who can stay inside the longest. The story originated as a one-page grant proposal about architecture that used digital video cameras to record different points of view, but after he heard about *Timecode* (the Mike Figgis film that used the four-camera idea to capture the lives of four Angelenos), Burns transformed his story into a slightly more orthodox narrative that features a central character and several intertwining plotlines.

"I don't know how I write. I come up with these characters and then I just build from there. But I know I'm comfortable with the episodic technique where you have a bunch of people doing parallel things. I block out the storylines and the characters and see how I can make them fit together ... When I made *waydowntown*, I didn't know anything about corporate culture, all I know is that they're pumping out way too many law students. I was more interested in how the plus-15s destroyed downtown Calgary. If you walk through downtown Calgary on a Sunday, it looks like a neutron bomb hit — the buildings are standing, but there's no one around. It's pretty sterile, so I thought it would make for a good backdrop for this story about a bunch of faceless people who have to work within it ... like ants in an ant colony. The drama doesn't come from events, but from the human interaction — and if I had to describe my sensibilities, that's it. I'm interested in drawing out characters through human interaction — without some life-threatening event, or psycho killer," he says.

"That's the beauty of making film in this country: you can do exactly the opposite of what's expected, just for the sake of it."

FILMOGRAPHY: *The Suburbanators* (1995) | *Kitchen Party* (1997) | *Fuck Coke* (1999) | *waydowntown* (2000).

Guy Maddin

Born 1956 — Winnipeg, Manitoba

© VILIAM

He doesn't know why people insist on calling him eccentric, but it's a cross Guy Maddin will carry until the end of his days thanks to his surreal body of work that includes *Twilight of the Ice Nymphs, Careful* and Canada's first cult sensation, *Tales From the Gimli Hospital*. In the eyes of his many fans, he's a Canadian pop icon — a martyr to the artistic cause — a saviour of the cinematic form. "Really," says Maddin, "I'm just a regular guy from Winnipeg who makes movies that aren't industry based ... and for that, I'm labelled an eccentric."

A former economics major who grew to love drinking and loathing himself during a brief stint as a bank teller, Maddin had no real ambition to become a filmmaker early on — although he did have an early brush with Hollywood fame when crooner Bing Crosby gave the little Guy a piggyback as a kid.

"In my twenties, I mostly just sat around and drank a lot. I slept. I took some film classes. But working in the bank was one of the worst things I've ever done. Every time someone quit, I'd get really drunk. The only

thing the future seemed to hold was a fate at the bottom of a ditch," says Maddin, who did find some comfort in the film classes and particularly the work of the Spanish surrealist Luis Bunuel. "I think if anyone inspired me to make movies it was Bunuel. You can see his influence in almost every one of my films. Magic realism appeals to my Winnipegger sensibility I guess ... I like being in my own private dream bubble."

Through film classes and his involvement with the Winnipeg Film Group, Maddin made his first film, *The Dead Father*, in 1986. A 30-minute film about a man trying to reconcile the death of his dad, Maddin had a chance to eulogize his own father — former manager of the Winnipeg Maroons (Canada's national hockey team in 1963) — and get a feel for the form. He was inspired to try again, and in 1987, he heard about a $20,000 development grant up for grabs through the Winnipeg co-op. Looking to his own Icelandic roots, he threw a proposal together about a group of ill-fated colonists who arrived on the shores of Lake Winnipeg in the dead of winter and slowly died of starvation and small pox. He got the grant and in 1988 *Tales From the Gimli Hospital* was released to a spellbound public. The film touched a nerve in the high-strung art-house circuit and Maddin was suddenly an *enfant célèbre*. *Tales From the Gimli Hospital* played an entire year to packed midnight screenings in New York, spawning a legion of fans and earning Maddin comparisons to such cinematic luminaries as Luis Bunuel, Sergei Eisenstein and David Lynch.

"I'm always pleased if someone likes the movies because they aren't what people would normally expect. I don't make films according to any industry standard ... which is why people call me eccentric. Finally, I'm just trying to express myself. I'm not trying to consciously make art by making the films in a certain way. I mean, if one were a novelist who used magic realism in the novel, they'd just call you a novelist. But when you do it in film, people call you an eccentric artist. It doesn't hurt to be called an eccentric, especially in this country. In Britain, the press told me I had my head stuck up my ass. In Canada, I don't get negative reviews, really. They just don't say anything. For the most part, my films don't even get reviewed here, but elsewhere, I'm fair game," says Maddin.

After the success of *Gimli*, Maddin set to work on his next feature, *Archangel*, with the help of his childhood friend and producer Greg Klymkiw (whose father was the goalie for the famed Winnipeg Maroons). *Archangel* shared the same thematic terrain as *Tales* and *Dead Father*: death, sickness, alienation and a confused sense of identity. Set at the close of the First World War, the movie is all about gaps and unformed identity. Having inhaled near-fatal amounts of mustard gas, a Belgian pilot, a Russian nurse and a Canadian soldier end up in the town of Archangel, a place of icy spires and snowdrifts. All the characters have forgotten who's who, and who they were in love with. John is in love with Iris, but Iris is dead. When John meets Veronkha, he thinks she's Iris — only to discover she's married to Philbin. Veronkha, however, can't remember she's married to Philbin, and falls in love with John. Everyone suffers from a collective form of amnesia, preventing any meaningful bonding between these drifting outsiders. Not long after the release of *Archangel*, which earned Maddin the U.S. Society of Film Critics' prize for best experimental film of the year, Maddin made *Careful*, another story laced with snowy landscapes, images born from the loins of Leni Riefenstahl and more death and disease.

Careful opened the Perspective Canada series at the 1993 Festival of Festivals (now called the Toronto International Film Festival) and screened in New York and Tokyo, raising Maddin's art-house profile to the next level — the level where you get commissioned by the BBC to make movies alongside the likes of Tim Burton, Jonathan Demme and Jane Campion.

In 1995, Maddin was invited by the BBC to make a short film poem inspired by the work of Belgian charcoal artist and Symbolist Odilon Redon titled *The Eye Like a Strange Balloon Mounts Toward Infinity*. The film was based on one of Redon's more famous pieces, which is pretty much exactly what its title suggests: a giant eyeball floating in space attached to a basket. Maddin recreated this image, only as seen from a steam engine chugging across the horizon. The film proved Maddin, who never received any formal training on a motion picture camera, had now mastered the art of capturing the archaic look and feel of early motion pictures using simple tools such as vaseline and handmade irises.

"I learned everything as I needed to. Film has really been an organic process for me ... like a mould that just keeps growing ... but I only touch the things I need to. I had to learn how to use a camera on *Tales from Gimli Hospital* because the camera guy lost interest in the project after the first day. I can't say I love cameras. I wouldn't want to spend the rest of my life with a machine, you know, and I find it quite tedious talking about the mechanics of filmmaking with technical people. They seem to think it's all about the camera. In a way, I suppose it is, but no one looks at a writer's pen in the same way. It's just a tool to tell a story," says Maddin.

"I was teaching English at the U of M [University of Manitoba] to make some money. I'm completely broke — which is the natural state for a filmmaker in this country — so I taught this course called Dreyer and Joan. We watched Carl Dreyer movies and Joan of Arc movies. Dreyer movies, especially *The Passion of Joan of Arc,* meant a lot to me. There's this Lutheran obsession in Dreyer films that I like. There's a bitchy intensity to it. They are personal films that communicate a larger message and that's what makes them so rich. I get so disappointed when the students write in third person about all this stuff because the whole point of film is to pull you in to someone else's point of view. I was always encouraging them to use first person," says Maddin.

"I think you can only make movies to please yourself, but that doesn't mean I don't want to make a movie that is truly watchable. In this country, it makes sense to make personal movies because it's just so hard to get the funding. You better believe in what you're doing if you're going to spend so much time and energy trying to make it. There's more money in the States or Europe, but I could never work in the U.S. Artists are weeded out of the system there at the plankton stage. Not even Sundance types are all that intriguing to me," says Maddin, who has big fans in the Four Corners area. In 1995, he was awarded the Medal for Lifetime Achievement by the Telluride Film Festival in Telluride, Colorado. He was the youngest person to receive the honour, which has been given to the likes of Clint Eastwood, Leni Riefenstahl, Gloria Swanson and Francis Ford Coppola.

"Now, I want to make a faster movie. I sat down and watched a whole bunch of American movies and I realized it all comes down to conflict. You have to have conflict in every single frame ... and not just with two people, but with several people. The more conflict, the faster the movie goes," says Maddin, who sat down with friend, mentor and number one fan, George Toles, to write a script that featured conflict in every scene.

"That's the next feature I want to make," says Maddin, who has made nothing but shorts — including the celebrated *The Heart of the World* — since 1997's *Twilight of the Ice Nymphs.* "Next time out, I'm going to leave all this meditative lethargy behind. I want to make a fast-paced film that's so fast, it's damn near electric ... like the protagonist, who has an accident with electricity. This won't be one of those classic passive Canadian protagonists, he'll be charged."

Maddin says he won't leave all the Canadian signposts behind. "I'm still interested in stripping things away and breaking up the narrative form to see what's behind the wallpaper. I love looking behind, but I also need the wallpaper. I need to be surrounded by wallpaper on all six sides ... I also need to be surrounded by red wine. I drink like a fish," says Maddin, deadpan. "You see, in a world where everyone has to be careful, I need simple things. I'm honest with myself. None of that passive-aggressive cowardly approach for me. I think you have to be honest with yourself, at least if you're making the kind of movies I make. There's a lot of myself in these movies. It's not all me, it's layers of me, like papier mache — they can be turned into anything," he says. "I make my own movies and I feel very lucky — even arrogant — about it. I'm an honest filmmaker. But that doesn't mean I don't want to explore different elements of myself. I'm not afraid of change."

FILMOGRAPHY: *The Dead Father* (1986) | *Tales from the Gimli Hospital* (1988) | *Mauve Decade* (1989) | *Archangel* (1990) | *Indigo High-Hatters* (1991) | *Careful* (1992) | *The Pomps of Satan* (1993) | *Sea Beggars* (1994) | *Sissy Boy Slap Party* (1995) | *The Hands of Ida* (1995) | *Twilight of the Ice Nymphs* (1997) | *Maldoror: Tygers* (1998) | *The Cock Crew* (1998) | *Hospital Fragment* (1999) | *The Heart of the World* (2000).

CHAPTER THREE

First Takes

OUR HOME AND NATIVE LAND

Now that we've explored our realist roots, guilt and the central terms surrounding modern Canadian criticism, it's time to move beyond the angular white frame and dig a little deeper into the earth beneath our feet. This chapter is an exploration of the First Nations experience, and what I believe to be the first layer of human awareness in our New World artistic tradition.

Long before American filmmaker Robert Flaherty's groundbreaking documentary *Nanook of the North* (1922) captured the lifestyle of the Inuit living on the frozen tundra of Hudson's Bay on film, Canada was seen as a land inseparable from its Native peoples — at least from the outside. Whether it was in the form of Cornelius Krieghoff's kitsch portrayals of the indigenous peoples in the cradle of colonized Quebec from the mid to late 1800s — paintings that illustrated women, or as he called them, "squaws," selling mocassins and young hunters burdened with dead bunnies — or that ill-fated kidnapping of Chief Donnacona to France to aid in Jacques Cartier's lobby efforts before the king, Natives have been exploited by white Europeans for various purposes.

Just watching poor Nanook eke out a subsistence existence in the frozen nothingness of the North, one sees Canada as a land of danger appealing to the Romantic adventurer. Remember, even the coldest landscapes look inviting when you are sitting in a plush velour chair surrounded by the warm air of a centrally heated theatre, and because of that

distance, First Nations cultures have been suitably dehumanized and gussied up by the white imagination, which yearns for a taste of "other." Other is anything that is different from self, or in this case, different from the dominant culture. Aboriginals have given Canada a sense of things exotic, even mystical, and for this reason, they and their cultures have been used as decor like so many Tiki Torches at Trader Vic's. In this respect, we are not that different from the Americans, who continue to appropriate indigenous cultures and artifacts for their chic, politically correct appeal.

Historically, however, Canada and the United States are very different in the way they approached the whole issue. Where America went out and "conquered" its indigenous peoples through a genocidal campaign that pitted "cowboys" against "Indians" and "settlers" against "savages," Canada's history of assimilation had more to do with religious battles for the soul than rough-and-tumble turf wars. There was no overt campaign to destroy indigenous cultures in this country, and no one was ever "conquered" technically through acts of war. In the Canadian imagination, we look upon our early interaction with the First Nations as something of a rough model in multiculturalism. Where Americans killed Aboriginals, Canadians supposedly cooperated — albeit for financial and spiritual profit. We learned how to hunt and trap and paddle canoes as a result of the relationships. We learned how to live in this cold, harsh and unforgiving climate and demonstrated enough faith to stick around and build a country.

For the American psyche the distinction between good white people and bad "Indians" became an intrinsic part of the identity process — and this was reinforced by Hollywood films. As Lee Clark Mitchell says in his book, *Westerns*: "... The Other in the Western forms a cultural threat ... Anxiety about this threat to culture, so central a feature in many Westerns, seems more or less an American preoccupation, explained in part by the recognition that American cultural identity originates as a matter of choice ... [and that] freedom of identification involves a corresponding fear of mistaken choice."[1] In other words, in order to found a country of heroes, one needs an enemy, and that's exactly what the early settlers found in the Aboriginal peoples living across the American West.

As we've seen, Canada is a nation where tensions are largely internalized. The enemy, the hero, the mediator and the victim are all integral parts of the Canadian psyche. For this reason, the Aboriginal experience in Canada is not nearly as easy to dissect as it is in the United States. In this chapter we will place the Aboriginal experience in the context of Canadian film. First, we'll take a brief look at some of the central myths that form the Aboriginal perspective; then we'll explore the portrayals and projected images of First Nations' peoples in non-Native film to see what the dominant culture extracts from the relationship. Following that, we'll move into an investigation of how Aboriginal people depict themselves, and how and why those images may or may not differ from the ones provided by whites. Finally, we'll identify another cyclical pattern that recurs throughout the Canadian film tradition and see how it

fits into the larger series of gears and sprockets we've detailed so far.

Dead Ringers and Sacrificial Mothers

"There are a lot of different myths surrounding creation in the Aboriginal tradition," says Montreal-based director Alanis Obomsawin. "But twins figure in a lot of them. They appear throughout the stories, in one way or another." Whether the twins are human in form or animal — as they are in the Kwakiutl myth, where they are salmon, the central spiritual and food source for West Coast First Nations — the twins figure prominently in the First Nations' collective psyche.

In Carl Jung's exploration of myth and its psychological impact on the subconscious, *Man and His Symbols*, he cites the research of Dr. Paul Radin. Radin was an American anthropologist who studied the Winnebago tribe for most of his life, attempting to decipher the mental state of man in preliterate societies. In Radin's article "Hero Cycles of the Winnebago," Jung says we can see four distinct stages in the evolution of the hero: "We can see the definite progression from the most primitive to the most sophisticated concept of the hero," he says of Radin's work, linking it to other hero cycles beyond the Winnebago. Indeed, Jung points out the Winnebago were a small and relatively little-known tribe, but their mythology was clearly part of a larger system. Elements of Winnebago myth can be seen throughout Canada in the stories of both the Algonquin and the Huron, reaffirming a sense of universality in the Aboriginal experience when it comes to the larger concepts of creation, life, death and heroism.

In the Winnebago's take on things, there are four distinct cycles in the evolution of the hero myth: the trickster cycle, the hare cycle, the red horn cycle and the twin cycle. Radin and Jung agree that these myths were developed in order to help societies deal with natural life processes through fictional invention. For instance, the trickster cycle relates to the earliest period of life when our world can't move beyond the walls of our own body. In the trickster cycle, everything is physical: "He has the mentality of an infant ... Lacking any purpose beyond the gratification of his primary needs, he is cruel, cynical and unfeeling."[2] In Freudian terms, this part of the cycle would be called "id." While the trickster generally takes the form of an animal, such as a fox or raven, it eventually transforms into a creature with human features and becomes the hare or the coyote. "The Hare is the founder of human culture — the Transformer." The Hare is the one who goes from animal to human, and as such, is the first to transcend the physical. Radin learned the Hare myth was so strong in Winnebago society that when early Christians tried to convert the nation, the members of the Peyote Rite (a part of Winnebago society) were reluctant to surrender Hare to Christ, since they already had a Christ figure in Hare. In Freudian terms, Hare would be similar to the ego construct: the beginning of self-awareness through a recognition of "other."

Red Horn, the third incarnation of the hero, is what Jung calls an "ambiguous person" — which should set off the alarm bells for our Canadian film explorer, because if there's one adjective that aptly describes Canadian film, it's "ambiguous." That said, Red Horn is a complicated guy. The youngest of 10 children, he is part human, part God. He has both the mental and physical strength to beat giants in games of wit and skill, but after his adventures are over, he is left alone on earth with his children, signalling the beginning of personal responsibility. As Jung says, "The danger to man's happiness and security now comes from man himself." Similarly, in the final phase of the hero cycle, The Twins, we see another call to consciousness. Jung writes:

Though the twins are said to be the sons of the Sun, they are essentially human and together constitute a single person. Originally united in the mother's womb, they were forced apart at birth. Yet they belong together, and it is necessary, though exceedingly difficult, to reunite them. In these two children, we see two sides of man's nature. One of them, Flesh, is acquiescent, mild and without initiative. The other, Stump, is dynamic and rebellious. In some stories of the twin heroes, these attitudes are refined to the point where one figure represents the introvert, whose main strength lies in his powers of reflection, and the other is the extrovert, a man of action who can accomplish great deeds.[3]

I am certainly not the first person to suggest Canada exhibits a few twin traits of its own. With that nagging split between our two founding European cultures, our white-indigenous duality, and our proximity to the behemoth of a nation next door, the Twin Myth certainly fits. If we apply it to the films we've discussed, we can see twin images in both *The Sweet Hereafter* (the doubled images of Bear in his parents' house, the physical similarity between Allison, Zoe and Nicole, who all fulfill a similar function in relation to Mitchell) and *Mon Oncle Antoine* (Benoit and the dead teenager in the coffin). Another obvious twin image in Canadian film can be seen in David Cronenberg's *Dead Ringers* (a story about creepy identical twin gynecologists). The value of the twin myth is clear to

Canadians, and if we could wrap our heads around the concept of twin systems, instead of a single uniform strand of existence, we might be better equipped to deal with issues of nationhood by seeing it as a two-pronged, or even three-pronged, outlet for expression.

First Nations mythology has more to teach us about our current reality, and about Canadian film, because women and the landscape are both central motifs — just as they are in Canadian film.

"In the stories of my nation, the land and women are often the same thing because both give life," says Obomsawin. "One of the stories that sticks with me most is the one about the wife who sees the Earth dying around her. There is no water, and the plants and animals are dying. She can't bear to watch, and so she begs her husband to kill her and drag her by the hair across the land. He refuses. But eventually, she wins out. He does what she wants and kills her. With a heavy heart, he opens her veins and drags her body across the Earth. The tears and the blood heal the Earth, and things begin to grow again. Her hair becomes the corn. Her sacrifice saves the Earth, and the people," says Obomsawin. "The land and the woman. They are central to the Aboriginal myth in almost every storytelling tradition I know. Women have the power. They have the babies. There is nothing more powerful than that."[4] I guess all that power proved too threatening to the first European settlers and missionaries because First Nations mythology was one of the first casualties of colonialism.

First Contact

In early Canadian literature, according to Atwood, "Indians were used in Canada for two main purposes: as instruments of Nature the Monster, torturing and killing white victims; and as variants themselves of the victim motif."[5] Things haven't changed all that much. But they have changed — in both Canadian and American cultures — in the wake of grassroots empowerment movements and the seismic force of political correctness that swept through and discarded old racist opinions from the establishment attics during the 1980s and early 1990s.

As a result, the white imagination of Hollywood has come to see the American Indian as a social victim in much the same way as Canadian literature did decades ago. From the cardboard villainy of Indians in old Westerns from the fifties, to the noble martyrdom of a socially minded effort like *Little Big Man*, and more recently to such homages as *Dances With Wolves* and *Geronimo*, we can see hints of revisionism taking hold, nudging Americans into a less divisive and slightly more humble perception of National Self vis-à-vis the Native Peoples who were destroyed in its creation. If we look at the smattering of Canadian films that feature Aboriginal characters — or the fewer still that were actually made by Aboriginal directors — we see where we've made progress and where the Canadian imagination continues to stagnate.

The most obvious — and most important — improvement is that we now have a body of film work created by Aboriginals, instead of white people telling Aboriginal stories. In the context of the identity process, this development cannot be undervalued because it puts the power of creation back in the hands of those who are being represented — an essential ingredient in the easily deflated identity soufflé.

For the most part, however, these Aboriginal storytellers have been limited to documentary work, and primarily documentaries produced under the auspices of the National Film Board. We could take this to be a bad thing because it ghettoizes the Aboriginal experience within a government institution (yet again) and limits not only the exposure of the art to a wider audience, but limits the content of the work to fact-based, documentary exposés of real-life scenarios. In other words, there is no potential for flat-out fantasy within the documentary form, thereby limiting the artist's imagination and, in turn, his or her ability for self re-creation. However, from what we've been able to glean so far about the identity construction process as it applies to Canadian film and the national identity, documentary film may well be the generic building blocks or foundation tools for creating a larger and more imaginative film tradition with its own narrative style and unique storytelling techniques.

Documentary Rebellion

As John Grierson himself was only too well aware, the documentary can be a highly effective tool. It can tell people "the real story" and as such, enlighten the masses about various forms of oppression. In Grierson's opinion, social enlightenment was the main purpose of documentary film and it remains so to this very day within the beige brick walls of the National Film Board, which continues to provide a voice to those who cannot or do not wish to be heard within the mainstream. We've already seen how this "tool of socialism" helped form early notions of the Canadian identity, and then how it played a pivotal role in the creation of the French-Canadian psyche through such films as *Les Raquetteurs*. We've even talked about films

Kanehsatake: 270 Years of Resistance (1993): Canadian soldiers face off against Mohawk warriors in Alanis Obomsawin's award-winning documentary look at the 1990 Oka Crisis, a long standoff in the woods that started with a blockade against a golf course expansion, and turned into a military action after a police officer was killed.
Photo: Shane Komulainen. Courtesy of the Toronto Film Library

like Arcand's *Au Coton* as further examples of the socialist tradition ingrained in the NFB. Simply, the NFB style of documentary film has occupied itself with the business of empowering those without a voice, and these days, the most outspoken filmmaker within the NFB system is Alanis Obomsawin.

Obomsawin is not only one of Canada's most prolific Aboriginal filmmakers, she may well be one of the nation's most prolific filmmakers — period. Beginning her career as a singer and storyteller, Obomsawin has made more than 20 documentary films chronicling the aboriginal experience in Canada. Of those efforts, few have made the impact of her 1993 film, *Kanehsatake: 270 Years of Resistence*. A very real story about one of the ugliest events in recent Canadian memory, *Kanehsatake*

brings us back to the hot days of August 1990 in Montreal, when the Mohawks on the Kanehsatake reserve just 20 minutes southwest of Montreal decided they would not sit back and watch their ancient sacred sites be expropriated for a golf course expansion.

Shortly after the Mohawks set up barricades to prevent bulldozers from pulling down the trees, another Mohawk settlement just a few kilometres away called Kahnawake blockaded the Mercier Bridge to commuter traffic. Within hours, the Sûreté du Quebec — one of the most infamous law-enforcement agencies in the country, known for its own brand of frontier-style justice — moved in with guns, and the standoff began. Before long, the army moved in and the situation erupted into a symbolic battle that dredged up

Rocks at Whiskey Trench (2000): Alanis Obomsawin returns to the Oka Crisis, but this time through the eyes of the women and children of Kahnawake, a community that showed solidarity with the Mohawks in *Kanehsatake* and barricaded the Mercier Bridge. When women and children were placed in cars and taken through the barricades as a safety measure, the convoy was stoned by white citizens on the other side. PHOTO LIBRARY OF THE NATIONAL FILM BOARD OF CANADA

every Aboriginal skeleton in Canada's closet.

Obomsawin was the only filmmaker permitted behind the barricades, making *Kanehsatake* the only source of information and images from the Aboriginal point of view. There were several newsteams standing on the other side of the barricades, but as someone who watched the event unfold more than 6,000 kilometres away on television, it was almost impossible to really understand what was going on — and why a small patch of land was worth dying for. More than six weeks later, the siege ended and the barricades came down, but nothing was solved as a result of the standoff.

In her follow-up documentary, *Rocks at Whiskey Trench*, Obomsawin revisits the people of Kahnawake in order to record the lingering emotional effects of the standoff, in addition to telling another ugly story of racist hate and acts of anti-Aboriginal violence. Where *Kanehsatake* focused on the events behind the barricades at Oka — where the contested golf course lies — *Rocks at Whiskey Trench* focuses on those Mohawks who showed solidarity and stood up in support by blocking the Mercier Bridge, a vital traffic artery in the cardiac knot of Montreal commuting. In particular, *Rocks at Whiskey Trench* deals with an incident that took place August 28, 1990, when the men behind the lines organized the relocation of women and children should things turn violent. As the motorcade of 75 cars crossed the bridge, thousands of angry non-Natives on the other side lay waiting, armed with rocks and stones. As the cars made their way through Whiskey Trench (so called for the Seagrams distilleries on either side) they were pelted from every angle, damaging the cars and in some cases seriously injuring the passengers inside. The police were present but made no attempt to stop the stone-throwing — leaving all the people of Kahnawake (including the indigenous peacekeeping force) sickened at the lack of compassion for the women and children.

As Obomsawin's lens settles on the people recounting the event, she finds the human angle the news cameras inevitably miss in the mad rush for sound bites. She shows us children who remember the crash of glass, and women who are still traumatized by the recollection of seeing their babies bundled in the back seat, covered in blood. When she goes out to interview the handful of non-Native people who were identified and charged with vandalism, only one agrees to be on camera — and he maintains he did nothing. At one point he says, "We built that bridge. That bridge doesn't belong to them." To which Obomsawin rebuts with a short aside on the Mohawk Ironworkers, who, needless to say, built the Mercier Bridge and were instrumental in building nearly every other iron-framed structure in Canada. (Obomsawin dedicates an entire movie to these men in *Spudwrench*, the story of a Mohawk ironworker who was also perceived to be the biggest and baddest Mohawk Warrior by the white media during the Kahnesatake standoff.)

By giving us these documentary accounts of real news events from her unique perspective, Obomsawin essentially revises history in the making. She picks up every stereotypical misperception of Aboriginals by whites and throws it right back at them. The tone is professionally measured, but unmistakably angry, which lends the films a sense of urgency as well as personality — an asset embellished by her own narration on every project.

More Film Warriors

Obomsawin is just one of many Aboriginal documentary filmmakers revising history and recording oral traditions for posterity and purposes of proselytization. There are several others — mostly working with the NFB, such as Loretta Todd, Annie Frazier-Henry, Dana Claxton, Daniel Prouty, Monika Ille, Catherine Ane Martin, Gil Cardinal, Gary Farmer (the actor/director), Barb Cranmer, Greg Coyes, Wil Campbell, Robert Adams, Doug Cuthand, Paul Rickard, Raymond Yakeleya, Clint Alberta and more. The common denominator among almost all of these filmmakers is a two-pronged desire to celebrate the culture while raising awareness of the threat of cultural extinction at the hands of mostly white, mainstream society. For instance, Todd's work has dealt with everything from recording the history of Aboriginal veterans (*Forgotten Warriors*) to an eye-opening biography of Chief Dan George that shows him to be a performer in the old Vaudeville tradition — not some rank amateur who stumbled into major motion pictures because he had the right hair. Similarly, Gil Cardinal's body of work includes films like *Foster Child* (a biographical tale of what it means to grow up in a foster home), *Children of Alcohol* (self-explanatory) and *The Spirit Within* (a look at Native spirituality programs introduced into penitentiaries and other institutions). In other words, these documentaries, for the most part, pull apart the highly romanticized, mythological proportions ascribed to Aboriginals by the bland, romance-hungry, TV-addicted white imagination.

White Man's Revision

Fortunately, the hypocrisy of the present day hasn't been lost entirely on white people. As we mentioned earlier, there have been several films from mainstream society since the sixties that attempt to resurrect the shadow of Native cultures on screen. While most of the American efforts have been *Dances With Wolves*-style apologies, the Canadian revisions have been rooted in realism — showing us flawed but nonetheless heroic human beings instead of cardboard martyrs. Sadly, most of these mainstream movies have been made by white people, but as the role of Aboriginal people has changed since early Canadian fiction, it's worth taking a look at how the modern Canadian imagination looks at First Nations people. Are they still, as Atwood suggested, filling a double role as instruments of Nature the Monster (torturing and killing white victims) or as variants themselves of the victim motif? Or, have they disappeared altogether as a motif now that they have been tucked away into postage-stamp size reserves, or else assimilated entirely through residential schools and conversion to Catholicism?

Indeed, it is hard to find images of modern Aboriginals on screen outside of documentaries and place-specific TV shows such as *The Beachcombers*, *Rainbow Country* and *Northern Exposure*. In fiction film, there are four prime examples of the Native experience that spring to mind: *Smoke Signals*, *Dance Me Outside*, *Black Robe* and *Map of the Human Heart*.

While all of them deal with the Aboriginal experience and contain plenty of Canadian content, not one of them could be called a purely Canadian Aboriginal motion picture. They are all international co-productions, collaborations with non-Aboriginals or, in the case of *Smoke Signals*, an American independent film. I could disqualify them from discussion in this chapter on principle, but that would make for a sorely ignorant take on the Aboriginal experience in North America. After all, as we saw in the previous chapter, we are a country that believes in pluralism, and First Nations' cultures play a large part in our mosaic. But once again, it's not possible to look at any culture in isolation. The whole map is held together by dynamic tension, or as Robert Lepage noted in the opening plaque to *Métissages*, his recent museum installation in Quebec City: "We are all, no matter what our origins, the offspring of *métissage* [mixed ancestry]."

Black Robe is probably the most enlightening from a Canadian historical perspective as it trains its lens on the Jesuit missionaries who came to New France during the 17th century with the bold and altogether ethnocentric aim of converting the Natives to Catholicism. From an Aboriginal point of view, this is the beginning of the end as Europeans not only expropriated the land but made every effort to expropriate the internal spiritual terrain as well, essentially separating Aboriginal peoples from their faith, their language and their land. In short, everything that made them who they were. There is a sad irony here regarding the French Canadians who continue to fight for distinct cultural recognition against the English "other," while ignoring their own history of cultural oppression vis-à-vis the First Nations. This has not escaped Robert Lepage, who includes an Aboriginal character in *Le Confessionnal* who is symbolically castrated by Anne-Marie Cadieux as part of a sex show in the opening moments in the film, and is later exploited as a sex object. *Black Robe*, on the other hand, is a serious, tragic drama, leaving little room for the type of ironic humour Lepage uses so well. Also, this Robert Lantos production was written by Canadian novelist

Black Robe (1991): Father Laforgue (Lothaire Bluteau) begins his voyage into the dark heart of the Canadian experience as he searches for his Jesuit brothers at a mission deep in the bush. Directed by Australian Bruce Beresford, *Black Robe* is a first-contact story that captures the gritty reality of colonization. SERENDIPITY POINT FILMS

Brian Moore and directed by Australian director Bruce Beresford — who may share the same colonial sensibilities as a Canadian and understand intercultural conflict with the same guilty European conscience — but follows a far more traditional narrative style and keeps the ironic humour to a minimum.

Built along the same lines as *Heart of Darkness* or *Apocalypse Now*, *Black Robe* follows the journey of young and idealistic Father Laforgue (Lothaire Bluteau) as he makes his way up the St. Lawrence River in a canoe. Fortified by faith and a zealous desire to spread the gospel of Christ, Laforgue finds himself in the midst of an intertribal battle between the Huron, the Iroquois and the Algonquin, who are paddling the padre's canoe ever further into the wilds of the hostile Canadian landscape, which appears to swallow the little canoe like a giant grey whale.

The movie begins with glimpses of heady optimism as we inhale the fumes of Laforgue's burning passion and see a small community beginning to emerge on the St. Lawrence (what would later become Quebec City). As autumn turns to winter, however, any sense of hope sours as Laforgue and the landscape emerge as complete opposites — a detail that is highlighted visually by the father's black robes against the white, snow-covered scenery. As the vast landscape dwarfs Laforgue along with his message, he looks like a man so removed from the world around him that he starts to resemble a psychotic on a city street. He talks to himself — as well as the dead at his feet.

No wonder the Natives around him think he's insane. Laforgue is a man so foreign to this place — both spiritually and physically — that the image is completely absurd, but coversion takes place nonetheless. And while his faith is incredibly moving, the results are predictably tragic. Laforgue ends up being the indirect tool for the slaughter of his Native converts, and in a darkly ironic twist, becomes their sole destroyer instead of their soul salvation. In *Black Robe*, then, everyone is a victim — establishing the tone for the Canadian experience for a long time to come.

An interesting aside to this discussion of *Black Robe* was the response from American critics, who all noted the "realistic" quality of the movie when compared to something as misty-eyed as *Dances With Wolves*. All the same, they didn't like the film that much because it was just such a downer. Certainly you could say the film had certain pathetic qualities, but by the end, you can't help but have a deep sense of respect for the brave souls who built Canada. In all that "nothing," they had the courage to build a little place to call home — and the faith to see it as a beginning of something much greater than themselves.

Map of the Human Heart

Map of the Human Heart is certainly no brighter than *Black Robe*, although it does present the Aboriginal in a truly heroic light until the ultimately tragic end. Directed and co-written by another child of "colonial" roots, New Zealander Vincent Ward, the movie is essentially a love story between two young people of Métis heritage. Through a series of flashbacks moving backward from present-day, we are told the story of Avik (Robert Joamie) a young, half Inuit boy living on the frozen tundra of the North (much like the famed Nanook — a reference that Ward doesn't miss in his framing of the vast white wilderness). Uprooted from his home and family by a white cartographer named Russell when it's learned he has TB, Avik is taken to a Montreal sanatorium (run by nuns) where he meets Albertine (Annie Galipeau). The two youngsters fall in love, but they are soon separated when Albertine is adopted, leaving Avik with nothing but Albertine's memory and a stolen X-ray of her heart and once-diseased lungs, which he carries with him into adulthood.

This transparent photographic image foreshadows the next movement in the film, which centres on the now adult Avik's (Jason Scott Lee) time as an aerial photographer during the Second World War. Without knowing it, both Avik and the adult Albertine (Anne Parillaud) are in London working for Bomber Command under the leadership of the apparently omnipotent white man with a talent for drawing boundaries, Russell (Patrick Bergin). Avik takes the pictures, Albertine analyzes them, and Russell decides which areas of the images will be obliterated by incendiary bombs. This is a pretty good allegory for the Aboriginal experience, with its inherent code of servitude, and the European propensity for violent, mass destruction. What makes it work dramatically is the added romantic connection between Albertine and Russell, introducing a perfect romantic — as well as cultural — triangle, reaffirming the idea of disconnectedness and that elusive sense of belonging.

When Avik and Albertine reconnect, we are transported with them to a place that transcends the ugly reality around them. Again, director Ward doesn't miss out on the visuals. By literally placing Avik and Albertine high above the madding crowd — first, on a giant white hot air balloon and second, on the catwalks above Royal Albert Hall — essentially he conveys that these two people do not belong in the world of warring white folk. This is not their battle and this is not their landscape, but because they are dislocated travellers, they are subject to the whims of the white world, where they are victimized all over again.

As you can well imagine, things don't work out for our two lovers — despite their near-complete assimilation into the white world. Albertine is a respected officer and Avik is a war hero, but they are both broken by their transplantation. Without roots, and without a connection to each other, they wither and die — which is how the film ends, as Avik returns to his home in the North to settle into the waiting stereotype: a drunk Inuit, talking about his glory days to perfect strangers. There is a dark sense of redemption at the end of this stirring tale, as Avik meets the same fate as his elderly grandmother when he sets himself adrift on an ice floe. It may be the end of his life, but as he drifts off into a frozen sleep, he is back in his own — albeit transformed — landscape, where he conjures the memory of his true love. From a purely narrative standpoint, both Albertine and Avik are clearly victims of a cruel white world that pulls them away from each other. But we cannot forget that they are also half white, and as such, a part of that world whether they like it or not. The real source of their victimization, then, is that they are trapped between two cultures, floating in a world without borders while the rest of humanity is obsessed with maintaining and protecting them, no matter what the cost.

Smoke Signals Across the Border

First Nations certainly have their own territorial borders, but they in no way reflect the straight-line landscaping of T-squares and sextants of the European world. As Obomsawin says: "The aboriginal reality is the same, no matter which side of the Canada-U.S. border you may be on. We've all been displaced and had our land taken away, leaving all of us with a similar experience." We can see evidence of this "borderless world" in a movie like *Smoke Signals*. A wonderful movie about reconnecting with one's roots and excavating one's culture, *Smoke Signals* is not technically a Canadian movie — even though most of the cast, including Adam Beach, Evan Adams, Tantoo Cardinal and Gary Farmer are all Canadian. The fact that most of us grew up with some representation of Aboriginal people in the classroom makes this movie feel familiar. The humour is highly ironic, the hero is atypical, the story is about underdogs and the film is rooted in the landscape — all of which contributes to the movie's sense of thematic familiarity. But that's where the similarity ends, because *Smoke Signals* is actually a very conventional story that remains true to Hollywood device, where endings are generally happy and closure is next to godliness. While the script was written by Sherman Alexie outside the box of expectation, the screenplay was workshopped at the Sundance Institute, where successful American screenwriters rework stories to "make them work" — or, in other words, fit the standard dilemma-climax-denouement dramatic mould.

There is nothing wrong with this, but in terms of dramatic structure, *Smoke Signals* has more in common with *Smokey and the Bandit* than the indigenous, oral tradition we see in shorts like Annie Frazier-Henry's *Totem Talk* — a quasi documentary that combines allegorical Aboriginal storytelling with computer animation for a nearly surreal viewing experience. *Smoke Signals* is relatively conservative and linear. Its flashback sequences are about as formally experimental as the movie gets.

Dancing Outside the Box

By contrast, *Dance Me Outside* is a truly Canadian movie. It was written by white author W. P. Kinsella (based on his collection of short stories, *The Fencepost Chronicles*) and was directed by white director Bruce McDonald. It also remains one of the few narrative features about the Aboriginal experience made in this country.

Set on the Kidabanese Reserve in Ontario, McDonald delves into subject matter that is more than familiar to the Toronto director of such films as *Roadkill*, *Highway 61* and *Hard Core Logo*: sex, drugs and rock 'n' roll. Here, we also deal with the extra burden of racism and white bigots, as the central axis of the film is the murder of a young woman (or as they say in police dramas, "the victim"). But this is not a victim story as such, even though the Native woman was murdered at the hands of a white punk. This is the story of a young generation looking for direction.

Separated into two weekends set a year apart, the film opens with Silas Crow (Ryan Black) and Frank Fencepost (Adam Beach), two dudes who listen to speed metal and dream of being auto mechanics. Cast in the same mould as Pete and Joey from *Goin' Down the Road*, who went down the road and found nothing but the same depressing reality waiting for them on the other end, Silas and Frank shun responsibility — which, in perfect Canadian form, makes Silas' now ex-girlfriend Sadie just a tad irate. Like many other Canadian women on-screen, Sadie (Jennifer Podemski) finds a sense of personal empowerment long before the men when she picks up the fight for Aboriginal rights. Now she doesn't want a boy, she wants a man who can translate his big dreams into reality. There is no shortage of dreams on the reserve. Silas aspires to be a writer in addition to being a mechanic, but his creative drive is stunted by his lack of willpower and confidence. All that changes, however, when a night out at the local dance hall turns ugly, and a racially motivated scuffle ends in the murder of a young woman.

One year later, we rejoin Frank and Silas to see how the murder spurred them toward both a greater understanding of themselves *and* creative expression steeped in rebellion. Silas writes about the murder for his mechanic admissions test, and he suddenly finds a sense of empowerment through the act of creation. Symbolically speaking, we have several Canadian archetypes unravelling simultaneously: we have the Native "victim" and the clash of two cultures embodied in the racist white punk who gets off with little more than a two-year sentence for manslaughter. These are what might be called the golden oldie themes within *Dance Me Outside*: good,

solid Canadian dichotomies where one culture defines the other through opposition, or in this case, oppression. But *Dance Me Outside* veers from the beaten thematic portage through two subplots in the underbrush: the marriage of Silas' sister Ilianna (Lisa LaCroix) to a white lawyer, and the reappearance of Ilianna's old beau and ex-con, Gooch (Michael Greyeyes). Through these direct bonds of love, the entire landscape shifts, and where there was once hate, there is now humour. For instance, at one point in the film, Frank and Silas poke fun at Ilianna's husband and give him a bogus spirit guide, which, being an earnest representative of Canadian institutionalism, he devours wholeheartedly. The white man is thus rendered the drunken fool. It takes confidence to pull back and laugh, and

Dance Me Outside (1994): Silas Crow (Ryan Black) and Frank Fencepost (Adam Beach) are two guys waiting for their lives to happen, which, eventually, they do. Based on W.P. Kinsella's *The Fencepost Chronicles*, *Dance Me Outside* has road movie sensibilities — only without the cars — thanks to its director, Bruce McDonald.
PHOTO: MICHAEL VENDRUSCOLO, COURTESY OF THE TORONTO FILM LIBRARY

even more self-possession to mingle with the perceived enemy.

Where *Dance Me Outside* leaves us then, is somewhere in the middle — the monotony of days that make up everyday life sandwiched between these two weekends, where humanity and interpersonal relationships have the potential to remake and recreate the political landscape.

Panorama Shot

In the big picture of film, we could say things have improved a great deal for Aboriginal people in Canada — but that wouldn't ring true. While Native people have made political progress regarding issues such as Aboriginal title, and have become a visible part of the Canadian political process in the wake of the failed Meech Lake Accord — when Elijah Harper (sole Native representative in the Manitoba Legislature) stood up with his feather and disapproved of Brian Mulroney's blanket offering in 1982, essentially pulling down the house of cards — there is still a great deal of room for improvement before we all reach anything resembling a fair and equitable society. Nonetheless, we do seem to be moving in the right direction. First Nations peoples now have the tools to tell their own stories — as a result of public institutions like the National Film Board and the creation of the Aboriginal Television Network. But as we noted earlier, these can be seen as government-funded ghettoes, and the stories are still mostly dedicated to revisionist documentaries, chronicling centuries of oppression at the hands of white society. These are important chapters in the history of a people to record, especially when the battle for recognition is just as pressing as it was 300 years ago. "If [non-Native] people were only a little more aware of the First Nations around them, things would be better,"

says Obomsawin. "So often, you can have an entire city living right next door to a reservation and they don't know anything about that culture. We can never be equal, or realized, if there is no desire for white people to learn about the world around them."[6] Anger can go a long way toward spurring the creative drive (as we saw in *Dance Me Outside*), but until it is transformed by an act of imagination — a leap into the universal space where art is born — it is not free expression, merely a recording of events.

As we've seen in previous chapters, one cannot move from an oppressed state to artistic freedom in one fluid movement. There needs to be a communal recollection of the past and a recognition of "where we are" before we can imagine where we'd like to be. In filmic terms, this means Aboriginals, as Anglos and Francophones did before, must move through the documentary, realism stage before translating their own storytelling techniques to the screen. From what we've gleaned so far, the cycle of filmic awareness evolves something like this: objective lens looks at other from a distance (institutional documentary); subjective lens looks at other from a more personal stance (revolutionary cinema direct); fusion of documentary and narrative technique (docudrama); subjective lens looks at imagined, but realistic other (auteur-driven realism); subjective lens creates everything before it without any constraints whatsoever in an attempt to reimagine the relationship with other (auteur-driven fantasy). This seems to be the path of film evolution, at least in Canada. As we noted in the previous chapter, picking up a movie camera is an empowering act. It puts the power of creation into the hands of the person looking through the viewfinder.

In the Atwood scheme of victim stances,

Deep Inside Clint Star (1999): Director Clint Alberta strikes just one of several poses he assumes as Clint Star — an alter-ego in search of a community — in his own documentary film with an unmistakable personal voice. Interviewing people he knows about everything from sex, oppression to history, Alberta revises perceptions of First Nations identity.

PHOTO LIBRARY OF THE NATIONAL FILM BOARD OF CANADA

First Nations peoples are just beginning to assume the fourth, "creative non-victim" position: they are revising history, forcing white culture to look at its own history and current-day propensity for oppression. What was missing, until the Spring of 2001, was the leap into narrative fiction, where complete recreation is possible and the artist's soul is free to express anything in his or her own way, using any type of traditional or avant-garde storytelling techique.

When Inuit filmmaker Zacharias Kunuk's debut feature, *Atanarjuat* (*The Fast Runner*) won the Camero d'Or at the 2001 Cannes film festival, it heralded the dawn of the next generation of First Nations' filmmakers. The film is based on Inuit legend and pays homage to the indigenous storytelling technique; it was also scripted entirely in Inuktituk and produced by an Inuit production team.

The film carries on the tradition of visual artists like Lawrence Paul Yuxweluptun, who has completely remade traditional aboriginal art forms to articulate modern stories of white oppression. A prime example is his massive tableau depicting the bargaining surrounding the recently inked (and soon to be challenged) Nisga'a Treaty which shows two Native figures cringing with exasperation while a pink, claw-footed, wormlike white figure with a bad comb-over smugly walks out of the frame with a briefcase. The forms are clearly inspired by traditional West Coast tribal art, but the themes and the execution are altogether modern. I can hardly wait to see a similar evolution in film, and chances are it won't take long. Young filmmakers like Clint Alberta, whose documentary *Deep Inside Clint Star* breaks open the stereotypes of Native youth, and screenwriter Stefany Mathias (daughter of the late Chief Joe Mathias), who workshopped a script about a young Native woman at Sundance during the summer of 2000, are two people who ooze confidence. As Mathias said in an interview shortly after she was accepted to the Sundance Lab: "We just wanted to make a movie, so we stood back and took it step by step. There is no room for negativity when you're trying to overcome the odds ... The most important thing is to believe in yourself. My father taught me that, and it's the one lesson I'll always remember: be proud of who you are. And I am."

Alanis Obomsawin

Born 1932 — Lebanon, New Hampshire

PHOTO LIBRARY OF THE NATIONAL FILM BOARD OF CANADA

One of the most prolific filmmakers in Canada and named outstanding Canadian of the year in 1965, Alanis Obomsawin could rightfully be credited with leading an Aboriginal revolution of the arts through her documentaries that cut to the very core of cultural tensions within Canada, and by grace of their universal appeal, the rest of the world.

"I get very excited whenever I make a documentary. I love the form because I'm very concerned about educating people about what's going on. So much history can be lost if no one tells the story — so that's what I do. I tell the stories," she says. "This is my way of fighting for social change."

The daughter of a hunting guide and a healer, Obomsawin grew up on the Odanak reservation (also known as Saint-François-du-Lac) northeast of Montreal and is a member of the Abenaki nation — from the word "wabanaki" meaning "land of the rising sun" or "dawn's land" — which, at the beginning of North America's colonial period spanned southward across most of what is now New England, and north to Maine and Quebec. As swelling European populations displaced the Abenaki people, they were forced off their ancestral lands and into reserves in and around the Quebec City area during the 1670s under the auspices of the Jesuit missionaries. The main mission in Silliery, on the north shore of the St. Lawrence, was eventually abandoned in favour of two major communities, the Odanak and the Wolinak, on the south shore.

Obomsawin grew up dealing with racism from the white community, but instead of turning inward with self-loathing, she dedicated much of her childhood to understanding and studying the history of her ancestors and learned what she could of the traditional songs and stories. She translated many of these stories to song, and made her professional debut as a singer on a New York stage in 1960. In 1967, Canada's Centennial Year, Obomsawin was approached by the National Film Board to be an advisor on a film about Aboriginal peoples. Motivated by her budding interest in film, with its potential to bring personal stories to a mass audience, Obomsawin made her first film, *Christmas at Moose Factory* in 1971. Produced by veteran NFB'er Wolf Koenig, *Christmas at Moose Factory* is a collection of children's crayon drawings showing different scenes of everyday life around the shores of James Bay. The voice of a young girl narrates the film, explaining what each drawing is, and how different — and in many ways how similar — life is for the residents of Moose Factory during the Christmas Season.

"My life changed when I was 12," she says. "My father died and I decided I wasn't going to get beat up at school every day by the other girls in the classroom. It was just a decision — just like that I said, 'no more.' And that's all there was to it. It stopped the next day."

While Obomsawin's work has always been steeped in an appreciation for her ancestry and a desire for recognition of Aboriginal cultures, her work took a decidedly political turn in 1984 with the release of *Incident at Restigouche*, a film that chronicled the raid by the Sûreté du Quebec on the Restigouche Reserve and the Micmac people who lived there. The government, upon hearing complaints from white fishers, was looking to restrict the Native fishery and gave the police permission for two armed raids of the community.

From that point on, Obomsawin's films have taken a hard look at the relations between white and Aboriginal Canadians — and discovered that things haven't changed all that much since Europeans began colonizing and displacing Natives centuries ago. From *Richard Cardinal*, a film based on the diary of a 17-year-old who killed himself after being placed and displaced in 28 foster homes, to *Poundmaker's Lodge*, a movie that deals with the cycles of abuse, Obomsawin makes movies about the people who fall through the social net and are promptly swept under the rug.

"Expression is as natural as breathing. It's something I have to do. But I make documentaries because I think it's important to show people how we live and who we are. There are so many white people who live right next to reserves but they don't know anything about their neighbours. They have no interest in learning about another culture," she says. "I'm fascinated by human beings. I love listening to people tell their stories. Everyone has one to share, you know. If you listen, they will speak, so my job is to listen."

While Obomsawin has made more than 16 films with the NFB, it was her documentation of the events at the Kanehsatake reserve in Quebec during the summer of 1990 that made her a household name in Canada. She was the only filmmaker to get behind the lines during what became known as the "Oka Crisis" — when Mohawks protested the expansion of a golf course into sacred burial lands by blockading a road and a bridge — resulting in the film *Kanehsatake: 270 Years of Resistance*. For most Canadians, Obomsawin's lens caught the blatant injustice of the situation that almost every news organization missed as government and police spin-doctors vilified the Mohawk warriors as terrorists with unlimited arms and ammunition. Obomsawin, on the other hand, showed us real people behind the bandanas — people who were willing to die for their cause.

"That was an important movie because it was the one story of injustice that the white media actually paid attention to. It was important to show the other side because no one else was going to do it. It was a story about the land, and how over the past 270 years it has been taken away from all the First Nations in North America," she says. "I think it empowered people. Anytime you tell someone's story, people don't feel so alienated. They feel someone actually heard what they had to say ... Our people are almost always ignored."

A recipient of the Governor General's Award in Visual and Media Arts for her "long-standing career and significant contribution to Canadian filmmaking," Obomsawin is also a member of the Order of Canada. She remains committed to salvaging the remnants of her culture, which is threatened by extinction. Less than three percent of the 1,900 surviving Abenaki people can speak the language, which is part of the Algonquin language group.

"In the last 30 years, there has been a lot of progress. They are starting to teach Native languages in universities, but there is so much work to be done. I'm very thankful to the National Film Board for giving me the chance to make these movies because it's all part of the process. I hope things will change and that white culture will embrace Native culture, but I don't think it will happen in my lifetime."

SELECTED FILMOGRAPHY: *Christmas at Moose Factory* (1971) | *Mother of Many Children* (1977) | *Amisk* (1977) | *Canada Vignettes: Wild Rice Harvest Kenora* (1979) | *Canada Vignettes: June in Povungnituk - Quebec Arctic* (1980) | *Incident at Restigouche* (1984) | *Richard Cardinal: Cry from a Diary of a Métis Child* (1986) | *Poundmaker's Lodge: A Healing Place* (1987) | *No Address* (1988) | *Walker* (1991) | *Le Patro Le Prévost 80 Years Later* (1991) | *Kanehsatake: 270 Years of Resistance* (1993) | *My Name Is Kahentiiosta* (1995) | *Spudwrench - Kahnawake Man* (1997) | *Rocks at Whiskey Trench* (2000)

CHAPTER FOUR

The Tangled Garden

REFRAMING EDEN

Take a look at the map. We're absolutely enormous. Canada is the second largest nation on the planet, and we have about half the population of the United Kingdom. We are so large, empty and expansive that the landscape itself is the primary fact of life in Canada. It certainly was in First Nations mythology, as Alanis Obomsawin's story of the woman begging her hubby to haul her bleeding body across the plains proved — somewhat graphically. For better or for worse, it's also been the central defining principle in the earliest European-based expressions of life in Canada.

Just as Susanna Moodie wrote about her experiences in the Canadian wilderness in *Roughing it in the Bush*, and Cornelius Krieghoff painted images of Habitant families sleigh-racing on frozen lakes, so it is that Canadian film focuses on the landscape and has since day one, when early producers like Ernest Shipman decided to shoot on location instead of in-studio.

Shipman produced one of the most successful Canadian pictures of all time (in adjusted dollars) with *Back to God's Country* in 1919. The film, which made a 300 percent return for its Alberta investors, starred Shipman's wife, Nell (an actress and writer in her own right), as one of the first-ever bona fide screen heroines who takes on almost manly proportions when she saves her husband — and herself — from the evil clutches of the villain, Rydal. Over the course of the 79-minute feature, we watch as Dolores LeBeau (Shipman) befriends animals in the wilder-

ness where she lives with her father (Roy Laidlaw). When Rydal disguises himself as a Mountie and tries to rape Dolores, the father ends up dead and Dolores is forced to escape with her true love on a whaling schooner — without realizing the captain is none other than (dum-dum-dum) Rydal! When the schooner is trapped in ice, Dolores is left to save the day by taming a wild dog named Wapi, hauling the disabled body of her husband onto a sled, and mushing miles to safety over the ice floes while Rydal, the villain, perishes alone in an ice cave. While this film is based on a story by James Oliver Curwood, Nell Shipman is said to have been the film's main creative force, establishing the importance of women and the landscape in Canadian film from the veritable beginning.

Even after Canada's nascent narrative film movement died in the 1920s — the result of increased American control over screens and production — the landscape continued to be a central feature, only now, it was as a backdrop for non-fiction documentary in such efforts as the NFB's *Pour la suite du monde*, *Les Raquetteurs* and dozens more. Even an animated piece like the celebrated Drouin film *Le Paysagiste — Mindscape* (1976), featured the landscape as a central device. Made using Alexander Alexeieff's pinscreen technique (where a board with several thousand pins creates a relief of light and dark shadows), *Le Paysagiste* shows a painter entering his own landscape painting — which begins to morph and change as different symbols connect to his subconscious, creating a landscape of the mind, or a "mindscape." By contrast, even a non-experimental, completely grounded narrative feature like Anne Wheeler's *Bye Bye Blues* (1989) includes the landscape as a central feature: the emptiness of the open prairie provides an emotional mirror to the heartache of the central character, Daisy Cooper (Rebecca Jenkins), whose husband has been imprisoned in a POW camp during the Second World War. As the seasons change and the wheat grows green and juicy under the hot sun, so does Daisy, who joins a swing band and falls for the charming band leader. The goofy comedy *Mob Story* (1990), a farce about an American crime boss who goes to Winnipeg to escape the "heat," includes a landscape-dependent running gag. Every time someone opens the door to the outside, a blast of dry ice smoke pours through to make sure everyone knows, baby, it's cold outside.

Peter Harcourt writes in *The Canadian Encyclopedia*[1] that the landscape is often the central character in Canadian movies. Then again, sometimes it is merely a spectre or just a running gag. But it is always present in the frame, and generally serves as a counterpoint to character. Why use trees and mountains to define character when you could just use a gun? Not an easy question, but in order to at least attempt an answer, we have to do more digging.

In this chapter, we will take a deeper look at our relationship with the landscape and how it has evolved over the years through our historical perceptions as well as artistic impressions. We'll take a speedy tourist cruise through the halls of Canadian art and build a lexicon of images, then check out how other Canadian artists relate to the world beyond their window. As we dawdle along the landscaped path, we'll rediscover some more obvi-

ous truths about the differences between the Canadian and American worldviews. We'll even see how similar we are to other Nordic nations posed against steel blue skies and white horizons. Particularly, we'll see how we've come to live with nature now that we have managed the very important task of survival itself, and as we do so, we'll also stumble across a few unique Canadianisms.

The Group of Seven

While Cornelius Krieghoff was the first painter to record Canada's landscape in all its frigid kitsch, the Dutch immigrant and novice painter brought a decidedly old-world lens to the images he committed to the canvas. Borrowing his form from the Dutch masters, Krieghoff painted the world in intricate detail with uptight, tiny little brush strokes and a reverence for pictorial accuracy. With his bright colours, vibrant reds and blues, not even his palette matched the bruised blues and muted greys of the natural landscape — not that anyone would have known better. His Old World style brought him immediate acclaim among the monied colonists, who were desperate to bring a modicum of worldly sophistication to their world of mud puddles, blizzards and bloodsuckers. His paintings were equally valued in Europe, where his quaint images of toqued Habitants clutching rosaries, Aboriginal men toting dead rabbits, Aboriginal women on snowshoes and wide open winterscapes were considered exotic for their depiction of a "primitive" lifestyle.

The Vancouver Art Gallery recently rounded up cratefuls of Krieghoffs and put them on display, and after walking from room to room and seeing the same images repeated over and over again — in exact detail — I noticed that Krieghoff was a very successful schlock artist who discovered the magic set of

The Blizzard (1860, oil on canvas) by Cornelius Krieghoff (1815–1872): The first European painter to document what Canada and Canadians looked like, Krieghoff was a Dutch artist who saw something quietly heroic in the people who managed to make a life for themselves in the cold Canadian landscape. Not surprisingly, snowshoes are often present in the frame. McCord Museum of Canadian History, Montreal

images that appealed to the populist palate. He was also an important documentarian of the era. No one else painted early colonial life in Canada in as much detail and over such a long period of time, and as a result, we can see the origins of our relationship to the landscape in his world. We see the stark contrast between interiors and exteriors, between the warm tones of bundled bodies, wood, smoke and old Catholic icons contrasted against the great white barren emptiness outside. There is something heroic in the contrast, because if we just saw the interiors in isolation, the people would look pathetic — like Van Gogh's freaky human tubers in *The Potato Eaters* — but because we know they are posed against nothingness, their very presence in the frame

lends them a sense of valour and courage. But as we've already discovered, Canadians don't have a predisposition for classical heroics — and Krieghoff's work, like that of other painters who followed, such as John A. Fraser and Horatio Walker, was an obvious Old World attempt at transforming the landscape into something manageable: a new and scaled-down backdrop for an Old World narrative tradition.

Early Canadian writers made the same attempt to transpose values and storytelling devices from the old country, and the results were invariably the same: a pile of corpses by the last page. It didn't work, because it wasn't in harmony with the landscape. It was precisely with that as his artistic aim that a young farm boy from Ontario named Tom Thomson turned his graphic talents to painting the great Canadian landscape, and paved the way for the famed "Group of Seven."

Franklin Carmichael, Lawren Harris, A. Y. Jackson, Frank Johnston, Arthur Lismer, J. E. H. MacDonald and F. H. (Fred) Varley were the first generation of Canadian painters who looked to the land for inspiration. Emanating from the metropolis of Toronto, these young men were struggling to free themselves from the formalist landscape tradition that was imported from Britain (like the bulk of English Canada's cultural industries). They did not want to paint typical European pastoral canvases that were so popular at the turn of the century: paintings replete with soft, white lambs, idyllic farm houses and sweet, blue skies. Instead, they looked to the work of Thomson, an older painter they met in Toronto. Thomson loved the North and painted it in a way that few had ever tried. Drawn in by Thomson's bolder strokes and blue palette, the men put their minds and brushes to creating an entirely new tradition that reflected the lifestyle and sensibilities of Canadians — a tradition that shared nothing in common with the castrated wilderness canvases from Europe, but a painting that was as rugged and wild as Canada itself.

To that end, they formed a support group of sorts — a collective of painters that shared the same aesthetic vision and purpose. In 1920, after nearly a decade of painting together, they formed the Group of Seven. Fittingly — at least in a Canadian survivor guilt sense — the creative allegiance came only in the wake of a death. Thomson, their close friend, mentor and artistic inspiration, drowned as a result of a freaky and somewhat mysterious canoeing accident in Algonquin Park in 1917. Thomson was an accomplished outdoorsman, and for the

surviving artists left behind, accepting his demise at the hands of the wilderness he loved so passionately created a gaping hole in their lives. They needed to patch that hole, and the formation of the Group of Seven became their therapeutic rebirth.

Their collective fascination with snow, ice and other northern themes was validated — at least personally — when they headed down to Buffalo to see an exhibit of Scandinavian artwork. In looking at canvases from Swedish painter Gustav Fjaestad, Harris and MacDonald saw a reflection of their own landscape in the heavy brush strokes and subtle shades of white, purple, yellow and pink snow. "This is what we want to do with Canada," MacDonald said at the time. Not all that surprisingly, the young rebel painters were hardly critical darlings in the early stages. A. Y. Jackson was at the point of moving to the United States after his paintings were slagged in Montreal as being "unrefined" — read "non-European."

When Harris painted a picture of a small, white, simple corner store because he liked the simplicity of the structure and the shadows of the trees, critics said he should have painted a mansion instead. When the painters

First Snow, North Shore of Lake Superior (1923, oil on canvas) by Group of Seven member Lawren Harris (1885–1970).
VANCOUVER ART GALLERY (PHOTO: TREVOR MILLS)

exhibited in Toronto, the established critics sounded a familiar bleat of disdain. One writer said he saw the birth of the "Hot Mush School" in the work that used such bold colours and manly, unfinessed brush strokes. Another, apparently uptight, critic named Hector Charlesworth wrote in *Saturday Night* magazine that J. E. H. MacDonald's *Tangled Garden* was far too large for its ordinary subject matter, and he accused MacDonald of "throwing his paint pots in the face of the public."[2]

Regardless of what critics of the day thought of these bold new canvases, there is no doubt the Group of Seven found a new, original and distinctly Canadian way of reflecting the landscape back at Canadians. The images found "the truth" of the raw and potent world around them, and they communicated it with fat brush strokes, open, untamed and classically unbalanced compositions. There was nothing "pretty" or "contrived" about the way they painted, nor was there anything pretty or contrived about the landscape. It was beyond their control and very different from them — which explains the near-complete absence of people in their work — but not beyond their comprehension or their experience. The landscape became the emotional mirror for the way they felt as individuals: alone in the wilderness, but not out of context. Human beings were not physically present in their tableaux, but their images were emotive, personal and undeniably connected to the human spirit. The land was clearly "other" — but it was not, necessarily, hostile. It is merely the other half of the human condition: the timeless, immutable backdrop for the ephemeral human drama. This clearly rang true somewhere in the Canadian subconscious, and as a result, they changed forever the way Canadians look at art and the landscape.

The Group of Seven's images are now a permanent part of our collective identity because they speak to us about where we live. From the dark clouds over heaving deep blue waves, to stark white snow and black rocks, to the startling contrasts and crisp shadows, to burning leaves of red and ochre unfolding into abstracted grey clouds, these paintings of the "Terre Sauvage" capture the rugged beauty all around us. But they do more than that. Through their abstractions, their open-minded and non-traditional approach to applying paint to canvas, the Group also opened up a completely new creative path in the Canadian psyche — one that we continue to explore and develop to this day. To borrow the words Jackson used to describe the paintings of his friend Tom Thomson: "Not knowing the conventions of beauty, he found it all beautiful."[3]

From the Group of Seven to Super 8

The Group of Seven — and their West Coast counterpart, Emily Carr — opened our eyes to the magic of the world around us through their collective vision of the natural world. That vision has taken root in the Canadian psyche. As a study by one-time Soviet conceptual artists Vitaly Komar and Alex Melamid titled "Canada's Most Wanted and Most Unwanted Art" recently proved, the Canadian public shows a preference for landscape painting over anything abstract:

The results of the poll were revealing: Our taste is surprisingly familiar to that of the American public, and not substantially different from that of the majority of Icelanders, Danes, Finns, French or Turks. There is a general interest in landscape painting. There are some intriguing regional variances in the response. While Albertans exhibited a notable preference for paintings of outer space, Maritimers had a slightly higher interest in paintings with a religious subject, and Québécois had a predilection for paintings with nude or partially nude people.[4]

While our preference for landscape echoes our roots in realism, and the work of the Group of Seven is generally filed under schools of "realism" for their recognizable pictures of mountains and trees, their very brushes transformed the landscape from three dimensions into a flattened, two-dimensional representation. Using entirely novel painterly techniques, these artists were able to transform the landscape creatively without attempting to actually go head to head with the elements. It was an abstract shift, and one that opened up a whole new territory of the mind because suddenly we weren't fastened to a strictly sensory relationship with the outside world. We could now look at the scenery around us and assimilate it mentally, as an idea — as an aesthetic that could be appreciated as somehow *separate* from the hard rocks and cold snow that inspired the images. This idea of artistic interpretation and projection is the central creative ingredient in photography, which, unlike painting is more of a mechanical process. What makes photography an art form is the person behind the camera, composing the shot, choosing to include some elements while deleting others. If we take the pioneering efforts of the Group of Seven and transpose them into the film world, we have to understand the role of the photographer. Fortunately such films as *J. A. Martin photographe, Calendar, Picture of Light, I've Heard the Mermaids Singing* and *The Grey Fox* offer images of people photographing the landscape, or photographing other people.

The easiest example to dissect is Jean Beaudin's 1976 effort, *J. A. Martin photographe.* Obviously, we know it's about photography, and we know the filmmaker was conscious of the camera as a symbol. Here we enter the world of turn-of-the-century Quebec to follow the lives of photographer J. A. (Marcel Sabourin) and his wife, Rose-Aimée (the legendary Monique Mercure, who earned a best actress prize at Cannes for the role in 1977), as they carry out their everyday duties, taking pictures and listening to stories from around the township. There is no classic dramatic structure to the piece: things simply happen, and our characters simply react. In this way, the film is clearly rooted in realism, which only makes sense when you consider Beaudin and cinematographer Pierre Mignot came from the NFB tradition. In addition to *J. A. Martin photographe*, Beaudin made a series of films on mathematics and later, an award-winning look at the psychiatry of vertigo, *Vertige* (1969), at the Board before he, like so many other frustrated Quebecers, decided to leave for the private sector.

J. A. Martin photographe finds Beaudin at the top of his proverbial game as he balances documentary distance with artistic intimacy, a split he brings to the frame through his two main characters, J. A. and Rose-Aimée. J. A. is your typical 19th-century male: taciturn, uptight, rigid and thoroughly chauvinistic when it comes to *les dames*. Rose-Aimée, on the other hand, is a woman trapped by time. Outgoing, opinionated, eager to help and steeped in a sense of community, Rose-Aimée spends little time thinking of what others think, and simply moves forward according to her own agenda. The movie is a study in the contrasts between these two people — and that's about all. The movie opens with J. A. preparing for his annual trip into the wilds of

J. A. Martin photographe (1977): Joseph-Albert Martin (Marcel Sabourin, who also co-wrote the script) and his wife Rose-Aimée (Monique Mercure) gently roll through this horse-drawn road movie from director Jean Beaudin that chronicles a photographer's voyage into the hinterland — and subsequent rebirth in the verdant lap of mother nature.
PHOTO LIBRARY OF THE NATIONAL FILM BOARD OF CANADA

rural Quebec, where he captures the events that define other people's lives, such as births, marriages and death. As he packs his hearse-like black wagon, Rose-Aimée gets in his face. She wants to come along for the ride, but J. A. adamantly refuses. Of course she wins, and the two set out on a voyage that will reposition their relationship as they finally learn about each other in profound and moving ways.

Like the horse-drawn carriage that pulls them ever closer to the bosom of the Québécois experience, the movie moves very slowly. For people weaned on MuchMusic's visual diet of 200 shots per minute, this is going to feel painfully relaxed. I know the first time I watched this heralded classic as part of a Canadian Lit class in university, my eyes glazed almost immediately as the NFB logo appeared and I settled in for what I figured would be yet another overly earnest ride into the Canadian condition. Snooze-a-rama. "*Why did I take this stupid class anyway?*" was the mantra simmering on my mental stove. As the wagon pulled out and headed down the road amid a forest of dappled green and brown, the warbled soundtrack squawked through the three-penny speaker. "*This sucks,*" was about the only thing I can remember before I surrendered to the boredom and began dozing. My professor, who had a flair for institutional discipline, coughed loudly just seconds later. There would be no sleeping in this class. I would watch *J. A. Martin photographe* and learn from it — come fail or high marks. I can't be sure when the beauty of the movie first hit me, but I think it was the sequence where J. A. and his wife lie back in a field of tall grass and smile at one another. There was something very human about this moment, and in the end, about the entire movie.

In retrospect, and after having reviewed the film a few times, that moment marks an important transition because it pulls J. A. away from behind the camera. For the first part of the film, we see him do nothing but pack and unpack camera gear, position his tripod, develop film and take pictures from behind a giant bellows, his head covered by a thick, black blanket. The camera becomes a physical symbol of his emotional detachment from the world around him, and his cool relationship with Rose-Aimée is merely a symptom of his larger worldview. He watches terrible things unfold through the lens of his camera — such as substandard living conditions, child exploitation and miscarriage — but he always protects himself from the harshness by mediating what he sees with the camera. When he emerges from behind the wall of the film plane and looks at his wife with his eyes instead of through the lens, we know he — and his perspective — have changed. We saw a similar detachment cycle in *Surfacing*, only it moved the other way. The professor uses the movie camera as a means of distancing and empowerment after he has been sexually humiliated.

Generally, landscape and photography work together in Canadian film. One represents the natural world, the other represents man's attempt at controlling, taming and containing that unbound beauty through the lens. The variable in the equation is the human being, the artist/photographer composing the shot. In Patricia Rozema's hallmark film, *I've Heard the Mermaids Singing* (1987), we see Polly (Shelia McCarthy) tooling around Toronto on her bike, snapping shots of things that catch her eye. All the images are made outside, amid the urban, park-checkered landscape of Canada's biggest city. Polly doesn't care if anyone sees her images or not, because just making them gives her so much pleasure. For Polly, a nervous-talking temp girl who lands a part-time gig at a downtown art gallery, photography is a means of empowerment. She can say what she sees, and what she thinks, without being forced to articulate it. In this way, Rozema reminds us of the transcendent power of art, but she also juxtaposes that power with the morally bankrupt world of "art commerce" — as it is symbolized by the character of the curator (Paule Baillargeon), a sexy woman who sells crappy paintings to ignorant poseurs. The whole system works, until Polly — the pure, unaffected artist — is devastated when the curator calls her work trite and empty. Suddenly we are forced to ask ourselves, what makes a picture good or bad? Who decides what's worthy and what is not? Who has the most power, the beholder or the beholden?

This is a central element to Egoyan's film *Calendar* (1993), another film that features an emotionally distant male photographer and his wife, *Calendar* has much in common with *J. A. Martin photographe*. In this slow, intimate story of a husband and wife who take a trip to their ancestral home of Armenia, Egoyan and his wife Arsinée Khanjian play the central roles — an obvious reflection of real life before the camera even turns the first frame. Egoyan plays the photographer who has been hired to take pictures of Armenian churches for a calendar, while Khanjian, as the wife, plays the mediator between the photographic image and the landscape itself. She is the translator. She is always in front of the camera. She is the one who is clearly a part of the landscape, while her uptight spouse sits rigidly behind the light-tight box, waiting for just the right moment to open the shutter.

Because the film takes place in Armenia, readers might question the film's inclusion in this particular chapter. After all, Armenia, with its flocks of sheep and ancient architecture, bears little physical resemblance to the Canadian landscape of snowcapped mountains and open prairies. However, the film's location doesn't take away from its "Canadian-ness" because not only is Egoyan a Canadian director, but the whole film deals with the very Canadian idea of dislocation. This is a story of the immigrant returning to a homeland he cannot understand. His wife makes the transition. She learns the language and becomes part of the landscape — both literally and figuratively. Meanwhile the photographer returns home to his sterile Canadian apartment completely alone.

Calendar does not end as "happily" as *J. A. Martin photographe* — even though it's a very amusing ride. The couple cannot get back together, and instead of a voyage of mutual discovery, the trip to Armenia — and most notably the landscape itself — pulls them apart. "It's not a question of wanting to go or not," Egoyan says in the film as his wife and the Armenian guide walk toward the horizon together. "It's much stranger than that. It's about watching the two of you walking away from me, into a landscape that I will photograph." Talk about a control freak: this pathetic loser isn't capable of getting past his own frame of reference. He is a perfectionist who believes he can control — or at least exercise symbolic control over — everything in his life, from his wife, to his profession, to his selection of dinner guests. His attempts are futile, of course, which gives him comic proportions — like Charlie Chaplin trying to hold up a house only to have it fall directly on top of him. As a result, the closer his wife gets to the landscape (virtually communicating with it through the local guide), the more he realizes she is beyond his grasp. He can't even pick up the phone when she calls, because that would be communication, and therefore a type of surrender.

What comes through in each of these examples is a symbiotic relationship between the female characters and the landscape, and a similar connection between men and the photographic machine. I guess the photographer girlfriend in Philip Borsos' *The Grey Fox* (1982) is a bit of anomaly on that score, but it fits the film's overall role reversal by showing us how much the great stagecoach-cum-train robber, Bill Miner (Richard Farnsworth), missed during his time in jail. In that film,

Calendar (1993): Ashot Adamian plays the guide to a photographer (played by Egoyan, who is notably off-camera) and his wife (played by Egoyan's wife, Arsinée Khanjian) as they roam around the Armenian country side photographing ancient churches. Egoyan often refers to *Calendar* as his most personal movie. For obvious reasons: he and Khanjian were the key cast and crew. COURTESY OF JOHNNIE EISEN, © EGO FILM ARTS

Miner represents the old, static landscape while his new sweetie represents the 20th-century mentality and all its changin' ways. There's a similar variation in *I've Heard the Mermaids Singing*, where the emotive Polly is the picture-taker and the uptight curator has the mechanical brain, an image reaffirmed by the installation of a closed-circuit camera in a mannequin's head to monitor the gallery activity. We never see Polly take a light reading or measure for focal distance. She just snaps pictures, and because she has an unmediated approach, her artwork defies the boundaries of the curator's limited worldview.

Opening the Lens

The equation works the other way, too, where the camera becomes a teacher all by itself. In Peter Mettler's film *Picture of Light* (1994), we watch as Mettler and a documentary crew voyage far north, into the land of the midnight sun — or, in this case, the long winter — to photograph the aurora borealis (the northern lights). They have aims of making a high-art documentary about the phenomenon, but as the equipment starts to fail in the extreme cold and the filmmakers are frustrated by cloudy skies without action, the film soon becomes a film about making a film. The landscape is the only reason why they trekked such a ludicrous distance, but sooner than later, that landscape pushes the crew into a completely new place. "We all went a little crazy," Mettler said of the experience. "It was like we all reverted to our animal nature, or else completely over-intellectualized everything. There was no middle of the road notion of sanity anymore." We can see what he's talking about as we watch the cinematographer punch a hole in the wall of his hotel to watch a snowdrift emerge, flake by flake, at the foot of his bed. In this way, the documentary crew

becomes fused with its subject on both a mental and physical level. There is no safe documentary distance. The movie is the landscape is the movie.

A similar collapse of distance takes place in the documentary *Project Grizzly* (1996). Even though this NFB documentary is "straight" in its approach to form and constantly maintains its objective distance, the arm's-length approach also echoes the catch-22 of the real-life protagonist: a man who is so in love with grizzly bears that he wants to develop a grizzly-proof suit so he can get up close without risking death. Think about the absurdity of the situation: a man is in love with a part of nature, but in order to consummate his love, he has to develop a completely artificial device that will not only disguise his humanity and make him look like a French tire mascot, but further separate him from the very nature he's so desperate to touch. This boy in the bubble strives for the best. He sells everything he has for materials and when he's finally finished, he tests his garment by having a pickup truck drive into him. Now he's ready for the wilderness. The only problem is the suit is too heavy to wear and impossible to walk in. The only thing he can do is have a vehicle drop him off in the middle of the woods, hoping he will see a bear. There is a beautiful irony in the story that makes it hilarious and tragic all at once. The filmmakers captured it because, like their subject whose bid at intimacy was undone by his bubble suit, they too maintained a sense of distance through the camera.

Regardless of the particular variations, the idea of capturing the outside world with a weensy little box is a metaphor for the human process of seeing, connecting and formulating worldviews. One can use the camera as a protective wall from a hostile world, or as a

Project Grizzly (1996): Troy Hurtubise stands tall next to his handmade grizzly-proof suit that he hoped to wear in the bush for some intimate encounters with the powerful animals he has grown to love. The outfit proves too heavy to walk in, but director Peter Lynch shows us the suit works when Hurtubise dons the armour and has a buddy drive into him with a pickup truck.
PHOTO LIBRARY OF THE NATIONAL FILM BOARD OF CANADA

medium of connection to another side of the human spirit. It all depends on who is creating the image, and what his or her feelings are about landscape, which represents "the other."

Us, Them and the Other

From what we've seen so far in Canadian art and film, landscape is central and immutable. It is not us — making it, therefore, "the other."

Our national relationship to the concept of "otherness" is one of the central spindles in our rotating notion of identity. Take a step in either direction from the Canada-United States border and the difference between our relationship to nature and theirs is immediately apparent. Roads in the United States are generally wider, smoother and straighter than ours. In fact, it was the armed forces who developed the manual for road construction in the United States and they approach it the same way one might approach a military operation. In other words, they pave over the landscape and plant flagpoles, conquering it at every turn while we tend to pave around it — adjusting to the landscape with curves and dips and culverts.

In Bruce McDonald and Don McKellar's *Highway 61* (1991) — which opens, incidentally, with a shot of a frozen body discovered in a bathtub outside — there is one scene in particular that establishes the different realities on either side of the Canada-United States boundary. Small-town barber Pokey Jones (McKellar) is in the car with Jackie Bangs (Valerie Buhagiar). As the camera captures the couple crossing the border, the Ramones kick in on the soundtrack telling us we're entering a louder, harsher kind of in-your-face country. As the two make their way down Highway 61— a unique roadway that runs from Ontario to the cradle of the American South in New Orleans[5] — Pokey's voice-over deals with the differences on the other side of the border while the camera focuses on a giant American flag, a bulldozer and wide roads littered with advertising. With a sweet, naive tone in his voice, Pokey simply says, "Things are different here ... in the U.S.A." And we know exactly what he means. America tames and controls the land, transforming it in the process, whereas Canadians are nowhere near so anthropocentric. We have no delusions about who's more powerful, and as a result, we defer to the landscape at almost every turn. I think this must be one of the main reasons why Canadians are generally pragmatic, conciliatory, tolerant and humble — not to mention good at winter sports: We've come to realize

Highway 61 (1991): Valerie Buhagiar plays Jackie Bangs in part two of Bruce McDonald's road trilogy that includes *Roadkill* and *Hard Core Logo*. In this film, two Canadians go south in an attempt to take care of some personal business, and end up discovering more about themselves in a foreign country than they ever did at home. SHADOW SHOWS

that you can't tame the wild. You can kill it. You can pave it under. You can poison it, put it in a cage and charge people to see it, but you can't make it your ally. You have to accept it for what it is, and hopefully, survive what inevitably becomes a love-hate relationship.

We've already seen how important the landscape is to the Canadian psyche. We've seen reverential images from the Group of Seven to codependent attachments to the landscape in everything from *Mon Oncle Antoine* to *Calendar* (in both films, the natural landscape makes the livelihood of the central characters possible, but it is also oppressive — like the asbestos mines in *Mon Oncle Antoine*). Landscape features prominently in other notable titles such as *32 Short Films About Glenn Gould, Roadkill, The Adjuster, The Sweet Hereafter, La Moitié gauche du frigo, Le*

Confessionnal, The Hanging Garden, Low Visibility, The Law of Enclosures, Picture of Light, New Waterford Girl, Mob Story, Black Robe, Lilies, Suspicious River, waydowntown ... and on, and on and on it goes.

Just recently, I was watching rushes (or dailies) of Anne Wheeler's latest project, an adaptation (by Wheeler and Charles Pitts) of an Alice Munro short story titled *A Wilderness Station*. For nearly 45 minutes I watched nothing but repeated takes of a lone, cloaked woman slowly plodding her way through deep snow under a bruised blue Manitoba sky. It's an image we've seen several times over in this country — the lone figure, small and black against the white or wooded background. It's also a regular menu item in Canadian art — not just in the pure landscapes of the Group of Seven, but in the catalogue of Quebec artist Ozias Leduc and such pieces as Newfoundlander David Blackwood's stark prints of ice floes and living ghosts, Alex Colville's hyper-real and flattened landscapes, Jean-Paul Lemieux's abstracted scenes of rural Quebec, such as *Nuclear Winter*, Wanda Koop's spiritually inclined *Shadow Man with Wreath*, and even Tom Forrestall's *End of a Winter's Day* all show a relatively small human in a broad, canvas landscape that is clearly "other." The human form and nature may occupy the same frame, but they are undeniably different, either in the way they are rendered through different techniques, colours or brush strokes, or else through composition. For instance, in the Lemieux painting, the human form (looking remarkably unhappy) is cut in half by the edge of the frame while the blue-white landscape of the city and a lone statue fill the rest.

Revisiting Nature the Monster

Typically, and certainly in the past, the nature of our relationship with the landscape was just another word for "victim." In *Survival*, Atwood says, "... Canadian writers as a whole do not trust Nature, they are always suspecting some dirty trick. An often encountered sentiment is that Nature has betrayed expectation, it was supposed to be different."[6] Atwood says part of this distrust could be due to the attitude that 18th- and 19th-century English writers brought with them from the Old World: a perspective of the natural world shaped by Edmund Burke's "cult of the sublime and picturesque," and later Wordsworthian Romanticism that likened nature to a nurturing mother who could reveal the wonders of the world to men who revered and listened to her. Inevitably, says Atwood, both Burke's and Wordsworth's views of nature were questioned by early Canadian writers who found themselves sucked dry by mosquitoes and

directionally confounded by close thickets of underbrush and impenetrable stands of trees. The result of this rude reality was that early English Canadian writers found their ideas about nature had to cleave down the middle, trapped somewhere between "faith in the Divine Mother and a feeling of hopeless imprisonment." The fears of nature were genuine. Countless early colonists perished from the cold and malnutrition. In some cases, they perished because other settlers lost patience with the extreme climate and decided to take out their frustrations on the man, or men, who convinced them to make the hellish voyage in the first place.

Consider the fate of Henry Hudson, who in 1610 tried to navigate the bay that now carries his name, looking for gold when his crew mutinied. Angry, bitter and disheartened after spending a harsh Canadian winter eating moss and frogs, they set Hudson, his son and the remaining loyal members of the Discovery crew adrift in a small boat — never to be seen again. Nasty, but not that different from Canadian expatriate James Cameron's story for *Aliens*, where the crew of a rescue vessel sent to save extraterrestrial colonists — whose desolate planet has been ravaged by the hostile force of "mother alien" — are forced to turn against their wishy-washy corporate leader (Paul Reiser) because he wants to stick around and capture the alien for weapons' research. I know Cameron is constantly referred to as an American director with "Canadian roots," if he's referred to as Canadian at all. To directors who remain in Canada, Cameron's unscalable ego is a source of amusement and in some cases, shame, because "I'm King of the World!" is such an affront to our humble Canadian sensibilities. But to me, *Aliens* and *Terminator* were movies that exhibited Canadian themes, even if they are pure Hollywood as far as production and execution go — which leads me to suspect that being "Canadian" is a concept that moves far beyond borders, and proves once again that indeed we do have an identity.

What makes a movie like *Alien* or *Terminator* Canadian, you may well ask. As I already suggested, there is a wonderful symmetry between the Hudson story and the plot of *Aliens*. Unlike the first film, Ridley Scott's *Alien*, which features an alien killing off members of a deep-space salvage crew, Cameron's original idea for *Aliens* focused on a colony. A bunch of unsuspecting Earthlings have set up an outpost far from home. Things are tough, but they have each other in this barren wasteland, but then even that is taken away when a whole tribe of beasts starts eating them and using their body parts for cocoons. No doubt this type of horror story would have rung familiar in Susanna Moodie's ears. She was certainly familiar with the idea of being in a foreign landscape where the creatures rip humanity apart limb by limb. That sounds Canadian to me, and so does the position of the woman in both *Terminator* and *Aliens*. In *Terminator*, Linda Hamilton is the "hero," as is Sigourney Weaver in *Aliens*. Both have to deal with an outside, hostile force, and as usual, it's only the women who truly understand the monster — the "mother alien" — the force of nature.

Colonial Baggage Claim

Almost all colonial cultures deal with similar nature-human tensions, and not surprisingly, when those traditions attempt a period piece, Atwood's victim stances reappear — only with a different accent. For example, in Jane Campion's *The Piano*, Ada (Holly Hunter), a mail-order bride from Scotland who moves to New Zealand, nearly disappears into thigh-deep mud every time she leaves her wood shack. There's also Australian director Bill Bennett's *In A Savage Land*, where Martin Donovan plays an anthropologist who contracts dysentery and dies a slow miserable death in New Guinea. There's also *Gandhi, Indochine, An African Dream, The Far Pavillions, White Mischief*, and many, many more. Almost every New World culture that looks to the Old World for its ancestry had to face the same harrowing period of readjustment in a very foreign — and typically hostile — environment. This is called "colonial baggage" or "the garrison mentality" — a condition recognized in literature to describe a state of self-alienation or exile. Afraid of the unknown that lay on the other side of the fortress walls, early English-speaking settlers essentially imprisoned themselves in wood structures to kindle memories of the Old World and nurture feelings of safety and the familiar. For this reason, Atwood's observations regarding early Canadian literature — as well as most early colonial literature — are just as valid today as they were 30 years ago. After all, the texts have not changed — but we, as a culture and as a nation, most certainly have. Film is the best place to look for these changes because the medium itself is modern and therefore much more likely to remain untainted by literary traditions of the past.

One of the strongest examples that illustrates just how far we've come in our love-hate relationship to nature can be found in Calgary-based filmmaker Gary Burns' *waydowntown*. The story of four office drones who challenge each other to stay within the air-conditioned and sealed office spaces of Calgary's downtown core using the plus-15 system of skywalks (a series of elevated walkways), *waydowntown* takes place in a decidedly urban environment. Each character is warm, well-fed, dressed in crisp business attire and perfectly safe from the elements at all times, placing them all in stark contrast to the early survivalists fighting to stay warm and scurvy-free back in the early days when Canadians were forced to eat moss and frogs. And yet, as the days wear on, the four urban "survivors" begin to exhibit all the signs of paranoia, disappointment and existentialist angst that poor Susanna Moodie did when she was roughing it in the bush. The only real difference is that Moodie was simultaneously awestruck and imprisoned by the natural world, whereas the four drones in *waydowntown* are voluntarily self-imprisoned and somewhat disgusted by the human-made mall: a forest of steel, glass and greasy food stuffs.

The film opens with a scene of our narrator, Tom (Fabrizio Filippo), making his way to work through the tunnels and glass elevators in the fused downtown core. One of his first stops is the underground parkade, where he smokes a big fattie in his VW Beetle before heading to the office. Before we even know what's going on, the images are screaming claustrophobia: Tom walks through a sealed office tower, ventures further into its bowels with a visit to the underground parkade, then isolates himself in this interior world in his own private bubble, the Bug. The only way Tom can really escape this industrial prison is to indulge in herbal escapism: after all, he can't physically leave the sealed confines because he's made a bet for $10,000.

The imagery and the scenario are telling us that Tom is a prisoner, a victim in the same tradition as all the other victims splattered and frozen across the Canadian landscape. Burns even includes the traditional dead animal in the opening few moments of the film, when Tom emerges from his car and picks up a dead mouse. Completing our inventory of "colonial baggage," Burns slams us over the head with a real ant colony as part of Tom's office decor as a symbol of this compartmentalization of nature. All the traditional colonial elements are here, but Burns subverts them all with a wonderfully ironic stance via Tom — our cynical junior executive who places himself outside the community in which he lives, if not physically in the outside world, then internally, in his own mind. The distinction is important, because it suggests the individual not only has free will but also has the ability to create his own reality. He can use his imagination, and Tom frequently does:

"When I was a kid, I always thought it was a pretty bad idea to connect all the buildings in the downtown core with walkways. My reasoning then was that it made it too easy to pick up the whole of downtown in one big clump and hold it hostage, as supervillains will. This left it up to the superhero to bring it down, and put everything back to normal ... I thought it might be fun to be in your office when the downtown is picked up, and hang in space under a protective bubble ... there'd be bedlam, rapes and killings ... but not from the supervillain or his henchmen, but from the inhabitants — the people I work with. Under the calm facade, I think most of these people would love to get back to the jungle ... Although, you gotta wonder why a superhero would bother saving us anyway. Superheroes have morals and a sense of decency, so he'd be disgusted by our behaviour and boot the whole works into the sun, which would be a shame, considering I'm just getting settled in here."

This excerpt deserves a bit of deconstruction

waydowntown (2000): Tom (Fabrizio Filippo) has a superhero moment as he appears to fly through the maze of Calgary's plus-15 skyway system in Gary Burns' award-winning feature about corporate life, dead end jobs and a bet about who can stay inside the longest. ODEON

because it sets up the rest of the movie, isolates the central themes, and shows us exactly how far we, as Canadians, have come in re-imagining our relationship with nature — not to mention the whole "National Experience." First, Tom hearkens back to his childhood, that so-called state of innocence before we all bite into the fruit of knowledge and find ourselves barred from Eden. Tom still has a connection to that place, he even remembers all the comic books he read that recounted the adventures of superheroes and can conjure those images in his mind. Despite the fact that Superman was born in the mind of a Canadian, superheroes — as literary or film characters — have never really found a spot in the Canadian psyche, making Tom's recollections a bit of an anomaly. The second notable detail in this opening

clip of voice-over is the distinction Tom makes between the supervillains and the inhabitants of the floating downtown bubble. He says the supervillains wouldn't be wreaking havoc — looting, raping, killing — but the people within the city would — "the people I work with." In this equation, then, the villain is not nature. The villain is not even a character. The real source of evil is — good golly — us! "Under the calm facade, I think most of these people would love to get back to the jungle," says Tom, throwing a question mark at the whole notion of evolution — not to mention the hero-myth that dictates how superhumans are automatically charged with saving humanity. Tom asks, "Why bother saving us at all?"

In a few short sentences, Burns breaks down the good-evil, right-wrong, dramatic balance. He says we are the ones without a sense of decency or any moral code. Any separation of good and evil is false. We are both and, therefore, ambiguous. Can there be retribution? In the case of *waydowntown*, retribution and salvation appear to lie in breaking free from the stale air and cubicles of office life. And yet, our four survivors have essentially locked themselves in these anonymous pens of their own free will. Why do they do this? Will they ever escape? These are the questions Burns asks throughout the film as we watch our little ants move through the industrial lattice of downtown Calgary. But they are also the larger questions we must ask ourselves every day as we drag our asses out of bed and head off to work in the anonymous confines of downtown towers, where we may feel alienated from our co-workers or feel lonely within the confines of our cubicles.

The effect is the same regardless of the actual backdrop: we feel oppressed by the environment. The only difference is that in the past, we were exiled to "wilderness stations" — now, we're exiled to "work stations." In the case of *waydowntown*, the characters are not oppressed by snow and death, but by mountains of paperwork and dead-end jobs.

This inversion may not seem all that important in light of the persistent symptoms, but it's nothing less than a complete redesign of the Canadian condition. When was the last time someone in our literary or movie tradition felt *unsafe* under the cool glow of a fluorescent tube? Certainly there were women in CanLit who felt more oppressed inside the cabin than outside, but that wasn't a result of the four walls and the warm fire — it was usually because there was some unpleasant, potentially violent husband or father figure inside waiting for them.

We'll talk about the women in a later chapter, but for now, let's accept that typically, the indoors have been seen as safe places, a human construct built for survival — a small but humble assertion of self in a hostile universe.

Waydowntown not only turns this idea inside out, but it takes it one step further when our de facto hero, Tom, decides the bet isn't worth it. He can't stand being inside any longer so he moves through the double doors and stretches out his arms, giving the stinky air of downtown Calgary a big, symbolic hug. Ah, the truly great outdoors. What a concept in a Canadian filmic tradition that includes the lengthy journey of a casket in the snow in *Mon Oncle Antoine*, the alienating white nothingness of *Kamouraska*, and the blanket of white ice that swallowed the school bus in *The Sweet Hereafter*.

Making this already notable transformation even more astounding is how Burns decides to end the movie. As our perfectly human hero walks into the natural light, he stops in his tracks when a two-litre pop bottle filled with marbles hits the ground in front of him. The marble-filled pop bottle is a recurring image in the film as the key to the outside world; throw the bottle at the shock-resistant plate glass window and it will shatter, allowing would-be suicidal freedom-seekers a brief, but highly dramatic, escape from the drudgery of a nine-to-five office existence. Burns introduces the escape route in the first few frames of the film through Don McKellar's character, Bradley (AKA "Sadly Bradley"), a longtime employee who decides he can't stand being a non-presence in the office wilderness, so he flirts with the "Romantic" idea of ending it all with a five-second drop into the middle of cool Cowtown.

When Tom sees the marbles at his feet, Burns changes the angle to an overhead zoom so that we're now taking on the perspective of

waydowntown (2000): Sandra (Marya Delver) breaks out of her glass cage and takes a deep breath of not-so-fresh down-town Calgary air after spending weeks inside. With the great outdoors representing a form of salvation, *waydowntown* marks an inversion of the Canadian stereotype, where nature usually plays the oppressor. PHOTO CREDIT

the falling projectile — in this case, the person who threw the bottle through the glass and is now hurtling earthward. It's not the McKellar character but the retiring "founder of the company," Mr. Mather (Harris Hart), who also happens to be a kleptomaniac. What happens next, in the final seconds of the film, is probably one of the most fundamental shifts in Canadian cinema I've ever seen: the camera zooms in on Fabrizio's eyeball, then shows us the reflection of the falling body with grey hair. The closer we get to the eyeball, the more suspicious the images become because we suddenly see a superhero, red cape flapping in the wind, flying to the rescue of Mr. Mather, who is then whisked off into the blue sky just as the tail credits begin to roll. The ambiguity of the ending ensures *waydowntown* meets

our original checklist for what makes a film Canadian, but the presence of a superhero, the open potential for a positive ending, and the very inversion of the inner and outer worlds — and where one finds safety in the crazy cosmos – combine to create a watershed moment in the history of Canadian film.

Naturally Bizarre

Even a film as dark and morose as Lynne Stopkewich's *Suspicious River* (2000), which bears all the earmarks of our traditionally Gothic interior and bleak sense of self, is a film that presents another shift in the way nature is used on screen.

Clearly, the river is the main symbol in the movie. Leila (Molly Parker) works at a motel by the river. When she has a smoke

Suspicious River (2000): Leila Murray (Molly Parker) is a motel clerk with too much time on her hands and too little adventure. To spice up her life a little, she begins seducing motel guests for one-night stands, including this charmer played by Callum Keith Rennie. MASSEY PRODUCTIONS, TVA INTERNATIONAL

break or a lunch break, she sits by the river and watches the swans drift by. This scene plays back to her memories as a child, a device that Stopkewich takes advantage of to fragment time and suggest the idea of parallel narratives. In other words, we are never quite sure if the kid Leila is talking to is just a kid she knows, or the projected memory of her childhood self.

The river, flowing thick and brown through her life, is the perfect symbol for this fluid idea of time and personal growth. Not only is it muddied from too much rain and turbulence, but it's constantly flooding. Water is generally a symbol of change that cannot be controlled. Water moves constantly in the most unpredictable of ways, and so does life. So no matter how much Leila would like to go

back to a certain time, she cannot. She must move forward: she must accept the fact that her mother was abused, that she must embrace her inner child and acknowledge her own pregnancy. She must integrate her past and present. Sadly, she can't. At least not at the beginning. Instead of moving toward integration and the river, she strays back into the hotel rooms where she has violent, humiliating sexual relationships with a variety of strange men. Only once she's been taken away from the river by car, to a faraway place in the woods, raped senseless — and very nearly killed — by a group of mono-dimensionally violent men, does Leila realize her separation from self and try to escape.

Once again, it's the inside that is oppressive and once again, it's nature that provides

Careful (1992): The face of dysfunction has a habit of staring back at you in almost any Guy Maddin movie, here, it wears many faces as the citizens of Tolzbad look upon one of the many horrors that surround them in their avalanche-prone mountain town. TORONTO FILM LIBRARY

the escape as Leila actually finds safety in the river itself. She escapes the murdering rapists by swimming to safety, and the motel, on the opposite bank. How much of this is real, and how much is imagined in the mind of our heroine is once again left highly ambiguous, reaffirming the film's Canadianess, but also revealing a far more open-ended approach to nature itself. Before, at least in literature, nature wasn't something that you could be ambivalent about — lest you fall into the river and drown or get lost in the snow and freeze to death. Nature could be ambivalent toward the human, but not, generally, the other way around.

As Atwood said in *Survival*: "Nature seen as dead, or alive but indifferent, or alive and actively hostile towards man is a common image in Canadian literature. The result of a dead or indifferent Nature is an isolated or 'alienated' man; the result of an actively hostile Nature is usually a dead man, and certainly a threatened one."[7]

Today, in Canadian film at least, the reality is slightly different. It is not Nature that is openly hostile toward man, but the highly constructed and very human urban environment — as we saw in *waydowntown*. Nature is still, certainly, a presence in the Canadian psyche, but as citizens of the 21st century, perhaps we have come to realize that nature represents our spiritual salvation just as much as it symbolizes our eventual physical demise.

In essence, we have reimagined our relationship to nature — which is no small feat when you consider how many characters in

CanLit were swallowed by frozen lakes and grizzly bears contributing to the whole "Death by Nature" CanLit trait. Sure, the landscape is still a threat to anyone inhabiting this awesome geography, but it seems the more we mature as a nation and a culture, the more we seem to be taking some sense of responsibility for our actions.

Be Careful Out There

For instance, in Guy Maddin's perfectly bizarre film *Careful* (1992), which looks simultaneously like a Sonja Hennie nightmare, a Leni Riefenstahl childhood dream and an Ingmar Bergman acid trip, the characters are constantly talking about the risk of avalanche. At one point the Electra-like Klara even says working in the mines is a good thing because "You can sing without starting an avalanche." Of course, once Klara actually articulates the word, there's little doubt as to how she will eventually meet her demise. Before she and Georg meet their mutual ends, however, an entire cast of characters is killed off through brutal encounters with nature: Johann throws himself off a snowy cliff after drugging his mother and fondling her flesh — a scene which Maddin intercuts with shots of a Maple Leaf flag. Klara kills her sister in the lake, and then brings her father to her snow cave in the hopes of claiming him for herself, only to be swept away in his arms when the portended avalanche finally rolls down the mountain. Not to be outdone by the ladies, Georg assumes the stance of a famed Nordic prince when he kills Count Knockters in a snowy dual to protect the honour of his dead father. Bereft of personal happiness in the wake of the count's death, Georg's mother, Zanita, kills herself in the

attic (the place once inhabited by Georg's eldest brother, Franz). Finally, Georg, without lover or mother, retires to the alpine snow cave and freezes to death — a coda to the first scenes in the film where the narrator tells us how people in this berg get their hearts pierced after death — like ice vampires — just to make sure they don't somehow thaw and come back to life.

There's no doubt the landscape plays a huge part in the denouement and dramatic scale of *Careful*, but there's a distinct difference between the Gothic side of nature revealed in early Canadian fiction and the way it is stylized, shaped and aesthetically reconfigured through Maddin's Gothically inclined lens.

The main difference is humour. Even though *Careful* is a pretty awful tale about incest in a remote mountain town, it's hard not to laugh at the melodrama. Everything is so over the top and so wonderfully subversive that Maddin makes the Gothic oddly comedic: "I have a hairball in my throat," says Zanita, the Bergmanesque heroine, overcome with grief. "I think I will swallow it." Swallow, indeed. Maddin symbolically swallows the Canadian tradition whole and transforms it completely, making nature almost benevolent compared to plain human evil and overcoming, with flying colours, a history of creative constipation in the face of the great outdoors.

Recreating images of nature and re-imagining our relationship with the elements is an undeniable sign of our cultural evolution. It proves that we have the power to abstract the world around us, and if not control it, at least assimilate it to a point where it is no longer so foreign and threatening, but simply an extension of ourselves.

PROFILE

Anne Wheeler

Born 1946 — Edmonton, Alberta

Exuding a sense of quiet, calm confidence, Anne Wheeler has been referred to as a "Dalai Lama-like" presence by the legions of young actors and filmmakers who have shared her many movie sets. Director of several features, including the critical success *Bye Bye Blues* (1989) and the commercial hit, *Better Than Chocolate* (1999), Wheeler has blazed her own trail through the wilderness — not just in film, but in life as well.

Growing up the little sister to three older brothers in the already hostile landscape of Edmonton, Wheeler says she was "determined to catch up" with her older siblings, regardless of whether the pursuit was athletic or intellectual. While the all-male sibling experience made Wheeler resilient on many levels, she was put to the test as a teenager: shortly after

the death of her father, she was raped and impregnated, and told it was illegal to have an abortion.

Wheeler's entire worldview shifted, and she began to question the status quo. After travelling the world and studying with a guru in India, she tried her hand at teaching and a variety of performing arts, including singer and stand-up comic.

"I guess I could be called subversive. But mostly I just ignore the status quo. I never put much weight on what other people think or how other people live their lives. I never even lived with anyone until I was 32," says Wheeler.

It was only after getting married and giving birth to twins that Wheeler's filmmaking career began in earnest, with a documentary short all about the ins and outs of oral hygiene.

From that bright and squeaky start, Wheeler soon found a group of film-minded Albertans and began writing the stories that brought her fame, such as *Great Grandmother* — a frontier woman's tale inspired by her own grandmother's journey to western Canada, and *A War Story*, another documentary with personal meaning. The film was based on the experiences of her father, Dr. Ben Wheeler, who had been a POW during the Second World War.

The National Film Board was impressed with her work. Soon, there was an NFB studio in Edmonton and Wheeler was on the verge of making her first feature, which she wrote, directed and produced: *Loyalties*, the story of a working-class First Nations woman (Tantoo Cardinal) and a middle-aged white woman (Susan Woolridge) who discover the complexities of their relationship after a revelation involving the sexual abuse of a child.

Wheeler returned to her Prairie roots once more for her next project, *Bye Bye Blues* — a wartime romance about an Alberta housewife who stumbles into her own identity while waiting for her husband to return from overseas.

Cowboys Don't Cry, the kids' film, *Angel Square*, and television movies followed, including *The Diviners, Mother Trucker — The Diana Kilbury Story* and *The Sleep Room*.

"I've never been to film school," says Wheeler. "I just think of the best way to tell a story. When it comes to character, I let my life experience tell me what works. And when it comes to camera moves, I'm usually open to suggestions."

When Wheeler isn't working on her own features, she's either writing, playing piano or directing one of the many TV serials shot in Vancouver, where Wheeler now lives.

"I'm on the good guy side. I want to reinforce the good in people. I don't really feel I'm on the frontier. But then again, who ever stands back to look when you're so busy planting and getting ready for the next winter," she says.

"The Canadian industry is great right now. We have so many talented people. We have excellent crews. But we still lose a lot of our talent to the Hollywood mentality. A lot of indie filmmakers have the same mentality in the U.S. though. It's always hard to find money to make a movie. It's even harder when there isn't a tradition of giving film-makers money, as there is in the U.S. But these are global problems," she says. "Denmark and India are telling stories that are close to their truth ... and they are commercially successful there. There are reasons to be encouraged. We're starting to see more real people. Think of a movie like *Secrets and Lies*; it's about real people and it did really well. Hollywood is in a bit of a rut. They can't come up with ideas anymore."

Wheeler says one of the best ways to avoid the pitfalls of cliché is to reinvent it at every turn and look for greys instead of black and white. "There are no villains in my movies. There are just people who make mistakes. That's because I basically believe people are good. We need to search ourselves and each other for understanding. Humour is good for that. I think, actually, that my sense of humour is responsible for my survival ... I think having dreams is great, but when they don't come true, just be realistic and push forward."

FILMOGRAPHY: *Loyalties* (1985) | *Cowboys Don't Cry* (1987) | *Bye Bye Blues* (1988) | *Angel Square* (1990) | *Better Than Chocolate* (1999) | *Marine Life* (2000).

Bruce McDonald

Born 1959 — Kingston, Ontario

KENNY HAYES AND SHADOW SHOWS

He's made a lot of movies, but Bruce McDonald will go down in history as the man who announced he would buy "the biggest chunk of hash" he could find after winning the $25,000 prize for best Canadian feature at the 1989 Toronto International Film Festival (then called Festival of Festivals). "What can I say," says McDonald. "I've never been all that interested in doing what's expected of me."

A true Canadian maverick, McDonald's career started in documentary and gradually shifted into narrative features after a solid stint as an editor on such films as Atom Egoyan's *Speaking Parts* and Ron Mann's *Comic Book Confidential* — not to mention crewing on Norman Jewison's nun story, *Agnes of God*. A proud Canadian, when McDonald originally set to work on his first

road movie, *Roadkill*, he wanted to make sure it was a Canadian take on the romantic genre and that his characters pointed north — not south, like they usually do. With that in mind, McDonald approached local Toronto playwright and theatre type, Don McKellar to write some pages — and the rest is history. *Roadkill* was the first Canadian film to burn the earnest, English-Canadian tradition in favour of hipster chic, and it quickly became a cult film for a whole new generation of Canadian moviegoers who were blown away to see such a cool reflection of themselves on screen.

"I grew up watching all kinds of American crap on television and loving it. I watched all those lame horror films like *Soylent Green* and thought moviemaking would be such a cool thing to do, but it's so much different than what you think it's going to be. Film is a very cerebral exercise that tries to access a very emotional space — it's a real challenge creatively because you have to use two parts of your brain all the time ... which can be a challenge, even on the best of days," says McDonald. "Film is such a fabricated medium. The main job of a director is to try and get an honest performance. The performer has to feel true in the moment, and that means they have to trust what you are doing. So you have to appear that you know exactly what's going on to put them at ease — but half the time you don't know what the fuck it is you're really looking for ... that elusive moment of truth. I'm completely insecure, but as a filmmaker you have to have a huge ego. You need both, and it's the collision of those two forces that makes it all happen."

Like a few other Canadian filmmakers we've run into, McDonald is also a fan of Jean-Luc Godard, the former critic who was at the leading edge of the French New Wave. "Godard should be our god. He pushed the envelope all the time and brought an incredible amount of creativity to the whole process. I try to push the envelope too. I'm always looking for the next layer of meaning, but you have to be careful not to get too precious about being an artist. You want people to understand at least some of what you are doing, and that's why it's usually a pretty good idea to have story editors and people you can bounce things off of ... But you can never be afraid to appropriate the material and make it your own. As a filmmaker, that's your job. You're the one looking through the camera — and I take responsibility for that."

McDonald is clearly fond of creative collaborations. He worked with McKellar on *Roadkill*, *Highway 61* and the TV series *Twitch City*. He adapted the work of W. P. Kinsella in *Dance Me Outside* and hooked up with poet-novelist Michael Turner to bring *Hard Core Logo* to the screen.

"I sort of look at it like a rock 'n' roll kind of thing. You know, one person writes the lyrics and the other writes the music and then you have a group of musicians to bring it all together on stage," says McDonald. "Some days I really wish I played in a band. You can get all that angst out in one night instead of fretting over it for months and months. In music, it's all about being in the moment but in film, it's about setting up a set of circumstances so the moment can happen — and hopefully happen in a way that feels convincing. That's what you try for, but it doesn't always work. You have to be open to something that you may not have planned for."

For instance, when McDonald realized he wouldn't be able to make the road movie he always wanted, which turned out to be *Highway 61*, he rolled with the punches and made *Roadkill* instead. The revenues generated from that film paved the way for *Highway 61*, and those shekels in turn gave McDonald

enough clout to finish his road movie trilogy (with a short break in between with *Dance Me Outside*), and create *Hard Core Logo*.

As someone who describes freedom as "driving at night listening to the tape deck, with a whole pack of butts and some beer," McDonald's passion for the road oozes from every frame of the rock-road-movie trilogy. Oddly enough, for a guy who loves to travel, he'd never really spent time in Vancouver before shooting the mockumentary, *Hard Core Logo*.

"People in Toronto told me Vancouver was small-town and that it was inhabited by a bunch of laid-back potheads. The small-town thing was wrong, as I discovered when I stumbled into this thriving East Indian community. The pot thing might be true, but people on the West Coast aren't as lazy as people think — they work really hard and then kick back ... It was a good education for me because I think it opened my eyes a bit about what life is really all about out here," says McDonald. "I also learned to love the muted, pastel light. It's a nice change to the stark sunlight and crisp shadows we get out east. It gives everything a totally different feel that I can really only describe as melancholy. I found that very interesting ... But I needed to know all of that stuff to make *Hard Core Logo* because it's a movie about time and place. There were other punk movements in other cities, but the Vancouver movement was such a weird, grassroots thing. It was like spontaneous combustion — it just blew up in everyone's face."

The symbolic shrapnel were bands such as DOA, The Pointed Sticks, The Modernettes, The Subhumans, The Young Canadians — and many more scrappy acts that played hard, lived hard and burnt out almost as fast as they appeared. Turner's book and McDonald's film offer a piece of that crazy time in Vancouver, but McDonald hoped the film would find universal resonance — especially as it came so close on the heels of Kurt Cobain's suicide.

"I guess all my movies deal with a sense of loss, but in very specific ways because I think the more specific a film is, the more universal it becomes. So *Hard Core Logo* is about the end of the band — the end of the dream." In an earlier interview with *Vancouver Sun* critic Elizabeth Aird, McDonald described *Roadkill* as the death of rock and *Highway 61* as the funeral, so *Hard Core Logo*'s obliteration of the last wriggling fibres of punk rebellion provided the end of the cycle, and a rather gloomy ending.

After *Hard Core Logo*'s less than stellar theatrical run, McDonald took a five-year hiatus from filmmaking and turned to television work and re-teamed with McKellar for *Twitch City*. He also made an ad for Levi Strauss that gave him a chance to tinker with sci-fi form, as well as *Scandalous Me: The Jacqueline Susann Story* and *American Whiskey Bar*, Noel Baker's adaptation of another Turner book.

McDonald says television is a good confidence builder because there's more money and less pressure, and now, he's going to put all that confidence and experience to the test. On the burner are *Pontypoole Changes Everything*, a horror movie based on a novel by Tony Burgess, which McDonald describes as a zombie movie made by Roman Polanski. McDonald also wrapped *Picture Claire*, a new movie (expected for release in late 2001) about a Montreal street creature who goes down the road to Toronto looking for a solution to a pressing problem. The film stars Americans Juliette Lewis, Gina Gershon and Mickey Rourke and is one of several new projects produced by Robert Lantos' Serendipity Point Films in the Canadian mogul's bid to bring bona fide commercial filmmaking to Canada.

"Money has always been the big taboo in Canadian film. You're not supposed to talk about how much money your films make — or don't make — because we're all supposed to be thinking on a higher plane. But we make crappy movies like everyone makes crappy movies. Sometimes, not even having your own vision is enough to make a bad script come together, so at the very least, I always try to tell a good story."

FILMOGRAPHY: *Let Me See* (1982) | *Knock! Knock!* (1985); *Roadkill* (1989) | *Highway 61* (1991) | *Dance Me Outside* (1994) | *Hard Core Logo* (1996) | *Pontypoole Changes Everything (2001)* | *Picture Claire* (2001).

CHAPTER FIVE

Probing the Negative

MOVING PAST THE FILM PLANE AND UNDERSTANDING EMPTY SPACE

"Canadians show a marked preference for the negative." —*Margaret Atwood,* Survival

In the previous two chapters, we explored how the early Canadian identity was forged in tandem with ideas of "other" — particularly the Indigenous "other" and the natural "other" as represented through images of the landscape. These two primary forces sculpted the inside of the Canadian condition with all the power of a glacial torrent released into sandstone: carving, churning and redefining the rock walls of the internal landscape in gradual increments. The cumulative effect of this dynamic tension isn't easy to read because most of the dramatic erosion took place slowly, beneath the surface. If we look hard, we can find clues beneath the thick brush strokes and blue pallettes of the Group of Seven and the grainy, snow-blown textures of Guy Maddin. We can see bits and pieces of broken selves, outsiders stranded in the wilderness and the vague outline of a national experience. So what — if anything — comes through as the defining emotional experience? Or, as Frye or Atwood might have asked: "Where is the emotional side of here?"

It's another one of those complicated questions, but the answer will take us to the next level as we drift downriver through our echoing canyon of eroded self, into the very heart of our Canadian identity. In this chapter, we're moving into the cave — the shadow world of negative space — the central spindle of the Canadian creative experience, and the pivot point in this book as we move from the external notion of "other" into an internal investigation of our cloven soul. Beginning with an overview of negative theory, we'll gradually move into increasingly abstract space and see how emptiness — or negative space — becomes a defining principle in the Canadian psyche, Canadian art and Canadian film. It may seem a little intangible, a little too abstract, but think of it this way: the hole may be nothing, but without it, a doughnut is just a pastry. So join me as we enter the hole and discover the mind-warping Canadian creative truth on the other side.

Negative Theory

"The word 'not' is really magical. It's a way of getting around everything we cannot conceive of. Not is nothing but the ghostly possibilities, because finally, everything simply is."
— *Joyce (Tilda Swinton), in Robert Lepage's* Possible Worlds

In a world that worships positive thinking, positive corporate bottom lines, positive temperatures and positive self-image, the very idea of casting the Canadian identity in a "negative" light wouldn't appear to be a great image builder — let alone a rallying cry for national pride. Nonetheless, from the previous examination we can see that we are defined by what we are *not*, more so than what we *are*. This may well be a survival mechanism we've developed over time to distinguish ourselves from the monolithic American nation next door. After all, whenever Canadians go overseas, our first instinct is to tell people that we are "*not American*" — to avoid any possible confusion, especially in light of the increasing wave of anti-American sentiment spreading around the world as the tentacles of monoculture and globalization pull away the foundations of cultural differences and notions of identity. Then again, when you "live in the shadow" of the most powerful nation on the planet, it's hard not to see oneself as "other" or "not that" before one can actually articulate what one "is."

I was never so sure of this as I was during the winter of 2000, when a beer company launched an ad campaign with a decidedly uncharacteristic patriotic bent. The spot featured a guy named Joe, standing in a mack jacket at a podium in front of (how perfect) an invisible audience. Waving majestically

behind him was a giant Maple Leaf. The scene was reminiscent of the American war film *Patton*, but in this case, it was transformed into something distinctly Canadian because instead of rallying the troops around all the virtues of the Stars and Stripes, Joe lists a number of things that make him Canadian, such as: "I have a prime minister, not a president ... I speak English and French, not American ... I believe in peacekeeping, not policing; diversity, not assimilation ... Hey, I'm not a lumberjack or a fur trader. I don't live in an igloo or eat blubber or own a dog sled ... And I don't know Jimmy, Sally or Suzy from Canada (although I'm certain they're really, really nice)."

On the surface, this was just a simple beer ad crafted from a trashpile of pop culture

Joe Canadian was born as a spokesman to sell suds, but his unapologetic celebration of being a Canadian — as someone who is defined by what he is not, instead of what he is — made him a mouthpiece for a new generation and its nascent sense of Canadian pride. MOLSON CANADA

references. It was aimed at selling beer, not a national consciousness, but it created a wave of Canadian sentimentalism as media types spun out of their swivel chairs trying to decode the meaning behind it all. The mack-jacketed Joe Canadian was deemed a hero of his time, a "national treasure," a watershed moment in Canadian history — at least for some media mavens — before the actor, somewhat ironically, left for Los Angeles to pursue his acting career.

The ad was a clear pronouncement of Canadianess — and that, in itself, seemed to be what struck a chord with the critics and the masses. But what was truly interesting about the whole Joe Canadian speech was the grammatical choice of defining himself through a list of negatives: "I am NOT a lumberjack or a fur trader ... etc." The word "not" is a term that finds meaning only in opposition to something else.

Canada has typically had a hard time articulating a sense of identity, even though there's absolutely no doubt in most Canadian minds that we are a nation, we know who we are and — despite what hay-making politicians, ambitious spinmeisters and media nitwits have to say — I believe we have little desire to be anything else. Our inability to articulate our sense of self has generally been misinterpreted as a lack of identity, but it's a bit more subtle. Tripping over language barriers and a tense history of conflicted cultures, we opted for silence — and that silence, or that perceived lack of an identity, is precisely what defines us as a culture, as a nation and as a people. We are, in a sense, what we are not.

North vs. South

The United States of America has a general obsession with affirming itself with flag-waving theatrics and jingoistic action movie juggernauts. This is the culture that gave rise to "the power of postive thinking" and the worship of giant corporate conglomerates that boast big, fat and very positive bottom lines. American movies, especially those created within the Hollywood tradition, are concerned with the "positive space." By that, I'm borrowing a term from sculpture: how the positive space (the chiselled stone) finds added meaning in relation to negative space (the empty air around the sculpture). Hollywood movies are all surface, and as a result, they can only focus on the thing (the bomb, the wave, the asteroid) and the hero's ability to tame it (because he is strong, macho and has a big gun).

The entire American myth revolves around the idea that a country was created out of nothing; that creation demands a certain amount of aggression against a potentially hostile world. Work hard enough and long enough, and you too can realize the American Dream and become a success. We saw this in our look at the Aboriginal experience in North America and in the treatment of the landscape in the previous chapter. The American Dream is all about self-assertion against the nothingness, about dominating nature, and for this reason, the American concept of nationhood is often referred to as "phallo-nationalism" because it places the male identity, and his seed, at the very centre of the national ideal. This idea of nation-building is embedded into the American cultural psyche as truth, and a truth that Hollywood has every intention of reaffirming and exporting to the rest of the world at every turn.

What all this boils down to is an "us" and "them" stance where anything that is not sympathetic to American values is a threat. We can see it in the run of Cold War sci-fi that demonized the outside visitor as a lethal life form, usually awakened from a deep sleep by ignorant scientists eager to further their own research at the expense of all humanity. In the American tradition, "us" is dominant. Anything beyond that is "other," and therefore threatening to the stability of the larger whole. Clearly, Canadians are not American — nor are we "positive space" thinkers. We are "negative" thinkers. We are a nation that believes in diversity, not a melting pot or a single ideology, which means there is no real grasp of "us" as a solid block of sameness. In the big "us" or "them" equation, we've clearly identified the "them" as the things "we are not" — but with the collapse and fragmentation of "us," there's a giant hole in the equation — a negative balance on our psychic bottom line. Or, put another way, we aren't the doughnut, we aren't even the Timbit. We are the hole.

Negative on Negative

The only way to really see what's been going on in the four walls of our mental theatre is to look at more Canadian movies and the one thing that unites them all — regardless of language — is negative space. Whether it's from a formal standpoint where the camera becomes the mechanical mirror selectively arranging positive and negative space before the lens, or a simple plot element about a missing family member, Canadian film is defined by an awareness of what's *not* there.

There is always something "missing" in Canadian movies. Sometimes it comes through in images of the vast, empty landscape. Often it's something tangible like a father figure as in *Surfacing, Mon Oncle Antoine, Lilies, Le Confessionnal, Back to God's Country, Maelström, Map of the Human Heart, Highway 61, Marine Life, Night Zoo* and *Perfectly Normal.* Sometimes it's something less tangible, like the missing child in Jeremy Podeswa's *The Five Senses* (1999), the aborted

fetus in *Maelström* (2000), or the burned out skeletal remains of houses in *The Adjuster* (1991). Sometimes the missing item is even harder to get a handle on because the lack becomes part of a metaphysical examination of the human condition, where one just never feels whole or complete, such as in David Cronenberg's *Dead Ringers* (1988) and *eXistenZ* (1999), or Don McKellar's *Last Night* (1999).

Because it's easier to understand this idea of "negative" or "gap theory" when the missing item was once concrete — when we can draw a chalk outline around the missing form — we'll start there with an examination of the movie that pushed me into an awareness of empty space and let me understand the beauty of Canadian film for the first time: *The Sweet Hereafter.* The story of a school bus crash that leaves a small town grieving over the loss of their children, this film plunges headlong into the aching chasm of loss.

When the film begins, the crash has already taken place (or as Heidegger might have said, "The terrible has already happened"). Though the music is fugal, we're not quite sure what the tragedy is until later in the film. In the meantime, Egoyan reveals the story layer by emotional layer, breaking narrative time and rearranging events to give us a 360-degree view of what's no longer there: the children.

In the opening few frames, we see only the bus: the mangled physical point of departure from our world to the sweet hereafter. We know there has been an accident, and we know that our time-travelling focal point, the lawyer Mitchell, is there to point the finger of blame. But only once Mitchell begins to fathom the depth of his clients' pain do we begin to see the children as they once were: sitting on the bus, happily singing songs as

The Sweet Hereafter (1997): Lawyer Mitchell Stephens (Ian Holm) is as frozen as the landscape around him, but he begins to thaw emotionally over the course of Atom Egoyan's film about a school bus crash that claims the lives of nearly all the children of a remote Canadian town. COURTESY OF JOHNNIE EISEN, © EGO FILM ARTS

the bus weaves its way through this snowy mountain terrain. Shot from a helicopter, the image of the bright orange vehicle snaking its way through the white landscape looks entirely surreal. The bus is brightly coloured and full of life, and as such, it stands in diametric opposition to the cold, white, moribund landscape. The screaming kids are the very embodiment of life rebelling against death, and then, it happens. Egoyan cuts to a shot of Billy (Bruce Greenwood), who was travelling behind the bus and waving at his kids who sat at the back of the bus. Through Billy's eyes we watch as the bus tumbles over the embankment and lands in the middle of a frozen lake. There is absolute silence. The surface tension of the ice keeps the bus in this world for just a split second — just long enough for us to hope nothing bad will happen — but that only serves to heighten our feelings of powerlessness when the ice fractures and the bus disappears into the watery black hole below. Everything that was joyous and life-affirming is swallowed whole by the landscape, leaving a giant gap in the hearts of the surviving parents — and the community at large.

The whole scene is edited in what might be called "real time," but it feels like slow motion — the way all life-altering events seem to unfold in some other plane where linear time stretches out into infinity, only to snap back with a sting when it's all over. The first time I watched this sequence, I remember thinking, Why doesn't Billy do something? Why doesn't he run down the hill like a madman, fly onto the ice and dive into the frozen water to rescue his kids? So what if the bus is already submerged in several hundred metres of water? I mean, he should try, shouldn't he? In any Hollywood studio film, no one dies without a superhuman rescue attempt. Had this scene been directed by someone like Steven Spielberg or Michael Bay, we would have seen a close-up of the ice on the road intercut with the bus wheels speeding along the pavement. Ahh, danger awaits — and the bus is full of children! Spielberg would have given us an image of a pretty little girl in a red dress, sitting like a little angel with her lunchbox. Then back to the wheels, the ice, then into the bus, where we'd see that same little girl in the red dress scream her little lungs out, "Daddy! Help!" as the bus rolled over in slow motion. Cut to the heroic father, hauling some giant ladder or scuba tank from the back of his pickup, racing to the lake below in a frantic bid to save his babies.

Sad to say, but I guess that's what I was subconsciously expecting: the classic hero model. Instead, Egoyan shows us a more realistic picture: Billy is powerless to do anything. He stands there frozen, in shock, unable to comprehend that his whole life could be so altered, so quickly. I didn't really understand how well Egoyan nailed that feeling of helplessness until last year, when on my regular walk, my dog bolted after a squirrel. I ran after him. I screamed for him to stop, and then, I saw the car. It was heading straight for him, and the little old lady behind the wheel couldn't hear my wails. I was powerless, and all I could do was watch as the car and dog collided — changing my little world forever. My dog, I am happy to report, recovered. But for months I couldn't stop thinking of what could have happened — and how I could have changed things. (A note: keep your dog on a leash around cars.)

All the characters in *The Sweet Hereafter* are haunted by the same thoughts and the same survivor guilt. The fact that most of the grieving is portrayed through silence, and the action is almost exclusively internal, lead some critics — mostly Canadian — to label Egoyan as cold and overly cerebral. Confused by his detached stance, and no doubt waiting for some Hollywood moment of dramatic verbalization that typically points the way to redemption, many viewers may have left the theatre unmoved. Personally speaking, I've never cried more. I walked out of the screening puffy eyed and damp — and just a little embarrassed at having uncorked my critic's bottle of emotion in plain viewing public. When I left the room and began talking to other audience members — especially the ones who weren't burrowing their noses into a stack of Kleenex — I couldn't figure out why some people felt nothing at all while I was weak from feeling so much. I began piecing the puzzle together, and by the time Egoyan's *Felicia's Journey* came out three years later, I had a theory, which I included in my review in the *Vancouver Sun* — and will reiterate here, as it essentially formed the critical foundation for this book:

... Inversion of film expectations is the heart of Egoyan's gift. Unlike the Hollywood formula, where emotions must be revealed on the surface to be understood, Egoyan works beneath the text. Where someone like Spielberg pushes you into a given feeling with manipulative, sticky moments, Egoyan pulls you in with silence. For this reason, Egoyan is constantly accused of being sterile, cold and too detached to conjure any emotional response. And yet, as far as I'm concerned, Egoyan is one of the most emotional filmmakers in the world

today. His films are about loneliness and unrequited human desire. Yes, they are also cold to the touch. But what better way to make you long for warmth than to throw you in the cold? Watching an Egoyan film demands a certain personal investment. If you are closed emotionally, you will come away with nothing. But if you risk openness, chances are you will genuinely feel the absence of love and walk away with a profound emotional experience that will change you forever ...[1]

Okay, so I was making an impassioned point — if not an all-out, on-my-knees plea — about people finding the patience and the right frame of mind to watch Canadian film. Maybe it went a little over the top, but after listening to many critics (my cherished and esteemed colleagues in the mass media) crap all over Canadian film for the past decade, I was ready for a fight. And if you can't already tell, I still am. I know a lot of the films we made in the past were hokey and tediously dull and institutional, but almost every Canadian film I've seen in the last ten years has stuck with me longer than any of the generic shoot-em-up genre movies that litter the nation's screens like so much empty plastic packaging. This started me thinking about a few things, like why do Canadians generally have worse things to say about our movies than anyone else? Whenever a Canadian film gets released in the United States., I skim the wires to see what the American critics have to say, and almost without fail, the nastiest reviews are not from Americans or Europeans, but from the long-serving Canadian critics who watch just as much Hollywood garbage as I do, but still find a challenging Canadian film less satisfying than a good car chase. To quote a line from a colleague's review of a recent Canadian movie: "I just don't get it." Exactly. Canadian films are fragmented and elusive at first glance. Without this solid notion of "us," we tend to look at the entire world as a series of "others" who define us through a process of elimination. It takes time to sift through these images of other, and as a result, identity is built through layers of awareness. This explains the popularity of layered narrative structures, broken linear time, and the perpetual alienation we see in Canadian film. It also explains the recurring theme in Canadian film that things will somehow be better elsewhere.

Roads to Nowhere

This is where we hop into our trusty, rusty Bricklyn (a Canadian car) and boot it into the great beyond. Well, we think it's great at any rate because at the very least, it isn't here. Canadians make a different kind of road movie. Where the American tradition took the epic structure of Homer's *The Odyssey*, a series of stories about an aging warrior desperately trying to find his way home to his wife and son in Ithica, and grafted it onto their phallocentric hero myth (which was easy to do, considering the automobile is one of the best phallic symbols out there), the Canadian road movie borrows the structure, but not the heroism. Where Americans find romantic heroics in the quests of outlaw heroes, the Canadian road movie usually subverts genre entirely, and symbolically (and sometimes literally) veers off the road before anyone has a chance to attain the Holy Grail or their rich homeland of Ithica. The characters are clearly in motion, looking to find some better place — but either they never get there, or the destination is a big disappointment.

The first real Canadian experiment with

Goin' Down the Road (1970): Joey (Paul Bradley), Betty (Jayne Eastwood) and Pete (Doug McGrath) hang out in a park in downtown Toronto, the Shangri-La that never materializes for these Maritimers in Don Shebib's classic road movie that's considered the starting point for contemporary, independent narrative fiction in English Canada. PACIFIC CINÉMATHÈQUE

the road movie was Don Shebib's 1970 classic *Goin' Down the Road* — which, like its Francophone cousin, *Mon Oncle Antoine*, is still considered one of the best Canadian films ever made. Though the scTV spoof of the movie may be more vibrant in the memory of younger Canadians (as it featured Garth and Gord looking for a pot of gold on Younge Street), it's worth taking a look at the movie that made Shebib one of the brightest talents in the nation before he drifted off into complete obscurity.

Pete (Doug McGrath) and Joey (Paul Bradley) are two hosers from the Maritimes who dream of something more than the familiar, subsistence existence they lead at home.

They want more than the endless cycle of unemployment lines and drunken coupling, so they pack up their beater Chevrolet and head out on the open road with hopes of finding great jobs and beautiful women in that Shangri-La called Toronto. They are positively giddy with excitement as they pull onto the Trans-Canada Highway, but when they reach their destination, Pete and Joey's bright hopes turn darker than an August thunderstorm. They are forced to spend their first night in a hostel. The next day they find a cheap, scummy apartment and Pete sets out on a job search. He wants to be an advertising executive, but as he has no experience, no education, no references, no training — he doesn't stand a hope in hell. To make ends meet in this central Canadian Eden, they find work in a bottling plant. Back on the lowest rung of the working population, Pete and Joey pick up where they left off back home. Joey picks up a waitress, Betty (Jayne Eastwood) and Pete, the upwardly mobile one, decides to leer at a woman beyond his reach. No sooner does Joey get Betty pregnant, than the boys lose their jobs. Laid off and depressed as ever, Joey starts to drown his sorrows at the bottom of one stubby beer bottle after another, while Pete tries to hang on to his pipe dream of a better life. When Betty is forced to quit work, the three of them move in together and hit the bottom. They try to steal a bag of groceries, only to be undone when a clerk comes out to stop them. They escape by pelting him with canned food, but by this point, the quest is long dead. Pete and Joey set out on the road with big dreams and a taste for adventure, but they end up back where they started: at the bottom of the socio-economic ladder. At least before, they had hope. Now they have nothing. Welcome to the great Canadian road movie, where the ride is free because it's all downhill.

Shebib captures the pathos of the descent in a blur of grainy, saturated blue and grey. The pictures are not pretty, but they speak to any Canadian because the quality of light is recognizably Nordic. Up here past the 49th parallel, light bends in a different way. We get cool, distant blues and longer shadows — not the high-key, flat colours that Hollywood made famous. Like *Mon Oncle Antione*, Shebib relied on natural light and real locations to give us a sense of time and place. This was not entirely intentional. Shebib originally intended to make a 16mm documentary about the economic decline of the Maritimes,

but like many other Canadian directors, he took a turn that led him in a different direction. We can only be happy he had the courage to keep going, because *Goin' Down the Road* was one of the first English-language Canadian films to show us who we were in all our flawed but remarkably beautiful humanity. It also featured those fabulous stubby brown beer bottles — and that alone makes it a Canuck classic.

Suburb-a-nation and Other Dead Ends

We get a similar nowheresville (but no stubbies) scenario in Gary Burns' *The Suburbanators* (1995), a road movie that literally drives around in circles. Burns once again plays with the monotony of the landscape and uses it to mirror the empty, dead-end lives of his characters, whose sole quest is to find some marijuana — another symbol of a trip into oblivion. A defiant middle finger salute to the American road movie tradition, Burns plays with the whole "phallo-nationlistic" way of thinking in two ways. First, he makes the cars ugly, or at least the diametric opposite of the American muscle car — he gives us a wood-pannelled K-Car, a public city bus, and a small, beat-up Japanese import. Second, he has one character utter the line, "Is your car your penis?" or "My car is my penis" several times over. Further throwing a spanner into the overhead cam engine is the lack of any free-wheeling highway driving. Characters simply putter around town, looking to score pot, repeating the same stories to anyone who will listen. It's a tedious existence, and clearly one they would love to escape — but as we all know, the quest is futile because no matter where you go ... there you are.

Burns includes a minor character in the film who does try to get a job, but like Pete, he

The Suburbanators (1995): Carrie Schiffler (left) plays Susan, one of the fleeting objects of desire who make spontaneous appearances throughout this Gary Burns film about a bunch of unfocused and unrooted people. Set against a sterile backdrop of strip malls, this is a road movie that essentially drives around in circles looking to score dope.
JOHN HAZLETT AND RED DEVIL FILMS

has no experience — and his efforts are doomed to fail. There is another minor character in the film who does seem to be moving upward and onward — a successful young novelist who offers two dudes a ride — but he only incites bitterness in the petty and jealous character of Carl (Stewart Burdett), who wishes he'd be more stuck up instead of being so self-effacing and humble. Either way, you can't win in this homogenous suburban wasteland. You can only survive and keep your sights low — that way, you'll never be too disappointed.

There is a similar thematic exploration in Philippe Falardeau's *La Moitié gauche du frigo* (2000). The story of a 30-year-old unemployed engineer named Christophe, this is a sassy feature film disguised as a "real life" documentary. When Christophe loses his job, he starts looking for a new one with his roomate Stéphane (Stéphane Demers) recording his quest every step of the way on his handheld video camera. From job training seminars to interviews, Stéphane records the gradual social effacement experienced by the unemployed — and Christophe's inevitable loss of self-esteem. At times his humiliation comes at the hands of Ontario Anglos. In a scene reminiscent of the opening for *Mon Oncle Antoine* and *Goin' Down the Road*, we watch as Christophe drives all the way to industrial Ontario for a job interview, only to be told by the arrogant English executive that there is no job. Deflated and disgusted by his own reflection, Christophe seeks escape. He heads out on the road again — and doesn't stop until he gets to Vancouver. The final sequence shows Christophe trying to regain his sense of self in

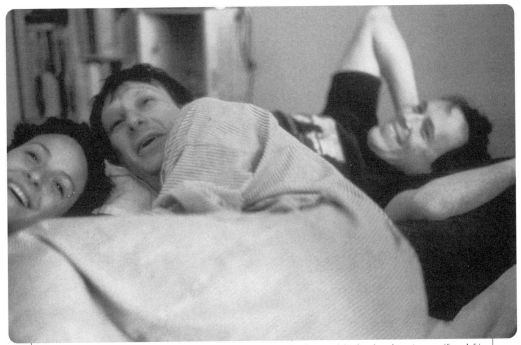

La Moitié gauche du frigo (2000): Philippe Falardeau's take on youth culture and dead-end road movies stars (from left) Paul Ahmarani as Christophe, an unemployed engineer, Genevieve Néron as a grocery cashier and Stéphane Demers as the best friend and camera-laden inquisitor who chronicles Christophe's futile attempts to find a job. FILM TONIC

front of the camera as he talks about his new life and his music career — only to have his ego punctured all over again when his new boss starts giving him crap about using the company car.

Highway to Hell

The cycle is almost always the same in the Canadian road movie: the hero decides life in his hicktown is too dull or without enough opportunity, so he heads out in search of the bright lights of the big city — where he believes there's a "pot of gold" with his name on it. Such romantic notions never last long in Canadian film, and so, by the end of the movie, the main character usually finds himself in the same place he started. This is not to say there is no sense of transformation in the Canadian road movie — there is. Even Pete

and Joey emerged from their experience changed men, just as Christophe and the boys from *Suburbanators* found themselves transformed by their adventures. The difference comes in the nature of that change. Where the classic romantic road movie shows us men or women finding a sense of newfound freedom, the Canadian road movie shows us men or women learning all about the impossibility of escape. The people in our road movies may start as dreamers, but they inevitably finish as realists.

The most complete road movie study can be seen in Bruce McDonald's auto triptych: *Roadkill* (1989), *Highway 61* (1991) and *Hard Core Logo* (1996). Paved and designed according to the classic rules of road movies — complete with a kick-ass, grinding rock 'n' roll soundtrack care of Nash the Slash, and the

Ramones, McDonald gets closer to genre than most, but things get real bumpy real fast.

In *Roadkill*, Valerie Buhagiar plays Ramona, a temp employee for a slimey rock promoter. Assigned to head to Sudbury in seach of the promoter's missing band, The Children of Paradise, Ramona doesn't even own a car, so she takes a taxi — reflecting her completely passive status in the face of authority. She does not drive, she is the passenger. When the taxi stops for gas, about halfway from Toronto to Sudbury, things begin to change in Ramona's life. She stumbles into the band and their on-board filmmaker (played by McDonald himself), who just "wants to make a movie about real life." After hearing a story about the band losing its lead singer, Matthew (Shaun Bowring), who just kind of lost his mind and took off, Ramona decides she has a better chance of finding the Child-of-Paradise-lost and bringing everyone back to Toronto if she joins them in the mobile home. From there, things get a little kooky as Ramona learns to drive, bumps into an aspiring serial killer (McKellar) and unleashes her inner self. Against a backdrop of giant nickels, dead rabbits and other Canadian roadside sights, Ramona finds her power (she learns to drive) — and emerges as a sole survivor in a shoot-out at the final destination, The Apocalypse Club.

In *Highway 61*, Buhagiar reappears — but this time, she is no innocent. Jackie Bangs is a hustler. She stole a load of drugs her boyfriend concealed in his electric guitar, and now she needs to get to New Orleans in order to sell the stash. The only problem is how. To move the drugs across the border, she exploits the kindness of a small town barber named Pokey Jones (McKellar). Pokey finds a frozen corpse at the beginning of the movie, and Jackie — fallen woman that she is —

Highway 61 (1991): Has coffin, will travel— that's Pokey Jones (Don McKellar) seen here with his parents' car. SHADOW SHOWS

decides to use the stiff to her advantage. She pretends the body is that of her brother, then pumps the drugs into the dead man's circulatory system when the undertaker isn't looking. With the drugs safely hidden, she convinces Pokey to drive her to New Orleans with the casket strapped to the roof. Pokey, who drives the car his parents left behind after their premature deaths, is excited to be leaving the barber salon. He's been called a "hero" in his town for trying to rescue the freezing victim with his hairdryer, and now he's ready to tackle a larger challenge and leave home. Here it's Pokey who is the complete innocent and Jackie who acts as the voice of experience. Not even the bingo-playing spectre of Satan, who is desperate to reclaim the body of the deceased so he can take his soul, stands in Jackie's way.

In true road-movie fashion, Pokey loses his innocence episode by episode: he leaves home, he crosses the border, he has sex and he accepts the death of his parents. On the surface, the story line has a lot in common with the larger road movie genre that takes the outlaw hero on a transformative journey from innocence to experience, but McDonald and

McKellar — the passionate Canadians who wrote the script — infuse every frame with a distinctly Canadian perspective that gently pokes fun at the American ideal. The landscape is littered with homogenous strip malls, and the people are downright creepy. One group of side characters involves a psychotic father who travels around the country with his three pre-pubescent daughters, hoping to make them child stars with their lame song-and-dance numbers.

Hard Core Logo follows a similar trajectory as it shows us a group of Vancouver punk rockers looking for their rock god, Bucky Haight (Julian Richings) — only to find their adventure turns into one very nasty trip with a nihilist ending. Joe Dick (real life rocker Hugh Dillon), Billy Tallent (Callum Keith Rennie), Pipefitter (Bernie Coulson) and John Oxenberger (John Pyper-Ferguson) are Hard Core Logo — a fictionalized band that reached the apex of subculture chic in the heyday of Vancouver's eighties' punk movement. Looking for his lost glory, Joe Dick convinces his former bandmates to reunite for a charity gig in honour of their idol, Haight, who Dick says was gunned down in Saskatchewan. The fundraiser was so successful that Dick urges his bandmates to join him on the road for a last farewell tour. Based on the book by Michael Turner, the film lacks a strong central line and detours into drug hallucinations and a variety of other dead-ends, but in its exposé of the young outlaws in search of their lost rebel souls, *Hard Core Logo* reaffirms the same bogus Canadian idea that things will somehow be better elsewhere.

While a movie as universally loved as *My*

Hard Core Logo (1996): The men, the music, the menacing expressions — Bruce McDonald pokes a hole into male bravado in this satirical chronicle of the Vancouver punk movement in the mid-1980s. From left: Callum Keith Rennie, Bernie Coulson, John Pyper-Ferguson and Hugh Dillon. SHADOW SHOWS

American Cousin (1985), Sandy Wilson's coming-of-age story set in British Columbia's Okanagan Valley that swept the Genies in 1986 was hardly nihilistic, it still revolved around the idea that life just has to be better elsewhere. Elsewhere was California — the land of the free and home to perfect studs like Butch (John Wildman), the cousin in the title, who isn't so perfect after all.

Another movie that picks up on similar threads of desperation for dislocation is *New Waterford Girl* (1999). The story of a talented young artist who craves to study in New York, the Allan Moyle film (from a Tricia Fish script) introduces another American into the mix who would seem to have all the answers. Unlike Mooney (Liane Balaban), the would-be artist, the tough-talking New Yorker Lou (Tara Spencer-Nairn) doesn't worry so much what other people think. She does what she wants, says what she thinks and doesn't focus on all the "negative" things that define Mooney's dead-end reality. Lou, like Butch, introduces a "positive" new way of American thinking to these small Canadian towns, and everyone looks to them as saviours. In *New Waterford Girl*, we even get a micro road movie when Mooney takes the transplanted New Yorker on a tour of the town. They head down main street and Lou is screaming and yelling at the pedestrians, a gesture of sweet release. Five seconds later, the car stops. The main drag is just a block long. So much for the romantic notion of the road trip. Not only are the cars rust buckets, but there's no highway to take you elsewhere. We see the same type of frustration in just about every road movie to come out of Canada. At times, it may look as though we believe in the outlaw hero myth, but we inevitably deny the romantic, throbbing-engine appeal of the road movie genre. The films clearly show us people desperate for escape and release, but even though they get in the car with all their hopes and dreams, the journey generally ends in disillusion.

The Emotional Landscape

As we've just seen, the road movie is a larger metaphor for an internal search for self. It uses concrete, "positive space" symbols such as cars, geography and physical movement to articulate emotional events taking place beneath the social veneer. As we continue, we'll leave the concrete symbols behind and strip down to the nitty gritty as we come closer to the wellspring of the creative spirit. Moving from concrete foes into abstract, internalized demons is not an easy transition to make, but artists do it every day. Using their creative energies, artists express their own internal landscape and recreate the external, concrete world with every brush stroke or click of the shutter. The world bends and shifts according to their perspective because it is artists who decide where to place the emphasis and where to draw the line between positive and negative space. For instance, a sculptor shapes both negative and positive space with each strike on the chisel: rock fragments fall off, reducing the piece's positive dimensions while opening up the negative space around it. The filmmaker also plays with negative and positive space as he frames each shot, deciding what to include in the frame and what to leave out. In the case of a musician-composer, it's slightly more complex because he must select the notes and organize them in empty, abstract space. For this reason, music is generally referred to as the most abstract art. Some even see it as the most advanced form of mathematics, as it translates the language of science — numbers, frequencies, sine waves and cycles — into an abstract art form with an unlimited ability to make us feel an entire spectrum of emotions. In other words, it is an abstract form that works in abstract ways.

In François Girard and Don McKellar's *Thirty Two Short Films About Glenn Gould* (1993), we watch as Gould — the most famous Canadian classical musician and arguably the greatest interpreter of Bach the world has ever produced — played brilliantly by Colm Feore, uses music in his attempt to reconcile his place in the world.

From the opening shot, which shows Gould as a small black dot in the midst of a flat, vast frozen snowscape, we know immediately that Gould is an outsider — or at least being positioned as one. We also have the defining Canadian image: the human being alone and vulnerable against the landscape, but there nonetheless — a thinking presence in the midst of emptiness; a rebel by default. As such, *Thirty Two Short Films About Glenn Gould* offers us a filmed example of our emotional landscape — or at least the artist's version of it — and earns a place in the Canadian film canon.

Before dissecting this film frame by frame, a note is needed about its overriding structure: The film borrows its structure from Bach's *Goldberg Variations*, Gould's signature piece, which he once described as metaphysical in nature: "I do not think it fanciful to speculate upon supra-musical considerations, ... for in my opinion, the fundamental variative ambition of this work is not to be found in organic fabrication but in a community of sentiment. Therein the theme is not terminal but radial, the variations circumferential not rectilinear, while the recurrent passacaille supplies the concentric focus for the orbit."[2] The writing style alone is an indication of Gould's hyper cerebral mental space, but the words themselves tell us exactly how Gould approached the variations as a whole. Gould says he believes the variations are all about "a community of sentiment" that is "radial" — not "linear" — in nature. In other words, *The Goldberg Variations* work around a central ordering spindle that is not necessarily uniform or concrete — but a chorus of emotion, a "community of sentiment." The same could be said of all Canadian art, particularly Canadian film. No wonder McKellar and Girard saw the Goldberg Variations as the ideal pattern to follow: through Gould's interpretation, they map the Canadian subconscious from an emotional perspective, and give us insight into the essence of the Canadian creative urge as it emerges from empty space.

The film opens with black title card and complete silence; then we see the white snowscape. Somewhere in between that black dot and the surrounding whiteness, music begins to filter through the gap. The figure approaches the camera, then stops. The screen cuts to black. Such is our introduction to Gould, and already we know he's coming from some alternate landscape that is cold and lonely.

After this introduction, the series of short films begin with "Lake Simcoe" — a short about Gould's first encounter with a keyboard in his parents' house by the lake on an old Chickering piano. "My mother tells me that by five, I had already decided to be a concert pianist ... While I was in the womb she played the piano continuously ... and it paid off." Gould (Feore) also tells us that it was his mother who played the key role in his life as it was she who introduced him to Bach. Already the familiar Canadian themes of the empty landscape, outsiderism, mother imagery and the creative womb have entered the frame, and we're barely a few seconds into the film.

As the fragmented narrative unfolds

Thirty Two Short Films About Glenn Gould (1993): Colm Feore disappears into the role of Gould and communicates the internal landscape of the famed pianist, often from behind a pane of glass or behind a fortress of microphones in François Girard's award-winning feature with a decidedly documentary bent. PACIFIC CINÉMATHÈQUE AND RHOMBUS MEDIA

short film by short film, the emotional importance of the landscape is impossible to ignore because almost every tightly composed clip contains an image of Gould poised against the outside world, either literally or figuratively. In the opening tableau of "Lake Simcoe," we see Gould on the dock, doing multiplication tables in his head with all the monotone passion of *Rainman*, while the camera circles around him in space. In "Forty-five Seconds in a Chair," Gould is sitting in a chair against three curtained windows, then the camera slowly dollies in to give us a close-up of his intense gaze. The next film is "pure documentary" and features an interview with Bruno Monsaigeon (musician and Gould collaborator), framed against a Parisian cityscape. When we return to Gould in the next

sequence, he is talking to himself in "Gould Meets Gould." There is no formal landscape element in this piece, but as we watch him perform the role of inquisitor and interviewee, we can recognize the internal split — the twins of self defining each other in opposition. After all, who else could possibly keep up with Gould's mind other than another Gould? For all intents and purposes, the man is an alien, and so in order for him to have a real conversation about himself, he'd need someone who could understand what he was saying — a sort of reflecting mirror to his own soul: a twin.

We return to pretty natural images in "Hamburg," where we see him play his new recording for an unsuspecting chambermaid. The first few shots in that Teutonic sequence show Gould at the window, looking out onto a cold winter scene, contrasted against the plush hotel room where he speaks on the phone to his management, explaining why he's not having much fun. "Practice" shows Gould in a basement rehearsal space where what little light there is filters through a few barred windows. It looks like a prison, and it is: this is the film where we begin to understand how unhappy Gould is performing. The next vignette, "The L. A. Concert," Gould's final live show, features Gould soaking his arms in hot water before making his way through a rat maze backstage. The following film is an interview with classical music icon Yehudi Menuhin, who reaffirms Gould's outsider, loner stance when he describes Gould as someone who created his own life and lived it to the exclusion of the rest of the world, while "trying to avoid every current of air from behind the protection of a scarf."

"CD318" shows neither Gould nor landscape. It is merely a duet between the piano action and the camera, the two tools of expression coming together without the "other" human half. The most articulate example of Gould's alienation in relation to the "other" or "outside" world can be seen in "Passion According to Glenn Gould," where we watch Gould listen to the playback of his recording while the technicians in the booth talk about the health merits of coffee with cream versus coffee with sugar. The boys in the booth are shot with live audio in regular time. The images of Gould on the other side of the sound-proof glass are in slow motion. From a crouched position on the floor, where he listens to the speaker behind a visual cage of music stands, Gould slowly stands up and lets the music take him away to a place far, far away. The outsider images get stronger as the film progresses, showing us how far Gould is

drifting away from the rest of humanity.

In "Truck Stop," the soundtrack offers us a brief reference to the times as Petula Clarke's "Downtown" mingles with the ambient sounds of a truck stop diner. When the camera settles on Gould's lone face at the dinette, we begin to hear what he hears: conversations in isolation, couples breaking up, kitchen sounds, knives on porcelain. In this cacophony of elements, Gould appeared able to hear everything distinctly and all at once, which only seemed to exacerbate his feelings of alienation. We see this again in "The Idea of North," where several different soundscapes fuse within Gould's free-floating mind.

The final few films show how Gould's internal dislocation finally catches up with him. When we hear him prophesy his own death, it's from a phone booth outside the city. Similarly, in "Leaving," we see Gould alone in his car as the rain beats down on his windshield. He is listening to his own music: it's on the radio, prompting him to stop the car and make another phone booth call to tell someone the exciting news. Time and time again, the imagery of Gould alone against the wilderness — be it mental, physical or spiritual — repeats.

From this multifaceted film portrait of a famous Canadian artist, we end up with a pretty good view of the Canadian emotional landscape as a binary system. Whether it's the inside world of the house posed against the outside expanse of the lake, or the inside world of Gould's brain poised against the technicians in the booth, the artist is the outsider looking in. The writing team of Girard-McKellar translates this idea into the very structure of the film because like the Goldberg Variations, *Thirty Two Short Films About Glenn Gould* is not a linear work. It functions as a series of emotional meditations on the same themes, and even incorporates the basic foundations of the Canadian film tradition as a whole into its superstructure. We have elements of documentary (the talking-head interviews), experimental film ("Variation in C Minor" features an image of a film optical track) and narrative auteurism (the film as a whole) in one package.

In this way, *Thirty Two Short Films About Glenn Gould* works because it never tries to "show" us the artistic experience (i.e., images of Feore pressing piano keys) — something McKellar says he was loathe to do because it cheapens the act of performance and turns it into a comparative acting exercise, where the audience looks at the mimicry instead of listening to the music and processing the emotional side of the film.[3] Instead, the filmmakers circle around their subject to show the space around him (note the circling camera moves) — and, in so doing, define the enigmatic man at the centre of the frame by showing us more of what he is not, than what he is.

Girard and McKellar's *Thirty Two Short Films About Glenn Gould* doesn't decode the mystery of the man. Nor does it answer all the lingering questions about why he left the stage at 32, nor explain his near-complete withdrawal from society. It is as open and amibiguous as Gould himself. As Girard told me after the film premiered at the Toronto Festival of Festivals in 1993, he never did figure Gould out — nor did he want to. "I wanted to leave the film as Gouldian as possible. I love doing things that don't fit into boxes. I think Gould did as well."[4]

Snowscapes

From the preceding analysis of *Thirty Two Short Films About Glenn Gould*, I think it's fair to make a few assumptions about Canadian film as we've seen it thus far: it is non-linear and fragmented; it prefers to tell stories through layers rather than straight lines; it revels in opposition and twin-mirror imagery; it is concerned with themes of alienation and has a tendency to show us the negative space around the subject to express character rather than indulge in contrived dramatic dialogue to articulate a specific mental state.

Because this chapter is concerned primarily with the last element — this abstract notion of empty space — let's consider the final, ghostly shot of Gould's figure in the vast snow-bound void. The image seems to symbolize the Canadian experience as a whole because it communicates alienation and silence, but is that figure truly alone? No, he can't be because we — the audience — are right there with him. We are the voyeur, he is the subject, and the camera is the implied "other" that frames Gould in space. The camera circles Gould, spies on him, follows him through labyrinthian buildings and even, in the X-ray sequence, sees right through him. The camera pokes and prods and bumps up against the image of Gould, but it never reveals his truth because in the end, it is just a camera — a machine that flattens reality into two dimensions.

This may seem elementary to some and obtuse to others, but the camera plays an important role in the evolution of Canadian film — and not just because it's the machine that makes it all happen. As we saw the first chapter, through the emergence of cinema direct and other "verité" forms, the way a camera moves through space has a huge impact on the final product. From an emotional standpoint, a shaky camera means something "real" and "direct" — while a static camera fixed to a tripod communicates a sense of institutional certainty and control. But we can take it further still: for instance, a camera can show negative space. In order to wrap our minds around that implausibility — that a camera can show us what is "not" in addition to what "is" — we need to look at the work of the world's most important experimental filmmaker, none other than Canadian artist Michael Snow.

As a painter and photographer, Snow was consumed with the idea of surfaces and the photographic collapse of the third dimension. To explore this reality-altering phenomenon, Snow created such works as *Walking Woman* (1961-1967), a series of five-foot cutouts of a female form that he made out of a variety of materials such as plywood and rubber, but always in two dimensions. He also cut off the top of the woman's head and the bottom of her feet, so it looked as though she had lost her body parts to an invisible frame. When Snow turned his attention to photography, he adapted the *Walking Woman* series in *Four to Five* (1962), a series of 16 pictures of the *Walking Woman* in a variety of urban environments. The aim again was to exaggerate the form's flatness in relation to her 3D environment, but also to remind his audience that the images of the Walking Woman in photographs were also flattened versions of the truth.

Snow's awareness of flat was just the beginning of his investigation into the metaphysical implications of photography. He also found a way of communicating the idea of "empty space" in the seminal experimental film *Wavelength* (1967). One long zoom shot with few cuts, *Wavelength* begins as a wide-angle shot showing the interior of an urban apartment and eventually zooms in to a tight close-up of a picture of waves on the other side. Metaphorically speaking, the viewer enters a space that looks familiar and recognizable as three-dimensional: there are walls, furniture, windows and as a result, a sense of depth. By the final frame, when the camera settles on that picture of waves on the other side of the room, we aren't quite sure what we're seeing because we've lost all sense of depth. We're looking at a picture of a picture of a natural landscape which hangs in the middle of loft in the middle of the city. Snow is telling us that cameras remove things from their natural context, they flatten all notions of time and space, and they frame reality into a tidy box. We don't think about all the things outside that box, because we can't see them — but that doesn't mean they don't exist. In *Wavelength*, we know the things outside the frame exist because the first shot showed us the whole room. As the zoom grows tighter, however, the objects on the edges of the frame begin to disappear. What happens to those tables and chairs? Have they disappeared completely? Of course not, but they are no longer a part of the positive space in front of the camera. In other words, everything the camera does *not* see can be called negative space (or, as it's called in film, "off-screen space"), just as the air around a sculpture is called negative space. Negative space defines positive space, positive space defines negative space, and depending on where you put the camera, you can alter the perception and boundaries of both.

We can see the effect of Snow's art in many Canadian films. In *Thirty Two Short Films About Glenn Gould*, Girard turns the camera into the inquisitive "other" trying to understand its subject. The camera spins around the pianist, slows him down, fragments him into different bits and pieces and even zooms right in to a close-up of his face in what appears to be a direct allusion to *Wavelength*, but it never breaks Gould's surface. The best it can do is show us the negative space around Gould — the studios, the rooms, the natural landscape and the people who knew him — to give us a better understanding of who he was, what fuelled his creative drive and how he found harmony in cacophonous contradiction.

An Identity Running on Empty

From this investigation into negative space we can see that Canadian film generally denies easy endings, linear structures and "positive" assertions of self in favour of ambiguity. From a sociopolitical perspective, this makes a lot of sense when you compare the way the United States emerged under a central ideology promoting capitalism and free will while Canada emerged as a pluralist model from the very beginning. The American identity has typically been a function of ideology — or ideologies. For instance, in the post-War 1950s in the United States, Communism was seen as such a threat that anyone who admitted to reading Karl Marx was considered a hostile force. Now, while there is no one, clear ideology to give Americans a homogenous profile, there are nonetheless myriad sub-ideologies or tribes to take its place. Canada, as a whole, never had a single guiding ideology to give us all an umbrella identity. We even look at the whole notion of pop culture tribalism — where people can find identity as part of a pre-packaged micro-group that likes one type of music, a given style or sport shoe — as something bordering on the absurd. This is not to say we don't try these identities on for size — we do. It's just that we don't give them the power to define who we are as people, because Canada is a country that puts the individual before ideology. For this reason, we've always had a hard time trying to find our ID at the door, because there is no concrete, "positive" language to describe it. We are a multitude of people, a rainbow of belief systems and a cacophony of voices.

The same holds true when we compare film traditions. In the Hollywood tradition, the film era began in studios or on redressed locations with surgically enhanced starlets. The images before the camera were clearly artificial and they dictated who, and what, was okay and who and what was "other" — and therefore threatening. The camera — by virtue of the fact that it points *at* something — is a natural "other" maker. Who and what is selected to be "other" in the American tradition is usually decided by a community of producers, script doctors, consultants, agents and other hangers-on deciding the final outcome of the process. In other words, there is not one single mind isolating the "other" — the outside force that plagues the hero, forces him to act, problem-solve and create. Instead, there is a community of people who believes in the same, shared ideology and in turn propagates that ideology through film. At the moment, it's not so much an ideology as it is a love of pure capitalism and shareholder confidence, but the results are the same: We end up with movies aimed at the lowest common denominator because they have the best chance of cashing in at the box office. Sadly, there is no room for ambiguity in the lowest common denominator, and so most American studio pictures are exercises in surface storytelling where good and evil do battle, and good always wins.

In the Canadian model, as in all other independent or auteur models, there is a clear, single-minded presence behind the camera, inserting his or her own worldview into every single frame. As a result, "the other" in Canadian film can assume a myriad of forms — if it assumes a form at all. Sometimes the "other" is the twin (*Dead Ringers*); sometimes it is a friend who changes before our eyes

(*Surfacing*); sometimes it is a dead body (*Mon Oncle Antoine*). Sometimes, and this is crucial, the defining principle is the mere absence of "other" — or the gap itself — that pushes the heroine into action as she searches for some sense of internal meaning. After all, without "you," I am "nothing."

That said, all notions of identity, and the very process of identification, comes down to who you are, who I am, and where "the other" fits into the equation. When the equation is repeated enough times in the same order — say Yankee hero wins again — then a natural pattern of expectation begins to develop in the mind of the viewer. This imprint then forms the parameters for that person's larger worldview, which in turn forms the basis of identity. When the cycle is repeated through time and generations, one ends up with a perpetual identity machine that reflects an entire set of values and ideas back at the viewer — and has the ability to articulate a uniform idea of nationhood.

With film, we often say, "I identified with that character" because that character mirrored something I could understand and relate to, or a situation I have already lived through. When images are projected before us, we will naturally look for any resonance between our experience and the drama unfolding on screen — but only when it's flattering. If we see a character that reminds us of the uglier side of our personality, we generally deny the parallel and focus on the flattering elements. In the American studio tradition there is no danger of the average American audience member finding him or herself identifying with the murderous Nazi spy or serial killer. They are trained to identify with the pre-fab protagonist.

Canadians, on the other hand, are highly aware of "other" — because, in a sense, we are all "others," whether we are Québécois in Canada, Anglo-Quebecers, First Nations, Westerners, farmers, fishers or new citizens. In fact, Quebec has come up with the curious grammatical construction "*nous autres*" — "us others" — to talk about themselves. Because most of us are outsiders of one type or another, we've built an entire society that protects the rights and cultures of "others." In socialist-minded, mosaic-model Canada, the "other" is supposedly as important as "us." As a result, when Canadians look at images of Canadian film, they may well recognize bits and pieces of their own experience in the reflected images of steel blue skies, Gothic trees and snow-covered tundra, but they will not find an overriding single vision of who "we" are. They will find a nation of individuals and a film tradition of auteurs articulating their own personal views. Every film we've looked at so far may share similar themes and motifs, but the films are as unique as the people who made them. Without a uniform jelly mould of ideologies and tribes to keep us together and give us shape, Canada always looks like a nation on the verge of dissolution. But I wonder if that's just another case of making silly comparisons to American culture, because if you think about it, a nation that gives each person the chance to express himself in his own way — without pushing uniformity — is much stronger because its strength lies in the individual, not the house of cards called ideology. To return to Glenn Gould's description of the Goldberg Variations one more time, the Canadian experience is not linear; it is a "community of sentiment" where, with faith and an open mind, we can find harmony in the cacophonous strains of individual identity and find meaning in empty space.

In Praise of the Big Hole

Since my "negative revolution" in the wake of *The Sweet Hereafter*, I've thrown the gap theory out to various filmmakers along the way. Some, like Robert Lepage, believed there was a lot of truth to the phenomenon in Canadian — and even Québécois — film, but he felt this emptiness was based in landscape, and therefore common to all Nordic nations covered in snow and poised against the cool, blue skies of the upper Northern Hemisphere. "I find this [negative space idea] as more of a Nordic trait," he said in an interview concerning *Possible Worlds*. "Film is light and landscape and this idea of negative space is something that you can find in other film cultures where there is a lot of empty space and the light is mostly blue-grey and casts long shadows."[5] Two years earlier I spoke to Lepage about his film *Nô* (1998), and asked him a similar question about identity. His answer was slightly different, but he was no less willing to acknowledge empty space and ambiguity as an ordering principle in the Canadian condition: "I'm proud to be a part of a culture that's indecisive, yes/no yes/no. It means we've learned to deal with things in a positive way. We don't pick up guns and kill each other, we cry, drink and make love. There is something very creative about ambiguity."[6]

For Don McKellar, the "empty space" phenomenon seemed to resonate. "Canadian film is about ellipses. My feeling with practically every American film is that it gives away too much," McKellar said in 2000. "I don't like the negative connotations to the word 'negative' but I think whatever you call it, it's a clear response to being bombarded by very unoriginal material. The majority of movies emerging from Hollywood these days is so incredibly boring. I get the feeling they are afraid to take a risk. There is no courage to

their storytelling. I don't want to sound snobby," he said. "It's not that I'm asking for better stories, I just want better storytelling. I don't want to walk into a movie theatre and know how the movie is going to end five minutes after the opening credits. To me, that takes away the pleasure of moviegoing."[7]

McKellar said if there was anything distinctly Canadian about his films — particularly *Last Night*, it was its ambiguity in the face of an absolute (i.e., the end of the world) and the need for the characters to reveal themselves. "Every character in *Last Night* must deal with the challenge of opening up. They have to see beyond the rituals they use to keep themselves safe. In this case they have nothing to lose because the world is going to end, but it's still so difficult to let go. That reluctance to open up reflects on us, as a culture, I think. But what, in the corniest sense, keeps them [the characters] going is a sense of being alive with possibilities."[8] What McKellar didn't say, but is implied in the film, is that the characters in *Last Night* are moving through an acceptance of their own looming demise. They are forced to come to grips with *not* being, and in the process, discover a genuine sense of meaning during the short time they have left. This imminent recognition of their negation leads them to assert themselves in a positive way — for what we suspect is the first time in their lives.

Like McKellar, you may think all this negative talk has no place in a celebration of Canadian film, but that's only because we've been brow-beaten into thinking "positively" by pop culture gurus ever since the 1970s. I think it's great to feel good and move through life with an optimistic attitude, but "positive" thinking leaves little room for the reality of life, which is often very difficult, if not tragic. Negative thinking becomes stigmatized as unhealthy and morose, which only makes our naturally melancholy moods socially unacceptable and increases the demand for happy drugs like Prozac and Zoloft and all the other members of the happy pill family that are just waiting to lull the blues to sleep. Personally, I find that kind of denial to be far more unhealthy than a natural gravitation to the dark side. Without negative, there is no positive — and without both, you have no tension — no energy. Whether you are talking about a double-A battery, a photograph or a mental outlook, the system is binary, and one without the other loses all meaning and value.

I believe this so-called "marked preference for the negative" is not only what makes us Canadian, I believe it's what gives us a broader perspective, an enhanced sense of creativity, a greater capacity to process the subtleties, and a profound appreciation for life. Because, if there's one thing we survivors are aware of, thanks to this dark and desolate landscape covered in snow and submerged in subzero temperatures, it's an awareness that one day, we too, will NOT be. And even that ultimate negative — death — is ambiguous. It could be the epitome of emptiness and an end to consciousness, but it could also be the portal to a different plane that lets us leap into the amorphous, conceptual space beyond.

PROFILE

Michael Snow
Born 1929 — Toronto, Ontario

© VILIAM

If there was ever a perfect image of the Canadian psyche, it's that of Snow. Born with the perfect name and a desire to make us aware of negative space, Snow may be a grandaddy in the context of this book, but as Atom Egoyan's foreword makes clear, his vision of the world has framed much of the Canadian film experience for generations past — and no doubt generations to come. For a guy concerned with the mechanics of framing, it's a fitting legacy.

Born in the very crust of the Canadian establishment, raised in Toronto's tony Rosedale district, and funnelled through its favoured institution — Upper Canada College — Snow was born to be a bank president. The fact that he became an artist makes him an original rebel, as his entire life's path turned him into a living artwork defined in opposition to institutional ways of thinking.

Already a painter and sculptor, Snow's formal film career began in 1956, when he joined George Dunning's Graphic Associates in Toronto and made the short film *A to Z* using cut-out animation — à la *South Park*. A jazz lover — and jazz musician — who wanted to push the boundaries, Snow moved to the very nucleus of the mind-altering art scene, New York City, in 1963. He did so to concentrate on his painting, but after he experienced the adrenalin rush of art frames that moved — particularly the work of filmmaker/film-critic Jonas Mekas — a refreshed Snow was blown toward celluloid. He used photographic elements to expand his *Walking Woman* series — a multimedia organic piece that he worked on from 1961 to 1967. (Eleven sculptures from this series were installed at the Ontario Pavillion for Montreal's Expo '67). He also turned out his second film, *New York Eye and Ear Control*, then made what is arguably his most important film of all, and most commonly used example of what "experimental film" looks like: *Wavelength*.

Screened in 1967 (Canada's centennial year), *Wavelength* made a big splash because it pushed people into a conscious awareness of the "frame," and in so doing, also pushed us to see the stuff that was "not in the frame." The film is all of 45 minutes long and executes what is essentially one very long zoom shot accompanied by repeating sonic cycles at different speeds.

In so many ways, *Wavelength* is the Hollywood anti-Christ: non-narrative, non-human, non-edited, non-dramatic and decidedly non-populist. You go from a wide shot of an apartment to a close-up of a photograph of waves on the opposite wall. That's about all the camera action you get. In the meantime, Snow inserts a variety of colour filters in front of the lens, changes the aperture, goes from positive to negative images and stumbles into apparently random human acts. A woman instructs two men to install a bookcase, someone turns on a radio, another woman opens a window and then, the veritable climax of the movie: a woman enters the room, picks up the phone and tells someone there's a dead body in the apartment. The film is packed with different layers of meaning, each with a multitude of interpretations. You could talk about *Wavelength* for days (if you were really pretentious) and ponder Snow's intentions, but the distinguished Canadian has been in the spotlight enough to offer his own words on the subject of artistic intent.

"The abstraction that's involved in making a two-dimensional image is a huge one, which we forget all the time. After all, I mean, they're flat. And it's amazing that we tend to concentrate on the suspension of disbelief part of it," he told arts writer turned tech guru Peter Wilson in 1994. "Apart from its image, what is this thing? How did it come about? Of what material is it made?" Such are the questions that fuelled an entire lifetime of artistic creation (including the suspended flock of Canada Geese in Toronto's Eaton Centre). Snow and McLuhan were on the same page with the whole "medium is the message" idea, only where McLuhan was focused on the intrinsic codes and value systems that go into the creation of a mass-market artifact, Snow was deconstructing the actual medium itself — giving the camera itself the starring role in every film he ever made. More proof can be seen in another Snow classic, *Standard Time* (1967): it's a 360-degree pan in a clockwise direction. Then there's *Back and Forth* (1969), where the camera moves — surprise, surprise — back and forth. Some of his more ambitious work combines all of these techniques, and maybe even a two-dimensional cutout of the human form to add extra contrast to his frames. For Snow, it's all about representation — and how the photographic image distorts the nature of three-dimensional truth, and so he plays with all the distortion knobs he can get his fingers on, from artificial light contrasting natural light, real colour vs. artificial colour, the real thing that is NOT the real thing.

If that's not proof of Snow's Canadianess — then consider this: his films are also concerned with language, and after being acknowledged as a leading experimental artist the world over with collections in the Museum of Modern Art and the Musée d'art moderne in Paris, he was trapped in the sphincter of Ontario's morality police for obscenity in the early 1980s (before his induction into the Order of Canada). Another Canadianism is the inaccessibility to Snow's work. He's never had a commercial release in over 40 years of filmmaking. Sadly, you cannot waltz into a Blockbuster Video near you and pick up any of Snow's work. You have to haunt cinematheques and galleries and hope one day, a Snow show comes to your neck of the woods.

My first Snow experience was at Expo 86 in Vancouver, where Snow created a series of 48 holographic stills called *The Special Image*. At the time, I was struck by the holographic images more than the whole piece. Those cheesy hologram eyeball watches had yet to appear in my berg, so it was quite a novelty to see a two-dimensional image that appeared three-dimensional. Little did I know that was the whole point of the exercise. But that's Snow's talent and the reason his work is so effective: they are so simple to look at, that you end up thinking about the things you see. It might not sound all that brilliant, but think about it. You'll be surprised.

FILMOGRAPHY: *A to Z* (1956) | *New York Eye and Ear Control* (1964) | *Short Shave* (1965) | *Wavelength* (1966-7) | *Standard Time* (1967) | *Back and Forth* (1968-69) | *Dripping Water* (with one-time partner, Joyce Wieland) (1969) | *One Second in Montreal* (1969) | *Side Seat Paintings Slide Sound Film* (1970) | *La Region Centrale* (1971) | *Two Sides to Every Story* (1974) | *Rameau's Nephew by Diderot (Thanx to Dennis Young) by Wilma Schoen* (1974) | *Breakfast /Table Top Dolly* (1972/1976) | *Presents* (1980-1) | *So is This* (1982) | *Seated Figures* (1988) | *See You Later/Au Revoir* (1990) | *To Lavoisier, Who Died in the Reign of Terror* (1991) | *Prelude* (2000) | *The Living Room* (2000) | *Corpus Callosum* (2001).

Atom Egoyan

Born 1960 — Cairo, Egypt

COURTESY OF JOHNNIE EISEN, © EGO FILM ARTS

Named in honour of the first nuclear reactor in Egypt, Atom Egoyan seemed fated to make a lasting impression. The first child born to Joseph and Shushan Yeghoyan, Armenian refugees living in Cairo, Atom, his sister and his parents moved to Canada in 1963 — where they set down roots in the gardening capital of the Great White North: Victoria, British Columbia. In order to make the transition smoother, the Yeghoyans opted for a phonetic spelling of their family name and opened a furniture store — despite their creative bent. Both parents had once studied fine art, and Joseph even spent time at the Art Institute of Chicago as a young man. They were one of the few Armenian families in Victoria at the time, and for the young Atom, a first-generation immigrant trying to find a place in the verdant bosom of British colonialism, an outsider stance came as second nature.

At first, like most kids whose parents have "accents," Egoyan rejected his roots and his mother tongue and tried to assimilate, which introduced the concept of contradiction as the central creative element in his burgeoning vision. As an outsider, he became sensitive to the idea of identity as something that is

socially constructed — not something that one simply inherits. His mental detachment can be seen in one of his earliest films, a short he did when he was 12 that involved putting a camera on a stage and shooting the audience as they smiled.

In his teens, he found himself drawn to the stark stage works of Samuel Beckett and Harold Pinter, which led him on a writing quest of his own that allowed him the freedom to create his own universes instead of living an anonymous life in the surreal and windy world of West Coast Canada.

At the age of 18, Egoyan moved to Toronto to study International Relations at the University of Toronto's Trinity College. Now able to create his own identity from scratch, he returned to his roots and joined the Armenian club on campus and rediscovered his mother tongue with the help of an Anglican priest. He also joined the campus newspaper, *The Varsity*, and wrote movie reviews as well as his own plays and fiction. A student of classical music, Egoyan also played guitar and studied opera — finding a sense of mental harmony with fugues. This musical experience is visible in all his films, which in Egoyan's own estimation appropriate a fugue-like structure with their repeated, melancholy motifs. Later on, Egoyan also directed and conceived several operatic productions, including *Salome* for the Canadian Opera Company (staged in Toronto in the fall of 1996 and in Vancouver in 1997), and *Dr. Ox's Experiment* for the London-based English National Opera in 1998.

In his first year at Trinity, he made another film, *Howard In Particular*, which picked up a few prizes at the big Ontario summer fair, the Canadian National Exhibition ("The Ex"). He was hooked, and followed up with other shorts, leading to his first

30-minute effort, *Open House*, with financial assistance from the Ontario Arts Council. Egoyan graduated with an Honours Bachelor of Arts degree in 1982 and joined the established local theatre troupe, Tarragon Theatre, as a playwright. When the CBC bought the rights to *Open House* as part of a series on Canadian pluralism, Egoyan had the necessary contacts and track record to make his first feature, *Next of Kin* (1984).

More TV directing work followed, with Egoyan directing things like *In this Corner* (an Irish-themed boxing movie) for the Mother Corp., as well as American episodics, such as *Alfred Hitchcock Presents* and *The Twilight Zone*.

With more directing experience under his belt and an understanding of how to make the most on a limited budget, Egoyan made his second feature, the self-produced *Family Viewing* (1987). He toured the festival circuits, where he was beginning to make an impression for his distinct style. When he finished *Speaking Parts* in 1989, he and the film were invited to the prestigious Directors Fortnight at Cannes. *The Adjuster* was accepted two years later into the same screening lineup, and Egoyan inked his first U.S. distribution deal. In 1992, Egoyan made the CBC-TV movie *Gross Misconduct*, a hockey story with a nasty edge as it dramatized the real-life story of Brian Spencer.

The cash and his building reputation gave him the freedom to take time off and go to Armenia, where he and his wife Arsinée Khanjian took a trip around ancient church sites with a video camera and a loose idea for a movie. *Calendar* came out in 1993, and was the first film to show a different side to the director. Where his previous films were somehow emotionally unavailable, *Calendar* pushed Egoyan to be personal. Not only did

he star in the movie with his wife, but he mocked his own persona — the detached artist/photographer/filmmaker who watches his wife fall in love with someone else before his eyes. "It's not a question of wanting to go [with her] or not, it's much stranger than that," says Egoyan's own voice-over in *Calendar*. "It's about watching the two of you walking away from me, into a landscape that I will photograph."

In 1994 Egoyan was off to Cannes again, this time in official competition with *Exotica*, the first English-Canadian feature in competition since Ted Kotcheff's *Joshua Then and Now* (1985). Egoyan's biggest feature to date starred a pregnant (with their son, Arshile) Khanjian as a sex-club owner, Bruce Greenwood as a troubled father mourning his dead daughter, and Don McKellar as an exotic bird breeder. "In telling the story of *Exotica*, I wanted to structure the film like striptease, gradually revealing an emotionally loaded history," said Egoyan in the throes of Cannes coverage.

When *Exotica* was released in 1994, it performed above expectations, pulling in $5,046,118 (U.S.) in cumulative box office receipts around the world — making it the most successful Egoyan film to date. The following year, in 1995, he ventured back to the Riviera to take part in the Cannes jury. He also made a cameo appearance in the Tom Arnold movie, *The Stupids*, before beginning production on *The Sweet Hereafter* — the film that ultimately changed Egoyan's filmmaking career and established English Canada as a skilled player at the film industry's poker table. Based on a Russell Banks' novel about a school bus crash that takes the lives of several children in a small B.C. town, *The Sweet Hereafter* picked up three prizes at Cannes — the Jury Prize, the Critics' Prize and the Ecumenical Prize — as well as two Oscar nominations for Egoyan's direction and screenplay adaptation. Suddenly, more people had heard the name Atom Egoyan than had ever seen his films. Egoyan's smiling face beamed around the world for a brief instant, but Canadian film had truly entered a new era: an era where we no longer apologized for our inconsistent track record and legacy of tax-shelter shinola. Along with Egoyan, several actors found their way onto the fame-bound bus — most notably Sarah Polley, Stephanie Morgenstern, Gabrielle Rose and Bruce Greenwood. People remembered these performances, and when I found myself at Sundance a few years later, in 1999, I had a conversation with an American casting agent for a major studio. We were at a screening of *Guinevere*, the Audrey Wells movie that starred Polley as a young, socially privileged outsider who gets involved with an older man (played by Stephen Rea). The casting agent said the only reason she came to the screening was to see Polley again. "She's so real, y'know? I mean, it's not just the teeth — it's the whole package. For a real waif, she has a lot of power, y'know? You can't find anyone with real teeth in Hollywood who isn't strictly a character actor ... or a dog, excuse me, canine performer." Even Wells, who introduced the cast and the film before the Park City audience, said she cast Polley because of her performance in *The Sweet Hereafter*. She also put her voice on the soundtrack of *Guinevere* because she was so taken with Polley's haunting vocals against Mychael Danna's layered soundscape.

Despite the film's incredible critical success, *The Sweet Hereafter* did not exceed *Exotica*'s box-office total, pulling in $4,306,697 U.S. Nonetheless, everyone in the world was hungry to ink a deal with the bespectacled Canuck, and Egoyan agreed to a Canada-U.K. co-production supported by Mel Gibson's pro-duction company, Icon Entertainment, and Egoyan's long-time supporters at Alliance-Atlantis (yes, look for Robert Lantos' name on the producer credits). The project was another adaptation, this time by William Trevor, who imagined a story of a young woman venturing from small-town Ireland to industrial England in search of her unborn baby's father. While she just misses an encounter with her irresponsible "true love," she does run into an introverted caterer named Hilditch (Bob Hoskins), who has sinister plans for the young and innocent Felicia. Filmed on location in the United Kingdom and the reknowned Shepperton Studio soundstages, Egoyan had his hands on the biggest budget of his career: a whopping $10 million U.S. (half of Julia Roberts' current per-picture salary).

The film *Felicia's Journey* opened the Toronto Inter-national Film Festival in 1999 amid a maelstrom of expectation. I spoke to Egoyan just hours before the opening. He was clearly frazzled. He was approving marketing materials and his father had just walked through the hotel room door as I turned on the tape recorder. "It's pretty crazy right now, everyone wants a ticket to get in ... but these [publicity materials] are important details that I just have to keep track of, as a producer, because they are so important for the release of a movie. I want to make sure the marketing campaign is accessible as possible," he said, looking at one version of the poster after another. "Every marketing campaign is different. We have one for English Canada, another for French Canada, another for Europe, another for the U.S. — it's a lot to keep track of, but I can't just let go. I feel I have to do as much as I humanly can before I let it out of my hands. For me, it goes all the way to DVD and video release — like will it be pan and scan or letterbox?" he says. "For better or worse, I've gotten myself into a position where people are beginning to expect a lot from me, and that means I have a lot more decisions to make," he continued. "I read in *Maclean's* today I have a publicist and driver. That makes me sound so important — even if it's only partially true."

Egoyan said his brush with L. A. fame was enough to convince him to stay in Canada, where we are "encouraged to live modestly and remain humble ... If I moved to L. A., I would make so much more money. But I wouldn't be able to direct the movies of my choice, and I wouldn't be able to direct them my way. It's a distinct lifestyle choice and right now, my creative goals seem far more important than my financial ones." Egoyan went on to talk about shooting in Ireland, and his first public screening there that focused on the abortion issue in the film. "It was all very moving being there. I had this sense of place, like this is where *Ulysses* happened. There was nothing like that at all in Birmingham — it was just a large, ugly, industrial town. It was real Jeff Wall territory, you know? But it was perfect for the film. It really was, because for me, the movie was about suppression and denial. I was fascinated by the fact that her boyfriend doesn't care about her at all. He's in denial. Hilditch is in denial and Felicia is in denial. If we make all these accommodations to perpetuate this state of denial, then where does real emotion come from? What is it — can there ever be a real bond between two people if they are both lying to themselves?"

Egoyan went on to talk about his current thoughts about the Canadian identity, and said the one thing he learned is that we go on and on about being threatened by American culture, but we're not alone. We're in the same boat with the rest of the world. "So much of our identity is formed by what we are not, but I think we know we are different. It's not just different from Americans. It goes deeper than that, and we fumble and make weird statements when we're in the face of the 'other' but I think we all have this nascent sense of confidence. We feel it, we just have difficulty expressing it — so we are defined by the other. It's kind of pathetic, but it's who we are ... and besides, I love our humility. In fact, when they put Arsinée on the front of *The Globe and Mail*, we were both stunned. It was just so, um, unCanadian to be treated like a celebrity that we felt really uncomfortable." A few hours later, Egoyan and Khanjian would have their bubble burst when a crowd-control officer almost declined them entry to the opening night gala, reconfirming their Canadian credentials — and no doubt, putting them back at ease because for most Canadians (at least the ones who know the rigours of the star machine), anonymity is often more precious than fame.

While Egoyan released the Beckett-based *Krapp's Last Tape* at the Victoria Film and Video Festival in Februrary, 2001, his next big features are slated to emerge in 2002, when both *Ararat* and the adaptation of Margaret Atwood's novel, *The Blind Assassin*, hit movie screens around the world — and clock an entire revolution of Canadian film.

FILMOGRAPHY: *Smile* (director 1972) | *Howard in Particular* (director, writer, editor, cinematographer 1979) | *After Grad with Dad* (director, writer, cinematographer, editor 1980) | *Peep Show* (1981) | *Open House*, director, writer, editor (director, writer, cinematographer, editor 1982) | *Next of Kin* (director, writer, producer, editor 1984) | *Knock! Knock!* (actor 1985) | *Men: A Passion Playground* (director, cinematographer, editor 1985) | *Family Viewing* (director, writer, producer, editor 1987) | *Speaking Parts* (director, writer, producer 1989) | *The Adjuster* (director, writer 1991) | *Montreal vu par ...* collection of short (director 1991) | *Thirty-two Short Films About Glenn Gould* (crew 1993) |

Calendar (director, actor, photographer, cinematographer, writer, editor, producer 1993) | *Exotica* (1994) | *Camilla*, actor (director, writer, producer 1995) | *Curtis' Charm* (producer 1995) | *A Portrait of Arshile* (actor, director 1995) | *The Stupids* (actor 1996) | *The Sweet Hereafter* (writer, director, producer 1997) | *Bach Cello Suite #4: Sarabande* (director 1997) | *Yo-Yo Ma Inspired by Bach* (director 1997) | *Babyface* (producer 1998) | *Jack and Jill* (producer 1998) | *Felicia's Journey* (writer, director 1999) | *Formulas for Seduction | The Cinema of Atom Egoyan* (himself 1999) | *The Line* (director 2000) | *Krapp's Last Tape* (director 2001) | *The Blind Assassin* (director, writer, forthcoming, 2002) | *Ararat* (director, writer, producer, forthcoming, 2002).

CHAPTER SIX

Sex & the Great Repression

GETTING HOT (AND STAYING COLD)

Now that we've isolated empty space and processed how it defines who we are, as well as who we are not, the next few chapters will look at how we try to mediate that empty space by building bridges to the "other" side. After all, even though we may feel empty and alone inside, we are part of a great big world that offers hope of salvation through community. Often we'll look to others to fill the gaping hole — but even there, the Canadian condition runs into problems. We have a hard time bonding because there's always something pulling us apart, such as sex, gender, language, ethnicity or death. Over the course of

the next four chapters, we're going to look at each one of our particular stumbling blocks in detail as they are manifested in Canadian film. In keeping with our cycle of moving from the concrete to the abstract, we'll begin with the most physical bonding mechanism: sex.

Yes, despite the frigid landscape we've slogged through, it had to come sooner or later. And here we are: the Weird Sex chapter. A lot has been said about all the kinky, dark, quirky and obsessive sex in Canadian film. From David Cronenberg's violent body collisions in *Crash* to the necrophilia of Lynne Stopkewich's *Kissed*, Canadian film has explored more sex-

Crash (1997): James Spader and Holly Hunter explore the leg room and adjustable steering wheel column of this luxury sedan in David Cronenberg's head-on collision with creepy sex that caused such a furore at Cannes, they invented a whole new prize to honour the director's audacity and innovation. ALLIANCE ATLANTIS

ual quirks on screen than Canadian society has ever had the courage to talk about out loud. This is probably no accident. As Canadians, we have an apparent cultural aversion to sharing the details of our bodily functions with others, and when it comes to the sex act itself — well, the less said the better. Not only does the state have no business in the bedrooms of the nation (thanks to the closest thing this country ever had to a sex symbol: the vaguely androgynous Pierre Elliot Trudeau), but no one else does either. We're repressed on both sides of the linguistic border. The French-Canadian soul is haunted by the Gothic complications of sex and the Catholic church, while the English-Canadian soul is burdened by Victorian codes of physical denial. Sex = Guilt in Canadian society, no matter which way you undress it.

Part of this guilt reflects our lingering institutional past — as represented by both the church and government. In the late 1990s, there was a wonderful example of this tightly sphinctered sexual approach when a parliamentary backbencher threw a political fit about the film *Bubbles Galore* (1996). This Cynthia Roberts feminist take on pornography featured a very long orgasm sequence featuring porn star Annie Sprinkle, and several other graphic porn movie devices. It also received government funding, which sparked a small brushfire in Parliament as right-wing members spouted off about the evils of the taxpayer paying for a bombastic but educational film about women and sex. (Lord knows, the average taxpayer doesn't waste money on pornography.) Not one of the members had even seen the film, but the very fact that it featured frank depictions of sex was

Kissed (1996): Molly Parker as necrophiliac Sandra Larson, draped over her favorite love nest in Lynne Stopkewich's scandalous feature film debut. While the movie certainly has its dark side as it crawls under the floorboards of the Canadian sexual ego, it also reminds us that nothing gives life meaning like a close encounter with death.
BONEYARD FILM PRODUCTIONS

offensive enough to merit a thrashing in the House of Commons. Clearly it's a natural reaction to be embarrassed when watching something as raw and animal-like as fornication. The guilt comes because we generally want to watch anyway. Whenever someone balls up enough courage to let a screaming sex demon fly in this society, we find ourselves transfixed and settle into a voyeuristic groove — which only makes us feel guiltier.

The rest of the guilt may very well be a function of our survivor guilt. Both survival and sex are normally considered life-affirming acts, and both cause the Canadian psyche to outwardly shrivel. We've already suggested some of the causes of survivor guilt in previous chapters, namely the burden of knowing that others died, and the non-socialist, non-pluralistic connotations of the "survival of the fittest" moral code. As Canadian actor Peter Outerbridge told me when I interviewed him on the set of *Marine Life*, a project he started just after appearing as a Russian rocket scientist in Brian DePalma's *Mission to Mars*: "The difference between Canadians and Americans is that they believe in survival of the fittest and we believe the strong should take care of the weak. I think we have to take care of others. It's the right thing to do, if only because it's really boring to think and talk about yourself all the time. We might look like capitalists on the surface, but deep down, we're socialist." [1]

Socially spurred survival guilt, or plain perversion? In this chapter, we'll focus on sex — lots of sex — and all its many perverse manifestations in Canadian film. Lord knows, there is no shortage of weird sex in our celluloid closet, and when I say closet — I mean it. We're as quiet about sex in general as other cultures are about homosexuality, which in itself affirms the guilt that sex has historically carried in Canadian culture. It also offers a

clue as to why there is almost as much gay sex in Canadian film as there is heterosexual copulation. We'll deal with all of this later in greater depth in the rest of the chapter. First, though, we'll look at gay sex, straight sex and all the variations therein. We'll also survey the major shifts that have taken place in the cinematic boudoir over the last few decades, and what's become of our long-voyaging guilt valise. We'll dissect and discuss our take on gender roles and look at how they, in turn, affect the types of sexual unions we see on screen. Finally, we'll take a broad view of the whole sweaty business and look at sex as the great Jungian metaphor for personal integration and where that leaves us as a culture.

The Dirty Deed

"I'm always so scared of being abnormal."
— Le Déclin de l'empire américain

One of the beautiful things about not talking about sex with any great regularity is the way it makes all sex uniformly "dirty." There is no distinction between what's "normal" sex and what's truly "kinky" sex when we barely acknowledge the act exists at all. This idea turned out to be one of the main comic engines in Denys Arcand's *Le Déclin de l'empire américain* (*Decline of the American Empire*), in which a group of upwardly mobile, educated professionals begin talking about their sex lives only to find out that "normal" doesn't exist. One is in the midst of a near-anonymous sadomasochist relationship with a biker type. Another is sleeping with every spouse in the house. "Whenever he talks about sex, he makes it sound ridiculous," says the wife about her husband, unaware of the fact that he's sleeping with her confidante. Similarly, the yuppy couple in David Cronenberg's *Crash* (James Spader and Deborah Kara Unger) appear to be

Le Déclin de l'empire américain (1987): This garden party image looks idyllic, but behind the pretty frames and polished, civilized veneer lie several ugly truths — and all of them revolve around sex. Can you guess who's sleeping with whom by looking at this picture of perfectly respectable professors and spouses as seen by Denys Arcand? SEVILLE PICTURES

the very model of conformity with their minimalist concrete apartment and luxury automobiles when in fact, they are suicidal sexual thrill-seekers desperate to experience a symbolic mutual orgasm with their automobiles. I could go on at length, but the truth about Canadians is, you just never know what their sexual habits are going to be because they are so seldomly discussed out loud. We are a sexually closeted culture.

The late critic Vito Russo wrote an entire book on the subject of closets. In his book and the subsequent documentary, *The Celluloid Closet*, Russo dealt with the latent signs of homosexuality on the American silver screen — essentially arguing that even though there are no overt homosexuals in Hollywood, the gay figure emerges one way or other, between

the cracks — no pun intended. If we analyze what Russo says about why America felt this need to hide the whole gay issue, we may be able to apply a similar logic to why Canada feels this need to repress sexuality in general, gay or straight.

As Russo writes under the title "Who's a Sissy?":

The predominantly masculine character of the earliest cinema reflected an America that saw itself as a recently conquered wilderness ... Men of action and strength were the embodiment of our [American] culture, and a vast mythology was created to keep them in constant repair. Real men were strong, silent and ostentatiously unemotional. They acted quickly and never intellectualized. In short, they did not behave like women ... The idea of homosexuality first emerged on screen, then, as an unseen danger, a reflection of our fears about the dangers of tampering with male and female roles.[2]

From what Russo gleaned on the subject of repression and the national identity with regards to our oh-so-potent southern neighbours, he makes a direct link between sexual identity and the national ideal. Reaffirming the logic behind the idea of "phallo-nationalism," America is generally a nation of masculine strength, not of hesitating girly-men who blur the boundary between the genders. If America wanted to ensure its beefy masculine image to propel the idea of the conquering wilderness hero, then the Canadian propensity for complete sexual denial could be reflecting our continuing national insecurity complex. We don't want to assert anything, in either official language, lest we upset the precarious balance of Confederation.

Sexual Realists

Despite our reticence to talk dirty in public, the Canadian psyche simply revels in sexual imagery on screen. Nothing graphic, mind you. Heaven forbid. Sex is more of a mental than physical occupation on Canadian screens, and a very popular one at that. If we scan back to early films, we could easily call ourselves sexual realists: people who are constantly contradicting, de-mythologizing and cerebrally deconstructing sex like some latter-day Gulliver, stumbling across a giant breast that is just too big, too real, too porous and too visibly hairy to see it as anything but a blob of human tissue — not some mythic globe of the great goddess.

Filmmaker Lynne Stopkewich observed: "The real difference between Canadian and American mainstream film can be summed up in an ad I saw when I was last in Los Angeles for 'Laser Vaginal Rejuvenation.' That, to me, is so completely bizarre. Canadians are constantly being labelled as sexually perverse or dysfunctional, but what could be more unnatural than getting cosmetic surgery to fix a natural process?" she asks. "That whole idea of correcting, perfecting and manipulating what is natural — to the point where it's unrecognizable — is so much a part the American psyche that they don't even see it as strange anymore ... But we, or at least I, do."[3] Stopkewich doesn't say it in so many words, but her comment echoes a common feeling among most Canadians that we have a more grounded approach to all areas of romance. Think about it: Where are all the great Canadian romantic comedies? All our sexy, melodramatic tear-jerkers about falling in love? There aren't many, but we're getting there. The year 2000 witnessed the premieres of such bona fide romantic comedies as Richard Roy's *Café Olé* and Clement Virgo's poignantly funny, *Love Come Down*.

In the past, we made comedies that include sex, as well as comedies that suitably deconstruct it. Films such as Yves Simoneau's *Perfectly Normal* (1990), which included this idea of a Canuck come-on: "It looks like you want to cover him with Mazola oil and ride the luge with him." Bruce McDonald's *Roadkill* and *Highway 61* are "comedies" that include romance, while John Hamilton's *Myth of the Male Orgasm* (1993) was a sassy precedent to Neil Labute's much harsher *In the Company of Men* (1997), which, according to Hamilton, "aimed to demystify the way men really talk about sex and women — without pulling any punches."[4]

When that movie was released — it was made without government funding – Hamilton said that he believed it would be popular with Canadians. "Why wouldn't it be? It's talking about sex. And it's talking about sex in a way that most people will be able to identify with." The movie had a respectable Canadian run, but it was hardly a testament to the romance in our hearts, which, despite much filmed evidence to the contrary, is something I believe we carry with us in great quantities — but we bury beneath bitter layers of emotional permafrost as a result of our dysfunctional national family.

We've already looked at some of the reasons for this cool approach. Fortunately, the sixties didn't pass us by, nor did feminism, nor did the swarms of people who showed up to watch Robert Lantos' landmark scandal, *In Praise of Older Women*, at the Toronto Festival of Festivals in 1978. From a society that was completely closed on the subject of sex, we're slowly opening up and letting all those wily sexual demons loose. Not surprisingly, the first such demons were dissected under the realist, documentary lens and dealt with things that should *not* be done. We witnessed the release of one of the most noted NFB documentaries of its day, the award-winning *Not a Love Story*, Bonnie Sherr Klein's vérité look at the hidden world of exotic dancers and prostitutes that introduced an articulate stripper who, after taking part in the exposé, realized she could no longer continue in her field. (Lindalee Tracey later chose broadcast journalism). Other public-service oriented movies followed, such as *Sexual Abuse — The Family: Sexual Abuse of Children: A Time for Caring*, and *Feeling Yes, Feeling No* (1984), a sexual abuse prevention workshop series for school kids. Another film to make some waves was Vancouver filmmaker Peg Campbell's *Street Kids* (1985), which used a docudrama approach that blended talking-head documentary segments intercut with dramatized scenes.

Other sex-demystifying docs followed, with Aerlyn Weissman and Lynne Fernie's investigation into the secret history of lesbian courtship, *Forbidden Love* (1993), Penelope Buitenhuis' candid look at the life of Canadian hostesses in Japan, *Tokyo Girls* (2000), and perhaps the very epitome of the clinical Canadian documentary dealing with sex and gender roles, *Two Brides and a Scalpel: Diary of a Lesbian Marriage* (1999), Mark Achbar's non-fiction look at a cross-gendered man who wants to marry a lesbian, as a lesbian. The film not only shows the legal marriage, but it also shows the surgical removal of the penis and the inversion of the penile sheath into the abdomen to create a vagina. (Now that's what I call a perfect example of our resistance to phallo-nationalism.) It's a wild ride, but what makes it enlightening instead of simply sensationalist is the way Achbar dissects the anatomy of gender from an emotional as well as clinical perspective.

Granted, we're still pretty clinical when it comes to sex. We've got Sue Johanson's *Sunday Night Sex Show* — a TV broadcast that features a post-menopausal woman posing wooden puppets to give us pointers on hot positions with all the rev and rumble of a mechanic talking about your fuel pump. We also have sex-oriented call-in shows, so anonymous sufferers can discuss their innermost sexual shortcomings with an audience of thousands. Although Canada is the birthplace of Pamela Anderson, Dorothy Stratten, Carrie-Anne Moss, Keanu Reeves, Natasha Henstridge or countless other sex symbols with all the va-va-voom of Neve Campbell and hairy-chest charisma of William Shatner, trying to find a "positive" or "normal" image of sexual coupling in Canadian film is very difficult — but not impossible.

In Praise of Older Women (1978): Maya (Karen Black) helps Andras Vayda (Tom Berenger) come of age in her very own way in this notorious movie that forced the Ontario film censor to pull out the scissors and the Toronto movie-going community to show up in droves. SERENDIPITY POINT FILMS

Coming of Age

While twisted, perverse and generally dysfunctional sex has been part of the Canadian artistic landscape for quite some time — and no wonder, considering how repressed we've been — it was in the closing decade of the 20th century that we woke up, collectively, to smell the sex. "Puritan filmgoers, brace yourselves, the Canadian portion of the 1994 Toronto International Film Festival is going to be hot," read Jane Stevenson's advance newser on the festival lineup for Canadian Press. "This year Perspective Canada is about sex. All kinds, all approaches, whatever makes life worth living. We've had some pretty sexy movies here in the past, but this year it's rampant," said Perspective Canada programmer Cameron Bailey, pushing the tried, tested and proven big red sex button to raise festival awareness for that year. Included in the 1994 lineup was Atom Egoyan's *Exotica*, a film about a man struggling to cope with the death of his daughter by developing an obsessive interest with a stripper; *Eclipse*, Jeremy Podeswa's debut feature that looks at the sex lives of several people on the eve of a solar eclipse in Toronto; *Super 8 1/2*, by Bruce LaBruce, which stars LaBruce himself as a burnt-out porn house star. By the time David Cronenberg's *Crash* came out two years later, our reputation as kinky Canucks was already well-established. And then came *Kissed* (1996), Lynne Stopkewich's tender coming-of-age story about a young necrophile, to forever cement the image of the quiet Canadian awash in sexual quirks.

Where does all this dark, twisted sexual imagery come from? If you're a Freudian, you naturally believe in all the Electra/Oedipal problems suffered by us poor Canadians. As an ex-pat Canadian who worked as a cultural attaché in Los Angeles once told me: "Canadian films are about nothing but smoking pot and sleeping with your mother." In a Freudian analysis, then, our sexual repression is the result of missing fathers and powerful mothers, or in the case of the Quebecois tradition, it's the result of the Catholic church's perceived emasculation of the male figure, leaving priests looking like women, or as *Parti Pris* editor Pierre Maheu said in 1964, *"pères en jupes"*[5] — fathers in skirts. If you're a Jungian, you could point the finger at the "shadow" — the repressed subconscious desperate for release. If you're a person who prefers a common sense approach, Canadian film's fascination for the darkly perverse could be seen as little more than a titillation tactic aimed at seducing the reluctant masses with the oldest trick in the book. I believe it's probably a combination of all these things. But what matters more than the root cause, at this particular point in narrative time, is the images themselves. It's one thing to agree that there's something perverse about the way sex is treated in Canadian film; it's quite another to look at the perversions themselves, which can tell us a great deal more about what's been repressed than any surface, historical dissection.

A quick survey of Canadian film on both sides of the linguistic border reveals a few common images in our collective sexual cellar, such as May-December couples, homosexuality, sexual displacement, incest, prostitution, sexual abuse and mental, if not literal, necrophilia:

Maelström (2000), dir. Denis Villeneuve: Bibi (Marie Josée Croze) is a young woman suffering from an image problem. Suffocated by her mother's fame and her brother's perfection, the film opens with Bibi getting an abortion, then getting drunk to assuage her guilt. She drives home, kills someone with her car, and then tries to escape using the only means she knows how: through anonymous sex with a stranger. From the blank expression on her face during the act, we can assume this is bad sex, and that for Bibi, the whole purpose behind sexual encounters is self-effacement, even self-destruction.

Crash (1996), dir. David Cronenberg: A cast of scarred characters gets a sexual charge from car crashes and particularly the mutilated flesh of wreck survivors. We see images of James Spader licking a long scar on the inside of Rosanna Arquette's leg, and more of him going down on Elias Koteas in the back seat of his car. Those are just a few examples. The whole movie is about revving your physical engine into oblivion with a carload of partners.

Kissed (1996), dir. Lynne Stopkewich: Sandra Larson (Molly Parker) shuns the attention of a good-looking, kind-hearted Matt (Peter Outerbridge) in favour of exploring the "other side" through the flesh of dead bodies. For her, sexual climax can only be achieved through necrophilic encounters. Similarly, in Stopkewich's second film, *Suspicious River* (2000), the lead character (once again played by Molly Parker) subjects herself to several violent sexual encounters with men in the motel where she works. In both cases, the sex seems to be a vehicle of emotional empowerment for the woman because she put herself in that place, with those partners, of her own free will.

New Waterford Girl (1999), dir. Allan Moyle: Our hero Mooney (Liane Balaban) is an aspiring artist who desperately wants to leave the small, oppressive Cape Breton community she calls home. After going over all the escape routes, she decides the only way to set herself free is to get pregnant — or at least, pretend to get pregnant. Up to this point the only chaste girl in the entire town, Mooney gives everyone the impression she's a complete slut — even though she doesn't have sex at all. In this Tricia Fish script, the only way for a woman to escape and pursue her creative destiny is to get "knocked up."

Live Bait (1995), dir. Bruce Sweeney: Our confused hero Trevor MacIntosh (Tom Scholte), is sexually unavailable to women his own age. There's something holding him back — and we're led to believe it's his own mother (Babz Chula). However, once he sets his eyes on an older female sculptor (a Louise Nevelson type played by Micki Maunsell, who looks at big hunks of metal and says things such as "We have to open this up a bit"), he realizes a sexual relationship with her and is emotionally healed. The movie ends on an undeniably upbeat note as he leaves his lover's bed, saunters back home, and smiles at his mother. Similar themes return in Sweeney's second feature, *Dirty* (1998), but this time the sex is far more obsessive, as the lead character can't let go of his infatuation for an older, drug-dealing woman. In the first movie, sex has healing powers — even if the bigger sexual picture is rather unorthodox. In the second film, sex is the disease, not the cure.

Careful (1992), dir. Guy Maddin: In this Gothic fairy tale, sex is the root of all evil. Carnal lust forces a young man to kill himself after drugging his mother and fondling her while

Live Bait (1995): Trevor (Tom Scholte) gets a kiss from mom (Babz Chula). BRUCE SWEENEY

she was sedated. It leads to one sister killing another because she's so in love with her father that she can't stand the idea of sharing his love with anyone. Sex also leads to the death of the supposed hero after he kills his mother's lover in order to win the heart of the same scheming woman who killed her own sibling.

Le Polygraphe (1996), dir. Robert Lepage: A multifaceted tale that revolves around the murder of a young woman in which everyone is using sex as a means of escape. A young actress heads home with a man she does not know, because she just witnessed a suicide on the Metro tracks. She and the man have sex. Later, we discover she auditioned for the role of the dead woman in a dramatization of the murder, and that the man she has sex with is a leading forensic examiner. Once again, sex, death and obsession are part of the same picture.

Ginger Snaps (2000), dir. John Fawcett: In this adventurous take on teen horror, we watch two late-blooming sisters undergo a transformation. At first, they are outcasts who amuse themselves by taking pictures of their own staged suicides. Later, after sister Ginger

(Katharine Isabelle) begins to menstruate, she slowly turns into a werewolf with an unsatiable sexual appetite and literally eats her partners alive. The functioning allegory here is that sex equals a complete lack of control, which has typically been one of the most frightening things for the control-freak Canadian psyche to deal with. Also, we see the same themes of sex and death revisited with the same grim results.

Exotica (1994), dir. Atom Egoyan: A tax accountant (Bruce Greenwood) begins to develop an obsessive interest in a young stripper (Mia Kirshner) who reminds him of his dead daughter. At first we think the man's a bit of a pedophilic freak. Then we realize that he is obsessed with this woman. His compulsion eventually pushes him to break through the non-contact barriers of the sex trade and talk to her as a human being because it reunites him with the spirit of his dead loved one. Egoyan's other films, particularly *The Adjuster* and *Family Viewing* (and in lesser ways in *The Sweet Hereafter* and *Speaking Parts*) deal with similar ideas of using sex as means of connectedness — a vehicle to escape from a state of complete alienation. Sadly, for all these haunted souls, sex provides no relief.

Exotica (1994): Where things come to a head.

It only makes the heart ache more for the things it can never hold again.

Cold Comfort (1989), dir. Vic Sarin: We watch as Paul Gross is saved from a blizzard by an odd tow-truck driver (Maury Chaykin), only to be held captive by his saviour and his equally odd daughter (Margaret Langrick), who appear to be romantically connected.

Lilies (1996), dir. John Greyson, **Le Confessional** (1995), dir. Robert Lepage, **Hanging Garden** (1997), dir. Thom Fitzgerald, **Better Than Chocolate** (1999), dir. Anne Wheeler: These are just a few examples of Canadian films where the camera assumes a queer point of view. This does not mean the films show us "weird sex" because they show gay mating. It means these movies push the viewer to alter his or her own "frame" around notions of homosexuality. This alteration of context is the essence of these films' inherent "weirdness."

The inventory could go on for pages and pages. There are so many images of weird sex in Canadian film that we can assume if sex is there at all, it's going to be a downer: a symptom of a socially rooted disease — not a happy communion of two souls who can't wait to explore each other's private parts.

If we turn our minds back to the theories of Carl Jung, who believed sex in dream imagery was a barometer of psychic health (because it integrates a person with his or her anima or animus, the creative impulse in the human spirit), then all the weird sex manifested in Canadian film suddenly makes a lot of sense, because it's not so much about sex at all, but about identity.

Sex & Identity

Sex (particularly heterosexual sex) is the ultimate symbol of unity and birth, but it is also a reminder of our death, as we reach the grand climax — experience brief transcendence — then collapse into a jiggling bundle of nerves and sweat and clammy dampness that does nothing but remind us of our physical essence. It brings opposites together in a physical embrace. The empty vaginal void is filled, the vulnerable phallus finds a safe harbour, and the force of nature itself is reaffirmed without any interference from that stubborn, and oh-so-distracting cerebellum. I know it's a reach, but if we translate this idea to film — which is a type of dream state in its own right, and quite literally a shadow world — then we can compare the dysfunctional sex in Canadian cinema to our fractured and continually frustrated national psyche.

In this respect, sex becomes a mirror to reflect the things we feel about ourselves as Canadians, but can't — for whatever reason — express. As Jung said, the "shadow" is not the whole of the unconscious personality — it only represents the parts that no one wants to talk about. "Whether the unconscious comes up at first in a helpful or a negative form, after a time the need usually arises to readapt the conscious attitude in a better way to the unconscious factors — therefore to accept what seems to be "criticism" from the unconscious."[6]

We've already established the fact that as Canadians, we're generally private, quiet and repressed on the subject of sex, just as we are quiet on the subject of national unity. Politicians are often looking to stir up a fear of "the other" — whether it's the evil English establishment, the flag-stomping PQ-istes, the "Asian invasion," or myriad other conveniently manufactured enemies. But in the real world — or at least the private world of most Canadians — national unity may well be a big concern, but it's not something you go around blabbing about ad nauseam.

Perhaps, then, we are using sexual imagery in film as a means of healing our inner "anima-animus" tensions. Maybe we are merely finding symbolic ways of integrating our national self. If we are, then we aren't so screwed up after all. In order to get to the root of the matter and figure out what's really going on with our anima-animus/yin-yang teeter-totter, we'll begin with an investigation into gender and dissect the assigned roles given to each sex in Canadian cinema. This exercise should shed some light on the larger relationship between the anima-animus, as well as offer up some clues as to why the unions betwen men and women in Canadian film tend to be so strange.

Women: Stronger, Faster, Smarter

"Like mother earth, women are the givers of life — and that makes them the most powerful of all."— Alanis Obomsawin.

One of the most notable new universals in both French and English New Canadian Cinema is the appearance of the strong-willed, highly competent and generally intellectually superior female character. The modern Canadian female protagonist bears little physical resemblance to the overabundance of "crones" that Atwood discussed 30 years ago in the pages of *Survival*. Back then, Atwood noted that most of the women in Canadian literature were over the age of 50. Not only were they "old" (she was in her twenties, remember), but they were a "tough, sterile, suppressed granite-jawed lot" who lived their lives "with intensity, but through gritted teeth and they were often seen as malevolent, sinister or life-denying." In archetypal terms, Canadian literature suffered a strange lack of Venus-like goddesses, but had an over-abundance of crones. Pointing to characters like Margaret Laurence's crotchety crone Hagar in *The Stone Angel* and the diseased mother in Alice Munro's *The Peace of Utrecht*, Atwood spotted an entire "Angry-Granny" group of "powerful, negative old women" in the pages of CanLit. She was absolutely right, of course. But just as these crones filled the pages of the burgeoning Canadian canon, another type of heroine was emerging on screen.

Before Laurence or Munro were even conceived, Nell Shipman was reinventing the Canadian female on screen. A sassy lass from Victoria, British Columbia, Shipman (née Helen Barham, b.1892) was born to a family of limited means but turned herself into an accomplished actress by the age of 16, eventually winning the attentions of Lothario impresario Ernest Shipman. The two married in 1910 and became a creative team, with Nell ensuring she had a starring role. In 1914, she directed and starred in her first film, *The Ball of Yarn* (1914). Then came *God's Country and the Woman* (1915), a film based on a James Oliver Curwood story about a woman who could traverse the arctic tundra with sled dogs, a character in whom Nell found her ideal alter ego. The movie was a commercial success, and when Ernest and Nell returned to Canada in 1919 to make *Back to God's Country* (1919), they were one of filmdom's most successful couples, thanks in large part to Nell's outgoing and creative energies.

The young, vital women Shipman plays have little in common with the "crones" on the pages of CanLit. Shipman created female versions of the romantic male hero, but cast in a feminine eye, because these heroines are at one with nature. The difference between the

page and the film images could suggest that the film medium itself presented a whole new way to frame the female experience — one that allowed for complete recreation without gender-role expectations.

Back to God's Country featured Shipman (also the screenwriter) as a young woman living in the North who was at home on the frozen tundra. She could trap, canoe and snowshoe. She even goes so far as to save her ailing husband from certain death while singlehandedly dealing with a bunch of no-goodniks. Shipman's character is the equivalent of the archetypal American male, with two crucial differences: She is not a man, and she is not a real conqueror; she gains her strength and mental advantage over the enemy by living in harmony with the natural world around her.

Film historian and Toronto film festival programmer Kay Armatage explored Shipman's heroic proportions in her article, "Nell Shipman, A Case for Heroic Femininity".[7] In it, Armatage establishes Shipman's unique approach to depicting the natural world as empathetic, not hostile: "Shipman routinely shifted the protagonist's position from the dog to the woman, and effected concomitant shifts in the working of the narrative as well. Thus into this circuit of commercial cinema, popular genre, animals and nature, Shipman inserts the new variable: Heroic femininity." As Dolores, the heroine in *Back to God's Country*, Shipman literally comes to the rescue of the abused dog (and saviour) Wapi, who is transformed into a gentle beast by a simple touch. "A new miracle of understanding," read the title card, "roused by the touch of a woman's hand." Armatage writes: "... Shipman played the leading role, always of the heroic stamp. Husbands or lovers were either absent or incapacitated: they fell ill, were injured, or were simply 'artistic.' Nell invariably had to save the day ... Her great sense of moral justice, and the instinctive connection with animals and nature: these are the signs of her essential feminity and simultaneously the source of heroism which allows her to resist the conventional narrative inscriptions of the woman protagonist as victimized and rescued."[8]

Beyond God's Country

Threads of Shipman's character continue to run through the contemporary tapestry of Canadian film. While the tax-shelter films of the seventies were as exploitative of the female form as their producers were of tax laws, the idea of the dominant female remains an integral part of the Canadian imagination. Even the work of expatriate James Cameron reverberates with the ghost of his formative years. His most interesting and well-rounded characters tend to be women: Linda Hamilton in the *Terminator* series, Sigourney Weaver in *Aliens*, Kate Winslet in *Titanic*, Jamie Lee Curtis in *True Lies*. For Canadian filmmakers who remain in Canada, the female character is even stronger — and generally less oppressed by a dominant, terminating, male force.

The most obvious shift from our crone-prone days has been the discovery of the autonomous Venus character. Not only is the modern Canadian female decidedly youthful, generally benevolent, physically attractive and outward looking, she is also fecund — physically and intellectually. She can bear children, even if she frequently decides not to. She's just as headstrong as her foresisters, but in an age where many of the women on the big screen are used as silicon-injected set decor, the Canadian female is one of the most realized characters in any film tradition going.

The power centre for these women is the empty, but potentially creative void within them: the uterus. Not only is this fist-sized

organ a perfectly portable and altogether symbolic empty void that plays into our "negative space theory," but it is a blatant symbol of one's creative potential. As New Age guru Deepak Chopra says: "We spring forth out of nothingness; nothing is the womb of life." In order to make the most of that nothing, one must possess self-knowledge. Then, and only then, will the act of creation be positive and constructive instead of a burden to those who made it. In this respect, there is a great deal of revolutionary power in empty space. An idea can change the world just as a child can change the nature of a relationship. All of these things give the female character an unprecedented amount of power in the distilled fictional universe of film. I think it's important to specify that it is the "character" and not the filmmaker that we are talking about here, because both male and female filmmakers in this country tend to give women similar attributes, which I find quite intriguing.

We can explain the rise of the powerful female character in Canadian film by using our handy-dandy negative space theory. Let me explain. If the average Canadian male character appears to be in the "sensitive-New-Age-guy" category because he's comfortable with ambiguity and "the hole inside," then it's only logical that the female whose own void mirrors that of the vast, empty Canadian landscape will be more in harmony with the natural world, and she will potentially be able to exercise more control, or at least have a more empowered attitude, to the world around her. One look at what happens when someone or something tries to invade that hole with an unwanted "positive appendage," and the whole equation becomes absolutely clear: she rebels against it until either the unwanted cargo, or the unwanted appendage backs down. In a situation where she is forced to carry the cargo, or allow entry to an unwanted appendage, she will either turn into the hardened crone or destroy herself. What follows is an exploration of some noteworthy films that deal with the woman and her womb.

The Handmaid's Tale

The most obvious example of this symbolic relationship between women, the womb and the locus of social control is in Margaret Atwood's *The Handmaid's Tale*, a novel that was turned into a film by German director Volker Schloendorff, from a script by Harold Pinter. When the book was written in the 1980s, America was in the midst of a cyclical return to the political right. Ronald Reagan had been elected president and there was a lot of talk about so-called "family values." Women were once again encouraged, thanks to Nancy Reagan's role-modelling, to reassume their matriarchal duty of maintaining the home and nurturing the family while men went off to do a variety of industrial, manly things. In Atwood's book, our main character Offred (even her name has been supplanted by that of the man's: "Of Fred") is one of the few remaining women in the fictional Republic of Gilead with a working womb. While other women have been rendered sterile as a result of toxic pollution, Offred can conceive, and so, when she is apprehended in the midst of an escape attempt from Gilead with her husband and daughter, she is forcibly turned into a handmaid — a woman whose womb will be appropriated by a wealthy woman who desires children. Offred has no control or say in the matter. She is now a human farm field, who will be tilled and sewn as "The General" and his wife, Serena Joy, see fit. Without giving away the entire plot of the worthy film, it's safe to say that Offred rebels against the oppression — but in her very own way. The ending of the movie is highly ambiguous, but there's the suggestion that things work out for poor Offred. At the very least, her inner void is never taken over by a hostile force.

Parsley Days

Contrary to Atwood's dystopian vision, maritimer Andrea Dorfman's bittersweet relationship comedy *Parsley Days* (2000) deals with similar issues — only without all the hard edges. In this release, which toured festivals with solid success but was later panned by some Toronto critics (which almost prevented its national run), Dorfman tells us the story of Kate and Ollie. Kate is a bike mechanic who teaches outreach classes, and her longtime boyfriend, Ollie, is "the king of contraception" — a public health worker charged with handing out condoms and touring schools to teach birth control.

As the film opens, we see someone handling a strip of multicoloured condoms as Kate's voice-over tells us: "I think a relationship is a lot like a condom: You look out at the world outside from behind your transparent shield and feel safe and snug. Your relationship is strong ... your relationship is the one that won't break." Just as the last words are uttered, one of the pretty condoms is pierced with a safety pin. Bam. Suddenly Kate finds herself pregnant and her world starts falling apart piece by piece. She realizes her safe relationship may be little more than an escape device. She might not love Ollie anymore. She's attracted to one of her bike students — the slow one. She is torn: should she stay with Ollie, the nicest guy in town, because she's safe and happy? Or should she come clean about the affair and see what happens? Or should she break up with Ollie and have an abortion?

Parsley Days (2000): Ollie (Mike Leblanc) and Kate (Megan Dunlop), falling out of love. SEVILLE PICTURES AND ANDREA DORFMAN

Yes, that's right: abortion. The United States rarely uses that word in any popular media — let alone a comedy, but up here in the Great White North, women have what's called free choice. In this country, where tolerance is hailed as the most important social virtue, women have complete autonomy over their own bodies, and so for Dorfman — as it is for most Canadians — abortion is simply part of the natural landscape.

In this case, it's also a part of the metaphorical landscape, because as Kate tries to solve her dilemma in a way that will have the least impact on others, she turns to her lesbian herbalist pal who tells her of parsley's "menses-inducing" properties. Kate is told she can induce her own naturopathic abortion if she injects several kilos of parsley a day ...

which she does, to great comic effect but absolutely no clinical effect. As the guilt builds within her, Kate finally snaps. She has to tell Ollie what's happened. She has to "be an honest person again." It's not the guilt of the affair that seems to be bugging Kate most, but the sad fact that she knows — if she is truly honest with herself —that she is going to break Ollie's heart (We know this because as she comes home, tormented about facing the music, she hears a newscast on the TV about a rash of "people dying of broken hearts.") In the end, Kate isn't just completely honest with Ollie, she tells him that she is no longer in love with him. She also has the abortion in the final frames of the film.

What makes this movie such a beautiful experience, and such a moving one, is the way it toys with our expectations. As Kate and Ollie sit there in the backyard, in the — what else, eh? — red canoe that is the running symbol of their love affair, we almost expect them to kiss and make up. And let's face it, most of us have been so programmed by the Hollywood romance formula (where opposites fight, then fall in love) that we find it impossible to conjure a love story where people simply fall out of love for no good reason at all. Affairs can end in Hollywood romances too, but usually only after someone meets an all-too tragic end in a plane crash, car crash, drowning, from AIDS, cancer ... whatever. The films where love affairs end not because someone has died but because people have grown apart, contradict the norm, and that negation of expectation is certainly one of the main ingredients in good drama.

Parsley Days is a good movie because it contradicts expectation without bending over backward to do so. Moreover, it's a good movie because it articulates the sense of loss we feel when a relationship ends — that sickening feeling of elation and sadness all at the same time.

New Waterford Girl

Mooney lives in Nowheresville (AKA New Waterford) Cape Breton. She knows everyone in town. She lives in a curtained "room" at the top of the stairs in the home she shares with her many brothers and sisters. Her mother, played by Mary Walsh (of *This Hour Has 22-Minutes*-Codco fame) is the dominant matriarch and her father, played by Nicholas Campbell (*DaVinci's Inquest*), is a deflated dreamer whose sole creative outlet is baking cakes. With these two parents as role models, the last thing Mooney wants is to end up trapped in the same procreative hell as her mom and dad. When the film opens, we learn that Mooney is a talented artist who has a chance of going to art school in the big city, but there's no money to facilitate the escape, so Mooney is left with few options. Either she can get pregnant and take the next train out of town like all the other gals who have been "knocked up" before her, or she can play the prude and exempt herself from the whole breeder business. Mooney sees no salvation in

New Waterford Girl (2000): Lou (Tara Spencer-Nairn) and Mooney (Liane Balaban). ODEON AND SIENNA FILMS

either scenerio, until she meets Lou, the outsider from New York City.

Lou (Tara Spencer-Nairn) is a feisty young woman who appears out of nowhere with her leopard-print sporting mother (Cathy Moriarty). Voluntary exiles in Cape Breton, the two are trying to escape the mom's deadbeat, abusive, boxing boyfriend back home. Within a few frames, Mooney (the outsider from within) and Lou (the outsider from New York) bond over their alienation and come up with a plan that may free Mooney from her destiny as a tethered baby-making machine: pretend to get pregnant, catch the train out of New Waterford, and never return. Suddenly the body part that was her biggest liability — the empty womb — becomes her biggest asset as Mooney borrows urine from pregnant friends and turns the town upside down with her sudden character swing.

The key to Mooney's empowerment is the way she takes control of her own reproductive organs. She isn't passively waiting for some boy. Both of these women take the proverbial bull by the horns and recreate their femininity in androgynous space. For instance, Lou's a girl — and second, she can punch the boys out cold. With Lou's help, Mooney goes out and controls the opposite sex to realize her own personal goals. This is a definite shift from the early models of women in Canadian Lit, who were victimized by their wombs and their creative abilities. Without autonomy over their own nature and control over the open and highly creative space inside, these women evolved into bitter crones. Now, it seems, women in Canadian film are using the mere potential for creation to their advantage. This does not mean children — it means a realization of one's inner, creative self.

Maelström

In the case of *Maelström*, our conflicted heroine Bibiane is awash in guilt over a recent
abortion. Mentally eclipsed by her mother's
fame and depressed by the failure of her own
business at the hands of her nasty and zeal-
ously rational, know-it-all brother, Bibi finds
herself free-floating. She is overcome and is
now emotionally paralyzed. At first, she looks
for comfort in the arms of an anonymous sexual partner she picks up at a rave. But because
she doesn't really care about anything anymore, they have bad sex and she becomes
even more fatalistic, more shut down and
more alienated from herself. Making things
worse, she drives home drunk, runs a man
down, then leaves the scene. When she meets
the son of the Norweigian fisherman she
killed with her car, she sees a possibility for
healing. On the surface, she is looking for forgiveness from the man who was hurt most by
her irresponsible act. But if we go a little
deeper (which this movie is wont to do, as it is
swimming in deep water imagery), we can see
that the budding relationship between Bibi
and Evian (Jean-Nicolas Verreault) is not just
about forgiveness, it's about spiritual integration: these two people are both lost souls.
Together they are found. Together, they have
meaning. The only problem is Bibi's bad deed
— a fact that director Denis Villeneuve drives
home symbolically when Evian throws the
ashes of his dead dad all over Bibi as she lies
in bed, the same bed the two of them made
love in the night before. Death, sex, guilt —
it's all here.

Perhaps had Villeneuve made this movie
at another time — or come from another generation (he was born in 1967) — he would
have ended his surreal love story with a
downer ending, the way most of us might have
expected. But Villeneuve resists. Not only does

Bibiane (Marie Josée Croze) and Evian (Jean-Nicolas
Verreault) put Maelström's water imagery to good use.
ALLIANCE ATLANTIS

he depart from our linear, four-walled tradition
of realism in the very first frames — when he
opts for fantasy and uses an ancient fish as the
narrator — but he goes the extra creative mile
and gives us a morally ambiguous but romantically sound "happy ending." The mise-en-
scène of the film remains highly realistic, at
least on the surface, but Bibi and Evian are
courageous and creatively open enough to
explore beneath the surface. They let the love
in — which proves to be stronger than any of
the negative energy around them.

Such romantic healing is a true novelty in
Canadian film, seen only on the rarest occa-
sions in such movies as *Last Night* (which is a
bit more ambiguous) and *New Waterford Girl*
— both of which are relatively new films
from young filmmakers. Is it fair to suggest
this new courage bodes well for our psychic
future, not just as individuals, but as a nation?

Villeneuve might have a problem with it.
The filmmaker considers himself "a confused
separatist" who yearns for a new, positive
start. However, in an interview at the Toronto
International Film Festival, where *Maelström*
premiered in 2000, Villeneuve also said he felt
Canada was essentially "a battle between two
cultures out to reject the other."

In order to heal the desire for mutual destruction, Villeneuve said the only solution was separation, "because at least that way, the two cultures could grow and flourish on their own."[9] I don't dispute the sincerity of Villeneuve's comments. But as we've just seen, the larger message of his film could be interpreted as being quite the opposite. It could very well be a shadow message of hope. Then again, it might just be sex — in which case, the very fact that we're talking about it at all is reason enough to rejoice.

There are a great many more examples of these new Canadian heroines who maintain control of their own inner space. She can be seen in everyone from Valerie Buhagiar's self-possessed characters in Bruce McDonald and Don McKellar's road movies, to the pregnant strip club owner (Arsinée Khanjian) in Atom Egoyan's *Exotica*. She is a ubiquitous feature at this point in Canadian film, and she has sprung from the cerebral loins of both genders.

If we see the female as the embodiment of our vast, empty landscape, then this new feisty femme fecund could attest to our changing attitude to the world around us. No longer foreign, cold and barren, she is able to give life — but only when she wants to. She can create, but only if she feels love. Now it's in her hands, not those of the predominantly male establishment. This, clearly, represents progress.

If we view the female as half the Jungian anima-animus equation of Self, then we can assume we are moving toward increased artistic expression, but, by the same token, a potential psychic imbalance as the female "anima" may well overpower the "masculine" animus. In order to get the full picture, we'll look now at the fate of men in Canadian film.

The Canadian Male

"Canadian men are nice guys."

— Jeopardy *host, and proud Canadian, Alex Trebek*

Some people, myself among them, have looked at the Canadian male on screen and felt pity. Pity these poor saps who don't get to carry guns and rescue maidens in distress. Pity these losers whose girlfriends would rather sleep with dead men, such as Peter Outerbridge's character in *Kissed*. Pity those freaks who need uniforms to make them feel big and powerful, like Tom McCamus in *I Love a Man in Uniform*. Pity even that hunk Paul Gross who is held captive by a crazy tow-truck driver (Maury Chaykin) after being hauled, half frozen, out of his half-entombed car in a snowstorm in *Cold Comfort*.

To people who have been trained to view heroism as the art of being bulletproof, the Canadian hero barely rates as a sidekick. He has no special powers, no clear insight into the ways of the heavens, no code name ... not even a special piece of snap-on technology that can turn him into a superhero at the push of a button. To outsiders, we've been lucky enough to coast on the manly red serge coat-tails of the RCMP, but we know they don't wear those cool uniforms unless they are on diplomatic duty, or out to impress tourists. It's all about appearances, and as Canadians, we tend to take a jaundiced view of anything that appears too perfect, or in the case of the RCMP, anything too institutional and earnest. Every once in a while, you get a movie like *Map of the Human Heart*, where the hero is an Inuit fighter pilot who falls in love with a Métis girl at the tuberculosis hospital in Montreal — but again, the man is hardly a winner in the classic American sense of the word hero. He dies a nobody on an ice floe.

In Atwood's decryption, the Canadian male is someone who cannot be redeemed by a heroic death, usually because he dies accidentally (by freezing or drowing). Certainly we could say the same still holds true in many cases. Canadian film is full of men who die accidentally, from the man who freezes to death in an outdoor bathtub at the beginning of *Highway 61* (because "he was no longer insulated from the harsh reality of the world around him"), to the conflicted hero in *Careful* who falls asleep in the snow cave, to the missing father figure in *Surfacing* who drowns looking for petroglyphs.

Measuring Ourselves

"Quite often I've noticed that Canadians always have the doughnut hole as the hero. He's not doing anything — he's the empty space in the middle. You'd never have an American hero like that. Not ever." — Guy Maddin.

If you just look at the surface of Canadian film, our boys don't quite measure up to the sizeable expectations surrounding the male hero myth propagated by the American movie industry, but as Atwood hypothesized, the very comparison may be a lingering symptom of our colonial past. If we look at the Canadian male in isolation, he doesn't look so wimpy at all. In fact, his very humanity and willingness to embrace ambiguity may render him far more heroic than anything we can see from the buff heroes in Hollywood.

The American mythology that we've been trained to absorb rhapsodizes about the achievements of the hero — concrete actions that not only affirm the man's place in the universe but also have the ability to transform the universe, even subdue and tame it with a human hand. As Russo said, "They did not behave like women."

In Canada, we clearly aren't so threatened by the idea of gender bending. Our women are often "manly" and our men are often "effeminate." In our universe, people are simply creatures who carry both "male" and "female" traits. As we've noted elsewhere, we are a cerebral culture, meaning sexual body parts may come second to brain. We distrust a clearly defined, and rather arrogant, approach to the cosmos because we are all too aware of how vulnerable we really are. We are all to apt to "drown or freeze" to death.[10] We are puny, near-powerless and ultimately subject to the forces of nature. Can you see a Canadian version of *Gladiator*? Hardly. But does that mean our men are weak and geeky? Hardly.

When I approached male Canadian actors at the 2000 Toronto International Film Festival with the geek theory, it became clear that the men who play these characters were for the most part opposed to the geek conclusion. At first, I figured it was just denial. But the more we talked, the more obvious it became that the whole geek theory had one giant hole in the middle.

The first misconception is to assume that these men are even trying to be larger than life. In other words, we shouldn't compare Hollywood's phallo-nationalist heroes with the Tim Horton doughnut-hole of a Canadian male — nor should we use the phallo-nationalist model as a measure of our identity, because we are, as we shall prove, a sexually ambiguous kind of people. Where they give us imported beefcake like Tom Cruise, Arnold Schwarzenegger and Russell Crowe, our hardest working male actors are people such as Don McKellar, who played the likes of an introverted, ambiguously sexual exotic bird breeder in *Exotica*; Tom McCamus who played a passive brain in a bottle in *Possible Worlds*, Bruce Greenwood, who in *The Sweet*

Bruce Greenwood plays the mournful tax accountant Francis, a man whose strength emerges slowly through silence, in Atom Egoyan's *Exotica* (1994). Here, Francis sees a reflection of his missing daughter in his niece, played by Sarah Polley. COURTESY OF JOHNNIE EISEN, © EGO FILM ARTS

Hereafter was forced to watch his kids die before his eyes, and Saul Rubinek, who plays a variety of atypical hero types in both Canadian and American movies. Let's not forget Jay Brazeau, who played the undertaker in *Kissed*, and Maury Chaykin, who played the chubby, dysfunctional musician in *Whale Music*. On the surface, it's probably all right to say that we fall on the goofier, negative side of the equation, but that's about the only thing we can say — safely — because the Canadian male is actually a great deal stronger than the American male once you get past the packaging and look at the contents.

"The men I have played [in Canadian movies] are incredibly strong," said Bruce Greenwood when I approached him on the geek theory. "If you look at *The Sweet Hereafter* or *Exotica*, the characters are in so

much pain — but they move through it because they are strong. They are not denying their feelings. They are trying to live with them. They adapt [with] some strange coping mechanisms, but they are strong enough to feel ... and I think that's psychically far more healthy than picking up a gun and blowing someone away. Don't you?"[11] Indeed. Beneath the so-called "wimpy" or "passive" exterior, these are men who are comfortable, or at least willing, to explore their emotional or feminine side. They do not feel an inherent need to conquer the wilderness and assert their destructive power, and as such, they stand in direct contrast to the all-conquering archetypal American hero myth. They are real human beings capable of great acts of bravery — only on a human scale.

According to Tom McCamus — who played

the vivisected George Barber in *Possible Worlds,* the nerdy bank employee with the secret cop persona in *I Love a Man in Uniform*, and the father who has an incestuous relationship with his daughter in *The Sweet Hereafter* — the males he portrays are not weak, they are "vulnerable" — and there's a distinct difference between the two. A weak person is ineffectual and easily crushed, but a vulnerable person is someone who is able to open up and expand his field of experience.

"The thing about us [Canadians] is that we apologize all the time. I think that reflects a certain vulnerability," said McCamus in a 2000 interview. "That's what directors are usually asking for, vulnerability. As a result, my character is not a guy who you'd look up to, but someone we can identify with. That doesn't mean to say we are wimps, perhaps it just means we have become more confident — that we can show a vulnerable side. I know George is an Everyman — in some ways, quite literally because he has this ability to process the thoughts of others in his disembodied state. He is many people all at once, and he is vulnerable, and vulnerability is a quality several Canadian leads males that I've played have."

Beyond the Mack Jacket
In addition to vulnerability, if we pull the Canadian male apart, trait by trait, the Canadian "hero" generally possesses one or more of the following:

» An inner longing that he may be unnable to articulate. Good examples of this can be seen in characters like Renzo (Michael Riley), the hockey player and beer-plant employee who dreams of being an opera singer in *Perfectly Normal*; the perpetually unsatisfied grocer (Simon Webb) in John Pozer's *The Grocer's Wife*, or the unemployed and perpetually unsatisfied Christophe (Paul Ahmarani) in Philippe Falardeau's *La Moitié gauche du frigo.*

» An ambiguous sexuality. Examples include Don McKellar's pet store owner in Atom Egoyan's *Exotica*; the bisexual James Dean wannabe played by Elias Koteas in *Crash*; Jeremy Irons' twins in *Dead Ringers*, and the lost Marc in Robert Lepage's *Le Confessionnal*. In the notes for Egoyan's *Speaking Parts*, he even specifies that Lance is "strikingly beautiful … almost androgynous". [12]

» A submissive relationship with women. Witness the run of male characters befuddled, and often threatened, by female sexual power: In Reg Harkema's *A Girl is a Girl*, a nice guy finds himself striking out with one woman after another because he just can't get a handle on the female experience. In Blaine Thurier's *Low Self-Esteem Girl*, a young woman is demonized by members of a Christian Youth group because she is too sexual and could very well seduce the strong and virtuous, sending them all straight to Hades. Other submissive male models can be seen in Anne Wheeler's *Marine Life*, where a younger man Robert (Peter Outerbridge) plays second fiddle to a few ex-husbands and a bunch of kids; Clement Virgo's *The Planet of Junior Brown* shows us a boy forced into submission by his mother and his unhinged piano teacher (Margot Kidder), and in Peg Thompson's script for *Better Than Chocolate*, the man is fully concealed in the cross-gendered character of Judy/Jeremy.

» A distrust of the physical world and the outward manifestations of "reality." My favourite example, and there are many, is the Ted Pikul character played by Jude Law in Cronenberg's *eXistenZ*. Pikul fears being disconnected to "civilization," and at one point, cries out for his "pink phone," which he keeps firmly tucked in his trousers. Of course the Allegra Geller character (Jennifer Jason Leigh) is in control and chucks the knobby pink phone out of the car window the minute it makes an appearance. (You have to love Cronenberg's gift for sexual imagery in every nook and flesh fold.)

» A potentially menacing other side. Witness the dad (Maury Chaykin) in Vic Sarin's *Cold Comfort*, who seems like the nicest goof until you see him forcibly confine Paul Gross in his gas station home, or Tom McCamus' mild-mannered bank teller who takes on the persona of a cop in David Wellington's *I Love a Man in Uniform*. Even Jeff Goldblum in *The Fly* fits the description when he begins to metamorphose into an insect, as does Larenz Tate's drug-addicted character Neville in *Love Come Down* when he loses control under the influence.

Taken together, these might not seem like particularly "heroic" traits — or add up to anything remotely resembling the classic hero myth. Rather, the resulting image of the typical Canadian male character is someone steeped in confusion, distrustful of others, potentially dangerous and ultimately subject to the will of the women around him. No wonder we think our guys are wimps. But if we go back to Atwood's last point and think about this man in isolation from other expected notions of masculine power, we can see a lot of "positive" elements in this rather "negative" — or anti-macho — male.

First, because he is ambiguously sexual and subject to the desires of women, he is symbolically in tune with the negative landscape around him. Standing in harmony with nature automatically lends him a power the

conquering male could never hope to have as he spends all his energies effacing the feminine and controlling her "natural" ways. By contrast, the Canadian male can spend his time and energy pursuing more "creative" pursuits himself, such as learning how to sing opera (as Renzo did in *Perfectly Normal*) or perfecting a stand-up routine (as Neville did in *Love Come Down*) or playing trumpet (like Pokey Jones in *Highway 61*).

In some cases, there is such a desire to commune with nature that the male comes up with absurd creative concepts, such as the grizzly-proof suit we see in the NFB documentary, *Project Grizzly*. The suit's a great idea, but it inevitably proves to be too cumbersome to be of any pragmatic use in the proverbial bush. This brings to mind another interesting element in the treatment of the male identity in Canadian film: if a man is trying to assume classical heroic proportions in the American mould, he is generally rendered ridiculous, if not completely insane. Again, this suggests that we know who we are, and it has little in common with the mythology we've been trained to assimilate through the Hollywood model. The Canadian man is more of a thinker than a doer, and as men are constantly referred to as slaves to their sex organ, the Canadian male's distinct separation from his reproductive system can be seen as nothing but a psychic liberation.

Director Reg Harkema hit the nail on the proverbial head when he talked about the process of making *A Girl is a Girl*: "When I started making *A Girl is a Girl*, I had no idea I was formulating a male response to evolving female sexuality, but that's kind of what happened. Men have been trapped by these historical and corporate ideas about women, as typified by fashion-magazine images. We actually bought into it, but now women are saying 'Fuck you, buddy!' And thank God. None of it is real … Unfortunately, a lot of men never get over that. And that's too bad because they are missing so much of what relationships are all about — two people trying to understand each other."[13]

Long-necks vs. Stubbies

In a typical Freudian analysis, the Canadian male's acceptance of a female point of view would be interpreted as "our men have no balls — or are castrated" because they do not priapically assert themselves. They are not eager to fill every vessel with a bit of themselves. In this analysis, the man would be marked by an unmistakable feminine edge. Once again, since the dominant culture in this society has determined that muscle cars, big tall skyscrapers, monster trucks, long-necked Buds, cigars, baseball bats and Fender Stratocasters are the Biggy Meal du jour, it's not surprising that the Canadian male has been the object of derision among men who identify more with an American way of thinking — and believe in the phallo-nationalist model. It's also not surprising that Egoyan is often criticized for his "cold," "passive" characters — after all, the more they are in harmony with the bleak, frigid landscape that surrounds them, the more they assume a feminine perspective.

If we take the Freudian analysis a bit further, then we can say the cold has shrunk our collective manhood into the proportions of a squirrel. Is this a bad thing? Only if you're intent on having sex in the snow or waving

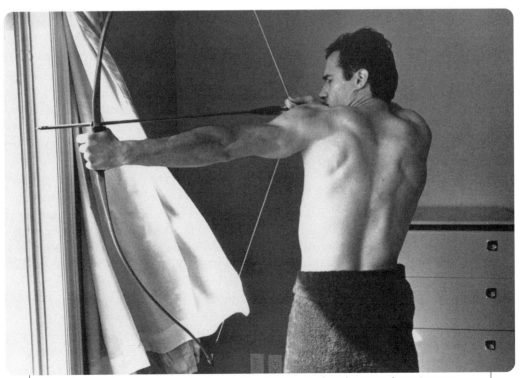

The macho hunter image is revised in Atom Egoyan's *The Adjuster* (1992), where Elias Koteas plays an insurance adjuster who draws his shaft at the nothingness that surrounds him — finding only a billboard that advertises his abandoned subdivision as a suitable target for his pointed actions. ALLIANCE ATLANTIS

yourself around like a flagpole. Most of us aren't. What's so wrong with showing that we are, indeed, subject to the forces of nature? When it gets cold, the thing shrinks, and so the man must either accept the fact and think of something other than his member, or make a fire. This places us in stark contrast to the likes of the sexually omnipotent James Bond, who can rescue a rich heiress from an avalanche one minute and have sex with her the next. As sexual realists, we clearly don't buy into that manufactured nonsense. We are only too well aware of nature's overwhelming force, which I think makes us more honest, more apt to survive, and far more open to the forces of creativity as they are embodied by nature herself.

One of my favourite barometers of manhood is the hunt motif. The traditional domain of men, and only men, the hunt is one of the most primitive, and therefore immediately telling, measures of manhood. Almost every man in American film is a hunter of some sort: he walks around with a gun, and shoots at the people who threaten his survival. In Canadian film, it's difficult to even find a gun, and when you do, its manly function is rendered absurd. Take the case of Noah Render (Elias Koteas), the title character in *The Adjuster*, who shoots his quiver of arrows into a giant billboard of a nuclear family at the entrance to his barren housing development. Another image can be seen in Jean-Claude Lauzon's *Night Zoo*, where the son and father reconcile over their last great adventure by breaking into the zoo and shooting a caged elephant. Certainly there isn't much of a macho challenge in killing an animal behind bars, but you can see other men do something similar in *Highway 61*, when the rock star character played by Art Bergmann decides to release a chicken in the mansion and issues

revolvers to all his guests. While other cultures may see the indoor chicken hunt as a manly activity, it's clear that McKellar has deflated the thick, hard, gun-barrel aesthetic with the prick of a small needle.

Copulation

How do these dissections of the Canadian female and the Canadian male translate into screen sex? Metaphorically, of course. Despite our desire to talk about sex and our unending fascination with exploring the most rugged of sexual terrains, we don't actually show the sexual act as much as most American films do. We are all familiar with the Hollywood drill: the saccharine strains of some Kenny G-soundalike generally flare up for the foreplay, settle into a slow rhythm, then explode in a tinny solo at the climax. The images are usually bathed in orange and red gels and the actors' body parts are shot in close-up isolation — a saliva-covered lip, the dart of a tongue, a clenched hand grabbing at the sheets in ecstasy. Clearly this is done to make the scenes look as sexy and as graphic as possible without risking an Adult, or NC-17 rating, but the final effect is something like watching sex in an abattoir: body part by body part.

Canadian sex is just as fragmented, but because it's used mostly for symbolic and not sensationalist purposes, the fragmentation takes place beneath the surface. Take *In Praise of Older Women* (1978) as a case in point. This scandalous Robert Lantos project is cleary one of the most graphically sexual films to emerge from Canada. It features Tom Berenger making love to a variety of willing women (played by the likes of Karen Black and Helen Shaver). There are plenty of wide shots and full frontal nudity, and the sex itself is rather "normal." There is nothing kinky about this coitus, but the lack of real emotional intimacy and a sense of commitment, between Berenger and his coterie of female admiriers is our hero's main struggle. He loves sex, but he's also a romantic searching for the one woman who will complete him — an older woman and mother figure who will hold him close to her bosom and relieve his existential angst.

Once *In Praise of Older Women* opened the floodgates, more sexual imagery poured through the system, seeping up from the storm drains and the kitchen sink — just like the poo-shaped parasite in *Shivers* (1975), which crawled through the pipes of a Montreal apartment building a few years earlier and entered a variety of hosts, boosting their libidos to Bacchanal extremes. In *Shivers* and in *In Praise of Older Women* — as in just about every film worth mentioning — the woman is in control of the union. Cronenberg's other films also give the women the dominant role. Check out the psycho ex-wife figure in *The Brood*, who transforms into a morbid she-wolf, spawning litters of deformed children that she pulls from her loins and licks in front of her horrified ex-husband, or the mind-screwing game developer Allegra Geller in *eXistenZ*, who ensures the male, Pikul, is penetrated at the base of his spine with her very own version of reality. Even the gender-bending in *M. Butterfly* gives the "female" the dominant role as the French attaché (Jeremy Irons) surrenders to her "feminine" powers, even though she is actually a man. Once again, we have gender confusion, anima-animus imbalance and a potent female.

Better Than Chocolate (1999): Christina Cox and Karyn Dwyer don't look much like Johnny Depp and Juliette Binoche, but sex, chocolate and taboo make for a rich mix of subject matter in this Anne Wheeler feature about two girls in love.
ANNE WHEELER

It only follows logically then that if we ever see images of the act, the woman is usually on top. In Don McKellar's Canadian Film Centre short, *Blue*, he cuts between an older woman reminiscing about her days as a blue movie star and an uptight, mild-mannered carpet-store owner (David Cronenberg) addicted to hardcore pornography. The older woman talks about how much "fun" she had acting the femme fatale, but she also says "my breasts hung better naturally, so I always tried to get on top." In the end, we find out the two are aunt and nephew, but neither one has a clue about the other's hidden sex life — affirming elements of fragmentation and repressed sexuality. More women on top can be seen in *Kissed*, where we watch Molly Parker mount several stiffs on the embalmer's table, or *Lulu*, where we watch the depressed Vietnamese mail-order bride attempt to make her impotent husband hard by rolling around on top of him — without success. Even Arsinée Khanjian's character in *The Adjuster* assumes a dominant position with regards to male sexuality when she bootlegs the porn films she is supposed to censor, then brings them home to her sister — essentially subverting "the institution" of the film classification office, as well as regaining the lost power of the gaze when she refilms the images of the "victimized" women in the porn industry with her very own camera.

Taping porn, mounting dead bodies, rolling around on flaccid male members: these are not what one might call images of healthy coupling. Something is broken in the symbolic bedroom of the nation: We can't seem to come together.

Things look different in the homosexual arena. There, both partners tend to share an equal sexual footing without necessarily buying into and following the heterosexual pattern. In the case of the gay male couple in *Lilies*, or the lesbian couple in *Better Than Chocolate*, there's a lot of rolling around and role-playing, but there's no dominant sexual partner. Ironically — and let's face it, we're good at irony — the gay sex tends to be "healthier" psychically than the heterosexual unions we see in Canadian film – perhaps because it doesn't demand an embrace of "other." Gay sex unites sameness — only on the outskirts of the mainstream perspective. We'll bring the binoculars to the queer peephole later on, but for now, we'll press our face to the fishbowl of the dominant, heterosexual society for the real freak show and see that almost all straight sex in Canadian film is downright bent.

Procreation Denied

As the inventory shows, the attempt at sexual union in Canadian film is undermined, either through endemic disease or through an act of will. As a result, there is a peculiar lack of progeny in a lot of Canadian film. Understanding why the procreative act is denied usually says a lot about a relationship, so we can expect it also says something about our Canadian psyche. So let's return to Jung — who understood the psyche and divided it into two opposing, but linked, halves. We see men and women struggling to understand each other: anima and animus desperate for mutual recognition. In Jungian terms, dysfunctional heterosexual unions indicate a symbolic schism between male and female traits within the self. The non-visible, and often repressed, female traits within a man (anima) are all about intuition, superstition, irrational thought and emotion. If the anima is repressed or denied, she can quickly turn into a femme fatale — a demon of death who threatens to undermine all that hard, cerebral work the man has put into creating his reality. A perfect example of the gender imbalance can be seen in Cronenberg's *Naked Lunch*, where the cerebral Dr. Benway (Roy Scheider) is revealed as a woman, Fadela, who peels off her breasts and face to show her hairy, man's chest.

In Jung's theory, if a man fails to meet the challenges posed by his anima, he'll be in for big trouble: "These anima moods cause a sort of dullness, a fear of disease, of impotence, or of accidents. The whole of life takes on a sad and oppressive aspect."[14] Hmmm. Accidents, lethargy, alienation, gender confusion, erectile dysfunction? Thus far, it describes the Canadian male in film perfectly.

The animus within the woman works in much the same way: it represents typically male characteristics such as reason, conviction and authority. Should the woman choose to deny her inherent masculinity, then she too will find herself facing down a death demon — a dark, dangerous stranger who will either rob her, rape her, kill her — or all three. "A strange passivity and paralysis of all feeling, or a deep insecurity that can lead almost to a sense of nullity, may sometimes be the result of an unconscious animus opinion."[15]

Once again, we can see a parallel between the way people see Canadian film and the way Jung describes the effects of an animus imbalance.

Given that we are a country steeped in historic tension between our two founding European cultures, between Upper and Lower Canada, evidence of psychic tension should come as no surprise. Our collective imagination has stunted any chance at mundane, missionary-style sexual union. As a result, we have a history of film that offers little in the way of a future. The children in Canadian film who are born, are often killed off (*The Sweet Hereafter*) or are declared missing (*The Five*

An Inventory of Sexual Dysfunction in Canadian Film

Necrophilia: The most famous example is Lynne Stopkewich's *Kissed*, where a young woman can only find sexual fulfillment with dead bodies.

Incest: In *Cold Comfort*, Maury Chaykin and Margaret Langrick play out a sexually charged father-daughter relationship. In *The Sweet Hereafter*, Sarah Polley and Tom McCamus play another father-daughter duo with a sexual history. While it's not incest, per se, the father in *Le Confessional* has sexual relations with his wife and her sister.

Impotence: In *Lulu*, Lucky is the physically impotent husband of a mail-order bride. In *Last Night*, Patrick (Don McKellar) is a man who suffers from mental impotence because he refuses to have sex on his last night on Earth because he doesn't want to have "bad sex" and have it be the last thing he remembers. In *Possible Worlds*, George appears unable to function sexually, but he can touch his lover in a way she remembers.

Asexuality: In *Thirty Two Short Films About Glenn Gould* we are led to believe that Gould was not sexually active at all, while most characters simply decline sex if offered.

Sadomasochism: Lynne Stopkewich returns to the land of sexual dysfunction in *Suspicious River*, where Molly Parker revels in regular beatings from anonymous sexual partners. In Denys Arcand's *Le Declin de l'empire américain* we have a professor engaging in S&M sex acts with her biker boyfriend.

Grotesque Fetishes: See any David Cronenberg movie, from *Videodrome* (where James Woods is burdened with a VCR in his chest cavity) to *Crash*, where his characters get off on scar tissue.

Sexual Self-destruction: Once again, we could look at *Crash*, where two characters see the sexual impulse and driving dangerously as interchangeable exercises. *Maelström*, where Bibi has anonymous sex to escape the guilt she has over the abortion and the hit-and-run.

Physical Sexual Deformity: Geneviève Bujold has two vaginas in *Dead Ringers*, which renders her unable to conceive.

Senses) or are aborted before they become children at all (*Nô*, *Parsley Days, Maelström*). If we relate this to the gap theory, then we can see "missing children" as a recurring motif symbolic of what could be seen as a latent or subconscious desire for unity.

We can see a concrete translation of this idea in Robert Lepage's award-winning feature, *Nô*. The film opens with, Sophie (Anne-Marie Cadieux), a Quebec actress at the Osaka World's Fair, getting the news that she's pregnant from a doctor (with her best friend, a blind Japanese translator). Lost and confused about what to do, she calls her partner Michel in Montreal. It's four o'clock in the morning and he's tired. It's also October, 1970, and just as Sophie is about to uncork the news to Michel, there's a banging on the door of Michel's basement apartment. It's his buddies — FLQ boys on the lam. Michel hangs up the phone. Sophie sits in her Japanese cubicle of a hotel room, oozing frustration. Sophie's stress about the growing fetus is mirrored by larger, external issues such as the long-term future of Michel and Sophie's relationship and the future of the nation as a whole. The fetus represents a world of possibilities, but it also symbolizes a potentially unwanted occupation of someone's private space — like a bunch of soldiers with guns in their hands standing on the street corners of your hometown. The film ends on a decidedly ambiguous note as Lepage fast-forwards to the 1980 referendum, when the people of Quebec were asked whether they wanted to remain in Confederation or opt for a symbolic divorce. The results were far from conclusive, and simply led to more referenda — and more relationship tension — down the road.

Gay Sex

"I like the politicalness of film. I think sex is great. I don't know why people get upset about sex with two women. Sex is a wonderful thing. Love is not a relationship between two people, it's a state of being. I aspire to being in a loving state." —Anne Wheeler

For all the dysfunction on the straight sex front, things look different when we look at the manner in which homosexual unions are portrayed on screen. Let's consider a few of the many relatively positive depictions of gay sex in Canadian film:

Outrageous!: This cutting-edge 1977 movie starring female impersonator Craig Russell features a psychotic (Liza McLaren) who leaves a mental institution to live with her gay hairdresser friend. The two outsiders find meaning and companionship together, which proves to have a positive, if temporary, anti-psychotic effect.

Better Than Chocolate: Anne Wheeler's film shows us two young, good-looking women who fall in love and have great sex. The sex is not destructive, despite one character's latent guilt and fear of disclosure. In fact, in this film (which is one of a few films to use nudity in an erotic way), the women find their creative powers are enhanced by the union, as we can see in the sex scene that has them painting each other with chocolate and rolling around on blank canvases.

The Hanging Garden and **Beefcake:** In the first feature from Thom Fitzgerald, *The Hanging Garden*, he shows us the path to accepting a gay identity as he brings a gay man home, where he encounters the ghost of his former, dysfunctional self. This film not only has a

The Hanging Garden (1997): Chris Leavins and Troy Vienotte play out and closeted versions of the same character in Thom Fitzgerald's award-winning movie that wrestles with issues of personal identity and the importance of going home to touch your roots. ALLIANCE ATLANTIS AND TRIPTYCH

happy ending, it's one of the few Canadian films that ends on a note of closure and healing. In his second film, *Beefcake*, Fitzgerald dramatizes the life of an early beefcake photographer in the fifties. The film feels really twisted in the way it makes the boys into sex slaves exploited by older men, but the sex itself is happy, escapist and altogether jubilant. They are proud gay men in a world that refuses to even acknowledge homosexuality as a reality in the world of muscle-building.

I've Heard the Mermaids Singing and When Night Is Falling:
In Patricia Rozema's first film, *I've Heard the Mermaids Singing*, Polly (Sheila McCarthy) is an idiot-savant artist who develops a crush on a gallery owner (Paule Baillargeon) because she believes the curator knows the inner secrets of art. When she discovers the gallery owner has her own lesbian lover (Anne-Marie MacDonald), she feels the pain of jealousy ... but as destructive as the emotion is, it eventually leads to a catharsis and bonding between the three women. Similar images of "good sex" — or at least sexy sex — can be found in Rozema's *When Night Is Falling*.

Lilies:
John Greyson's adaptation of Michel Marc Bouchard's Quebecois play, *Lilies*, shows us a gay couple who fulfill the full romantic cycle: they fall in love as children, fight for their love together as teens, then tragically lose each other at the hands of a jealous peer

Lilies (1996): Danny Gilmore and Jason Cadieux burn up the screen as Vallier and Simon in John Greyson's adaptation of Michel Marc Bouchard's play about a group of prisoners who help a friend avenge the death of a gay lover.
ALLIANCE ATLANTIS AND TRIPTYCH

— who is so threatened by their devotion and commitment that he destroys one of the them in a fire and leaves the other to rot in prison, wrongly incarcerated for the death of his true love. It might not have a happy ending, but the relationship between the two men is healthy and sincere, affirming all the positive elements of love and bonding. Gender, in this case, is a universal because all the parts are played by men — even those of the women — because the film is set in a prison, where the inmates put on a play to force the aging criminal (now a priest) to confess his guilt.

Being at Home with Claude: As it opens with the corpse of a murdered gay lover, this Jean Beaudin effort appears to break the "positive image" rule, but for all the pain and homicidal misery in the movie, there is no doubt how

much the two men love each other. They are passionate about their affections. They are connected in ways far beyond the surface, and it's their connection, not their difference, that finally leads to the Romeo and Juliet ending.

There are other postive examples of gay sex to be found in Canadian cinema, and while they all deal with the same Samsonite luggage of repression and self-loathing, they tend to assert a more "positive" sense of self-worth in the final frames. Why gay sex gets a better shake than straight sex should be easy to explain at this point because it reaffirms, symbolically, what we've already come to understand about the larger systems at work in Canadian cinema — particularly our attempts to reconcile all the varying manifestations of "other" that occur in Canadian society at large.

With difference all around us, alienating us at every turn, isn't it only natural to gravitate to sameness?

In Jung's mind, the real reflection of self could be found in a dream character of the same gender. "It is particularly in contacts with other people of the same sex that one stumbles over both one's own shadow and those of other people. Although we do see the shadow in a person of the opposite sex, we are usually much less annoyed by it."[16] In other words, a homosexual encounter in a dream is not a homosexual encounter at all, but a confrontation, and potential reconciliation with the repressed shadow self ... or, in the case of Canadian film, a confrontation and eventual reconciliation of repressed notions of identity.

In Rozema's *I've Heard the Mermaids Singing*, we can take the symbolism to a surface level because one woman is Québécoise, the other is Ontario Anglo. On the symbolic level, we can see the frequency and relative health of homosexual couplings as a sign of psychic healing, because it reflects an understanding of selfhood — and we all know we can't love someone else until we've learned to love ourselves, eh?

PROFILE

Patricia Rozema

Born 1958 — Sarnia, Ontario

© Viliam

Though she had never seen a movie until she turned 16, Patricia Rozema entered the Canadian film scene with a big bang — and spawned new, creatively charged life amid the once-barren landscape of Canadian film. The film was *I've Heard the Mermaids Singing*, a 1989 release that was loosely based on the filmmaker's personal history.

Raised in a traditional Calvinist home under the watchful eye of her Dutch parents, Rozema learned about the emancipatory powers of the imagination at a young age. While she wasn't allowed to watch TV or movies, the young Rozema delighted in drama class and went to theatre camp. When she turned 16, Rozema saw her first movie — *The Exorcist*. The movie made an impression: Rozema had nightmares for weeks, and she eventually rebelled against the church — and all authority figures — that came between her and her heart's desire.

When she left home to study, Rozema started sampling art-house fare and began to understand the whole fascination with film. "Movies taught me that you can empathize with almost anyone," says Rozema. "Whether it's Fanny [in *Mansfield Park*] or Polly [in *I've Heard the Mermaids Singing*], I've tried to give people a sense of what it would be like to walk a few steps in someone else's shoes ... someone they may not even notice otherwise. Maybe it's the remnants of my religious upbringing, but I do try and insert a sense of social justice into the work ... for instance, to me, *Mansfield Park* is a story about servitude and slavery. Other people may have a problem with that, but that's how I read the book and so that's how I shot the movie," she says.

After graduating from Calvin College in Michigan with a degree in English and philosophy and a minor in journalism, Rozema headed out to do a round of practicums in Chicago and New York, then aggressively launched herself at the CBC — which was prepping a new magazine-format news show called *The Journal*. "It's kind of obnoxious really, but I have no shame if I want something," she said in an interview with Janis Cole and Holly Dale in the book *Calling the Shots* (1993, Quarry Press). Rozema's shameless self-promotion paid off. She got a job with *The Journal* and began working at the CBC broadcast centre in Toronto. Emotionally pinned by journalism's rigorous pursuit of facts, Rozema spent her spare time writing scripts — most of which were declined for development funds. When the cutbacks came to the CBC (as they do almost every year), *The Journal*'s budget was slashed and Rozema was turfed. Left to lick her wounds, she continued writing and eventually landed some cash to make her first short, *Passion — A Letter in 16mm*. The film won a Silver Plaque at the Chicago International Film Festival and Rozema was off to the cinematic races. *Passion* was the story of a successful career woman, and the minute she finished it,

Rozema knew she wanted her next project to focus on professional failure — a typically Canadian underdog. With the character of Polly taking shape in her mind, Rozema started working on the script for *I've Heard the Mermaids Singing* while working as a third AD (assistant director) on David Cronenberg's *The Fly*. When Cronenberg was done, Rozema fleshed out her script (then called *Oh, The Things I've Seen*) and in 1986, she and a former Xerox administrator named Alexandra Raffé applied to the newly created Ontario Film Development Corporation for production financing. Even though the script was seen as "precious" by the paper-pushers, the women got their cash and with just $362,109 Rozema and Raffé (co-producer) set to work. Neither woman had made a feature film, but they were given free rein to do whatever they pleased, which explains — in large part — the film's complete lack of institutional baggage, and its potent imagination.

No one expected the film to make much of a ripple, let alone a splash, but when Rozema was invited to screen her debut feature at the Directors' Fortnight at Cannes, everyone in Canada took notice. The standing ovation supposedly lasted more than six minutes — which is rare for any film in France that does not star Jerry Lewis or have Celine Dion on the soundtrack. Rozema was an overnight sensation, but just when it looked as though life couldn't get any better, her next film flopped. *White Room* (1990) was a complex, meditative piece about a young man experiencing a psychotic break. Norm (Maurice Godin) is trapped between two worlds: the one in his head, and the one out there — in the "real" world. After witnessing the murder of a rock diva, Norm suffers from incredible bouts of survival guilt. Hoping to purge his baggage, he goes to the funeral and meets a woman in black (Kate Nelligan), who may or may not hold the key to the mystery. Rozema describes Nelligan's character as another Canadian archetype: someone who has "much to offer, yet doesn't dare say it."

Made for a little over $1 million, *White Room* was one of the most expensive publicly funded films ever made in Canada. When it failed to light a fire at the box office, Rozema's self-confidence spiralled downward. From the top of the pops to the bottom of the barrel in just three years, Rozema began a whole new round of soul-searching and threw herself into a collaborative project: *Montreal vu par ...* (1992), a series of short films celebrating Montreal's 350th anniversary. One of two Anglo directors (the other being Atom Egoyan), Rozema offered up *Desperanto*, a vignette that featured Sheila McCarthy as an uptight Toronto housewife who visits Montreal and crashes a fancy Francophone party — only to make a complete ass of herself. The title's play on the word "Esperanto," the universal language that never quite took off, offers a clue to the film's deeper meaning as Rozema explores issues of language, culture and identity with a tourist's wanderlust.

After the Montreal project, Rozema took a breather and returned to lesbian themes for her next film, *When Night Is Falling* (1995), the story of a classical mythology professor at a Christian college who falls for a female circus performer. The film did well on the arthouse and gay and lesbian circuit, and Rozema was back in the pink. Turning her attention to music, she made two films with classical themes: *Bach Cello Suite #6* and the collective TV reel, *Yo-Yo Ma Inspired by Bach* (which also featured segments from Atom Egoyan, Niv Fichman, François Girard, Kevin McMahon and Barbara Willis Sweete). The

latter won Rozema an Emmy Award in 1997 and after a decade of see-sawing on the Canadian culture meter, Rozema was finally a fish swimming in the big pond.

After sizing up her many offers, Rozema's next film was truly international in scope: an adaptation of Jane Austen's *Mansfield Park*, produced in part by The Arts Council of England and her old pals from her glory days in Cannes, Bob and Harvey Weinstein — the brothers behind Miramax who bought *I've Heard the Mermaids Singing* after it premiered at Cannes. A "hybrid" of a film that combines elements of magic realism alongside perfectly rendered pieces of period drama, *Mansfield Park* reinterpreted the classic work and made the heroine Fanny Price a loose reflection of Austen's own persona.

"I think I respected the spirit of the book and its vital writing style, not to mention the majority of the plot. But no movie is ever going to be a perfect adaptation of a book — they are so different. You're changing forms and, as a result, you have to change the ingredients. I had to cut certain things and flesh out others. To do that, I could only rely on my own gut feeling about what I thought the book was about," she says.

Rozema followed up *Mansfield Park* with another adaptation, Samuel Beckett's *Happy Days*, which she made for Irish television, and the short film, *This Might Be Good*, which she completed as part of the Toronto International Film Festival's Preludes series.

FILMOGRAPHY: *Passion: A Letter in 16mm* (1985) | *I've Heard the Mermaids Singing* (1987) | *White Room* (1990) | *Montréal vu par ...* (1991) | *When Night Is Falling* (1995) | *Bach Cello Suite #6: Six Gestures* (1997) | *Yo-Yo Ma Inspired by Bach* (1997) | *Mansfield Park* (1999) | *Happy Days* (2000) | *This Might Be Good* (2000)

John Greyson

Born 1960 – Nelson, British Columbia

ALLIANCE ATLANTIS

He's here. He's queer. He's John Greyson — one of the most courageous visionaries to spring from our frozen loins since the late, great Claude Jutra threw himself into the abyss of *Surfacing*. From his audacious debut, *Zero Patience*, which attempted to unravel a knotty history of prejudice and fear in the wake of the AIDS epidemic, to *Uncut*, his low-budget experimental look at Pierre Trudeau and the rite of circumcision, Greyson has never shied away from hot topics. If anything, the B.C.-born filmmaker seems to have a heat-seeking flare for making films that consciously challenge the status quo.

"I can get very angry about things," Greyson said shortly after *Zero Patience* premiered at the Toronto International Film Festival in 1993. "I look for ways to channel that anger in the most creative way I can. But there is a lot to be angry about, so I take pot-shots when I can, like the jabs at the media in *Zero Patience*. The rest of the time I try to find a way of looking at the problem from a different perspective so I can understand it all a bit better."

In *Zero Patience*, for instance, Greyson looked at the blame-game. When a gay flight attendant was labelled as "patient zero" for his alleged role in the spread of AIDS, Greyson looked at the stubby finger of blame and traced it back through history, where 19th-century scientists tried to figure out the mystery of life by dissecting everything to the last cell, while any hint of sexuality was buried under several bolts of heavy cloth.

"When you're dealing with a pressing social issue where death intrudes all the time, it's hard to maintain personal focus. There's a lot of rich material, but it's often hard to find the distance you need just to make the movie — otherwise you're in creative paralysis ... In the end, I hope the tone of the film is strong, I just hope it doesn't feel like one long polemic because AIDS has touched a lot of people, and it deserves a human treatment."

Greyson, who developed the script for *Zero Patience* as part of his stint at the Canadian Film Centre, says his compassion and conviction is part of his Canadian identity. "I think Canada is a very socially conscious country — or at least we like to imagine ourselves that way — so social awareness and identity are two things that go hand in hand for me."

After his parents moved from Nelson, British Columbia to London, Ontario, Greyson gravitated to the fringe and saw himself as an outsider — an artist in embryo. When an art teacher introduced him to performance art and video cameras, Greyson knew he wanted to make movies because it involved so many different types of creation: visuals, the written word, music, et cetera. In 1978, Greyson moved to Toronto and explored his sexuality, which lead to his coming out to his parents in 1980.

"I like writing because it's the most creative part of the process, but I also like directing too because it's craft oriented and you get to work with different people." Greyson said after the release of *Uncut* in 1997. Half the time just getting a project to the shooting stage is an act of creation in itself because it is so hard to make a movie in this country, and things aren't getting any easier. It seems like things were just taking off, and then it all fell apart. Canadian films still only represent two percent of Canadian screen time, and we're all fighting for that two percent. I think if we make the films available Canadians will see them, but first we have to get over our prejudice about Canadian film. We have this idea that Canadian films are going to suck. For some reason, we just never became big fans of our own culture — which really sucks, because we make films for adults, where America makes films for 14-year-old boys."

Greyson says *Lilies* is a perfect example of a film that would be hard to make in the United States because of its adult themes. The story of a gay prisoner who confronts an aging bishop about a past tragedy, *Lilies* featured an entire cast of men — many in drag — exchanging romantic glances and sizzling kisses. "*Lilies* was a film I made for other artists. It was all about how people create things — their past, a play, themselves — and that creative energy is what I really wanted to bring to the screen. I loved how it didn't move in a straight line — Michel Marc wrote a thoroughly bent play, and that's what attracted me to it in the first place."

Greyson says he's happy and proud and living an "out" lifestyle, but he still marvels at how homosexuality has the ability to ruffle so many feathers. "When I was at the Film Centre in 1990, there was this whole debate about outing people, and whether it was fair or not. There was also concern about censorship ... and that's how I got the idea for *Uncut*. Somehow Trudeau and circumcision seemed like a natural fit," he says in a perfect deadpan.

"In the end, it's all about identity — and feeling comfortable to be yourself, and expressing yourself."

Another film Greyson envisioned during his stay at the Canadian Film Centre (for advanced film production) was *The Making of Monsters*, a story based on the real beating death of a Toronto librarian in High Park in 1985. The film was seen as a surreal revelation on the realist Canadian film front for its portrayal of Bertolt Brecht as a catfish, but was pulled from circulation after the Brecht Estate found the portrayal of the late leftist playwright unflattering.

The Law of Enclosures was a different kind of tragedy, says Greyson. "It's about the everyday kind of tragedy, when relationships end." While the themes were familiar, Greyson took a slightly different approach to the narrative because it was written by American novelist Dale Peck. "I couldn't just hijack the text and say, okay, this is what the movie is about. The book was so beautifully written and the characters were treated with such sensitivity that I wanted to bring all the feelings to the screen without over-sentimentalizing the drama. So I tried to find ways where I could introduce tension within the frame — in the composition, in the landscape, so I didn't have to push the characters into these false moments. I mean, there are a lot of differences between the book and the movie. In the book, Bea (played in the film by Sarah Polley and Diane Ladd) is a big-boned gal with dark hair — and clearly, Sarah is not that person. Every change I made, I talked over with Dale, who I can't say enough good things about."

The story of a middle-class couple on the first and last day of their relationship, *The Law of Enclosures* covers an entire lifetime in the space of a few hours — but not compressed through the magic of moviemaking.

Instead, the movie unspools through a series of recollections that highlight where these people were in their youth, and where they are now, as mature adults.

"There was a sense of loss in the book that I found really touching. It's about what happens to love — and searching for something that just isn't there any more. In a way, it reminded me of a film I love: *The Sweet Hereafter*. I really loved the way Atom conveyed that sense of loss without getting maudlin. In a way he showed me the road I wanted to take with *The Law of Enclosures*."

Shot in four weeks for $2.2 million, *The Law of Enclosures* is set in Sarnia, Ontario — the surreal industrial city that sits across the border from the United States. "I liked the border element, because it introduces this idea of two sides — two perspectives, which is what the whole story is about. Also, Bea and Hank are spoon-fed everything. I think our relationship to the mass media, and particularly the American mass media, is very similar. We don't question enough of what we take in," he says. "Besides, there's something about Sarnia that resonates with people — even people who've never been there — because it's so industrial."

As for the shifts in character, Greyson says he changed the way his characters fight in the movie. "In the book, the fights are awful and they go on and on. It would have been a really loud and obnoxious film if we'd translated the fights to the screen the way they were written. In the end, we found that silence was a far better way of communicating the tension ... because really, the story is about the effort they didn't make to keep the relationship going," says Greyson. "The film focuses on the first and last day, so it ends up having this palindrome structure, which is very much like the film — so even if the novel is American, I think the film is very Canadian because it doesn't show you everything. It's about the things you don't see, the things we don't do, and how those lost efforts lead to the end of love."

FILMOGRAPHY: *The Perils of Pedagogy* (1984) | *Kipling Meets the Cowboy* (1985) | *The Jungle Boy* (1985) | *Moscow Does Not Believe in Queers* (1986) | *A Moffie Called Simon* (1987) | *The Making of Monsters* (1991) | *Urinal* (1988) | *Zero Patience* (1993) | *Lilies* (1996) | *Uncut* (1997) | *The Law of Enclosures* (2000)

CHAPTER SEVEN

Crashing Into the Language Barrier

THE POLITICS OF WORDS

We've seen a history of frustrated attempts at physical union in Canadian film. Now we'll turn our attention to the more abstract concept of political unity, and see how our desire for psychic integration often runs up against the language barrier.

Up to this point, I've not only desegregated English and French cinematic "traditions," but steered away from using politics as a blade to dissect Canadian film. I've avoided a head-on encounter with the "p" word because part of me is just plain chicken to enter a circular debate that makes everyone look petty and arrogant. Any discussion of Canadian politics generally devolves into a Confederation tug-of-war, where we all take sides and decide if the country is a legitimate nation made up of a diverse group of peoples, or a giant lie propagated by morally bankrupt businessmen looking to advance their own careers, and is now little more than a make-work project for the Department of Canadian Heritage — which is out to crush Quebec sovereignty once and for all. Zzzzzzzz.

The rest of it has to do with the relative paucity of political film in the Canadian film closet — especially outside Quebec. Even in Quebec, the overt political film was more of a 1970s phenomenon than a running theme.

Inspired and empowered by their rebellion against the institutions of the Catholic church and the Anglo-centric Canadian government in the wake of the Quiet Revolution, we witnessed an entire generation of young Quebecers including Gilles Carle, Claude Jutra,

Jean-Claude Lord and Michel Brault pick up movie cameras and recreate themselves and their reality. We can see this conscious affirmation of self in everything from the ethnographic, proto-separatist tone of movies such as *Les Raquetteurs* (1958), by Gilles Groulx and Michel Brault, *Rose et Landry* (1963) by Jacques Godbout, *Pour la suite du monde* (1963) by Pierre Perrault and Brault, *On est au coton* (1970) and *Gina* (1974-75) from Denys Arcand, to the overt anti-Confederation, pro-Quebec stance of films such as Fernand Dansereau's *Faut aller parmi le monde pour le savoir* (1971), Jean-Claude Labrecque's *Les Smattes* (1972), Lord's *Bingo* (1973-74) and Brault's *Les Ordres* (1974).

The evolution of awareness and directorial presence in these films moves according to the same model we pinned down in the "First Takes" chapter: Objective institutional documentary; personal or revolutionary documentary; docudrama; realist auteur-driven narrative; non-realist auteur-driven narrative. As we saw in "Probing the Negative," this filmic evolution mirrors a rise in self-awareness and creative emancipation as it sets in motion a loop of identification whereby the people create images of who they are, which in turn informs later generations of where they came from.

English Canada missed out on a great deal of this revolutionary thinking — at least on the surface. You can barely find a reel of political stories on the big screen of English-Canadian cinema. Yes, there have been a few small screen

Claude Jutra (1930–1986): The creator of the realist narrative *Mon Oncle Antoine*, Jutra declined the Order of Canada as a separatist gesture.
PHOTO LIBRARY OF THE NATIONAL FILM BOARD OF CANADA

signposts, thanks in part to the efforts of the atrophying, but still vital, CBC, which has given us stories about pivotal political figures such as *Riel* and the recent made-for-TV project, *Canada: A People's History*, a long-overdue — and sorely earnest — docudrama chronicling the birth of our nation. While I applaud any effort to bring us closer to ourselves, the sad truth is that for the most part, whenever English Canada has tried to give us a sense of "who we are," we end up with anesthetized images of kitsch Canadiana like *Anne of Green Gables*, the story of a sweet, mischievous orphan in Prince Edward Island. The story may have had depth as a novel, but it turned up in one dimension in the TV translation.

Since I've mentioned Anne, it's worth pointing out that orphans are another popular motif in Canadian film, right up there with abortion and Canadian beer. A few examples include: *Anne of Green Gables, Map of the Human Heart, Le Confessionnal, Highway 61, Perfectly Normal, Lilies, I've Heard the Mermaids*

Singing, In God's Country, Night Zoo, Surfacing, Maelström, Suspicious River, Mon Oncle Antoine, The Planet of Junior Brown, Les Muses orphelines — just to name a few. In the context of nationalism, the orphan is a potent image of dislocation and outsiderism, as it suggests the lack of a family structure and a larger identity. The orphan does not belong to a specific group or clan, which mirrors the core of the Canadian identity as a culture steeped in ambiguity and otherness. Most critics see this as a bad thing because it fails to raise a flag to one specific people or nation, and as a result, Canada has been seen as a failure in proactive nation-building. We don't measure up to the phallo-nationalist standard because orphans suggest a break in the patriarchal cycle: son needs to find daddy in order to understand himself. I'm not going to deny that the theory seems to make sense, but it's a pretty colonial way of thinking, and I believe we've moved beyond that as a culture — at least subconsciously.

In recent years, we've been able to subvert some of that orphan Canadiana with darker subplots. One of the most interesting and poignant images of the orphan can be found in Jean-Claude Lauzon's 1992 masterpiece, *Léolo*. The child in this film isn't even a real orphan. Leo Lauzon has a mother and a father, but he can't accept his birthright. He doesn't even accept his French-Canadian identity, preferring to believe he's the son of an Italian fruit-packer who ejaculated into a crate of tomatoes destined for North America. Leo believes his mother fell into this Old World seed and conceived him, suggesting Léolo is a self-created work of fiction made flesh. Fantasy is what nurtures Leo, and pulls him out of the fragmented, dilapidated reality in which he finds himself. The escape is purely internal, but it's an escape nonetheless — and a perfect symbol of our internalized identity and our apparent

The Divine Ryans (1999): Jordan Harvey plays Draper Doyle Ryan, a Montreal Canadiens hockey fanatic who pushes himself into the darkest recesses of his family's closet to find the truth behind the circumstances surrounding his father's death. RED SKY ENTERTAINMENT

inability to articulate our broken psyche in words.

Another subversion of orphan kitsch can be seen in Stephen Reynolds' *The Divine Ryans* (1999), where everything looks perfectly quaint as we watch a young boy indulge in his love of hockey alongside his father in 1960s St. John's, Newfoundland. Everything in Draper Doyle Ryan's life seems to be lifted from a Canadian version of a Norman Rockwell painting, but when his father dies suddenly — and the whole town shuts up about it — all that earnestness we've grown to loathe evaporates in the crucible of truth: Draper's daddy was — egad! — a homosexual. (No wonder we have no Rockwells).

These are just two examples of films that show how notions of identity are buried in silence, but there are many others — and they occur on both sides of the linguistic barrier. And yet, despite the presence of these many shared truths and thematic connections — as a people defined by the landscape and living next to the megabroadcast tower next door — language remains the main source of division between Canadians. Not just between English and French, but between "established Canadians" and "new Canadians," and between First Nations peoples and the mainstream culture that resulted in the sad legacy of residential schools, which separated the people from their culture and their heritage. Whether it's the presence of a bilingual sign in Quebec or the "Asian invasion" that had isolationist British Columbians in a panic about house sizes, the language barrier has played to our ugly, xenophobic paranoia and won every time.

Because it's a politician's trick to play on difference, I've conscientiously resisted the urge to treat English-Canadian and French-Canadian cinema as separate entities. Yes, there are obvious and distinct differences between the two cultures — but the films offer more similarities than difference. Besides, Canada is a nation that is much broader and much more vital than a simple confluence of two stale, muddied Old World rivers. We are changing all the time, and all of us, regardless of place, appear to be moving in the same general direction as we slowly gain the confidence and sense of self to rejoice in who we are.

Nascent Canadian Pride

Over the past few years in my discussions with Canadian directors I've noticed a decidedly more upbeat tone when it comes to the identity question. When I spoke with Don McKellar at the 2000 Toronto International Film Festival, he said he was a proud Canadian and he'd noticed how other film-makers, such as Jewison and Cronenberg, were also blooming with latent pride. This new pride doesn't seem limited to directors; even audiences are starting to respond more positively to Canadian film (and their reflected image on the screen). "It was truly amazing how everyone got it. No matter where we were in the country, people laughed at the same places and had the same reaction as they left: they could all relate," said film-maker Catherine Annau of her film, *Just Watch Me* (1999). An NFB documentary on the children of the Trudeau era, *Just Watch Me* is an insightful and often hilarious study of

language issues in Canada and whether or not Trudeau's dream of a bilingual nation was a good idea or a futile endeavour. What Annau discovers through her filmed testimonials of separatists, federalists, Francophones and Anglophones is a group of people with distinct ideas and well-formed political opinions. There is no unifying stance — no homogenous take on language or overwhelming political conclusion — but all of the interviewees echo similar sensibilities in their ability to see the other side of a situation, their intellect and their sympathetic relationship to the world around them. With so much resonant beauty beneath the surface, focusing on something as mutable as language seems like a deadend in the quest for self.

Languages, like all organic concepts, change and evolve to better meet the expressive needs of a people. English, an amalgam of other languages, has adapted more successfully to change than any other spoken tongue, and as a result of its Darwinist ability to mutate, it has emerged as the dominant language in the world today (even though Mandarin wins in the number-of-speakers category). As linguist-philosopher Noam Chomsky maintains, there is something called the "universal grammar" — an inherent brain structure that allows kids to acquire language in much the same way, regardless of where and what their mother tongue sounds like. All the same, language remains an artifact of culture, and for this reason, it's worth taking some time to understand the linguistic dynamic in this country and how it's shaped the nation so far.

The Silent Self

For all the attempts to fix the problem, the unresolved language issue has taken a toll on the Canadian economy, Canadian politics and

Just Watch Me (1999): The cunning and charismatic Prime Minister Pierre Trudeau dreamed of a nation that was functionally bilingual. In her NFB documentary, *Just Watch Me*, Catherine Annau turns the lens on a generation of Canadians who learned both official languages, with mixed results. PHOTO LIBRARY OF THE NATIONAL FILM BOARD OF CANADA

most importantly, the Canadian psyche. Afraid to speak, our expression of self is stuck somewhere south of the epiglotis — a bolus of identity just waiting to come out.

I was never so aware of this abscess as I was at the funeral of Pierre Trudeau in the fall of 2000. The newspaper I work for, the *Vancouver Sun*, sent me to cover the event as it unfolded in Ottawa, and later, in Trudeau's hometown (and mine), Montreal. As I stood outside the Parliament Buildings alongside thousands of other Canadians, waiting to catch a glimpse of the casket draped in the red Maple Leaf, I found myself sandwiched between a group of university students from Ontario and a family of loyal Liberals. The university students, all young women, said they admired Trudeau for having the courage to dream of a united Canada. They weren't sure

if it was working out so well, but the man gave us an idea of who we were in the world. Trudeau established the Canadian identity abroad, even if he left it in tatters back home. After three hours, the journalistic questions were exhausted. Every time another camera came our way, pointing a fuzzy microphone in our direction, the comments were inevitably the same mix of respect and doubt. There was nothing new to say. Every pundit in the country had offered his two cents on the subject — and none of it was all that revelatory, as feelings were reduced to adjectives. Once again, I felt something was missing. The cameras and the sound bytes were only catching a glimpse of what was actually going on out there in the line-up of mourners. It was frustrating, because as a journalist, you're always looking for the right quote to sum up a situation —

those magic words that will make everything come together. It wasn't happening. Not in Ottawa, and even less so in Montreal, where the coffin arrived midmorning to a small crowd gathered outside central station. Talk about emptiness. After the throngs of people in Ottawa, the turnout in Montreal was so thin. People crossed their arms as the cortege drove by. Some waved. A few people cheered, but this was no joyous homecoming. This was dead silence.

The next day, standing outside Notre Dame Basilica, where the ceremony took place, I began to put the pieces together when one idiot started yelling out inane comments as the guests arrived. Perhaps thinking he was at a college football game instead of a funeral, he offered the crowd a taste of his lame humour. It wasn't the comments that made me cringe as I stood next to him, but the language. He was an Anglo — and he was talking out loud! "Shut up, you moron," was the only thing going through my head. "Shut up. Shut up. Shut up. You're playing up that selfish, stupid Anglo stereotype. Why can't you mourn in silence, like the rest of us, pal?" I was driving myself crazy trying to will him to shut up, but the blabbermouth was unstoppable and completely clueless. I looked around as others rolled their eyes, but none of us said anything. We were too afraid. Besides, what if someone should learn that I, too, am an Anglo? Sure I can pass, but the truth is, I'm a Montreal Anglo — and I carry the shame for centuries of injustice. If I do not speak, I am invisible. I fit in. So I do not speak. Nor, I believe, does anyone else — except for clueless and selfish hooligans.

This fear of expression lies at the core of our identity, and because it's difficult to articulate, people have mistakenly concluded that we have no sense of self. But we do. In fact, throughout that surreal long weekend, I was struck by how much all of us — every single Canadian I spoke to (and there were hundreds) — were feeling deep down inside. We know who we are. We feel it, but we just can't find the words to push it out — so we keep it all inside, where language cannot betray feelings and where politics cannot undermine self. Yet again, it's a process of negative affirmation where what we don't say is far more valuable than what we do.

Filmic Fraternity

This long history of linguistic-based political tension has emerged in different ways in Canadian film, but for the most part, it translates as heroes battling internalized demons, orphans, dead babies, dysfunctional relationships with the externalized "other," and a host of other aberrations.

Thirty years ago, the political terrain was not nearly so ambiguous because it was all reduced to a simple equation: oppressive Anglo culture versus the romanticized Québécois ideal. Most of the French-speaking filmmakers of the era, such as Gilles Carle, Claude Jutra, Pierre Perrault, Michel Brault and the young Denys Arcand were part of a new, politicized artistic community that aimed to give the people a representation of themselves: an outward identity that could establish *Les Québécois* as a people on the world stage.

In his recent book, *Quebec Nationalist Cinema*, Bill Marshall — a Glaswegian French professor who spent time in Quebec and liked it a lot — went to great lengths to make a case for the emergence of a Quebec "nation" through film images. His arguments are not that different from the ones contained here, as he includes a discussion of everything from sexuality to feminism. He makes a lot of very interesting points and I agree with many of them, but he omits one important element in his lengthy treatise: he fails to acknowledge the other half of the Québécois reality — the Canadian twin — and that is English Canada.

Constantly using the United States as the cultural foil — "Quebec cinema and culture have only the American connection to work with, and its presence is more massive, the relationship more unequal."[1] — Marshall places the balance of "other" to the south, when given the bifurcated history of Canada, the other "half" is clearly English Canada. The two linguistic and cultural traditions have emerged in tandem, in lock step, in opposition to each other — providing each with a ready-made identity.

In a sense, the film traditions in this country have emerged much like the twins in First Nations mythology: they began together, contained in the same creative womb at the National Film Board, but began to cleave into separate forces with the birth of the auteur-driven documentary (*cinéma direct*), which permitted the filmmaker to use his own, not the institution's, voice. Like the twins, our two film traditions explore similar thematic terrain — alienation, isolation, a sense of emptiness or being incomplete — but now that they have separated and gone their own ways, there is little chance of ever reuniting the two children, just as there is little hope of uniting the nation without embracing difference over sameness. It's hard to see the similarities because politicians eager to divide and conquer have concentrated on difference instead of similarity, but once you get past the language barrier, certain things begin to resonate across the country. They may not echo the very same concerns, but they follow the same beat. English and French Canada give each other meaning as yin-yang components of the larger whole.

Finding the Meaning in Other — Defining Other

The sex chapter highlighted the opposition between the sexes and elaborated on the sexual dominance of women, who emerged as well-formed, autonomous individuals as a result of their constant opposition to the mainstream, male culture. An enemy gives you a purpose and a whipping boy and makes the struggle for identity all that much easier. "*On ce pose en s'opposant,*" (we stand in opposition, or we place ourselves in opposition) were the words Quebec filmmaker Richard Roy used to describe this particular Canadian-Quebec phenomenon when I interviewed him at the 2000 Vancouver International Film Festival. Roy was there for the international premiere of his new English-language film, *Café Olé*, a romantic comedy about a Chilean refugee and the video store clerk who can't get her out of his mind. Roy, who credits the original quote to Hegel, said the saying was quickly adopted in Quebec as a rallying cry against the forces that oppressed Quebec nationalism, particularly, English Canada.

It is interesting to note that Hegel also said, "World history is not a place for happiness. Periods of happiness are empty pages in history, for they are the periods of harmony, times when the antithesis is missing." The antithesis has never been missing in the Canadian reality. We began as a nation of opposites and we continue to be one, which is why everyone who's ever bothered to look at the big Canadian picture — from Northop Frye to Peter C. Newman — has isolated the idea of dynamic tension as the core of the Canadian experience. Frye put it this way: "The tension between this political sense of unity and the imaginative sense of locality is the essence of whatever the word 'Canadian' means. Once the tension is given up, and the two elements of unity and identity are confused or assimilated to each other, we get the two endemic diseases of Canadian life. Assimilating identity to unity produces the empty gestures of cultural nationalism; assimilating unity to identity produces the kind of provincial isolation now called separatism ..."[2]

In this context, *Mon oncle Antoine* and *Les Raquetteurs* are "provincial" pieces of art, as they explore the quotidian quality of life in rural Quebec and show us a culture beginning to assert itself through opposition. Other examples of the English-French tension can be found in movies we mentioned earlier: *Bingo* (1974), Lord's story about a young French-Canadian rebel named François who sees his hardworking dad as a victim of an Anglo capitalist system and becomes a militant in the name of Quebec liberation. Brault's *Les Ordres*, a collage of vignettes about five people who were taken into custody as a result of the War Measures Act, draws a line down the centre of his frame, often literally, as he shows us innocents behind bars and corrupt power-freaks on the other side. Pierre Falardeau's *Octobre* (1994) is a dramatization of the October Crisis from Laporte's kidnappers' point of view; it shows how human and empathetic these characters are in comparison to the ignorant governors in office. In this reel, we see how the poor terrorists were suckered into believing they were looking at victory, when in fact it was yet another betrayal at the hands of Robert Bourassa. Even Denys Arcand's *Gina* (about a textile worker who is exploited by a film crew and her employer) and his politically charged *Rejeanne Padovanni* (1973) have strong socialist, and one might argue, separatist messages as they firmly establish "the other" as the morally bankrupt Anglo establishment. Nearly 30 years after the October Crisis, we still see images of "The People" emerging from Quebec. But instead of politically charged reflections, we get more relaxed, less didactic efforts like *Les Boys*, Louis Saia's record-breaking 1997 release about a bunch of aging hockey hosers who have only one aim: beating the rival bar team at the coolest game on earth.

November: The Linguistic Landscape After November

After three referenda, and the rise of the French-speaking business establishment in Quebec, the line between the haves and the have-nots can no longer be drawn along linguistic lines. Also, the truly romantic notion of starting a whole new country from scratch — complete with a just socialist agenda and celebratory flag-waving in the name of the people — has lost a lot of its lustre in the wake of scandals, the xenophobic theatrics of the hardline PQ, and the overall movement toward borderless free trade. Without the English, the next generation of Québécois filmmakers has no easy villain — which means the linguistic border is blurring more and more all the time.

Just as Francophone director Richard Roy made the bold step of making an English-language film — and a romantic comedy, to boot — other Québécois directors are taking on projects in English, and English directors are taking on projects that originated in French. Continuing the trend Jutra started a long time ago when he agreed to direct *Surfacing*, and later *By Design* in English, Denys Arcand has made two English-language films as well: *Love and Human Remains*, and most recently, *Stardom*. François Girard's first feature was the highly regarded English-language *Thirty Two Short Films About Glenn Gould* and his second was the multilingual

The Red Violin. Léa Pool, who has lived in Quebec for the past 25 years, released her first English-language effort, *Lost and Delirious,* starring Piper Perabo and Jessica Pare in summer 2001. Then there's André Forcier, who has made several films in Quebec (*Comtesse de Baton Rouge ...*) but is writing two films in English. "They are stories that I like and have personal importance — one is set in 1926, and it's the story of a guy who wants to go to Hollywood. The other one is a satire about Longueil," says Forcier, who sees no inherent cultural problem in switching tongues. "English has a musicality to it. So does French. But they are different. That's what I like about living here, but everybody in this country is an outsider as long as filmmaking is a commercial undertaking. While I want to make more films, and make money, I don't think I'm concerned only with commerce ... I want to make films that say something about life, and who I am. For me, film is an autobiography of the mind."

Even Denis Villeneuve, the celebrated Genie-winning director of *Maelström*, has indicated that he wants his next film to be in English: "There's only so much you can do when your film's audience is limited to the number of people who either speak French or want to read subtitles."

Robert Lepage also dipped his feet in the cool puddle of Anglo-Canadian culture recently with his adaptation of *Possible Worlds*, the John Mighton stage play that explores the realm of consciousness through the point of view of a brain in a bottle. Lepage says there was never any real question of adapting the play into French. Not only would that limit its potential audience to French-speaking nations and art-house film lovers who don't mind subtitles, but things would get lost in the translation.

A language comes with its own structure and ideological structure and its own logic. French logic. English logic. There's a relationship, I think, between the musicality of the language and the kind of sensibilities that can be expressed through language. What I found [with Possible Worlds] was that I was far more artistic in a language that's not my own. That's what art is about. You become very selective of the words you are choosing and ask yourself questions of the language you are working with. It's a more artistic thing to do. Working in a foreign language became interesting to me. How does someone who paints decide where to put the paint? How do you paint with words, a certain emotion? How do you convey that idea?

Languages come with a history. That's why you can't say, "Just translate it into French."

Actors in an English-speaking world don't work in the same way [as] in Latin-speaking cultures. In English, people are listening. That's why they say audience. In Latin, it's spectator — seeing. How we perceive acting has a lot to do with our own cultural understanding of the world through language. As a general culture, based in language and text, French culture is generally more visual. It's all about the show. The dialogue isn't so important if you have a good show. Even if you do have good dialogue, the text-based things won't work as well as visuals ...

I work in England. I have tea in the afternoon and I take vitamins. Really, I feel comfortable there. Quebec City culture is closer to London culture. We force ourselves as Quebecers to connect with France, to connect with French bloodlines, and I find that interesting because culturally, Quebec is very close to English culture. This came as a shock to me, after studying at the conservatory [in Quebec] and then going to Paris. Emotionally, you get to London and it feels so close to home that it's quite disorienting.[3]

For all the Québécois directors moving into the world of English film, there are a few notable moves on the other side of the linguistic equation. Arto Paragamian directed scenes in the French-language film *Cosmos*, and John Greyson, an English-speaking director based in Toronto, took on the challenge of adapting Michel Marc Bouchard's French play, *Lilies*, to the screen in English.

This type of cultural cross-pollination is enough to give some media types in Quebec perforated ulcers. For years, the small community of French-language journalists (who were politicized by the October Crisis and the latter-day PQ-istes) kept the fortifications strong. But suddenly, money and the quest for wider markets pulled down the cultural drawbridge — voluntarily. As if losing the supertalents of Celine Dion to schlock rock wasn't pain enough.

In the words of *Le Devoir* culture critic, Odile Tremblay: "Québécois filmmakers jumping to English is nothing new. They are simply more visible today ... The danger is that we could lose our best French talents in the ocean of the language of the other. There is also the danger that in choosing English work, we may sweep our national realities under the carpet."[4]

Tremblay essentially says that Quebecers are in danger of losing their collective identity when the best and the brightest begin to work in English. This assumes that French Quebec is not strong enough to withstand the language of "the other" — namely Hollywood — but it fails to acknowledge that English Canada has been dealing with that exact problem since its inception, and it continues to survive. In recent years, I'd go so far as to say we've not only survived but thrived. For years, Canadian critics and culture-watchers sounded the alarm, predicting that a truly Canadian film tradition might be too much to hope for given our small budgets and the dominance of Hollywood product. And yet, English-Canadian cinema has never been better — or any more Canadian.

Interestingly, the new films coming out of Quebec bear many of the same thematic birthmarks as their English-Canadian counterparts: alienation, self-doubt, survivor guilt, weird sex, dislocation and an overwhelming sense of something missing, or what we examined earlier and defined as a sensitivity to negative space. Moreover, these typically "Canadian" themes have emerged in direct relation to the disappearance of the overt political message movies that defined early Québécois cinema. There are no easy demons left in Quebec nor in Québécois film now that the English are little more than a silent minority herded into the political background (and Trudeau is dead). The new demons in Quebec are far slipperier because they don't come from the outside. Without an easy nemesis, identity can't simply be created by notions of "not" — it must be excavated through an internal process of self-realization. To quote the alternative title to David Cronenberg's film *Shivers* (1975), which — incidentally — was shot in Montreal just a few years after the October Crisis, "They Came From Within."

Decline of the Church —
Internal Demons

Showing us the transition from the external to the internal demon, Robert Lepage's *Le Confessionnal* (1995) takes place in two separate times: at the height of the Duplessis era in 1952, and the summer of 1989, when tanks rolled through Tiananmen Square. The film opens with a shot of a bridge in Quebec City and a voice-over telling us: "Where I grew up, the past carried the present on its shoulders like a child." Immediately, Lepage tells us how the ghosts of the past have shaped the present face of Quebec — and particularly Quebec City, where the famed battle on the Plains of Abraham unfolded all those years ago. But this is not a movie about French and English. On the surface, the film is about one man's quest to find the truth of his paternity. Marc (Patrick Goyette) is a former championship swimmer who wrestles with suicidal tendencies because he doesn't feel as though he truly belongs to the world around him. He is dislocated, and despite his obvious "French-Canadian" roots, he is an exile within his own community.

Raised by his aunt and uncle along with his little cousin Pierre Lamontagne (Lothaire Bluteau), Marc knows that his mother killed herself shortly after his birth and his father may have been a priest. At least, that's what all the townspeople believed and gossiped about whenever his back was turned. Now Marc is a grown man and his little brother/cousin Pierre has returned home from studying art in China to take care of the family estate in the wake of his father's death. When he arrives, we learn two things: the dad died from complications arising from a neglected diabetic condition which also left him blind (an important symbol of the past, as it relates to the father figure), and Pierre was in his mother's womb when Alfred Hitchcock's

I Confess received its world premiere before an audience in Quebec City. The Hitch classic, starring Montgomery Clift as a priest who knows more than his vows allow him to reveal, was shot on location in Quebec City, and fittingly, the film becomes the central filmic device that connects the past to the present. It also serves to show us Quebec before and after the Quiet Revolution, as *I Confess* was shot in the days of the Duplessis regime, and establishes the father's, and the church's, dominant role.

The connections between *I Confess*, the father, Hitchcock and Marc's paternal quest may seem completely unfathomable, but as the plot thickens with blood plasma and repressed guilt, we realize they are all clues to Marc's paternity. Seamlessly cutting back and forth between 1952 and 1989 (using a technique we also saw in *Le Polygraphe*, where Lepage holds the camera in place with a character from one era, then slowly dollies to a new point to show a character from a different time in the same space), Lepage begins linking the past to the present with plot details and the odd lateral jump. When Pierre goes back to the house he grew up in, he walks through the empty rooms and notices the outlines of where the family pictures once hung. The pictures are missing, which backs up the gap theory once again, but Pierre's memory conjures them back into place, allowing the flashback sequence to begin.

Using a tracking shot down the central aisle of the neighbourhood church (where they shot scenes for *I Confess*), we move from the time frame of the funeral to the Duplessis era as the voice-over echoes the words of communion ... with particular attention paid to the word "blood," which is the central motif in the entire film — symbolically, visually and in terms of narrative.

We see Pierre's family sitting in the pews, and a young woman with a look of horror on her face. We follow her to the confessional, where she seems so traumatized by her sin that she can barely spit it out. The young priest assures her that she is not confessing to him, but to God, who is all forgiving. With enough prodding, she surrenders the information, which we cannot hear ourselves. Instead, we get the reaction shot of the priest turning a ghostly white.

Back in the present time frame, we cut to a different type of confessional: the gay bath-house where Pierre begins to look for his long-lost brother. Floating over the cubicles like an angel with a penchant for linear flight, Alain Dostie's camera shows us several men in their small rooms, completely alone. There is nothing erotic or even sexual about the baths: it is an anonymous place for empty encounters. This is the antithesis of the idea of "community" that defined Quebec during the Duplessis era, when everyone knew everyone's secrets. When Marc and Pierre do finally meet, it is in the surreal, almost heavenly clouds of the spa's white steam — a symbol of death, and ultimate rebirth.

This idea of the break between the past and present, between communities and isolation, is brought back into frame with Pierre, who tries to paint over the outlines of the missing family pictures with deep red paint. In the background, the massacre at Tiananmen Square plays out on the television — reminding us that we are not only living in global times, where images can be transmitted in milliseconds around the world, but that history is not static. It changes through recollection, and once-great and all-powerful leaders will often have their legacies defaced and challenged by the next generation. Mao's body may lie pickled under a sheet of glass at Tiananmen

Square, but the reverberations of his time in power continue to shape history. The same holds true for Duplessis, who preferred to keep the people of Quebec tied to rural economies and under the church's control. That way, there would be no class struggle to fragment the people, no intelligentsia to challenge his authority, and a perfectly untouchable villain in the English elite. It was a manageable equation and a way to keep "the people" together, as a manageable clump, instead of a sprawling population of diverse individuals who see the world in different ways.

The ramifications of Duplessis' time in office are the back half of *Le Confessionnal*, and this is what I mean by internalized demons, because Lepage doesn't pick up the Duplessis era rhetoric that vilifies the "other" Canadians (whether they be Jews, immigrants, Protestants or plain Anglos) — although he does allude to the xenophobic nature of the era when the conniving assistant to Hitchcock (played by Kristin Scott Thomas) tries to secure the church locations by appealing to anti-Semitic feelings.

The point is, history cannot be erased — nor even painted over. Pierre tries to pour several coats of paint over the past and it constantly bleeds through. The outlines of the old family pictures continually reappear, leaving Pierre increasingly frustrated. For Marc, the situation is even more pressing. Without a father figure, Marc has no tangible connection to his past, and therefore his personal identity is compromised. He is angry and lost. He doesn't even have sex to please himself. Instead of sleeping with his stripper girlfriend (Anne-Marie Cadieux), he partners up with an odd, rich older man at the Hôtel Frontenac who seems to know more about Marc than he lets on — the mysterious Monsieur Massicotte (Jean-Louis Millette). Distilled into symbolic forms, we have two men who feel completely dislocated. Pierre knows who his parents are, but feels entirely removed from the world around him, while Marc has been looking for his father for years with no results — leading him to hate the world and distrust anyone who wants to be near him.

The tragedy of the whole story is that Marc did, in fact, know his father. He was actually living with his real family, but the combined forces of Catholic guilt and emotional blindness left him emotionally orphaned. In other words, the real villain was not some outsider who knocked up his mother and then took off. The villain was in his own family: the pain came from within.

The ending to the film is highly ambiguous, with Pierre walking across the same bridge — this time with Marc's child in his arms. He clambers over the rail and says, "Let's play tightrope," as the voice-over repeats the opening lines: "Where I grew up, the past carried the present on its shoulders like a small child ... " This scene could be interpreted in a variety of ways — as a sign of optimism because this time, someone is taking care of the kid, or as a sign of pessimism because they are right back where they started. No matter which side you fall on, there's no doubt Lepage is offering a warning — a clear signal that you must know who you are in order to move forward. Not even blood can solve the riddle of identity. Most of all, one needs self-knowledge and a willingness to ask questions of the silent force of history, which has a lot to reveal if one has the patience — and the internal strength — to see past the painted-over outlines of truth. The demon in *Le Confessional* is not Anglophone culture, it's not even the Catholic church, but someone much closer to the family structure — the patriarch.

Other Québécois filmmakers have used a similar "psychic McGuffin" by introducing what appears to be an easy, externalized demon, only to show us the real source of guilt, shame and self-doubt comes from within. In *Le Déclin de l'empire américain*, the film begins with a female professor, Dominique (Dominique Michel) strolling down the halls of a university, talking to a journalist about her book, which asserts the Western Empire is crumbling as a result of declining values, self-indulgence and the "indifference" caused by social comfort. The people in this film are smart, affluent and decidedly a step removed from the political activism that defined the Québécois intelligentsia in the days of The Quiet Revolution. Also, the very fact that the film opens in an institutional context would appear to pose academia as the logical replacement for the church — where faith has been replaced by intellect. In other words, these people are not attached to any collective identity that unites the people under one ideology — such as the church or revolutionary intent. Marshall and other critics have read this intellectual detachment as the result of losing touch with one's cultural truth: "... This is a post-traditional society, in which there is no longer a moral centre or collective social or political project ... The diagnosis ... is of an absence or void where historical memory is and 'truth' in traditional society, or even modernity, was once located."[5]

Marshall helps to reaffirm our gap theory, but he neglects the presence of another institution: academia, which has just as many rules of conduct and grandiose aspirations of answering the world's problems as the Catholic church. Universities are cloistered environments where questioning is good, but only up to a certain point, and when we first

Le Confessionnal (1995): Pierre (Lothaire Bluteau) stands behind the man he always thought of as a brother, Marc (Patrick Goyette). The two men think they are cousins, but there's more to family identity than meets the eye in this Robert Lepage film that unfolds in two time periods against the backdrop of Quebec City.
MR. TAKASHI SEIDA, CINÉMAGINAIRE AND ALLIANCE ATLANTIS

encounter the characters in *Le Déclin de l'empire américain*, we can see how confidently they approach the world as a result of their privileged place in society. They clearly feel they are freethinkers, exercising free will every step of the way, but they are still in a box — as the continuous use of interiors reaffirms. The first shot tracks through endless gleaming corridors, and even when two of the women stretch before a workout, they are on the enclosed playing field of the school stadium. Also, when they head up to the glorious landscape outside the city for their delicious dinner, they stay in the house and yammer. The landscape is all around them, almost begging them to join in, but they maintain their

distance at every turn. The only sequence shot outside that takes advantage of the soft, natural beauty of the Eastern Townships is where Dominique talks about how men fall in love with fantasy — not truth — and once the fantasy has been unveiled through the act of sex, it loses all its appeal. In this scene, Dominique is in harmony with the natural world as she debunks the whole romantic ideal. Through her actions, she also corrupts the institution of marriage — having screwed several male spouses in the room.

Some critics have pondered Arcand's intent and slagged the film for being misogynist and too ambiguous with its political message. It seems they cannot tell if the film is serious in the treatise of its title or not. My take on it is that Arcand gave us a satirical take on intellectual pomposity. He shows us this group of college profs going on endlessly about their importance and intellectual superiority, when really, they're all victims of yet another institution: stuck in four walls, unable to see even the barest truths that stare them in the face. Fall of the American empire? Sure, it could happen — and so what? The world will continue. As the final shot shows the house covered in snow, several months later, we are finally on the outside amid the landscape — where we can see just how small and unimportant all these mind-games are in the big picture. The landscape is immutable, but these egotists on the inside have convinced themselves they have a role to play in the unfolding of history. What hubris! If the empire does fall, they have no one to blame but themselves. They are the ones lapping up the luxury and losing themselves in distraction. Once again, the demon is internal, not external.

Similar models of internalized demons and inward guilt can be seen in *Maelström* — in the self-loathing character of Bibi — and in Jean-Claude Lauzon's *Léolo*, which takes place almost exclusively inside young Leo's head. The difference with these two films is their use of fantasy. Where the earlier, politically charged filmmakers externalized the identity problem, Villeneuve and Lauzon turn it all back inside — where they can find some control through their own powers of creation. Villeneuve, who was born in the 1960s, shows us a woman who is torn apart as a result of her own actions but finds symbolic atonement through the death of an ancient fish. The image is surreal, but healing. Similarly for Lauzon, the gifted Québécois filmmaker who died in a plane crash in 1997, salvation could be found through creation. Even though Léolo retreats

into his silent, internal world at the end of the film — and will no doubt be institutionalized for the rest of his life — we get a sense that he is in a better place because it's a world he made. There is only love and beauty in that world, and so he chooses to live there: "Because I dream, I am not what I am," is his constant refrain. Sure, the evil kid that picks on Fernand, Léolo's older brother, is an Anglo, but his taunts reveal an internal weakness within the hulking character of Fernand. Fernand is ripped — a walking clump of sinewy muscle, but when the nerdy bully makes fun of his form, he is crushed because he lacks internal self-esteem. The bully was just the catalyst; the demon was there all along.

In *Léolo*, language becomes a device to deal with this internalized tension — not in an English-French dynamic, but rather, an artistic, creative one. Leo writes his thoughts in a journal, where they are perused by "the word-tamer," played by none other than one-time nationalist politician Pierre Bourgault. (Watch for Denys Arcand, who also makes an appearance as the hospital director.) The word-tamer is the one person in the real world who understands Leo's fantasies, and while he makes several efforts to integrate Leo into the world, he proves unsuccessful. Leo gives himself over to the fiction he created in his own mind. To the outside world, he is gone. But inside, he is found: He created himself in the dark hole of his own imagination. This internal view stands in stark contrast to the externalized political tracts of the early 1970s, where characters were relatively monodimensional vehicles used to express a black-and-white political reality. Because it was really only Québécois filmmakers who even attempted to express these linguistic tensions, the resulting films functioned along the lines of Hollywood genre — where heroes (the

Nô (1998): Sophie (Anne-Marie Cadieux) and Hanako (Marie Brassard) attempt to decrypt the many linguistic, political and relationship messages swirling around them at the 1970 World's Fair in Osaka, Japan in Robert Lepage's award-winning film inspired by his own play, The Seven Streams of the River Ota. Alliance Atlantis

romantic Québécois freedom fighters) where heroic because they battled the oppressor (the evil Anglo empire).

The clearest example of the distance travelled can be seen in Robert Lepage's film *Nô*, which takes us back to October 1970. The film intercuts time and place between Montreal (shot in black-and-white) and Osaka (shot in colour), allowing Lepage enough worldly distance to offer a complete historical revision. Where the other films that dealt with the October Crisis, either directly or indirectly, turned the FLQ into warriors for a just cause, Lepage shows them to be a bunch of incompetent goofs who blow up their own car when they set the timer on the wrong time — and what better symbol of self-destruction could there really be? Moreover, they can't even write a manifesto in grammatically correct

French, which further erodes the idea of linguistic and cultural purity. Lepage plays with language all the way through this movie that includes two translators as central characters — the blind Japanese translator and her Canadian boyfriend from Vancouver. We constantly hear the cacophony within the translation booth at the Osaka World's Fair, and languages begin to blur and bend into each other, cross-pollinating and changing. In the great big colour world outside Quebec, there is enough room for the two translators to fall in love and marry in pluralistic Canada, but back in black-and-white Quebec, the movie ends with Sophie and Michel watching the referendum. They are old lovers now — and a decade after the opening sequence, they are finally having the long-delayed discussion about the future: should they have kids, or not? We don't know what they decide, but they are both ready to move forward — which I interpreted optimistically as a sign of affirmation and acceptance. They are both ready to take responsibility for their own problems and their own lives instead of taking the easy way out and pointing the finger of blame at someone outside the circle. This, combined with Lepage's comic distance, proved — to me, at any rate — just how far we've progressed on the road to cultural maturity on both sides of the linguistic border.

"We've moved on as Quebecers," Lepage said after the film won the Toronto Festival of Festival honours for best Canadian feature, but was tepidly received at home. "But the October Crisis is still something that people treat very seriously. The idea of making a comedy about it was very offensive to some people in the Quebec media, who did not like the way I portrayed the FLQ. I remember listening to Jacques Lanctôt — a former FLQ member — on the radio ... He said, "*ça resume*" — it starts again. The people are being ridiculed. But not everyone is ridiculed. He just didn't like the fact that I made fun of the FLQ — who have always been portrayed as heroic martyrs in Quebec. They don't even like showing representations of bourgeois Québécois. They believe in showing "the people" — but I don't recognize myself in these people ... When I am in Quebec, I am a Quebecer, but when I am away, I am a Canadian — a world citizen." That pretty much says it all.

Denys Arcand

Born 1941 — Deschambault, Quebec

TORONTO FILM LIBRARY

Perhaps the first Canadian filmmaker to achieve true celebrity status, not just in English and French Canada but around the world in the wake of *Le Déclin de l'empire américain*, Denys Arcand still gets a rush out of getting a last-minute reservation at his favourite restaurant.

"As a filmmaker you become semi-famous for six months — every four years. I can't say I don't like that. I'm not addicted to fame or anything, but it's nice to think people are listening when you open your mouth to say something," said Arcand after the release of *Stardom*, his 2000 film that centred around a young female hockey player from rural Ontario who becomes a supermodel quite by accident.

Before Arcand found a global sense of community, he struggled with identity issues. The eldest of four kids, he grew up in a strict Catholic household. His mother wanted to be a Carmelite nun and his father was a St. Lawrence River pilot in Deschambault. With the hopes of making a better life for his family and exposing his children to a better education, Arcand's father moved the family to Montreal in 1954.

The move to the city brought Arcand closer to sprawling urban movie palaces, but film was frowned upon by Arcand's father, who saw it as a pastime for the poor having watched able-bodied men linger in the half light of movie houses during the Depression. Arcand was nonetheless transfixed by movies, preferring them to books. His first exposure to flickering shadows was back in Deschambault, where his uncle owned a 16mm projector and would regularly rent concert films and play them for the neighbourhood.

In Montreal, however, the young Arcand was being groomed for a place of social importance. He attended a prestigious Jesuit college and earned his masters in history from the Université de Montréal. History, he said, was the only subject that interested him, and the only thing he felt he could stick with long enough to earn his graduate degree and please his parents. While at school, his interest in theatre and film flourished, prompting Arcand to try his hand at producing a short film, *Seul ou avec d'autres* (*Alone or With Others*) in 1962. The National Film Board offered equipment and a few key personnel to make the film happen, and Arcand soon made the acquaintance of Michel Brault and Claude Jutra.

"I was completely seduced by the lifestyle," he said. In Brault and Jutra, Arcand saw two young, politicized and worldly men who appeared to be riding the wave of the future. He wanted to be just like them. Brault even encouraged the young Arcand to try his hand at writing a script, which he did. It was called *Entre la mer et l'eau douce*, and years later when Brault actually made it, it featured Geneviève Bujold in her first movie. It told the story of a folk singer who moves to Montreal looking for his big break, but finds nothing but heartache. Arcand was looking for a big break himself, and after graduating, he applied to the

National Film Board, Société Radio-Canada (CBC) and *La Presse* (the major Montreal daily newspaper). The only response came from the NFB, who saw the young history major as the right person to help research a series of films on the history of Canada aimed for exhibition at Expo 67. There was only one problem: Arcand didn't agree with the version of history he was being told to document. He remembers endless rewrites, but he stuck with the film board long enough to complete a few short films on "national parks and how to play volleyball."

In 1966, Arcand was feeling the yoke of institutionalism and left the NFB for the private sector to make commercials. In 1967, he took a job at Expo 67, the Canadian centennial celebration and World's Fair. Arcand was suddenly part of an increasingly large new bourgeoisie. At 27, he appeared to have all the creature comforts: a nice sportscar, a house and a chunk of significant cash in the bank. Around this time, he married Denise Robert — who would later become his chief production partner and an established, respected producer in her own right. Everything should have been going great, but Arcand felt he was hitting a creative wall. He was in the scene and checking out parties, but he wasn't thinking. He wasn't writing. He wasn't challenging himself or his potential, so he dropped off the radar. He lived at home for a year, vowing never to return to film unless it was for a project he truly cared about — a film with real meaning.

In 1969, he went back to the NFB, where he reconnected with Jutra and Brault in the famed cafeteria, and he began work on a project about disenfranchised textile workers in Quebec. The film, *On est au coton*, was an exposé of working conditions and labour exploitation in developing nations at the hands of a morally bankrupt (American) establishment. The film was making waves — too many, in fact, to release on schedule at the height of the October Crisis in 1970. The reel was shelved because it was too "biased." Dejected and disheartened once again, Arcand refused to give in and decided to make a film about the 1970 provincial election that saw Liberal Robert Bourassa elected Premier of Quebec. The film, *Duplessis et apres*, was hardly an objective news account of the campaign. It was full of creative associative techniques, such as showing a picture of Bourassa speaking while the audio track featured a classic, patronizing speech from Duplessis to his flock. Arcand was making a political point, and it was that little had changed in the province despite the much-ballyhooed Quiet Revolution under Jean Lesage. The church's influence had declined in the preceding decade, but the people were still patronized by authority — and leaders were inevitably more concerned with their own legacy than improving the lives of their citizens. Arcand was isolating a cycle of radicalism, followed by conservatism, and back again. Decidedly anti-establishment and a little to skeptical of authority, *Duplessis et apres* was shelved as well, prompting Arcand to take his leave of the NFB for a second time.

Arcand made his first "commercial" movie in 1972. It was called *La Maudite galette*, an irony-laced thriller about a working-class couple who decide to murder a rich uncle and take off with the loot. Of course, things go wrong: the husband is shot dead during the robbery, and the wife takes off with a lodger who takes the cash and brings it to his parents. The wife reappears, prompting the two to kill each other. Only the parents are left alive, and they take the cash and the car to Florida. The message is ambiguous at best, cynical at worst

— much like the endless crop of modern Tarantino redux where a sense of nihilism is mistaken for substance. For Arcand, at least, the cynicism seemed to be well-founded, and it fired his creative furnace for another feature about the corruption of ideals and the seductive power of wealth.

Rejeanne Padovani was made for $135,000 and premiered at Cannes in 1973, where Arcand was referred to as a "beautiful and strong fur trapper" by the French. The story of a dinner party set against a backdrop of road construction and political tenders, the film has been compared to Jean Renoir's *Grand Illusion* and *Rules of the Game* for its long takes and deep focus, not to mention class-war subtext. In *Rejeanne Padovani*, the title character is the exiled ex-wife of a gang boss and highway contractor who returns home during a dinner party. Her ex is entertaining a bunch of politicians who were influential in giving Padovani the contract for building the Ville-Marie expressway while the maids and servants have their own, alternative party unfolding in the basement. When Rejeanne returns to reclaim her children after taking off with the head of a rival Jewish cartel, she is "rubbed out" and later, quite literally, "paved over." Once again, exile, alienation and fractured families take the foreground as overt discussions about the volatile political situation in Quebec are left to simmer as subtext.

In 1975, Arcand returned to familiar socialist ground for *Gina*, the story of a stripper who is carted off to a textile town by her gangland bosses. There, she runs into a documentary crew that is shooting the "real struggle" of the women in the textile factory — particularly the story of Dolores, a textile worker who does her best to tell the crew what they want to hear, namely exploitation stories about strikes and being fired on by the cops. Gina, the stripper, has sympathy for the documentary crew as well, and when she takes their side at the bar, she ends up on the bad side of the local snowmobile gang. They feel so threatened by her strength that they gang-rape her to get even (while "O Canada" can be heard in the background, as part of the network TV sign-off). More violence follows as her biker bosses take revenge. All this happens underneath the lazy eyes of the documentary crew who leave Louiseville behind, having changed nothing. Here, Arcand acknowledges the separation between the shooter and the subject, showing us that even a "documentary" version of the truth is slanted, if not altogether deaf and blind as a result of institutional thinking. In short, there is no real hero in Arcand's early films — there are only failed attempts. Nobody, it seems, can change the world through honourable means.

Arcand's next project was a documentary about the 1980 referendum, *Le Confort et l'indifférence*, which he made with the NFB. Once again, Arcand's decidely anti-establishment stance was palpable and the film was considered scandalous because it compared Trudeau's federalist forces to Machiavelli. The sovereignists disliked the film because it mocked the people for being taken in, and the federalists didn't like it because it made them out to be shrewd, cold-hearted tyrants. Perhaps what many considered most offensive about *Le Confort et l'indifférence* was the film's reluctance to make any blatant political statement at all when so many people were desperate for artistic rallying points. Art had to be political if it was to have merit, and for a while, Arcand was perceived as being a softening separatist — a traitor to the cause — because his eye on Quebec politics was becoming increasingly jaundiced. It was a sad, pathetic joke that was hurting everyone.

Arcand returned to fiction, and made a cheesy feature based on the ever-popular Plouffe family — *Le Crime d'Ovide Plouffe*. Apparently resuscitated by the emptiness of it all, Arcand returned to the typewriter to write the script for *Le Déclin de l'empire américain*.

Picking up the same multiple personality story as John Sayles' *Return of the Seacaucus Seven* and Lawrence Kasdan's *Big Chill*, Arcand's *Decline* brought a uniquely "Canadian" spin to a tale of adults sifting through memory and experience in an attempt to find meaning. All the characters (four men, four women) are well-educated intellectuals who are so smart, they have lost touch with the gritty reality of life — only to have it hit them in the face. Everything looks perfect, but beneath the surface, everything's messed up. They make beautiful food, but take no pleasure in eating it. They talk about sex, but find no pleasure having it. They are smart and rich, but lack common sense and life fulfillment. Once again, Arcand tells us that appearances are deceiving — and those who seem to have it all together are probably the biggest screwups of all. Intellectually superior and far more sarcastic than other films in a similar vein, *Le Déclin de l'empire américain* became the first international Canadian cinematic success story. Not only did it win the FIPRISCI prize, the Critics' Prize at Cannes and an armload of Genies, but it was nominated for an Academy Award for Best Foreign Language Film, making Arcand a household name overnight.

In his next film, *Jesus of Montreal*, Arcand took the story of Christ and transposed it to modern-day Montreal, where a group of actors are putting on a passion play on Mount Royal. Lothaire Bluteau plays the sad-eyed Jesus, who is committed to putting on a creative and controversial version of the stages of the cross. But just as the creative juices get going, the establishment forces of the church — which we see to be hypocritical because even the priest is sleeping with one of the actresses — take control and shut the play down. Creativity is the martyr, and corporate greed and institutional thinking are the tyrants. Arcand said at the time he believed "the Catholic heirarchy is completely opposed to Christ's purest teachings."

Jesus of Montreal was another domestic and international success, and it netted Arcand another foreign language Oscar nomination. From there, he decided to try his hand at English-language film and adapted Brad Fraser's play, *Love and Human Remains*, to the screen. A story of urban angst and identity crises, the multi-layered film centres on a gay waiter and his feelings of insecurity. Set against a backdrop of a city wrapped up in paranoia because a serial murderer is on the loose, *Love and Human Remains* is an edgy and ambiguous story where sex is the sole means of interpersonal communication, and even that has been turned into a dark force as a result of the outsider — the "other" — the faceless serial killer who thrives in these anonymous urban landscapes.

Love and Human Remains was a moderate success, but it opened Arcand to a barrage of criticism from Parti Québécois (PQ) faithful who saw his language shift a betrayal to the movement. Arcand took time off to recharge his batteries and returned with another English-language (in fact, multilingual) effort, *Stardom*.

"If you look at *Stardom* or *Jesus of Montreal*, you can see a message, but it's not the kind that tells you how to live your life. Maybe they are telling you to be careful about not making the same mistake — or not taking things too seriously. Look at our culture that reveres celebrities like religious icons. Look at Lady Di — do you know who she really was? No. But you feel like you know her. This is the lie of the camera, and the lie of celebrity. You never find any truth or deeper meaning, you just get the picture. And for many people, this is enough. In *Stardom*, I simply try to make people conscious of the lens — conscious that they are watching through someone else ... in this case, they are watching through Robert [Lepage]."

Ask Arcand if he feels there are any similarities between his work and that of English-Canadian filmmakers, with specific regard to structure and the recurring idea of "gaps" in the webbing of the film, and he sits back to reflect. "You know, I never even thought about it much, but I guess there could be something to it. There might be something we share in our constant resistance to American genre film. But I'm too close to see what I do objectively. I'm the filmmaker, you are the critic. If you can explore this gap idea further, bolster it a little, you will have a book I'd be interested in reading."

FILMOGRAPHY: *Seul ou avec d'autres* (1962) | *Samuel de Champlain: Québec 1603* (1964) | *Champlain* (1964) | *La Route de l'ouest* (1965) | *Les Montréalistes* (1965) | *Volleyball* (1966) | *Parcs atlantiques* (1967 | *La Maudite galette* (1972) | *Québec: Duplessis et après ...* (1972) | *Réjeanne Padovani* (1973) | *Gina* (1974) | *On est au coton* (1976) | *Le Confort et l'indifférence* (1982) | *Le Crime d'Ovide Plouffe* (1984) | *Le Déclin de l'empire américain* (1986) | *Jesus of Montreal* (1989) | *Montréal vu par ...* (1991) | *Love & Human Remains* (1993) | *Poverty and Other Delights* (1996) | *Stardom* (2000)

Robert Lepage

Born 1957 — Quebec City, Quebec

ODEON

A Renaissance man with a modernist's flair for reinventing media, Robert Lepage is one of the most exciting visual narrators in Canadian cinema — a talent that may be explained by his entrance to film via theatre.

Born into a working class family that had already adopted two English-Canadian children, Lepage was always interested in performance, a passion that eventually led him to Quebec City's *Conservatoire d'art dramatique*. He was an engaged student, and when he graduated in 1977, he could write, direct, act and execute elaborate stage designs — but had no particular area of expertise. After a three-week workshop with Alain Knapp in Paris, he returned to Quebec and formed Theatre Hummm with Richard Fréchette.

The two produced award-winning work and from there, Lepage hooked up with Théâtre Repère, an established troupe, where he would stage works such as *Tectonic Plates*, *En Attendant* and *The Dragon's Trilogy* — which toured across Canada, the United States and Europe. (It even hit the *Chicago Tribune*'s top ten shows.)

In 1988, filmgoers had their first look at him in the role of Pontius Pilate in Denys Arcand's *Jesus of Montreal*, but he soon disappeared behind the scenes again when he was appointed to the National Arts Centre in Ottawa as head of the French Theatre.

After leaving Ottawa in 1990, Lepage turned to more personal pursuits and wrote, acted and directed his second solo show, "Needles and Opium," a piece dedicated to exploring altered states of mind and involved scenes of Lepage flying over the stage. The show toured everywhere from Budapest to Zurich, Baie-Comeau to Vancouver.

In 1992, he attracted more international attention with his productions of Bela Bartok's *Bluebeard's Castle* and *Schoenberg's Erwartung*. The dedication, hard work and touring culminated in his biggest coup in Canadian theatre history: he became the first Canadian to direct a Shakespeare production at the National Theatre in London with *A Midsummer Night's Dream*.

The same year, he was the subject of a BBC documentary by Hauer Rawlence titled "Who's that nobody from Quebec?" He also played himself in Patricia Rozema's segment in the film anthology of Montreal, *Montréal vu par ...*

If he wasn't an international star already, his reputation as a mixed-media innovator was flashed across the pop firmament when he designed and directed the stage show for musician Peter Gabriel's cutting-edge *Secret World* tour, which performed 119 shows in 19 countries.

In 1994, Lepage founded the theatre company, *Ex Machina*, which was the foundation for such critically praised productions as *The Seven Streams of the River Ota*.

Lepage made the leap into directing feature films with *Le Confessionnal*, which premiered at Cannes in 1995 and went on to become Canada's entry for the Oscars. For all the success, Lepage says he prefers the theatre because he can work with actors longer during the rehearsal process.

Soon after, he made the Genie and FIPRESCI prize-winning *Le Polygraphe*, a movie based on an earlier play penned by Lepage and Marie Brassard. The film is a frame-breaking piece that focuses on the after-effects of a high-profile murder. One character is suspected in the killing, another dissected the body, and yet another is auditioning for the role of the dead woman in a filmed dramatization of the tragedy. *Le Polygraphe* blurs the line between reality and fiction, which seems to be a running theme in Lepage's oeuvre as it also formed the metaphysical backbone of his 2000 film, *Possible Worlds*, based on the stage play by John Mighton.

"Technology is changing the way we see the world ... I've always welcomed a new gadget because every new gadget brings with it a new idea that is trying to be expressed. With a sampler, for instance, you have the recorded version of the real thing — but then you can manipulate it and turn it into something else. The new tools of the film industry, such as video, bring new ideas — not just new solutions. They form a whole new esthetic," he says. "I'm very interested in exploring these new technoligical frontiers because they change the way we see the world — the way we perceive reality."

Despite his love of gadgets and an interest in exploring the metaphysical space between the film frame and reality, Lepage says he still prefers theatre to film because the interpretation can be a communal endeavour, from rehearsal to performance.

"Theatre is far more collaborative than film," he says. "Even though film is a very collaborative thing because you have so many people contributing to the project, finally, it's the director who decides what will be in the frame. The more you make films, the more you can control what will happen. You can predict the effect of a given scene depending on the angle you use, and so on ... That's why I tend to do a lot of storyboarding, so I can predict the outcome." Lepage says in theatre, it's exactly the opposite because the entire piece is played out before a live audience.

"But this is what I'm beginning to appreciate about film: the playfulness that results when you borrow the rules of theatre and change them. Film has elements of theatre, architecture and literature, and all these great disciplines come together to form a braid within the narrative ... they play a part in the storytelling, a part that may well have more impact on the viewer than the story, but not on a conscious level," he says.

"We're brought up in a culture where we're bombarded by media technology making all these images user friendly. When you've worked in film for a while, you can become more archaeologically specific about what you're being exposed to. You can pull apart what the message is."

In 1998, Lepage directed *Nô*, another film inspired by his previous theatre work, in this case *The Seven Streams of the River Ota*. In *Nô*, a two-part story that takes place simultaneously in Osaka and Montreal during the days surrounding the 1970 October Crisis, black humour abounds, but so does love and compassion, making for a balanced — but perfectly ambiguous journey. The film met with tepid reviews when it premiered at the Montreal festival, but it picked up the prize best Canadian feature and the Toronto Film Critics Association Award at the Toronto festival. Lepage says the mixed reaction in Montreal was probably the result of his characterization of the FLQ, who appear in *Nô* as a Laurel and Hardy types. "The October Crisis is part of

Canadian-Québécois history," Lepage says. "And sometimes it's healthy to look at history in a humorous way ..."

Lepage is also ambiguous when it comes to politics, calling himself neither a formal separatist nor a federalist, but a world citizen who sees the new European political order as a model worth emulating. The idea of one currency and a myriad of social realities — each with its own set of laws and protections — appeals to Lepage, but politics are not his passion. Creating dynamic art with a group of others is what Lepage loves most, and so it is that you can spy his name on the head credits of many films, and his face in front of the camera in others — such as *Ding et Dong* and *Stardom* (in which he plays the ubiquitous videographer).

"I was never interested in doing just one thing. I think it's important to be able to change your perspective as an artist. You have to have the freedom to see things from all the angles, otherwise you don't really understand what you are looking at. You would never know if something is flat, or three-dimensional if you stood in the same place ... I get very excited when I see something familiar in a different way. It reminds me that change is possible."

FILMOGRAPHY: *Jesus of Montreal* (actor, Denys Arcand, 1988) | *Montreal vu par ...* (plays himself in Patricia Rozema's "Desperanto," part of the anthology, 1992) | *Ding et Dong* (actor, 1992) | *The Confessional* (director, 1995) | *Le Polygraphe* (co-writer, director, 1996) | *Nô* (co-writer, director, 1998) | *Possible Worlds* (director, 2000)

Denis Villeneuve
Born, 1967 — Gentilly, Quebec

YVES RENAUD AND ALLIANCE ATLANTIS

While Denis Villeneuve began making films shortly after graduating from the Université du Quebec à Montréal in 1990, he only showed up on the mainstream radar in the wake of *Maelström* — his 2000 Genie-winning film about a woman on the verge of a guilt-induced nervous breakdown.

Having grown up in the small town of Gentilly, a small town near Trois-Rivières, Villeneuve moved to Montréal to study filmmaking at the Université du Quebec à Montreal. Eager to try his hand at bigger projects, he entered Course Destination Monde — a competition sponsored by the Société Radio Canada that sends aspiring filmmakers around the world to learn the tools of the trade alongside industry veterans.

Villeneuve won, and spent the following months making short films. Upon his return to Canada, he landed a contract position with the National Film Board, where he worked for two years and was cherished as a rebellious throwback to the board's wilder days.

Villeneuve says he was struck by the two separate communities within the NFB. "I was so surprised so see what happened at lunch hour. You had half the cafeteria speaking French, the other half speaking English. They didn't mix. You might be working with an Anglophone on a project, but socially, everyone stuck to their own linguistic group. I found this very strange," Villeneuve said in a 2000 interview.

"[The two languages] give us a rich culture. But I feel anger from both sides. English Canada feels rejected and Quebec feels that no one is listening. I think maybe we need to work on building some mutual respect first, then think about politics after, because right now, there is a real problem with communication."

A self-described "confused separatist," Villeneuve says his first feature was his most political film. Titled *August 32nd on Earth*, the film revolves around one man's breakdown in the middle of the Utah desert. It screened as part of *Un Certain Regard* at Cannes in 1998, and Villeneuve was invited to represent Canada at the Oscars in 1999. It picked up awards at festivals around the world, but it never got commercial theatrical distribution in English Canada — let alone in the lucrative U.S. market.

"*August 32nd on Earth* was my chance to say something and it was my comment on the Quebec neurosis. Why can't we make a decision? That was my most political movie and now, I don't want to talk about politics anymore. I want to talk about real life — or at least about emotion. That's why I made *Maelström*," Villeneuve said. "I am a confused separatist. There are two cultures out there trying to destroy each other. I always thought separatism was a good thing because it might give both cultures a chance to grow — and a chance maybe to come together without frustration. But I'm not so sure any more. People have become sarcastic about Quebec nationalism because the financial argument is stupid — and the rest of the world, especially Europe, is moving in the opposite direction ... So I am confused."

Shot in blue hues and steeped in a gritty sense of realism, *Maelström* deals with several levels of survivor guilt as a young woman named Bibiane (Marie Josée Croze) has an abortion at the beginning of the film. Feeling alone and unwanted by her super-achiever family, Bibiane gets wasted at a party and bowls over a pedestrian on her way home.

With so much angst at the surface and so much guilt swirling beneath the dialogue, *Maelström* would appear to bear all the signs of angsty kitchen-sink realism that defined Canadian cinema for so long — if it weren't for one jaw-dropping visual: the narrator is a fish, an animatronic contraption with big black eyes and a sad, gaping mouth who talks to the audience directly and unveils the characters' secrets with deadpan aplomb.

"The fish is my attempt at lyricism. He's quite funny, I think. But people might not know what to make of it, because traditionally, we don't feel comfortable with lyricism because we have this sense that it is not real. For me, it was a way to break the rules a little and experiment with the form without really getting in the way of the story," said Villeneuve.

"I don't think about what the rules are anymore. I wanted [*Maelström*] to be emotional — a story of the heart, not the head. I think when you make a very documentary-style film, it might be harder for the spectators to relate to it emotionally, so I opened it up with this lyrical device," he says.

"If people see me as a traitor for making a film in English (which I want to do) it just makes me feel sad. I want to be a filmmaker. This is all I ever wanted to do, and when you make a film with subtitles, your chances of success become very narrow."

Despite the linguistic compromises he may be forced to make down the line, Villeneuve still thinks it's preferable to work in Canada. "We have the luxury in this country of making very different kinds of films. This gives us a real advantage over Americans, because they can't see anything outside their own world. They have no idea what it's all about. They watch their own films and read their own books and watch their own TV. They don't need to know what's going on outside their country, but we can't help it," he says.

"We have to find originality. We can't compete with traditional forms so we have to do something different. We have to be more creative ... and I think we're getting there ... I don't watch a lot of English-Canadian movies. In Montreal, clearly, we have more European films than English-Canadian ones, but I enjoyed *The Sweet Hereafter.* I saw it at Cannes, and even though I am not a big movie cryer, I cried at that one. I don't know why. I think I was very tired and I missed my kids," he says. "I look at Egoyan and I feel hope for the industry. But he makes films without subtitles ..."

"If there are any similarities between English Canadian and Québécois film it would be the connection to realism — and form. In Egoyan and Cronenberg, I see an interest in form — we have a very strong documentary tradition and that has enabled us to experiment and play with the rules. But I think overall, that English cinema is far more cerebral.

"Right now, our cinema is going through a depression. People are shooting like TV. This new generation is more amused by cinema than by a need to explore. There's a lack of interest. A lack of research in photography. In the sixties there was a lot of research on the subject of filmmaking. People were looking for something. And they made beautiful films. I think there was a tendency to be inspired not by life, but by the conceptual. In the eighties, people were looking for something. I think there was a tendency to take inspiration from concepts, not real life. There was a lack of authenticity. Now we have a better rapport between the two and I hope it continues. I hope we continue to explore fantasy — but that doesn't have to come at the expense of authenticity."

FILMOGRAPHY: *La Course Euro-Asie* (short film, 1991) | *Rew FFD* (short film, 1994) | *Cosmos* (a film anthology with short films from six directors, 1997) | *August 32nd on Earth [Un 32 aout sur terre]* (feature, 1998) | *Maelström* (2000)

CHAPTER EIGHT

Pluralist Perspectives

SEEKING SALVATION IN THE MOSAIC MODEL

The wheels began turning in the midst of a lunchtime conversation with Davor Marjanovic, the director of the Genie-winning film, *My Father's Angel*. As we talked about the film and the difficulty a Canadian may have grasping the depth of the horror witnessed in the Balkans, Marjanovic told me the long, drawn out misadventure he undertook to bring this story to the screen. It made no sense. Here was a story about the immigrant experience — the fundamental reality of this country — and he couldn't get a nickel to develop the script. As I cast my mind into the musty recesses of my memory, I realized the irony of the situation: We are a country built on immigration and yet, as a result of the funding mechanism and its bureaucratic gears, it's very difficult for first-generation immigrants to tell their own story. Deepa Mehta experienced the same troubles as Marjanovic when she tried to make *Sam & Me*, her first feature about the Canadian immigrant experience from an Indian perspective.

As I listened to Davor's story, the catch-22 of the Canadian funding system became abundantly clear: We consider ourselves a pluralist nation and we want to make films that reflect the Canadian reality, but we lose first-generation stories because the creators aren't "Canadian" enough. As a result, we end up with second-generation stories. These may well be powerful in their own right, but we end up missing the moment of first contact — when the amorphous notion of the Canadian identity comes face to face with a well-sculpted Old World idea of self. First contact stories are incredibly important because through the eyes of the new Canadian, we get the closest thing to a cohesive understanding of our own identity as they size up the customs and expectations and attempt to join the fold. New Canadians build an abstract of "Canadiness" where the rest of us — having been born into this reality — barely question the four walls that surround us.

Marjanovic was certainly questioning. A Sarajevo-born director who moved to Canada in the midst of the Bosnian War in 1993, he had been the brains behind a popular television satire — translated as "Top List Surrealists" — and was considered one of the well-to-do movers and shakers in Sarajevo society. He moved to Canada because he was flipping through a 1968 encyclopedia and stumbled across the entry for Vancouver. "I read that it was a beautiful city of 100,000 people — mostly fishermen," he says. When Marjanovic arrived, he found a thriving,

My Father's Angel director, Davor Marjanovic (centre). Bob Asketer and tva International

multicultural metropolis of more than a million — few of whom knew anything about nets, fish or trolling. Together with his wife and children, Marjanovic became one of the thousands of immigrants who abandon their roots and move to the wide-open Great White North. It was a difficult transition emotionally, financially and culturally, but Marjanovic was intent on making it work. As his wife continued her architecture studies, Davor began working on what he hoped would be his first Canadian feature film. The script revolves around a Bosnian Muslim who moves to Vancouver with his wife and his son. The wife, a survivor of the Serbian concentration camps, is a broken spirit, and the father prayed every morning on the bathroom floor

that an angel would come to relieve her suffering. The son was emotionally functional, but he was already an old man in a teenager's body, aged by the monstrosities of war he witnessed "back home."

As I listened to Marjanovic recount the story, I could think of other people I knew personally who had similar experiences of being dislocated by war and ending up in Canada. Every time you turn a street corner in a major Canadian city, you are bound to bump into a new Canadian with a horror story about their former homeland. Davor Marjanovic was one of these people, and he wanted to share his experience with the rest of the nation — and the rest of the world.

It took five years to secure the necessary

Fire (1996): Shabana Azmi and Nandita Das star as sisters-in-law living in the same house, struggling against the same oppressive gender expectations. Each one feels she has failed in her duty to nurture and conceive, but together these two outsiders find meaning in this controversial look at untraditional romance in traditional India from director Deepa Mehta. SEVILLE PICTURES AND DM FILMS

funds to make *My Father's Angel*, and they only materialized after Mort Ransen, the director of *Margaret's Museum*, decided to take Marjanovic's story under his wing. "They didn't know who I was," says Marjanovic of his first encounter with Telefilm. "I told them I wanted to make a movie and they said, 'Who are you?'"

Trying to Fit In

"The Canadian experience for immigrants seems programmed for failure."
—*Margaret Atwood*, Survival

On a purely bureaucratic level, Mehta and Marjanovic's stories tell us that while it's not impossible to make a movie as a new immigrant in this country, it's certainly not easy. Chances do improve for the second generation, but if you look at the already small number of readily accessible Canadian films floating around out there, the number of reels dedicated to the immigrant experience is pathetically small. As we have seen, there are a great number of English-language movies about alienation and self-effacement. There are also plenty of French-language films about guilt and a longing for community. What makes the lack of immigrant-themed movies all the more striking is that all the themes we've seen thus far — survivor guilt, negative space, desolation, alienation, self-loathing, linguistic tension and philosophical doubt — all make sense in the context of the immigrant experience. After all, if this country was originally settled by people who were homesick, then the immigrant experience is square one on our hopscotch path through history. Think about it: our tradition started with Susanna Moodie — a woman who wrote *Roughing it in the Bush* as a giant red flag to warn other potential immigrants away from the wilds of the New World. The first

Europeans hated the harsh landscape of Canada and desperately tried to recreate elements of home, without much success. So we may scratch our heads about why, oh why, we feel so dislocated and abandoned, but if we frame all those emotions according to an immigrant perspective, it all comes together. We may exhibit or even relish in our dislocation and abandonment from an existential perspective, but for the new Canadian, all that angst is par for the course.

Different Visions of the New World

America never seemed to acknowledge immigrant angst. Stories that emerge from Hollywood all focus on the attainment of the Hollywood Dream, where newcomers are given the chance to thrive in the land of opportunity without once feeling the pangs of lost history.

In Ted Kotcheff's filmed version of the Mordecai Richler novel *The Apprenticeship of Duddy Kravitz* (1974), we can almost isolate the exact point where the entire Canadian film tradition veered away from its American cousin. The movie (and the book, obviously) chronicles the rise of a street-smart Jewish kid from Montreal to the upper ranks of the nouveau riche. In order to make it, Duddy (played here by the very young Richard Dreyfuss) lies, cheats and stabs people in the back to get ahead. He has no clear moral framework to weigh him down, only ambition and a positive sense of self. In short, Duddy doesn't really fit the classic Canadian hero mould. Not only is he Jewish (and there's a curious lack of Jews in Canadian film, on both sides of the camera), but he is a winner in the classic American sense of the word. Duddy ain't no creative non-victim; he's a shark with an ego who's not afraid to assert himself. As Atwood notes in her analysis of the novel in *Survival*,

The Apprenticeship of Duddy Kravitz (1974): Operating in his own world, and by his own rules, the socially ambitious Duddy Kravitz (Richard Dreyfuss) is one of the few Canadian screen characters to take big risks and dream big. Making him even more of an anomaly: he's impervious to feelings of guilt. This Ted Kotcheff adaptation of Mordecai Richler's famous novel is a genuine Canuck classic. TORONTO FILM LIBRARY

he is a hero cut against the "American pattern," and his only shred of Canadianess lies in the form of his "promised land" — a scenic chunk of the Laurentians. In the Hollywood model, it would have been a vault full of money and a brand new Corvette.

The fact that Duddy is one of the few Jewish heroes in Canadian cinema and one of the few "winners" in the classic sense of the word are probably not unrelated. In Simcha Jacobovici's documentary based on the book by Neal Gabler, *Hollywoodism: Jews, Movies and the American Dream* (1998), the filmmaker argues that the American Dream didn't formally exist until it was created by the handful of Jews who founded Hollywood. Without access to the upper reaches of establishment

society, the Carl Laemmles, Louis Mayers, Warners and Sam Goldwyns of America decided to create their own little world in the arid sands of southern California. After leaving centuries of persecution, pogroms and religious oppression, the Jews who built Hollywood were hoping to create a new society without religious or ethnic borders. They saw assimilation as the end of violence, and so promoted equality in whatever primitive way they could imagine — whether it was through unintentionally racist portrayals of blacks or moral fables of the underdog hero. The bottom line was always tolerance and the idea that anyone's dreams can come true. The studios repeated this message over and over again, no doubt hoping to put an end to persecution by whitewashing over difference. As we all know, this was a nice idea that never quite worked. Race riots are still a large problem in the United States. Hollywood is often criticized for its homogenous worldview, particularly by Spike Lee, who sees no place for a black perspective in the mainstream.

In essence, the golem the early studio chiefs fashioned from the California dust — this hulking Hollywood model they hoped would protect them — has turned around to bite them in the fanny. The biggest disasters to befall American society have all come from within, and while Hollywood is not directly to blame for race riots in Cleveland and Compton, or the destruction of the Federal Building in Oklahoma, or the massacre of dozens of teens in schoolyards across the nation, it's hard to ignore Hollywood's role in the social order. Hollywood promotes equality through homogeneity, but if you're a black American living in South Central, it would be hard to swallow this as truth. Similarly, Hollywood promotes the victory of the little guy against the oppression of the State — not to mention the glory of gun ownership, which helps explain horrors such as schoolmates shooting each other and an American serviceman blowing up a building full of people in America's heartland. Sure, the American Dream was a nice idea, but it's a far cry from the ugly reality of life in what remains a highly stratified society where the gap between rich and poor is probably greater than in any other place on Earth.

Canadian cinema never had a critical mass of Jews in the film business to fuse this message to the larger cinematic tradition, perhaps because the Jews in Canada weren't entirely frozen out of the banking and business communities, as they were in the United States. Ironically, they assimilated into Canadian society without losing their Jewish identities and made contributions across the board. Who knows, maybe the small size and relative sluggishness of the Canadian industry may be related to the lack of a Semitic critical mass. Hard to say. All we know for sure is that *The Apprenticeship of Duddy Kravitz* is the first and last immigrant story of its kind in Canada, and it shows us a man who came from nothing — and not here — to make something of himself in the New World.

Homesick Horrors

Later immigrant-themed movies to emerge from Canada, such as Mina Shum's *Double Happiness*, Clement Virgo's *Rude*, *The Planet of Junior Brown* and *Love Come Down* (2000), Istvan Szabo's *Sunshine* (which qualified as Canadian for the Genies — despite its Hungarian director), Davor Marjanovic's *My Father's Angel*, Srinivas Krishna's *Masala* and *Lulu*, and many of Atom Egoyan's films, such as *Calendar*, are far more "Canadian" in their treatment of the immigrant experience than something like *Duddy*. In these films the characters are displaced and alone, and they often feel overwhelmed by the new, peaceful and altogether foreign world that surrounds them.

Of the lot, *Lulu* (1996) is by far the most grim example of the Canadian experience. It tells the story of a Vietnamese mail-order bride named Lulu (played by first-time actress Kim Lieu) who finds herself in Canada living with an impotent husband ironically named Lucky, played by Michael Rhoades. Lulu is quiet and beautiful and works at the make-up counter of a downtown department store — no doubt a symbol of the external "good, brave face" she is forced to put on in this technically free but personally oppressive new home. There, she gets regular visits from her husband as well as a documentary filmmaker

(Manuel Aranguiz) who wants to interview her about her life journey from Old World to new ways. Lulu refuses, knowing that her boy-man of a husband will get jealous, but eventually she complies after the director makes his case: "I am a refugee too. I need to do this. I can't go back to my country. I used to be a revolutionary. Now, the history of my country doesn't need me anymore. I want people to know about us," he says. "They should hear our stories."

The next time we see Lulu, she is standing in front of a French Revolution tableau depicting Liberté in flowing toga, revealing her life story and the details of her real love affair with a man who was imprisoned before she arrived in Canada. It's clear Lulu still loves that man, but now, she is in this hellish new place, with her parents who resent her for taking them away from their roots in the twilight of their lives. "First, you brought us shame," they say. "Then, you brought us here."

There is no victory for Lulu. Her marriage leaves her without a sense of matrimonial meaning as a result of Lucky's erectile dysfunction. Eventually she seeks physical solace from Lucky's friend. Her parents feel she has betrayed the family by uprooting them and then placing them in the sterile surroundings of a nursing facility. Making things even more difficult is the burden of survivor guilt Lulu carries with her, knowing that the man she loves may well be dead. When someone notices she doesn't talk all that much, her sole reply is, "That way, no one can blame me for anything." Not a bad policy given the preponderance of prairie politicians who feel they can gain points with their rural constituents by blaming immigration for the given problem of the day.

Like I said, this is one of the darkest of the modern takes on immigration on screen. Not even *Masala* (1993), Krishna's first feature, was nearly as grim. In *Masala*, the immigrant experience is relayed with such humour and filmic ingenuity that it's hard not to be won over by the film's bounding energy. Here Krishna himself takes on the lead role of an angry and bitter petty gangster whose parents died in a plane crash (a clear allusion to the Air India bombing). Relocating to Toronto, he lives with his uncle (Saaed Jaffrey), a greedy man who embodies everything rank and corrupt in North American society — namely a preoccupation with money instead of spiritual matters. As in *My Father's Angel*, *Lulu* and *Double Happiness* (as well as others), the key figure in the transition to the New World is the "Canadian" romantic partner. In this case, it's the daughter of a postie, whose mother talks to her favourite God, Krishna, through the television. This is no ordinary Krishna, however; this is a displaced Krishna who shows up wearing hockey jerseys. The symbolic parallel, then, is obvious: the God Krishna represents the Old World's traditional and spiritual values facing assimilation, while the New World is embodied by the greedy uncle and the confused, alienated and completely disoriented young man, Krishna, who struggles to reconcile his missing Old World connection (his parents) with his new, foreign environment (Toronto).

The plot itself shares a lot of common ground with *Lulu* and *My Father's Angel*, but *Masala*'s willingness to jump off the realism bridge that connects Canadian cinematic tradition to the rest of the world is relatively novel — or at least it was when it was made in 1993. Before then, it was hard to find movies that injected pure fantasy into gritty dramatic denouements, but in the past decade, the practice has become increasingly common.

Masala (1992): Rita Tikkoo (Sakina Jaffrey) and Anil Solanki (Herjit Singh Johal) exchange glances in Srinivas Krishna's brilliantly subversive comedy about religion, cooking, terrorism and salvation. Krishna brings Old World traditions and New World individualism together, showing us the wacky, but potentially life-affirming magic of multiculturalism.
CINEPHILE/TORONTO FILM LIBRARY

Masala blurs the line between fantasy and fiction. Other movies that play with the line include Thom Fitzgerald's *The Hanging Garden* (1997), which features a talking sculpture of the Virgin Mary, and *Maelström*, which features a talking fish. In all cases, one might argue that the lines are blurred for the same reason. Namely, to show us the difference between traditional and modern beliefs. In *Masala*, the television set becomes the vehicle for firsthand chitchats with the God Krishna. In *Hanging Garden* (which is not an immigrant story, but deals with similar outsider themes as the protagonist is gay), the talking Virgin Mary represents Grandma's religious faith, as well as her fragile connection to reality. In *Maelström*, the talking fish tells us all

about the life of the early Norweigian fishermen — the songs they sang, the wars they fought and the fish they caught.

From these surreal symbols we could conclude that Old World ways are richer in fantasy than the quiet, grounded and all too vérité reality of life here in Canada — or at least they look that way to the next generation, who may either romanticize the mystical customs of their ancestry in a search for personal identity or attempt to erase that old identity in a bid to assimilate into the Canadian landscape. Fortunately, because Canada prides itself on being multicultural and pluralistic, the pressure to "fit in" is not a part of the larger social system. In the United States, people are urged to throw themselves into the crucible called the American People. In Canada, we like spice — or masala — even if it means a little trouble (which, incidentally, is what "masala" means colloquially), and that's generally what the immigrant encounters when he or she arrives in Canada: a new place that throws all Old World ways out of whack, prompting a sense of dislocation and blurred boundaries.

Importing Old-World Optimism

My Father's Angel is relatively optimistic, despite its incredibly bleak subject matter. In Marjanovic's story, we watch as another family uproots itself and moves to Canada — more specifically, from the jewel of the Balkans, Sarajevo, to the jewel of the Canadian pacific, Vancouver. Ahmed, the father — played by Genie-winner Tony Nardi — is what one might call in perpetual crisis mode. His wife, Sayma, is averbal and emotionally catatonic as a result of being raped several times a day for months on end by Serbian soldiers. Now Sayma (Asja Pavlovic) sits at the table with a faraway look in her eyes, rocking back and forth. Every once in a while, she'll scream — but that's the extent of her current linguistic skill. Meanwhile, Enes, Ahmed's son (Tygh Runyan), has given up on school because he can't seem to find any common ground with the other Canadian teens because he's witnessed the horrors of war firsthand. What makes Marjanovic's film so strong is the way he keeps the viewer trapped in a siegelike state, even though the film takes place entirely within the safe and perfectly scenic confines of Vancouver.

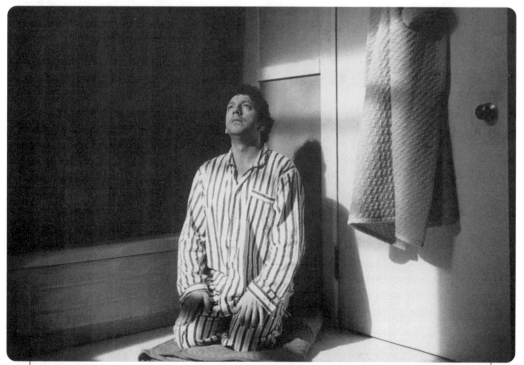

My Father's Angel (2000): Tony Nardi won a Genie for his performance as a Bosnian war survivor and new Canadian, Ahmed. He prays on the bathroom floor every day, hoping an angel will save his catatonic wife from the hell she lived through in a Serbian prison camp in Davor Marjanovic's hard-earned first feature about the immigrant experience.
BOB ASKETER AND TVA INTERNATIONAL

"We put my mother's body on the plane to Vancouver, but her mind is still in Sarajevo," says Enes in the opening lines of the film, establishing the idea of mental dislocation from the outset. To further this idea, Marjanovic throws Old World problems at these New World arrivals by forcing an encounter between Ahmed, the Muslim, and Djordje (Timothy Webber), a former Serbian soccer star who now drives a delivery vehicle in Vancouver. Dazed and confused after learning that Enes is not going to school, Ahmed is walking down a back alley and mistakes the headlight of Djordje's car for the angel of his prayers. The collision brings both men's destinies together, pushing these former enemies to make a new start in the New World. Letting go of old baggage is never easy, especially when your wife has been spiritually and emotionally broken by her imprisonment and sexual abuse. Not surprisingly, Ahmed — upon recognizing the face of the once-famous athlete — turns away from Djordje, calling him the devil.

As for Djordje, things aren't all that easy for him either. He was famous in his old city; now he is perceived as little more than an immigrant courier who gets reamed out by his boss at every turn. Like Ahmed, who was once considered a rich man in the old country, Djordje has lost the core of his personal identity in the transition — and now, through the eyes of Serbian victims Ahmed and Sayma, Djordje is forced to examine his cultural identity as well. Is he a "devil" as Ahmed says? Could his Serbian brothers and sisters have committed the atrocities they are accused of by the Western press? He can't believe it, nor can his wife, who meticulously collects the morning papers off people's doorsteps so they can't read the "lies" about Serbs. Even thousands of miles away from the epicentre of this

longstanding ethnic strife — even in the middle of such soothing Pacific beauty — the explosive suitcases linger. The real challenge is not with the two older men, but with the two sons: Enes and Vlada (Brendan Fletcher), Djordje's boy. Sadly, they too have absorbed "the poison" and hate each other. This would be the bad side of the mosaic model: Just as Old World identities are given enough room to re-root, Old World prejudices also survive the voyage and reestablish themselves in the next generation. Once again, it would seem as though the immigrant experience in Canada is doomed to fail, but not altogether.

The new landscape and the new culture count for something: they present enough of a blank page to offer some sense of hope. That's exactly what Marjanovic gives us when he makes Djordje examine his Old World roots and realize that perhaps the newspaper reports of "ethnic cleansing" may have been right after all. Perhaps the old identity could be improved with a little Canadian peacekeeping effort: and in the final sequence Ahmed carries the lifeless body of his wife through the streets of Vancouver and Djordje steps in to help, stopping cars and clearing the way for the impromptu cortege.

Clearly *My Father's Angel* repeats the now-familiar Canadian themes of survivor guilt, dislocation, alienation and, to a certain degree, existentialist angst — as seen in the character of Enes, who can't quite adapt to the placid Canadian lifestyle after experiencing the horrors of war. For all the bad vibes, however, Marjanovic's story leaves room for optimism and the possibility that one day, life may be better for this broken family now that it's able to symbolically bury the past and heal.

The Dangers of Assimilation
While it may be possible to bury the past, it's

important to leave a grave marker so you know where to go when you're looking for home. As followers of the mosaic model, Canadians believe it's important to know where you come from — as identity cannot simply be repackaged every time one moves. One can pretend, and be a chameleon, but the consequences of such assimilation — as all forms of cultural denial — are generally quite nasty.

I remember goin' down that road for an entire week during the 1999 Toronto International Film Festival, when it seemed the entire world was making movies about identity and transference and cultural appropriation. American filmmaker James Toback made *Black and White*, a movie about white kids assimilating black hip-hop culture. Another American independent, Jim Jarmusch, made *Ghost Dog*, a movie about a black man who finds a moral code in the lifestyle of the samurai, and Hungarian Istvan Szabo (along with Canadian producer Robert Lantos) made *Sunshine*. When I spoke to Toback about issues of cultural integration, he was clearly very excited about the new bridge between white and black America: "Hip-hop culture has a beat that's fat and broad enough to include everyone ... I spent the sixties in James Brown's house as the sole white guy, and I loved the experience. I learned how to make love like a black man. That's good. I can't see anything wrong in cultural crossover. It's healthy."

When I spoke to Jim Jarmusch about the same topic, he saw culture as more of a clash between "the people's culture" and "the corporate culture." In Jarmusch's mind, the human moral code has been supplanted by corporate greed, which means the people must find a way to reimagine their relationship to those in power:

People need a sense of identity. I don't have a tribe per se — but I know I don't fit the mainstream, so it's more like a tribe by default. I'm not black, but I have some feelings of identification with urban black culture because it's all around me. I don't want it to sound like hipsterism — but corporations don't care about anything good: it's a culture of greed ... I'm sitting here with a credit card in my pocket and I know that I'm a part of the corporate reality. We're all a part of it. And sometimes I let myself get really negative about the whole thing. But then I remember that things change all the time — you know, like John Cage said, 'Don't try and change the world — you'll just make it worse.'

Contrary to these relatively New World takes on culture, Szabo's stance on cultural assimilation was distinct in its cautionary stance: "I think [assimilating] is the worst thing anyone can do ... I don't think you can truly do this — escape who you are. If you do, I don't think you can ever be truly happy, because you have no identity at all. You belong to no one."

Lantos, the Canadian movie mogul (well, the closest thing we have, at any rate) who discovered his own Jewish roots only as a mature adult, said the reason he wanted to make *Sunshine* was to show people just how important it is to not surrender your past. "Istvan and I both share a similar history," says Lantos. "We both come from assimilated Jewish roots. It's a story many share but few want to really talk about. That's why this film had to be made."

The story of a Jewish family that makes a bid to assimilate in the hopes of breaking into the anti-Semitic core of the Austro-Hungarian establishment, *Sunshine* chronicles what happens to the Sonnenschein clan once

Sunshine (1999): Gustave (James Frain), Valerie (Jennifer Ehle) and Ignatz Sors (Ralph Fiennes) were the ideal family, until they cut themselves off from their roots in an attempt to help Ignatz attain a higher standing in the Austro-Hungarian civil service in this near century-long family saga that spans three generations and two world wars.
ALLIANCE ATLANTIS AND SERENDIPITY POINT FILMS

they convert, and change their name to the less Semitic-sounding Sors. The film features British actor Ralph Fiennes as the patriarch through three generations: first as Ignatz, the social-climbing lawyer who puts the wrecking ball in motion when he abandons his roots, then as Adam, an Olympic fencer. Adam is put to death by the Nazis, who remove his clothes then hose him down with water in sub-zero temperatures until he freezes to death. Adam was a Hungarian idol, but the Nazis and the collaborators in the Hungarian government didn't care. They knew he had Jewish roots and that was enough to warrant a death sentence. The last incarnation of the doomed family is Istvan, who is so unrooted that he has no moral centre anymore, and he betrays a friend. *Sunshine* is a tragic and con-

voluted story about the dangers of homogenization and globalization. It shows us what happens to a proud, working-class family who sacrifices everything in a bid to "fit in": they are spiritually and almost physically erased from the face of the Earth.

Salvation in the City

There is a place that offers some protection from the forces of conformity. It's the same place you go when you're at home and life is making you lonely: downtown. The city is a place where almost everyone is an outsider, which is why people can find a tiny place to call their own within it. Robert Lepage remarked that when he walks down the streets of multicultural Montreal, he feels waves of optimism about Canada's future. "You can see people, all kinds of people, living side by side, speaking different languages, and it seems to work. Whenever I'm there, I find myself thinking that maybe it can work. Maybe we can all live together, but that's just Montreal — where they almost have no choice but to try." Whether it's Montreal or Toronto or Vancouver or Calgary — or even New Waterford — the urban environment can bring outsiders together. Just as the natural landscape shaped the emotional frame around most early Canadian films and early Canadian literature, so does the urban landscape shape the emotional world of the New Canadian. The immigrant almost always lands in the midst of a city, and so it's not all that surprising to see urban environments provide the backdrop for most pluralist stories in.

In *Lulu, Masala, My Father's Angel, Rude* and *Sam & Me*, the city becomes the emotional foil. When the main character is cold and alone, the city simply turns its concrete back. When he is happy and alive, it is because within the monotonous grey of the urban landscape, he has found a splash of local colour to remind him of home. The one image I can't get out of my mind is from *Sam & Me*, where the young "hero" Nikhil lives with a group of other Indian men in a cramped Toronto rooming house. They eat on the floor and share the same one room, but every weekend they play cricket in the dirt-covered back alley and reminisce about being back home. These scenes in the backyard form a stark contrast to the urban angst and suburban repression we see in the rest of the film: It's the only time we see the characters smile or laugh.

In the big picture, then, the city becomes a type of microcosm for the larger nation, where people from diverse groups come together as part of one society. Where Canadian film veers away from other cinematic traditions is that

there is usually a place for all types of people within the city — especially those who don't fit in anywhere else. They may have to kick away at the dirt, or open a secret door in a boarded-up building, but they can usually find a place where they feel comfortable being themselves — a place where they can recreate their old home, or recreate an entire family. This could be the dusty cricket field we see in *Sam & Me*, the multicultural take on addiction we see in John L'Ecuyer's *Saint-Jude* or the basement in Clement Virgo's *The Planet of Junior Brown* (1997).

In Virgo's film (which was originally made for TV but is available on video), we see an entire array of dysfunctional people. There is Junior, the talented piano player without a piano. There's his dissociated mother who was essentially abandoned by her husband, and then there are all of Junior's oddball friends, like the burn victim who lost his family (note the orphans) and the young woman who ran away from home because she was sexually abused by her middle-class dad. All these people are outsiders of some kind, but they create their own world in a boarded-up basement, complete with a mechanical solar system of their very own. Together, they find a sense of community and meaning. They support each other and love each other, proving that even an outsider can find a place to call home — if not in the outside world, then at least within his own.

Love Come Down (2000) was Virgo's follow-up to *The Planet of Junior Brown* and it shows us another community of outsiders all looking for family. Neville (Larenz Tate) is a drug-addicted delinquent and his half-brother Matthew (Martin Cummins) is the great white hopeless — a boxer with an almost perfect winless record. Spawned from different fathers, the boys have different skin tones (Neville is

Love Come Down (2000): Martin Cummins and Larenz Tate star as Matthew and Neville, two half-brothers with one giant survivor secret between them in Clement Virgo's urban story of love, family and the search for grace.
EQUINOX ENTERTAINMENT

black, Matthew is white), but they carry the very same piece of luggage: a nice, sturdy black trunk that keeps the truth of their Jamaican father's death concealed from prying eyes. Inside that black box, guilt and identity become one, which is why, when we first meet them, Neville and Matthew are spinning around in circles, trying to escape their own reflection. Joining this dance party of dysfunction is Nico (Deborah Cox), a woman with her own identity baggage: She is the adopted black daughter in a white Jewish family. Everyone's personal identity is confused. There is no black and white approach to selfhood, no magic answer to the meaning of life, and Virgo makes this abundantly clear by blurring all the racial and ancestral boundaries that are supposed to tell us who we are. Making things even more confused is his decision to turn the entire melo-

drama into a comedy, which not only subverts genre expectation — a Canadian specialty — but introduces a foreign element into the Canadian landscape, and that is God. In Virgo's world, there is a god, and so there is also forgiveness. Existentialist comedy does exist. It's generally called absurd — as are many Canadian movies. Classic comedy demands divine intervention. It circles around the sense that everything will be okay because the universe is ordered and God is watching to make sure everything unfolds as it should. Virgo even offers up a tangible symbol of God in Sister Sarah (Sarah Polley), a former junkie who now tries to help other street kids and users kick.

"All my films are about finding grace," says Virgo. "I can get angry and feel very lost, but that's when you have to leave yourself open — that's when you have to find the faith to believe in grace. Otherwise, you become a very bitter and closed person and I don't think you can access your own creative centre when you're so closed down. I think you have to be prepared for the release, and just let it happen." Because forgiveness, or grace, plays such a large part in Virgo's creative vision, his heroes are always flawed or broken. "Maybe it goes back to this idea of the harsh landscape, but I think one of the things that makes my films truly Canadian are the broken survivors I like to focus on. There is no perfect warrior in a leather jacket in my movies, they're all just trying to get by — they're all just trying to heal ... and if they do, it's because they found grace through their brother, or their so-called fellow man."[1]

Outsider bonding is clearly a big theme in Canadian film. *Sam & Me* is a story of a young Indian man who finds a meaningful friendship with an aging Jewish man longing to go home to Israel. *The Planet of Junior Brown* is about an obese piano prodigy who finds companionship in the company of other social outcasts. *Love Come Down* is a story about outsider brothers with different skin tones. *The Adjuster* offers more of the same, as the immigrant outsider, the social outsider and the sexual outsider all occupy the same landscape. Even Cynthia Scott's beautiful film, *The Company of Strangers*, shows a group of older women with little in common except age learning about each other when their bus breaks down.

American films, and almost all other national cinemas, generally offer stories of the outsider being integrated into the dominant culture, where they are finally accepted and assimilated. Lacking a dominant monoculture and a pre-hung identity that goes along with it, Canada has become a quilt-work of identities. Outsiders bond together, and together they discover a community that helps them reach out to other outsiders.

For this reason, Canada has never asked New Canadians to ditch their old identity at the door. The thread of pluralism runs through our entire quilt, meaning that you can be Indian and Canadian or Chinese and Canadian at the same time. The Canadian identity — at least as we imagine it — is broad enough and open-minded enough to allow for difference. There is no need to sacrifice one identity for another because in this country, there's room for everyone. If we were phallo-nationalists, this would be impossible because the phallo-nationalist model relies on homogeneity — not difference — as a measure of nationhood.

Before we move forward, I'd like to remind you of the Kwakiutl twin myth I mentioned in *First Takes*. According to their legend, when a mother gives birth to twins (seen as salmon), she must have another child to give the twins a tail, because forever contemplating their place vis-à-vis each other, the twins are unable to move forward upriver. They need someone else to come up behind them to push them along, lest they stagnate and die before reaching the spawning grounds upstream. I love this myth, because if Canada is a twin country — forever contemplating its other half — then the New Canadian would represent the tail, a completely new force pushing us forward all the time and releasing us from the static equation of diametric opposition.

From the films we've seen so far, the equation seems to work. In *Maelström*, Bibi finds salvation through the son of a Norweigian fisherman. In *New Waterford Girl*, Mooney breaks the dead-end reproductive cycle thanks to the help of a punch-happy American. Similarly, in *My American Cousin*,

Double Happiness (1994): Jade Li (Sandra Oh) is trapped, both mentally and physically, between two worlds. One one side, there is her internal drive to explore her own individuality; on the other, the traditional forces of home and her family, which constantly seems to be checking in on her personal life in Mina Shum's feature debut. MINA SHUM

the outsider opens up a whole new terrain of possibilities.

Second Generation Twins

The real test of identity usually takes place in the second generation, as the children find themselves trapped between two traditions: that of their parents and that of their new home. Once again, we end up with a twin dynamic — and once again, the twins are internalized: two different identities struggling to find harmony.

Atom Egoyan's films hum with the dissonance generated by two different world views, but for the most part, the tension is communicated beneath the surface — through eastern musical scales and a creepy sensation that things are somehow out of place. The dynamic is easier to grapple in

Mina Shum's *Double Happiness*, a story that deals with second-generation issues on the surface as it tells the story of *Jade* (Sandra Oh), a young Canadian woman who falls in love with a white guy but can't find the strength to tell her traditional Chinese parents that she's leaving the family fold.

Based on Shum's own experience growing up in Vancouver, where she played in a rock band and acted before picking up the camera at the University of British Columbia film school in the late 1980s, *Double Happiness* tells the story of a spunky chick who has her own ideas about life, love and happiness. Jade is saracastic and hip and at the age of 22, she's decided she wants to be an actress — but there's just one hitch: Her family wants Jade to get married, have kids and work for the family's greater well being. With hopes of landing her the big Kahuna, they begin fixing her up with the community's most eligible bachelors — particularly Andrew, a clean-cut lawyer who could make any mother cry into her teacup with joy. Andrew is relatively happy for the date, but he too has a secret he cannot share with his traditional parents. Together, they try and fake a relationship to keep their families happy, but when Jade meets Mark, everything changes. Jade is forced to confront who she is, and the person her parents wanted her to be.

> I will always be interested in stories about identity. The identity crisis issue is of personal importance to me ... Those are issues that I'm still dealing with and so they come out in my writing. I'm a Chinese Canadian — that's part of my identity. But I also watched The Flintstones and had a Star Wars blanket. I can't deny either part of my culture.

When I interviewed Shum, who was born in Hong Kong and moved to Vancouver with her family as a child, she discussed the basis for her storytelling:

> I knew I was Chinese, but China was a place very far away from where I was. I could never really be there and belong. It was a mental concept more than anything. I can't deny that I am a part of Canadian culture, but this is a place where people will often judge you by the way you look ... We all have preconceptions about people. I was out walking at night down Queen Street in Toronto and these guys looked at me and said, "We're going to kick you in the head, you stupid Chink!" and I couldn't believe they were talking to me and I said, "But I'm a girl!" — like it mattered. Besides, how did they

> even know I was Chinese and not Korean or something?
>
> We don't like to think there is as much prejudice as there is in Canadian society, but it's there, and usually, it's below the surface ... When I'm writing, I'll have three or four characters in my head at once. They all take on different sides to my own personality and I can hear them talking to each other. I also keep a journal where I write everything down and then analyze it. All that stuff becomes part of the characters' internal dialogue, which is the place I really want to take people ... In cinema you can really plug people into your brain in a visual, aural and dramatic sense. As an independent filmmaker, I can make sure that the audience gets exactly what I've intended ... You can't do that in an American studio system, where everything is reduced to the lowest common denominator. They whitewash everything.[2]

In Shum's second feature, *Drive She Said*, she externalizes the internal identity struggle. In that film, which focuses on a bank teller who is happily kidnapped by a bank robber and taken on a road trip, one of the destinations is "China City" — the abstract made concrete. This is an important transition, as it pushes the internal identity crisis out into the landscape where the individual can form a connection to place, and potentially, an understanding of where she/he "fits in" to that external environment.

When Shum was writing the script for *Drive*, she said she was consciously thinking of using the landscape as a foil for character, but not in a realist way. "I wanted to make a film where I'd set people up against a landscape that reflected them in an expressionist way. So we used a lot of graduated filters and made the grass kind of blue and the sky orange. I was inspired by Wim Wenders' exaggerated shots of landscape. It was a real attempt at manipulation."

Given everything we've mapped so far in the wilderness of Canadian film, any attempt to move away from our realist roots signals a paradigm shift in how we see ourselves and how willing we are to re-create the world with an artist's hand. Even if the landscape remains oppressive, if we've been able to paint it a different colour, or leave a personal imprint on it in some way, we've still achieved a form of creative control and self-determination. This is important, because it signals a certain amount of artistic confidence. We allow ourselves the freedom to imagine something other than what is.

The Magic Future

In *Cosmos* (1997), producer Roger Frappier's jam session for six young Québécois directors — Jennifer Alleyn, Manon Briand, Marie-Julie Dallaire, Arto Paragamian, André Turpin and Denis Villeneuve — the collective and pluralist element has been incorporated into the filmmaking act, as well as the content. Here, we take a cab ride with the mystical Greek cabbie, Cosmos (Igor Ovadis), who engages his fares in quasi-Socratic dialogues that are aimed at holding this six-stranded braid of a film together. In Villeneuve's tale, a film director gets in the cab on his way to a hyper-styled TV interview and Cosmos asks him what his movie is all about. The director, an artsy type who is clearly far more comfortable keeping it all inside, says his film is about fragility, vulnerability and time stretching out. In other words, the artist is making a film about his own relationship to himself — his own fragile creative identity which he is trying to articulate in front of a waiting public, but he simply cannot bring himself to spit out the words.

When he gets to the TV studio, they completely remake his external facade by dying his hair and making him look ultra-chic, but when it's time to "turn the negative switch" (as the Veejay calls it) and throw him into the light, he bolts. He can't bring himself to let it all out.

The other stories deal with similar communication blocks and internal crises: one follows a mysterious man who appears to be killing people; another deals with a couple on the skids; the next shows a star-crossed romance, and *Boost*, Manon Briand's (*2 Seconds*) effort deals with a woman trying to distract her buddy before he gets the results of an AIDS test. The final chapter, directed by Arto Paragamian, deals with Cosmos the cabbie, whose car is stolen, leading him on a wild goose chase to the middle of nowhere. "It's all about agriculture," says Cosmos, offering his personal take on cosmology and the meaning of life. In one way or another, all these stories revolve around the search for expression and the desire to communicate inner truth, but every character is stuck except Cosmos, the immigrant, who literally becomes the vehicle of their personal emancipation.

The Red Violin (1998) abstracts the immigrant "other" even further by turning this tool for personal catharsis into an inanimate object: a violin with a mysterious red paint job. For any object to play the protagonist, it's got to be pretty special, and on this score screenwriter McKellar and director Girard don't let us down. The violin is a symbol of passionate love and artistic obsession, as it was a gift made by an Italian violinmaker for his unborn child. The wife, the child and the violinmaker all perish, but the violin lives on — transforming all those who draw the bow over its ancient, aching strings. The other half of the story relates to identity: The violin

The Red Violin (1998): Greta Scacchi must compete with a musical instrument for the sole affections of her lover, Frederick Pope (Jason Flemyng) — a perpetual fiddler — in François Girard's multi-lingual epic about a centuries-old violin that makes its way to a Montreal auction house, where the past meets the future. ODEON AND RHOMBUS MEDIA

comes to a Montreal auction house in a bulk shipment from China. No one knows exactly what it is until an American specialist, played by Samuel L. Jackson, puts the pieces of the puzzle together and authenticates the instrument's lineage.

True to Canadian form, *The Red Violin* is something of a fractured fairy tale — a confluence of stories all leading to the same, ambiguous end. One story focuses on a tiny orphan, a weakling outsider who finds his soulmate in the violin. The two make beautiful music together. They even sleep together, but when it comes time to perform in public, the child, almost predictably at this point, collapses into a wee puff of taffeta and satin because like so many other Canadian-made heroes, he cannot make the leap into the exter-

nal world. In another chapter, the violin finds its way into the hands of a violin master who unleashes his animal passion on the instrument, as well as on his lover — often at the same time. In his case, the violin — which is almost synonymous with the red-haired violinist's sex organ — proves to be the tool that pries him from the arms of his paramour, as he loses the ability to separate his passion for the music from his passion for sex. Obsession has blurred the lines and the violin usurps his lover's place.

In symbolic terms, the immigrant "outsider" violin becomes the de facto villain in the eyes of the betrayed girlfriend — and so she shoots it in a cliché fit of jealous rage. This chapter does not really seem to fit into the complex weave of the story, and while some

Red Violin director, François Girard. ODEON AND RHOMBUS MEDIA

critics have suggested that it's simply too melodramatic and silly to work (a comment I agree with), it's worth noting that it's also the only chapter that compromises the position of the violin as mystical, miraculous outsider that has the power to heal internal pain through love. There's no doubt that particular narrative thread is the most jarring of the lot, and the symbolic knot may explain why — although it's hard to tell just what was more disturbing: the violin's compromised position, or that of virtuoso soloist Frederick Pope (Jason Flemyng), who fingers the strings in mid-coitus. Things improve, at least symbolically, in the penultimate chapter of the violin's odyssey in China, where it is persecuted for being a part of the old, elitist world order during the Cultural Revolution. Once again, the violin is an outsider — and a potentially dangerous friend — as it embodies the act of individual creation and personal expression over the forces of lockstep fascism.

By the end of the film, we have feelings for the little red violin. When violin expert Charles Morritz (Samuel L. Jackson) and the technician (Don McKellar) put it through a series of acoustic tests, it looks like a lab rat getting vivisected. It's disturbing, and so is the ending because we don't have any feelings for

the uptight, obsessed violin expert (Jackson). He is cold and ruthless and egotistical, and he's the one who walks off with the jewel under his arm. It just doesn't seem fair for a putz like him to swindle the others out of the goods, but he's the American — and naturally, he wins — whether we like it or not. The instrument is taken out of Canada. Its identity is erased and its magical catalytic power to unleash internalized expression will be harnessed by a no-goodnik Yankee. Well, that's my reading of it, at any rate. Whether Girard and McKellar had such subversive aims is hard to know for sure, but McKellar did tell me the ambiguity at the end was certainly purposeful. As for Girard, he was trying to say a lot of things through *The Red Violin* — but they had more to do with internal, Canadian linguistic politics than anything anti-American:

To me, the most important element in the film is the idea of connecting cultures. I live in Montreal and so language is hard to ignore. I want people to connect and I want people to understand each other, but in Canada, this hasn't been so easy. French and English Canada can't understand each other. There are historical reasons for this — our long history and postcolonial attitudes towards each other. We have our fair share of problems. There's a fair bit of misunderstanding where French and English Canada are concerned. We have yet to understand each other because we can't get past the language barrier.

There is so much out there. The world is full of noise. But that's what this movie is about: It is about language — not just how music is the "universal language," but how one instrument can be played by several hands, in several different ways, and maintain a certain integrity of purpose because it was created with passion. To me, that's truth ... More so than my other movies, The Red Violin *is about the whole picture — about detail versus global impression. Through the creation of this movie, I learned that human expression is often far more powerful than language itself. Language is merely the symptom of our desire to connect ... Too often, we perceive it the other way around. Language affects the way we think, the way we process information, but it can often lead us to the wrong conclusion if we aren't paying attention to the feelings behind the words.*[3]

Girard is one of the few Canadian directors who actually speaks openly about language issues and politics without trepidation, and so his comments about *The Red Violin* bring another facet to the immigrant-as-other symbol. For Girard, the time-travelling immigrant violin has the capacity to unleash expression, but it also has the capacity to rise above language — the ubiquitous Canadian pothole that throws us off course at every turn.

"Music is also a language and a way of thinking, but it is far more abstract ... and so I had to make [the cast] understand that it's not about the violin ... it's not even about the music ... it's about what we leave behind as people. If you leave behind truth and passion — and love — it will survive and resonate with other people."

PROFILE

Deepa Mehta

Born 1950 — Amritsar, India

DILIP MEHTA AND SEVILLE PICTURES

Drawn to all types of conflict, whether it be personal or political, Deepa Mehta patrols the horizon of everyday reality like a Canadian peacekeeper: watchful, empathetic and ever hopeful that she can make a difference every time she maps a landmine of intolerance. In the past, those landmines have included everything from ethnic tensions, such as in *Sam & Me* (between Jewish Canadians and Indo-Canadians) and *Earth* (between Hindus and Muslims), or gender inequality, as in her sexually charged lesbian-themed *Fire*, as well as *Camilla*, Jessica Tandy's last film in which she stars as a violinist who is creatively and spiritually squished by her tubby jackass son.

"I like stories that tell us something about the world we live in — not always as we think it should be, but as it really is," says Mehta. "If people don't like what the films show, then they should be looking at the world they created — not threatening to burn the theatre." Mehta's comments were hardly hyperbole. When *Fire* screened in India in 1998, one fundamentalist organization was so offended by its overt lesbian themes and feminist slant that they threatened violence.

"To me, *Fire* was about politics. It deals with questions of identity and who has the right to tell you who you are. This is politics — and for women, life is often a very political existence. The lesbian element is just an extension of that search for identity — but now it's been turned into something political. So you see, you can intend to do one thing — but someone will see something else. All I can tell you is that I never intended to make anything quite so controversial, but now that it's caused a reaction I hope it will raise the level of discussion and promote debate because that's the only way you can deal with oppression: by talking about it out loud."

Born in Amritsar, about 25 kilometres from Lahore, Mehta grew up around conflict in post-separation India. The wounds from the 1947 partition were still weeping and Mehta found herself asking questions that no adult could readily answer. "For the longest time, I can remember asking, "Why do people do this? Why do people hurt each other?" she says. "I never found an answer, but at least by forming a human connection with these people [in the movie *Earth*], I realized we all have the same potential within us. We all have the ability to kill. Knowing that such a possibility exists may not answer the question 'why?' but it does provide comfort by reminding us that we can all think about such things and perhaps use intelligence and compassion — instead of violence — when the next situation arises."

Mehta's desire to understand through film may well have been forged by her first years as a documentary filmmaker in India. Originally hoping to be a doctor who could heal the broken souls and broken bodies she walked by every day, Mehta abandoned her dreams of medicine to pursue a philosophy degree at the University of New Delhi. When she finished, she stayed on and joined a group of Marxist documentary filmmakers. Mehta knew a lot about film already. Her father was a film distributor and exposed her to a variety of reel worlds as a child, so the transition from abstract philosophy to the concrete medium of film came quite naturally.

"Film is very interesting to me because it has its own language that is universally understood. This eliminates many of the problems we have in trying to understand one another, which is one of my main interests: what separates us from each other? Is it age, culture, language, birthplace, religion? There are so many ways to pull us apart, but film tells stories in a way everyone can understand. It can reflect how you feel about something and how you see the world. So it's very rich that way. I'm always hopeful that it can make a difference."

Despite Mehta's boundless hope for a better world, she often tells stories with rather bleak, or at best ambiguous, endings. When she first showed *Sam & Me*, her first feature that earned kudos at Cannes (an honourable mention), to an Indian audience, they were stunned by the rather downer ending. "They were expecting a happy immigrant experience and this was not so optimistic. It was an honest portrayal of what really happens, which no one seems to talk about."

Mehta moved to Canada in the early 1970s shortly after she met her former husband, Paul Saltzman, while he was making a documentary on the High Commissioner in India. Mehta was researching the High Commissioner's daughter and the two soon found common ground in their love of film. Together with her brother, Dilip Mehta, a news photographer, the three founded Sunrise films. With little more than a script and a lot of energy, Mehta and screen-writer Ranjit Chowdry set out to make *Sam & Me*. They had no money and the funding agencies were reluctant to sponsor a film from a recent immigrant. They persevered, and the movie about an oddball friendship between an aging, demented Israeli-Canadian desperate to return to the promised land and a young Indian man looking to start a new life came together.

After *Sam & Me*'s success, Mehta did some work for George Lucas, shooting TV scripts for *The Young Indiana Jones Chronicles*. She then landed *Camilla*, a "big-budget" ($11 million) Canadian feature that starred Bridget Fonda and Jessica Tandy. The experience of directing a veteran like Tandy was challenging, but Mehta took it all in stride. Even when the film failed to live up to expectations at the box office, Mehta was suitably philosophical. "Don't be a slave to the system. No matter what system it happens to be. The only thing that really matters is how you feel about yourself and your own work — fortunately, it's also one of the things in life that you can control ... Of course, I want the films I make to be successful, but getting them made is the biggest success of all. When I made *Sam & Me*, I really didn't care if it made a penny. We made it, and that's all that mattered."

Mehta picked herself up, dusted herself off and headed back to India for her next project, *Fire* — the story of two disillusioned wives who find emotional comfort in each other's arms. The film didn't do much when it was originally released in Canada, but after the controversial run in India, *Fire* was re-released in select cities. Her next film *Earth* proved even more successful with critics and audiences alike, as it examined the most painful chapter in Indian and Pakistani history: the 1947 partition into two nations. Adapted from the autobi-ographical novel *Cracking India* by Bapsi Sidwa, *Earth* tells the story of Lenny, a young girl living in Lahore with her mother, father and beautiful nanny, Ayah. Until the partition, everything in Lenny's life is Edenic. She lives in a lovely middle-class home, she gets ice cream from her nanny's many suitors and everyone — be they Muslim, Hindu, Sikh or Parsee — live peacefully side by side. When the blade comes down on Mother Earth, however, everyone starts to bleed.

"I think you have to approach these stories with trepidation. But you have to approach them, and I thought by focusing on Lenny — a young girl caught in the middle — I would be able to find the fair and empathetic ground I needed to tell the story." Like *Fire* and *Water* — the final, and equally controversial instalment in Mehta's elemental trilogy which shows how widows were essentially discarded from Indian society in the 1930s — Mehta says all her stories are about the essence of identity.

"It's about where you live and where you feel at home. And from there, how you reflect your neighbourhood and your neighbourhood reflects you. I live in the Annex [a downtown Toronto neighbourhood] and just by saying I live in the Annex, people know what kind of person you are, a rough idea of your salary and even your political affiliation. That's what I'm talking about — what gives you a sense of identity, what makes you who you are."

FILMOGRAPHY: *At 99: A Portrait of Louise Tandy Murch* (documentary short, 1975) | *What's the Weather Like Up There* (documentary short, 1975) | *K.Y.T.E.S. How We Dream Ourselves* (documentary, 1985) | *Travelling Light: The Photojournalism of Dilip Mehta* (documentary, 1986) | *Martha, Ruth & Edie* (co-direction project with Norma Bailey and Daniele J. Suissa, 1988) | *Sam & Me* (1991) | *Camilla* (1995) | *Fire* (1996) | *Earth* (1998) | *Water* (2001)

Léa Pool

Born 1950 — Geneva, Switzerland

TORONTO FILM LIBRARY

From scrawling on blackboards in her native Switzerland to calling the shots on feature films in Canada, Léa Pool has travelled a great distance both physically and emotionally since abandoning her teaching career to study communications at L'Université du Québec à Montréal. When Pool left Geneva in 1975, she did so with the simple aim of learning to shoot video so she could teach her students what to do. She never dreamed of making movies, let alone becoming one of Canada's premier directors, but once she discovered the medium's ability to act as a type of psychic paint stripper, Pool was hooked.

Beginning with a small, co-directed documentary short about a bellhop in a hotel, *Laurent Lamerre, portier*, Pool made an impression off the bat and was given a chance. *Un Strass Café* (1980) was her first solo project — an experimental short made with the support of the National Film Board — and established Pool's artistic perspective early on. Shot in black-and-white, the film deals with urban alienation as it shows images of the cool Montreal cityscape set to a soundtrack of fragmented spoken word. Through these impressionist visuals, Pool tells the story of two people looking for love — but they never meet. Pool remembers that first film as a very "intense personal experience" because she was working alone until the moment she screened it before an audience. "It was all me ... It was a good exercise because I think I needed to be alone to find my style and to understand what I was doing without any guidance," she says. "I learned film can just pull you in a certain direction, and when it does, you should probably follow it even if you aren't too sure where, exactly, you are going."

Pool's first feature, *La Femme de l'hotel* (*A Woman in Transit*), explored similar themes. In that film, which won the International Critics' Prize at the Montreal World Film Festival and best Canadian film at the 1984 Toronto Festival of Festivals — in addition to a host of other honours around the world — we not only see the return of the hotel motif (a visual penchant she shares with Atom Egoyan), but another story that deals with fragmentation and personal identity. The film revolves around three female characters and true to reflexive Canadian form, the pivotal figure is a filmmaker, Andrea (Paule Baillargeon), who returns home to discover she is a stranger in her old hometown. The other two women are symbolic foils to Andrea the creator. One is a suicidal older woman mourning the end of a love affair; the other is an actress in Andrea's musical. Pool says the intention was to fragment the self into three parts: the conscious, the unconscious and the one forced to negotiate both at every second, the filmmaker herself. It was a complicated, surreal weave, but it worked, and Pool was suddenly hailed as a bright light in the Canadian marquee (even though half her films have never been released theatrically in English-speaking Canada because distributors don't think Anglo-Canadians, or Americans, appreciate subtitled movies).

With good reviews and a budding reputation, Pool began work on her next film, *Anne Trister*, a story that closely mirrors Pool's own life. In the story of Anne (Albane Guilhe), a woman who leaves her native Switzerland to start a new life, Pool began to unpack some of her own neatly packed parental baggage through the artistic process. Pool is the product of a mixed marriage: her father was a Jew who lived as an exile in his wife's country, leaving Pool and her brother with a cloven identity. When Pool moved to Montreal, she — like Anne — fell in love with a woman, and began to create a new self in the proverbial New World. *Anne Trister* didn't excavate all of Pool's excess luggage, but it was the beginning of her creative journey inward.

Her next film, *Straight for the Heart* (*A Corps perdu*), followed the same thread but it was more of an abstract statement on her own life as it told the story of a photojournalist who returns from an assignment in war-torn Nicaragua to discover both his male and female lover have left him — for each other. Broken and betrayed, Pierre turns his lens on the city of Montreal and finds nothing but more fragmentation. Dislocation and alienation are favoured motifs in Pool's oeuvre, but she never forgets the power of love — which has the capacity to fill the gap and bring people together. "If there is anything that I hope for [when people see my films], it's for people to relate to the characters so they know they are not alone. Everybody has feelings of alienation, but they have to know they are not

the only ones," she says. In her 1994 film, *Desire and Motion* (*Mouvements du désir*), Pool sets her contrapuntal themes of love and alienation against the vast Canadian landscape, as a train carrying two broken souls chugs its way from Montreal to Vancouver. A perfect Canadian metaphor, the railroad that brought the country together becomes the vehicle through which two lost souls find mutual understanding.

Pool's most personal film to date is her recent (1998) effort, *Emporte-moi* (*Set Me Free*). A coming-of-age story about the child of a Jewish-Catholic marriage, the film stars Karine Vanasse as Hanna, a kid who can't reconcile two different worldviews. Her Jewish father is a slightly unhinged intellectual who feels the world is out to destroy him, and her mother is a martyr who spends her days in a sweatshop to pay the bills, then comes home at night to type up her husband's prose. Hanna's only escape from this hellish existence comes in the form of Godard's *Vivre sa vie*, which Hanna watches over and over again in the quiet silence of the movie theatre.

"With *Emporte-moi*, I wanted to make a film that showed how difficult it is to be that age. Everything is very confusing, but you are trying to understand who you are so you look inside yourself for answers. The challenge in making the movie was to make this internal struggle apparent on the screen, so I show Hanna watching this strong woman [Godard's Anna Karina] in the theatre as a way of showing you who she would like to become. But outside the theatre, things are much more difficult," she says.

"It's definitely my most personal film. It's about my mother and my father and my life. My mother saw the scripts. I wanted to show them to her because it was important to me that she understood what I was trying to say, and it brought us closer together. In so many ways, the movie was a relief. It pushed me to think of things I did not really want to look at before. But making the movie, I was able to see my life from a distance. This was not just my story, it was now the story of Hanna and I could watch her and care for her as a character — not a memory," she says.

The coming-of-age story was only half the identity baggage that Pool was given a chance to unpack in *Emporte-moi*. Pool says she didn't even think about the religious baggage until she was in her thirties, when she began to feel the urge to explore her father's roots. She went to Israel and got in touch with what she describes as her "exile" side.

"We think we live in a non-religious time, which may be true. But it's not possible to escape your religious roots. The exile identity question is one I always have with me. The Jewish part of me is the exile; my father was not allowed freedom of movement. That leaves a very strong imprint on your memory. There is also the suffering. As a Jew, my father suffered for the lost generation. He was a Jew who did not die. I never thought these things affected me, but it was so deep in me ... it was subterranean. It's still difficult to talk about," she says.

What Pool does talk about, with glee, is her affection for film and the way it can bring poetry and sensuality into the darkest places. "But there is light, too," she says. "I don't just want the dark; in photography you need the light. Film is also light ... In terms of style, I just try and give a very strong point of view. Only then can you find this larger emotional scale. But for a strong point of view, it's so important to open oneself so you can get the universal. That's why I like very simple shots ... I have nothing left to prove, I'm a good filmmaker. I can relax a little. I don't need the fancy camera moves to find new ways of filming. I can relax a little now and enjoy the pleasure of living."

FILMOGRAPHY: *Laurent Lamerre, portier* (1978) | *Strass Café* (1980) | *La Femme de l'hôtel* (*Woman in Transit*, 1984) | *Anne Trister* (1986) | *À Corps perdu* (*Straight for the Heart*, 1988) | *Hotel Chronicles* (1990) | *Montréal vu par ...* (1991) | *La Demoiselle sauvage* (1991) | *Mouvements du désir* (*Desire in Motion*, 1994) | *Emporte-moi* (*Set Me Free*, 1999) | *Lost and Delirious* (2001)

Clement Virgo

Born 1966 — Montego Bay, Jamaica

EQUINOX ENTERTAINMENT

Clement Virgo describes his approach to film-making as a "happy accident that you wait to happen." One of the few Canadian filmmakers to bring God into the picture, Virgo believes in fate — even when it comes to the contrived art of making movies. "You never know exactly what's going to happen. You can prepare. You can pray. But when it comes down to the moment, you have to be open enough to see what's in front of you. Sometimes the shot you want might not be the right one — so you have to create a new shot. It's always about rolling with the punches."

In Virgo's case, one could almost take that literally. A fan of the boxing motif, which appears in *Rude* and *Love Come Down*, Virgo's films generally involve a tense conflict. Usually the tension is between family members, but it often gets projected into the larger outside world in various ways, such as boxing, gang violence, or even self-destruction through substance abuse.

"Ultimately, all storytellers reflect on life.

And for most people, life is hard, so the people in my films are always trying to overcome some obstacle. There's nothing all that unique in that, but I do believe in God, and so all my films involve a search for grace ... And that goes for the film as well as the process. I trust the artistic process completely. There are a lot of people I know, and a lot of very famous film-makers in general, who want to control every-thing — you know, like Kubrick. I feel I'm more like Truffaut or Godard, I let the passion for filmmaking guide me. I don't try to control the process at all — it's about letting go."

As a kid in Jamaica, where he lived until the age of 11, Virgo remembers watching movies in a four-walled hut without a roof. "The floor was grass and I could lie down and look up and see the stars. I can remember watching Sergio Leone movies and Karate action films. They were all pretty cheesy, but the experience was really magical. And for me, movies still are really magical. That's why I feel incredibly lucky — I get to have so much fun," he says.

As a teenager living in Toronto, Virgo's passion for film intensified with regular visits to the downtown theatres, where he soaked up the strange masterworks of Fellini while gorging on American popcorn movies. As an outsider, he identified with the likes of Jimmy Cagney in, of all things, *White Heat.* "You feel so bad for him at the end when he goes down like that, but I liked that he wasn't your arche-typal hero. He was a bad guy that you rooted for. I think I've been affected by that. I don't have archetypal heroes in my stories, either. My films show heroism, but in that antiheroic way," says the man who thought he'd never get a chance to direct movies (and briefly entertained a career as a window dresser). After a few years in the company of man-nequins, Virgo experienced something of an epiphany while watching Spike Lee's *She's Gotta Have It*. If a young black man in the United States could make movies, then why not him?

Virgo's first short film was an empowering excerise, he says. It's also a testament to his unorthodox approach. *A Small Dick Fleshy Ass Thang* was made at the Canadian Film Centre (with Virginia Rankin) during one of two summer programs he took part in and, as the title suggests, Virgo revelled in breaking a few bodily tabboos — as well as a few phallonationalist ideas.

"I like making films that have sex and bodies and all those very human things in them. I think we are so hung up on sex that we don't know how to enjoy it. Canada has never really been what you'd call a sexy nation. Not even our bands are sexy. Look at Barenaked Ladies, they are almost anti-sexy," says Virgo. "Maybe it has something to do with our documentary past, that we're always trying to show things as they are, in some authentic way, instead of romanticizing anything ... Maybe it has something to do with our harsh landscape and always being cold, I don't know, but it's hard for us to come together ... if you know what I mean."

When he first moved to Canada with his family to settle in Toronto, Virgo remembers watching old NFB reels in school and being struck by the different landscape. "There were so many images of snow. Everything looked like *Nanook of the North* — which was another movie we all saw. I'm definitely influenced by all that."

For all the differences between his native Jamaica and the Great White North, Virgo says the cool Canadian psyche doesn't frustrate him. If anything, he finds it inspiring because it leaves so much room for interesting drama. "The city is not the arctic, but it's an equally cold landscape for a lot of people — the difference is there's a lot more colour in the city. I'm Jamaican-Canadian and the influence of Jamaican culture is everywhere in Toronto," says Virgo, who sees racial issues as symptoms of the larger human condition. Virgo's films deal with racial tensions and feature a variety of ethnic performers, but race issues are never the central creative spindle. Things spiral inward in Virgo films, allowing him to avoid blanket generalizations when really, it's all just about people trying to find ways of living together — whether it's black and white, male and female, or just outsiders bonding with other outsiders.

"It's all a part of me. I feel Jamaican, I feel male, I feel Canadian," he says. "That's why I love being Canadian — you can be all those things and more. And if I can bring anything to the film tradition in this country, I hope it's sex. I would love it if Canadians suddenly became the sexiest people on the planet. I'm working on it, but I think we need a little more self-confidence. We can't be embarrassed. I mean, I'm wearing a T-shirt that says *Love Come Down*. I'm promoting my movie but a lot of Canadian directors are almost ashamed to be self-promoters. We're afraid of being cocky Americans. You go down to L.A. and people will tell you things like 'I'm the best goddamn screenwriter in the country...' and they mean it. That's a little obnoxious, but it works for them and if you ask me, there's nothing wrong with being a little cocky, and I think we have every right to be more boastful than we are."

FILMOGRAPHY: *A Small Dick Fleshy Ass Thang* (1991) | *Split Second Pullout Technique* (short, 1992) | *Save My Lost Nigga Soul* (1993) | *Rude* (1995) | *The Planet of Junior Brown* (1997) | *One Heart Broken Into Song* (1999) | *Love Come Down* (2000)

CHAPTER NINE

The Incredible Weight of Being

TALKING PHILOSOPHY WITH THE GRIM REAPER

We started out so grounded. Firmly fastened to the earth with a tripod and rooted to reality through a documentarian's eye, early Canadian film emerged from the womb of creation with a desire to simply open our eyes to the reality around us. It crawled across empty white landscapes dotted with tiny black shapes on the horizon, tugged at the apron strings of our ancestral histories and established point of view — all in the hopes of telling us who we were, and what we looked like. We reached into empty space to feel the walls of our identity. We set out to explore the open space, and brushed up against different notions of "other" to find community. Now, we're going to deal with the biggest other of all: the empty hole that's usually six feet deep, Death itself. Death is an intrinsic part of the Canadian landscape and as much a part of our national psyche as weird sex and snow imagery. From the opening funeral shot in *Mon Oncle Antoine* to the proliferation of West Coast drug-culture movies that deal with the nihilism of narcotic abuse — not to mention every David Cronenberg movie ever produced — death lurks behind the curtain in Canadian film. In the context of negative theory, it's not hard to see why the Grim Reaper is a recurring character in our cinematic history, because death is the antithesis of being; it is the essence of what we are *not*.

Pondering the great beyond, and in the process the meaning of life itself, is a highly abstract occupation. It can begin with a concrete recognition of corpses, but as thoughts about death mature, they generally move toward metaphysics. We go from body to brain, or the concrete to the abstract, much in the same way that the Canadian film tradition has evolved from a documentary to auteur-driven fiction. We started out grounded but as the years wore on, and awareness of our own image increased, the camera freed itself from the so-called sticks (that's film terminology for a tripod, eh?) to become a free-floating appendage that could walk side by side with a filmmaker along a stream of consciousness. As consciousness turned inward, films began to ask harder questions. They challenged us to rethink reality. Time began to twist and warp. Camera techniques and methods of film recording began to polymorphize: steadicams, cranes, dollies, helicopters, digital video, video, animation, computer animation ... even the unholy force of special effects. We recorded those who were visible and dug into the social folds to find people who weren't.

The film tradition that started as a single cell amoeba — a social experiment in the institutional corridors of the National Film Board — mutated into a hulking multicellular consciousness trying to understand its place in the world. Rigid institutional minds feared its differences, for it was never all that pretty. It was also hostile to any attempt to cage or control its creative spirit. Threatened, they lobbed barbed insults, and ridiculed its primitive technique and grainy imagery. Like *The Blob* or *The Thing*, they saw this mutant art form as a pinko experiment gone awry and some, who were reluctant to embrace the change the creature represented, tried to kill the struggling life form, fearing it would destroy the towns and townspeople — leaving nothing but death and destruction in its wake now that it was thawing out, and could think for itself. Alas, the poor creature was simply misunderstood.

It used to be perceived as being over-sentimental and earnest. Evolving up here in the emptiness of the frozen north, The Thing called Canadian film has often been accused of having a reptilian heart and a cold, cunning mind. Either way, at the big prom of film traditions, we're the weird wallflower — standing outside the coupled dancers, processing why we don't fit in — and usually, it's because we prefer being right where we are. While the "popular" films of the day flickered across the theatres of the nation and the world, showing off their pearly white caps at Oscar time, almost all Canadian films unwound a day or a few days at a time in the darkened corners of cinémathèques and art house cinemas — a deformed child that no one dared acknowledge, just like the nonverbal son locked in the attic in Guy Maddin's *Careful*. In the tower, it found company in the likes of other exiles — the French New Wave, German expressionism, American experimental film, English kitchen-sink drama and the Nordic existentialism of Ingmar Bergman — but it still longed to be acknowledged by its own family and loved for what it was ... as well as what it was not.

It was us, but it was also "other" in its refusal to stay inside the lines of the Hollywood model, and it confused some audience members to the point of trepidation. For some, it's the lack of a happy ending — or any easily recognizable ending at all — that creates

the stumbling block. For others, it comes down to the common refrain: "They're just too cerebral to be moving." This is particularly true of English-Canadian cinema, which is not only burdened by the internalized Canadian experience but by the language as well (which, as we saw in the previous chapter, bends toward the analytical side of the spectrum as opposed to the emotional one). For the average moviegoer, this means Canadian film presents more than your average number of emotional and rational challenges to the audience as it often refuses closure, revels in ambiguity, obsesses about death and plays with notions of linear time and personal identity until they lose all sense of familiarity or meaning.

After a steady diet of easy-to-swallow, escapist entertainment from Hollywood, we've absorbed a lot of their conscious resistance to death. American starlets never age. American heroes are bulletproof. Canadian women are gorgeously earthy. Our guys rarely carry guns — but they often end up dead. Death, loss, destruction — who needs it? No wonder a lot of Canadians turn up their noses at the intellectual brainteasers concocted by our filmmakers: obsessing about death doesn't seem like much fun.

The purpose of this chapter is to coax you into thinking otherwise. After all, there is a lot of pleasure to be had in the process of processing, and through a meditation on death, we have a better appreciation for life. Over the course of the next few pages, we'll exhume some concrete images of death and gradually move into an investigation of a more abstract or metaphysical relationship with the great beyond in our continuing search for psychic wholeness. We'll look at some of the "tougher" Canadian films and discuss what makes them so challenging. In some cases, it's narrative structure; in others, it's content. Underlying most of them is an awareness of death and a desire to reconcile the two competing forces of nature. Only by integrating both can one reach a "higher plane" — or, what is generally referred to as "a state of enlightenment." In other cultures, this is religious experience. In ours — now that Canadian society has distanced itself from the institutions of the church (Quiet Revolution) and the state (Newman's take on the Mulroney years) — it's very often a philosophical exercise. Without a god, or blind faith in the concept of heaven and the afterlife, it's up to the individual — and the individual filmmaker — to negotiate the metaphysical distance between life and death.

The Needle and the Damage Done

Before we head down the tortuous road to metaphysics, we'll begin with a look at some concrete examples of our relationship with death as absolute "other" in Canadian film. The best illustrations of our tangible nihilist streak can be seen in the microcosm of West Coast Canadian film — particularly the work of young Vancouver filmmakers. Famed for its Downtown Eastside, where the majority of Canada's heroin addicts gather for their daily dance with death, Vancouver has its fair share of demons, and like their brethren booting around the rest of the country, they live deep inside. Exploring the crevasse of addiction has become a favoured West Coast motif. We can see characters battling the same bout with self several times over in movies like Martin Cummins' *We All Fall Down* (2000), Kirsten Clarkson's *Horsey* (1997), Ross Weber's *No More Monkeys Jumpin' on the Bed* (2000), Bruce Spangler's *Protection* (2000) and even the Vancouver police department's well-received documentary, *Through a Blue Lens* (1999).

In the same way that politics and language drove a hole through the soul of central Canada and gave it a sense of definition, so it is that heroin, crack, crystal meth and all the pharmaceutical escape routes drill a hole through the West Coast character — which typically lacks the easy linguistic "other" against which to define itself. The externalized oppressor in these movies can be an abusive partner or a family tragedy, but the coping dynamic is usually uniform — at least in symbolic terms, because it's all about self-escape and a need to flirt with death. Addicts essentially do nothing but escape who they are. Effacing their very identity with every injection, they too are defined by the holes — the series of needle sites that constantly need feeding.

In *Protection*, former social worker and first-time feature film director Bruce Spangler shows us the cycle of addiction through the eyes of a child protection worker, Jane (Nancy Sivak). Bordering on burnout, Jane is losing touch with her job, her colleagues and her own self — a point Spangler makes in the opening frames of the film as he shows us Jane in her car, making her way across the Pattullo Bridge to the City of Surrey. The image is shot in negative, an effect that dislocates the viewer immediately and sets Jane up as an alien, driving through a rain-soaked moonscape. As someone assigned to guard the next generation, Jane is supposed to be a force of life, but as a representative of a government institution chained to filing cabinets and triplicate forms, Jane eventually finds herself becoming a passive voyeur as the Grim Reaper closes in on her caseload.

Another film that breaks linear narrative, *Protection* deals with one central plot element from a variety of perspectives to give us a multilayered, impressionist take on everything from bureaucratic fatigue to addiction to maternal love. The ordering storyline revolves around Jane and Betty (Jillian Fargey), a heroin-addicted mother who can't seem to kick regardless of the hours spent in therapy, family counselling and rehabilitation centres. When Jane decides to check up on Betty as part of her regular follow-up visits, she finds a whole new knotted maggot's nest of problems: Betty and boyfriend Don (William McDonald) are still using; Betty's son has a black eye; Betty's daughter says Don comes in to her bedroom at night and touches her; the house is a mess and there's no food in the refrigerator. The professional alarm bells sound in Jane's head: the children are not safe. She must perform an apprehension. Like almost any mother, Betty wants to keep her kids. She truly loves them — but when it comes down to a choice between her children (the concrete symbols of affirmation and pro-creation) or the drugs (the concrete symbol of self-destruction), Betty inevitably chooses death because she is too weak, too diseased, to choose life. *Protection* is a truly tragic story made darker by its ambiguous ending, which suggests nothing will ever change. This is a "real life" approach and Spangler's shaky digital video-cameras tell us as much through cinema-direct style.

Similar realist techniques can be seen in *No More Monkeys Jumpin' on the Bed*, another digital movie about addiction — only with a hint of humour — and *Through a Blue Lens*, an NFB-funded documentary about Vancouver's Downtown Eastside drug addicts photographed by the police officers who deal with the victims of the syringe-facilitated sickness every day on the job.

Another example of wrestling with the drug-demon of death can be seen in the more sophisticated cinematic language of Martin Cummins' *We All Fall Down*. Shot with a professional look on 35mm stock by Cummins' work

buddies from *Poltergeist* — the Vancouver-spun TV series — the film does not have the same shaky-cam style as its lower-budget brethren, but it's still firmly rooted in reality.

Loosely based on Cummins' own battles with the needle in the wake of his mother's death, *We All Fall Down* breaks the internal demon of death into two different characters. There is Michael (Darcy Belsher), a man who was abandoned by his dad as a kid and just recently lost his mother, making him a lone, grieving orphan without any sense of family or sense of purpose. His symbolic mirror, or twin, is Kris (Cummins), a good-looking user and good-time Charlie. The more alienated Michael feels, the closer he gets to Kris and the very precipice of heroin addiction. Does Michael have the strength to save himself? That's the question that drives this well-scripted story forward and gives it a good engine of dramatic tension as it pits the corrosive death force against the fragile thread of life in every frame.

For Cummins, *We All Fall Down* was more than a first film project; it was art therapy that gave him a chance to deal with his own ghosts in a creative way.

"After acting in 88 hours of television, I needed to do something creative, otherwise I would have taken a gun to my head,"[1] Cummins said in the wake of his directorial debut after it premiered at the 2000 Toronto International Film Festival. "This movie has been sitting in me for quite some time and making the movie was like bringing some sort of closure to that chapter in my life. Also, part of the disease of addiction is secrecy, and now everyone knows I was a user. I don't have to carry that around any more so it feels like a huge release just finishing the film — and the way we shot it, with people I know, like Helen [Shaver] ... it made it all feel like a family effort. It was exactly what I needed because family was what I lost. My mom died, then my granddad died two months afterward. I couldn't fucking cope and I used dope as a Band-Aid, but ultimately, it only made me sicker ... I guess we do it all on purpose. I look at my son and he says things like: 'You know, Dad, soon the sun will come out and we'll ride our bikes.' And really, it's that fucking simple. But for some reason, we choose to complicate things. We create drama in our own lives because we aren't comfortable without it."

Cummins' comments remind us of two things: the healing power of creative expression, and the phenomenon of the split self. Without tension, the internal twins would fuse into a formless blob without any forward momentum, which may explain why a lot of these junkie stories emerge from the moist loins of the coastal rainforest. Out here on the fabulously scenic West Coast, we are often accused of being too laid-back and lazy. It's a bit of an unfair generalization, but there's some truth to it because far removed from the dynamo of Ontario-Quebec tensions, the West lacks an easily recognizable "other" to wind its spring — and so we look for some essence of life by embracing death at the pointy end of a syringe.

Independent American filmmaker Bill Brown saw Vancouver's obsession with disaster and negative energy in a slightly different way in his film *Confederation Park* (1999). A solo road movie that explores the Canadian landscape from a southerner's viewpoint, Brown travelled from one end of the nation to the other with a little camera and an outsider's perspective. The results were memorable — and rather unique — as it's not often that we get a chance to see how America sees Canadians as different, instead of just a funny-talking version of themselves.

When Brown turned his lens on Lotus Land, he was struck by our fascination with the dark side. We talked about earthquakes and floods and revelled in urban decay. To him, it made no sense, because to the naked eye, British Columbia is Eden (if you don't believe me, look at the landscape shots in *Rupert's Land* and feel your jaw drop).

As though recognizing the positive is a jinx in itself, we prefer to keep quiet. Or as Brown says, "Living in paradise makes people nervous." [2]

The Last Ride

In *rollercoaster* (1999), Scott Smith's beautifully acted tale about teen suicide, we encounter a group of young people who break into an amusement park called Wonder World (Vancouver's Playland) off-season to off themselves. Darrin (Kett Turton) and Chloe (Crystal Bublé), Stick (Brendan Fletcher), Justin (Brent Glenen) and Sanj (Sean Amsing) are all teens living in the same group home. One day they steal a car and break into a boarded-up and bankrupt amusement park for a little fun — or in the case of Darrin and Chloe, two young lovers who have made a suicide pact — for a final goodbye. To Darrin, a young rebel robbed of stable family life, death looks like the ultimate act of rebellion — and it makes him giddy. As they wander around the empty, dilapidated park, which provides a beautiful symbol of the kids' lost innocence, Darrin revs with excitement at the thought that soon, he'll be worry free. The others, particularly his best friend Stick, aren't so convinced — but they say nothing to sway Darrin from his purpose because he's so clearly alive just thinking about the moment where he will *not* be. In a beautiful example of negative theory and our nagging linguistic hang-ups, the kids play a game called

rollercoaster (1999): Brendan Fletcher, Sean Amsing, Crystal Bublé, Kett Turton and Brent Glenen play a group of troubled kids who break into an amusement park and lose their innocence in director Scott Smith's debut. GIRAFFE PRODUCTIONS

"Opposites," where you have to answer a question in the exact opposite way that you intend. For instance, in one sequence that features Stick talking to his best buddy Darrin: "I hate you, Darrin. I fucking hate you!"

As we'd expect, there's a lot going on beneath the surface of this Canadian film. We have the tension of the suicide pact, a disturbing encounter with a pedophilic guard, a lingering abortion question (Chloe is pregnant) and one character's personal battle as he comes to grips with his homosexuality. In this complex weave, death becomes the defining force that will either swallow the characters whole, or push them past their own barriers into self-acceptance. The choice is theirs, but either way, whether they choose the swan dive from the top of the roller coaster or a quiet return to the land of the living, they leave

transformed by their dance with death. In his director's statement contained in the press notes for *rollercoaster*, Smith says he was fascinated by the subject of teen suicide pacts and wanted to work within the metaphorical landscape of an abandoned amusement park: "I felt the emptiness of a space once home to so much delight was a perfect metaphor for the loss of childhood and the rides themselves for the volatility of existence ... In making this film, I have come no closer to 'unlocking' the mystery of suicide. The film does, I think, provide some insight into the appeal of escape suicide, just as the escape of the amusement park provides us with relief from everyday life."

Nordic Sensibilities

There is nothing uniquely Canadian about our philosophical film bent and cinematic obsession with death. The drive is universal and is the common denominator for the human condition, which must — by its very existence — reconcile the relationship between the internalized sense of consciousness and the external, concrete reality in which it finds itself. Given that our reality is cooler and emptier than most, it's not surprising to find similarities between Canadian and Scandinavian, or Nordic, film traditions in the way we approach larger philosophical questions about the meaning of life.

Certainly to an outsider, Canadian film bears remarkable similarities to the work of Swedish director Ingmar Bergman, playwrights Harold Pinter and Henrik Ibsen, and in some cases, even German filmmakers such as Rainer Werner Fassbinder or his heir to the Teutonic film throne, Tom Tykwer. We share the same landscape and the same quality of light. Through the lens of a camera, our realities are bound to look similar. This explains why people like Robert Lepage say the only similarity between English-Canadian and Québécois film is the landscape itself — which simply reveals a shared northern sensibility and not much more. It also explains why, when Catherine Annau showed *Just Watch Me* to American audiences, their response was: "That's the way I see all northern cultures." There's no denying our philosophical stance has been influenced by the landscape north of the 49th parallel. It pushes us to recognize how small and fragile we are. It can also push us into an extreme state of alienation — where we experience a greater awareness of the void and Death himself.

I remember reading Ingmar Bergman's autobiography, *The Magic Lantern*, and being struck by his temporary descent into madness in the wake of a tax problem:

The breakdown came Monday morning. I was sitting at home in the big room on the first floor, reading a book and listening to music ... I felt nothing ... and now I was deep down in an emotional vacuum, painless and free of emotions. I closed my eyes. I thought I had closed my eyes, then there was someone in the room and I opened my eyes. In the sharp light, a few metres away, I was standing looking at myself. The experience was concrete and incontestable. I was standing on the yellow rug looking at myself sitting in the chair. I was sitting in the chair looking at myself standing on the yellow rug ... This was the end, there was no return.[3]

The psychotic break that Bergman experienced in the wake of being questioned by police pushed him out of himself into that "other reality" that is not governed by the senses. In that other reality, he was lost. He couldn't even write, but as time wore on and he relaxed into the unchallenging rhythm of the mental home, he began to reach outward.

"I don't know what made me break out of this hermetically sealed security ... Every morning, I walked for an hour in the park, the shadow of an eight-year-old beside me; it was both stimulating and uncanny. Otherwise, this was a time of violent torment. My suppressed anxiety shot up like the flame of a blowlamp ... Demons were raging. I thought I would be torn apart by internal detonations ... I went on to attack my demons ... I had declared myself guilty without being guilty, craving punishment so that I would receive forgiveness and release as quickly as possible."[4]

I see a lot of "us" in that descent into loner hell as it hitches up to our thematic raft so far: Bergman talks about the split of self, about negative space or "the internal vacuum," and walking alongside a younger, innocent version of himself. The words prompt mental images of Pierre taking Marc's child across the bridge in *Le Confessional* and just about any sequence in a Cronenberg movie where the main character looks in the mirror to see a shape he does not immediately recognize as his own — like when Jeff Goldblum checks his hairy reflection in *The Fly*. The similarities are clearly there, reaffirming the importance of landscape in shaping a cinematic vision — but there are subtle variances that separate the Canadian film tradition from its Old World ancestor. Over time, in this cinematic Galapagos, we have evolved into a different animal altogether. As we continue to move through this chapter, we'll explore the metaphysical landscape of Canadian film. We'll examine different ways in which Canadian filmmakers have negotiated their relationship to the great beyond of otherness and emptiness. We'll also dig into the different layers of cinematic form to see how the filmmaking process itself mirrors the metaphysical quest. Hopefully, we can better understand this beast we made so we can bring it in from the cold for a long-overdue warm embrace by the ol' hearthfires of home.

Shooting Monsters

I made a reference to old-fangled science fiction movies at the beginning of this chapter for a reason: Monsters are always incarnations of ourselves — the shadow self, the demon within — and they appear with regularity in cultures that fear "the other" as a threat to a highly traditional, and often fundamentalist, society. During the Cold War in the United States, science fiction films with creepy, ooey, gooey, formless mutant monsters like *The Thing* were so popular they became a genre unto themselves. At the time, there was a deep fear of saying anything political in the United States, lest one be branded a Communist sympathizer. Also, people were just beginning to come to grips with the fact they now had the capacity to destroy the planet. In other words, there were externally generated fears about subversion and Soviets, but there were also internal fears, and no doubt deeply repressed guilt, about the monster of nuclear war that America had unleashed on the world. To deal with this new world order, America brought out the blamethrower and created an externalized enemy: the invading monster out to kill humanity.

Canadian film has its share of monsters, too, thanks to David Cronenberg. But even though our ghoulies might bear some physical, slime-covered resemblance to the creatures that emerged from the American subconscious during the Cold War, they negotiate a

different philosophical dilemma. Our monsters do not emerge fully formed and hostile to maintain a psychic balance (or "positive identity") the way Hollywood constantly constructs villains to maintain a homogenous and heroic stance. Canadian monsters almost always come from within.

David Croneneberg and the Cartesian Question

For the longest time, David Cronenberg's fascination with lumpy prostheses, phallusshaped parasites, anal penetration and the animal side of sexual metamorphosis actually had him labelled a commercial sell-out within the Canadian film clique. Critics in the early years saw his use of fantasy and fictional devices as a betrayal to the more authentic documentary tradition. His crimes were only deemed more offensive when his films turned out to make more money than any of those crafted by his earnest compatriots. And while the king of Canadian horror has certainly experimented with the vat of American genre film, there is always something undeniably Canadian about the way he uses weeping sores and rubber schlongs to articulate his philosophic stance to the Canadian reality: the monsters, or monstrous protrusions, generally manifest themselves as part of the protagonist's body. We may be distracted by these cancerous lesions and pus-filled sores — and see them as a plain horror device — but make no mistake, they represent death. Cronenberg's creative engine is fuelled by an obsession with death, and particularly with the way the human body is pulled apart by the Grim Reaper's bony hand before the mind has a chance to catch up.

Cronenberg is an atheist and a disciple of Cartesian theory, which means he believes all reality stems from our physical presence —

The Brood (1979): Samantha Eggar unveils the truth, and her canine, corporeal transformation in David Cronenberg's bizarre horror movie about empathic, deformed children that was released with the tagline "The ultimate experience of inner terror." LAUREM PRODUCTIONS

our flesh and blood. René Descartes (1596-1650) was a mathematician who sought an empirical foundation for all knowledge and is best known for his declaration "I think therefore I am." In his famous essay, "Discourse on the Method of Rightly Conducting the Reason, and Seeking Truth in Sciences," Descartes begins by saying that "being possessed with a vigorous mind is not enough; the prime requisite is rightly to apply it."[5] Descartes knew there were several conflicting theories about the nature of the universe and man's place in it, so he decided to doubt them all. The only truth he could come up with was based on his own

experience: He was thinking, therefore, he must exist.

If the physical presence is the first Cartesian fact of life, then Cronenberg's bodily distortions take on a whole new meaning. They aren't just creepy violations of the flesh, they reshape the afflicted character's perception of reality — and in turn, reframe existence as a whole. All the organic grotesqueries inevitably ooze death, transforming their victims one flesh flap at a time. The motif is nearly universal in Cronenberg's filmography. In his first feature, *Shivers* (which was also known as *The Parasite Murders*), and the thematically portentous *They Came From Within* (1975), Cronenberg shows us a blistered banana of a prop pushing up through the drainpipe and penetrating unsuspecting apartment dwellers. Once firmly inside "the victim," the blob begins to alter his or her relationship to the outside world. Even though it's really cold outside, and the Montreal location (The Starliner Apartments) looks as warm and inviting as an operating room, the Starline residents get hot in this hard-edged, prisonlike apartment. We learn it's all the result of — yes! — a scientific experiment gone awry. A researcher developed the parasite in the hopes of getting people to love each other a little bit more — only to find out that the parasite turns people into libidinous but homicidal sex freaks. Yep. The thematically dynamic duo of sex and death get another spin on the dance floor, picking up where they left off with weird sex — and going deeper.

For all the thematic resonance in Cronenberg's work, *Shivers* marked the first perversion of traditional notions of Canadian movie-making by introducing fantasy and directly referring to sexual acts. It was panned. But in a metaphorical way, it got its own revenge as it showed what happens to people living in repressed societies: they develop hidden, potentially destructive outlets to indulge their natural cravings. From the cool landscape to the way the residents of the Starline prefer to keep to themselves, *Shivers* was a definite comment on uptight Canadian culture and stifling WASP codes of behaviour, and so it is no surprise to find our first fantasized mediation of "other" — in this case, the monster — "comes from within."

After *Shivers*, Cronenberg's eye was cast: his thick-glassed gaze was focused on themes of death, repression, internal conflict, twisted manifestations of creativity and the physical

means through which we process reality. Adopting a fantasy or sci-fi stance in the films, Cronenberg was able to turn everything inward. He could create anything he wanted to in his own private fantasy world. If he was thinking weeping wounds, he could make a movie about them. As a result of this leap of creativity, one is never sure what is actually happening in a Cronenberg movie, and as with most Canadian filmmakers, that seems to be the whole point of Cronenberg's art. He creates a universe that looks familiar — if not wholly authentic — then he slowly pokes holes through his screen with clawed hands, showing us that beneath the clean veneer, something strange and twisted is suckling at the teat of imagination. He even uses that very suckling image in *The Brood* (1979) as he unveils the protagonist's ex-wife as a psychotic mutant she-wolf who gives birth to damaged, violent, dwarflike children who function as empaths. If the mother is happy, the children are quiet. But when mummy gets threatened or angry, the creepy kids begin bludgeoning unsuspecting adults — symbolically taking revenge on all those adults who neglected their inner children, and their inherent creativity.

The thematic mechanics are always the same: the "other" — the creative self — has been internalized to the point where it's desperate for release, turns bitter and transforms itself into a monster capable of ripping right through the flesh of the host to get out. People are always popping out of rubber cocoons fashioned by art director Carol Spier in Cronenberg movies, whether it's in the form of a hostile VCR in *Videodrome* (1983) or an Underwood cockroach in *Naked Lunch* (1991). The sheer artifice of the costumes and special effects, combined with the suspension of disbelief it takes to enter a world in which heads explode (*Scanners*) have reduced the intellectual impact of Cronenberg movies, leading many to believe he's just another schlock artist out to make a buck off gore-swilling teenage boys. While that may well be true in some respects, there was one recent Cronenberg effort that was trashed by intellects and teenage boys alike — and continues to be one of my favourite movies of all time.

EXistenZ (1999) was the most complete philosophical treatise Cronenberg ever put to film, and one of the few films in his cinematic cabinet of Dr. Caligari that didn't rely on long, throbbing monstrosities — which probably explains why the film was not as popular with teenage boys as producer Robert Lantos and Cronenberg would have liked.

Set in the not-too-distant future, this Cronenberg effort picks up on the latest trend in entertainment — and what is currently the largest piece in the entertainment industry pie: the $7-billion U.S. video-game industry. An addiction-forming activity that produces different brainwaves, video games are an interesting watermark in the pool of pop culture. They are not "productive," nor are they all that educational. They are the height of escapist entertainment — and modern society can't get enough of them. In this case, they aren't video games as such, they are video games taken to the next level: the processor is all inside your own skull cavity. You play the game via a biological plug-in that interfaces directly with your central nervous system, meaning there is no screen or control pad — only your body and the messages from your brain.

In the opening sequence of the film, we are introduced to the new game, eXistenZ, and the woman who created it, Allegra Geller (Jennifer Jason Leigh), a superstar game designer and a complete introvert. (At this point, it should be noted that our powerbroker is a woman, and a woman who seeks freedom to choose — two details that reaffirm the film's Canadian sensibilities.) Allegra is addressing a focus group of sorts: a bunch of gamers who have been selected to give her latest creation a complete demo. The meeting seems to be a big secret, and people are searched as they enter a room that looks a lot like a refitted church — the windows are leaded and stained glass, but there is no sign of an altar or crucifix, just a big blackboard with the word "eXistenZ" written on it. From this, we can gather that this not-too-distant future is a world where religion and other formalized belief systems have been usurped by escapist forms of entertainment. (Like I said, this is a *not-too-distant* future). But even on that score, eXistenZ (the game) aims higher

Naked Lunch (1991): There's no shortage of surreal images in David Cronenberg's adaptation of William S. Burroughs' quasi-autobiographical novel that revels in hallucinogenic episodes featuring typewriters that turn into cockroachs and a variety of other metamorphosing bodies. ALLIANCE ATLANTIS

than mere escapism. According to Allegra: "The world of games is in a kind of trance. People are programmed to accept so little, but the possibilities are so great." Ahh ... The possibilities! There are so many courses of action, but as a result of corporate brainwashing in the name of creating better consumers, we've lost touch with that all-important notion of free will. Allegra wants us to rediscover the idea of free choice — and so her game creates a variety of scenarios that prompts the player to make a series of decisions.

Nothing too revolutionary in that: even current video games demand decision-making skill. Where eXistenZ deviates from the multitude of familiar game titles, though, is the level of immersion, or what's referred to as "flow." When you plug the game into your "bioport" — an anus-like socket at the base of the spine that accesses your central nervous system — you suddenly lose all sense of what is "real" and what is imagined. You enter an alternate reality.

In the context of the film, this means we are never quite sure which level of reality we're dealing with. Are we in the "real" world or are we in the "game world" — or neither? Cronenberg gives us no easy answers, because that's the crux of his entire oeuvre: can you trust what you see? Can you trust your senses? If not, how does one know anything at all with any certainty? How does one live?

These are the same questions that preoccupied Descartes, and they form the foundation layer of meaning in eXistenz as the characters move through a similar series of "doubt tests" trying to understand the nature of experience, and particularly, the nature of

eXistenZ (1999): Allegra Geller (Jennifer Jason Leigh) attempts to explain the ins and outs of virtual realities to a reticent Ted Pikul (Jude Law), a marketing assistant desperate to cling to the version of reality he's familiar with, even though there's no way he can truly tell if his version of reality is live or eXistenZ. AVA GERLITZ AND ALLIANCE ATLANTIS

the game they are playing. Likewise, the audience is pulled into this Cartesian guessing game as Allegra and Ted Pikul (Jude Law) begin their adventure.

For those who haven't seen the movie, here's a brief synopsis: Allegra unveils her new system, but after an attempt is made on her life, she and the public relations assistant, Ted Pikul hit the road. Allegra worries about the health of her biotech game after the attack, and she cajoles Ted into plugging into the system with her. As the two fugitives explore the game terrain, they realize there's a war going on between "the realists" and the gaming giant Cortical Systematics. The only question left for the viewer, then, is, what's real and what's not? We can never really tell, because as an audience, we are also locked into a single frame of reference when we look at the movie screen, and Cronenberg is constantly shifting gears and changing realities throughout the picture. In the end, we aren't sure if the characters are truly alive or simply software creations designed to emulate real human beings. In this way, Cronenberg's mediation with death is completely abstract as it pushes us to question what existence means from a completely cerebral place. The flipside of this inquiry into the nature of life is therefore an investigation of death, and how it translates into the alternate reality of the game:

PIKUL: I don't want to be here. I don't like it here. I don't know what's going on. We're both stumbling around together in this unformed world, whose rules and objectives are largely unknown, seemingly indecipherable, or even possibly nonexistent, always on the verge of being killed by forces we don't understand.
GELLER: That sounds like my game all right.

PIKUL: That sounds like a game that's not going to be easy to market.
GELLER: But it's a game everyone is already playing.

Cronenberg loves playing this Cartesian game of "guess what's real," and it recurs in almost all of his work, from *Videodrome* (1983), which blurred the line between TV broadcasts and reality, to non-authored projects like *Naked Lunch* (where drugs blur the line for the William Burroughs character), *Dead Ringers* (where twins, and their twin realities, become the central motif), and including *M. Butterfly* (1993) (where a man falls in love with the female image of an opera star, only to discover the diva is a man).

EXistenZ is the cumulative result of all this reasoned searching, which may explain why the film was deemed so convoluted by a lot of people. It's designed to make you question, and if you leave the theatre thinking a little bit more about life, or TV, or pretty much anything, chances are the film did what it was supposed to.

Says Cronenberg in an interview contained in the graphic novel version of *eXistenZ*: "One of the excitements of course about getting into the game in [*eXistenZ*] is to find yourself questioning what reality is: to what extent we create our own reality, to what extent are we all characters in our own game and we do play certain roles and can alter them and shift them to a certain extent, and as you get older you begin to realize — it becomes a very strong and very palpable thing that people define their own characters almost as if they have written them."[6]

When *eXistenZ* was released in the spring of 1999, it was one of the most ambitious launches in Alliance-Atlantis history — complete with a simultaneous American and

Canadian release. Usually, Canadian films are released in Canada first, where they are supposed to gather steam and good press, then make the leap into the cutthroat U.S. market. I had a feeling *eXistenZ* would do very well, not only because I liked it a lot, but because, as a part-time video game reviewer, I knew how close Cronenberg was to lifting the veil on one of the most disturbing entertainment trends to hit us since TV. Video games are mind-altering, highly addictive and potentially harmful entertainment products. But we all love to have fun. We love to escape and think of nothing, and video games are the fastest-growing segment in entertainment industry, not to mention one of the major factors behind personal computer sales. I believed *eXistenZ* captured the gaming world in the big picture, and as a result, would become a touchstone for the times.

I was wrong. The movie didn't fail at the box office, but it had a hard time competing against a similarly themed movie that came out just a few months earlier called *The Matrix*. (There was also a third movie that was released around the same time called *The Thirteenth Floor*, which was by far the worst of the three efforts, but nonetheless suggests the mood of the moment was to question, question, question.)

Because *eXistenZ* and *The Matrix* came out so close to one another, it's worth making a few comparisons. *The Matrix* (which, incidentally, starred two Canadians, Keanu Reeves and Carrie-Anne Moss) was about an alternate reality, called *The Matrix*, created by a race of machines who used human beings as their main energy source. In order to keep the humans quiet and orderly in small pods, the machines implanted memories and lifestyle programs into their heads so they would believe they were actually running around,

working, partying and playing in the big city instead of sitting lifeless in a pool of jelly. The humans have absolutely no say in their fate. They are merely prisoners until they "wake up," are spewed out of the system and become outlaws. And we all know what happens when you are an outlaw in a big-budget American movie: you end up shooting a lot of guns, which is exactly what happens in *The Matrix* as our renegade heroes attempt to pull the system down from the inside. *eXistenZ* deals with a similarly internalized style of thought-control. Once people are immersed in the game reality, they lose touch with their own sense of free will. This is illustrated in one scene at the restaurant where Pikul and Allegra chow down on mutant fish:

> *PIKUL: I do feel the urge to kill someone here.*
> *ALLEGRA: Who?*
> *PIKUL: I need to kill our waiter.*
> *ALLEGRA: Oh, well, that makes sense. When he comes over, do it, don't hesitate.*
> *PIKUL: But everything in the game is so realistic. I don't think I really could.*
> *ALLEGRA: You won't be able to stop yourself. You might as well enjoy it.*
> *PIKUL: Free will is obviously not a big factor in this little world of ours.*
> *ALLEGRA: It's like real life ... there's just enough to keep it interesting.*

While this passage clearly shows our distinct, deadpan sense of humour, it also shows us that free will is an important part of the plot. The people in *eXistenZ* are willing participants in the false reality. The people in *The Matrix* are not — they are simple victims. From an intellectual standpoint, Cronenberg's diagram is far more interesting because it places all the decision-making power in the hands of the individual, who, in turn, gives away all of his or her power in exchange for some mind-numbing entertainment. Granted, it's an equation that is far more difficult to reconcile than the good-people-bad-machine diagram in *The Matrix*, but once again, that's the beauty of Canadian film: it pushes us to think for ourselves, and in doing so, reminds us of all the things that make us human — namely, our ability to think, our ability to exercise our own free will, and the desire to laugh. I've always laughed at Cronenberg movies — just as I laugh at the cheese factor in most horror movies. I don't know if I'm supposed to or not, but I think that Cronenberg, as a good Canadian, has included a funny bone in his goody bag of body parts. I mean, how else am I supposed to read the scene where Pikul gets sexually aroused by Allegra, then gets all nervous about the idea of leaving reality? "That's my pink phone," he shouts as he plunges his hand into his trouser pocket to answer the ring. No sooner does he fish his pink thing out than Allegra tosses it out the window. "What did you do that for?" screams the nerdwink Pikul. "That was our lifeline to civilization!" I have no doubt Cronenberg, like all men, has his very own pink phone that he carries with him in his pants, strapping him to civilization, and all other constructs of reality, particularly the one that matters most: the body — the living, breathing, but oh-so-temporary negation of death.

Rubik's Cubism

In Vincenzo Natali's debut feature, *Cube* (1997 — made at the Canadian Film Centre for $700,000), we move through a similar mind-maze as Cronenberg's, as six people find themselves trapped in a giant cube for no apparent reason. The film opens with a close-up of an eye. We hear a strange, jarring sound then the camera pulls back to reveal an entire man — just before he falls to pieces. Razor-wired into tiny, bloody cubes, the man is the first of many victims in this mystery thriller with an existential bent.

Like *eXistenZ*, and as we'll see later on in *Possible Worlds*, *Cube* takes place in no specified time period. From the high-tech set design and the "*Star Trek* plasma drive" sound effects churning in the background, we know it's sometime in the future — but there is nothing to link the story in any tangible way to the world we know, no force pulling us out of this carefully constructed alternate reality. We see connections all over the place, and we can relate to all six prisoners, but only through behaviour as they try to find their way out of this ever-changing cage which guarantees death to those who attempt an escape.

Because they are human, escape is of course the first thing on their minds once they hook up and put their talents together. The aim of this game — which is like a sci-fi *Survivor* — is to make it to the end of the show without getting sliced, poisoned, stabbed or voted off for talking too much. There is no object to the cube other than survival, and none of the people seems to have done anything to deserve such horrendous punishment — which only adds to the film's Canadian (and existential) value. Some of the inmates — such as the tough cop (Maurice Dean Wint) — seem better suited to the rigours of the cube than others, such as an autistic savant (Andrew Miller). After a few senseless tirades about how unfair it is to be stuck in the cube for no good reason, the resourceful humans decide to work together. Showing the human capacity for cooperation, they all work as a team, deciphering the mysterious numbers on the threshold of each compartment and navigating their way through the maze. As their numbers dwindle

Cube (1997): Nicole De Boer plays Leaven, a mathematical genius who helps the ragtag group of randomly chosen inmates try and escape their cube-shaped hell in Vincenzo Natali's feature film debut that won over audiences in Europe and Japan, but met with only tepid success back home. FEATURE FILM PROJECT

and they watch each other die off, we get all the melodramatics of the *Poseidon Adventure* combined with the existential angst of Albert Camus.

The movie's dramatic tension comes from the relationships between the humans and the way they choose to deal with their highly hostile environment. They are all alone, and where another film tradition might have played more on their urge to backstab, Natali and screenwriter Graeme Manson seem to make a concerted effort to maintain their civility for as long as possible. This not only helps them survive a little longer, but it ensures the contrast between the humans and their environment is as strong as possible.

Cube is a human drama disguised as a science fiction movie, and because the behaviours rang true for me, I was completely seduced by the film — as were many others around the world. This little existentialist study became one of the more successful Canadian releases of 1998.

"It was a fun movie to write," said Manson in an interview after the film had a successful run in France and Spain. "It was like trying to figure out a giant puzzle. I'm a sci-fi fan, but I've never really liked the modern tradition where it's really just a shoot-em-up in space. I like the *Twilight Zone* style of sci-fi, where you're never quite sure what's real and what isn't. It's a mind-trip, not a special-effects clearinghouse. I think that's what the Europeans were relating to. They get off on the film's existentialist edge. In Japan, where the film also performed well, I think they responded because they live in stacked boxes — and this somehow struck a chord of familiarity. They understand the idea of a compartmentalized existence."

Ironically, Canadian audiences didn't seem all that interested in *Cube*'s abstracted, empty spaces and compartmentalized image of existence. The film met with tepid reviews from many critics, who faulted its cerebral edge. As *Toronto Sun* critic Bruce Kirkland wrote: "The weakness is that, despite quality actors, the six characters are in search of an author. None is fleshed out enough, and inter-actions are often as mechanical as the cube itself. The emotional involvement in *Cube* is minimal."[7]

Possible Heads in Severed Worlds

Where Natali's *Cube* opens with a shot of a man being "cubed," Robert Lepage's *Possible Worlds* opens with a shot of a murder scene where the victim's head is cut open. Based on the stage play by John Mighton, this English-language debut from Lepage opens with the strange murder of George Barber (Tom McCamus), a smart man who was found dead in his apartment — without a brain. Surgically removed with the utmost precision, the brain becomes the main focus of the police investigation. Meanwhile, on screen, we are in George's head and witnessing the events of what we believe to be his past life unfold.

As veteran consumers of the filmed image, we have no problem with the idea of breaking the line of time (with a death) and then moving backwards along that line, plot-ting different points through flashbacks. We see it all the time on television and movies. So

Possible Worlds (2000): Tom McCamus plays George Barber in Robert Lepage's investigation into the nature of reality, and the potential for a man to lose his head, but continue to function in a near-normal fashion. ALLIANCE ATLANTIS

when Lepage leads us into the narrative with the murder, then picks up bits and pieces of George's life and puts them on screen, we can only assume Lepage is using flashbacks to help us figure out who might have killed the poor man.

Did I ever say assumptions are danger-ous in the context of Canadian film? Well, they are. No matter how much you think you know about a given director or a given sub-ject, chances are things won't quite measure up the way you expected, particularly if you are basing your assumptions on Hollywood conventions.

That said, what we believe to be George's

flashbacks on screen are not flashbacks at all. They are George's current perceptions. Just as Descartes came to the conclusion that his mind and his body were two entirely separate things, so it is that George Barber finds himself separated from his corporeal reality. His brain has been removed from his body, but it's still alive and functioning within the confines of a glass jar. George doesn't know he's been butchered. His brain is creating its own reality throughout the film, and those are the images Lepage brings to the screen.

For the viewer, it's yet another demanding film because George's perceptions are gradually losing touch with all linear notions of time. One minute, George is sitting in a bar flirting with a female stockbroker; the very next, the same woman is sitting across the table, dressed in a lab coat at a hospital cafeteria. As the movie progresses, the lines only get blurrier — and the narrative grows more confusing.

The first time I watched this movie, I was struck by its visuals and its broken sense of time in a rather dissociated way. The second time I watched it, however, it all came together. I picked up the clues Lepage leaves in the frame to point us in the right direction: the glass, the water, the stainless steel surroundings and the bubbling coffeemaker all point to the lab where George's brain gurgles up consciousness. Once I was able to stop worrying about what was actually going on, I could sit back, enter the human drama and watch George, the everyman, attempt to piece these fragments of understanding together to create a new reality. Now when I think back on the film in my mind's eye, it is the emotions I remember most — just like George. George may have been set adrift in a sea of memory and conflicting planes of existence, but the one thing that remained constant

throughout his ordeal was his love for his wife (played here by Scottish actress Tilda Swinton). Love was the one thing that made his life worth living, and now that he's little more than a brain in a jar, preserving the memory of that love makes death a necessity — as his wife proves when she comes in to unplug him in the final sequence. So once again, I have to differ with popular opinion on the "coolness" and overly cerebral quality of Canadian film. There are plenty of human emotions rattling around in every frame; it's up to the viewer to invest a little of his or herself in the picture in order to reap the biggest rewards.

Breaking Surfaces

Personal investment is a tough one for us overtaxed Canadians, and it's one of the leading reasons why Canadian film isn't doing better than it is. People aren't all that willing to make a point of watching Canadian movies and they also have a genuine fear of investing real money in them (which, given the poor performance of most entertainment stock, may be another sign of our intelligence). I'll let the stock promoters and producers push you to invest the cash; for now, I'm only interested in pushing you to invest the time to get past the frame and explore the incredible landscape within Canadian film — and for once, I'm not just talking trees and snow, but I'm still concerned with death.

When Egoyan was formulating his film *Speaking Parts*, he realized he loved the idea of a television show within the film itself. "[The TV show allowed me to] take an issue that was fictional, but create a format that people are used to identifying with. On real TV talk shows, there's this level of interaction between the audience and the guests. In *Speaking Parts*, I'm preventing the audience from reaching that normal level of interaction because I've assigned conflicting roles to all of the characters they are seeing. The resulting confusion on the part of the viewer is something that thrills me. The viewer doesn't quite know what it is he's watching ..."[8]

Egoyan breaks the cinematic frame all the time. He plays with different photographic media and makes them part of the inherent narrative of the film. For instance, in *Speaking Parts*, Clara (Gabrielle Rose) watches video images of her dead brother in the video mausoleum and the people in the hotel use a video conferencing device to talk about their project, which turns out to be a script written by Clara about her dead brother. Video and film images intercut, mix and mingle, and as a result, so do the frames of reference. We don't know where we are at each moment in time,

nor do we know whose perspective we're watching from. Images simply run into other images, informing each other in the process, and pulling the film apart at the seams. Most Hollywood directors hate to see the seams or cuts in their movie (with the exception of Steven Soderbergh, who also loves fragmenting narrative to dislocate the viewer), but many Canadian filmmakers have a distinct taste for breaking frame — and opening up the film surface. The philosophy behind this type of fragmentation is surrealist in nature, and it plays to our dream memories — the movies in our mind that let us time-travel every night.

While surrealism — proper — followed some 20 years later, the roots of the surrealist movement can be traced back to the work of Picasso, who began experimenting with

Speaking Parts (1989): Claire (Gabrielle Rose) sits in a high-tech video mausoleum, where she watches images of her dead brother in a futile attempt to reconnect with his presence. The use of video images takes on more than artistic significance in this Atom Egoyan movie about the nature of loss, and the use of flattened, distorted photographic images to negotiate the space between being and not being. COURTESY OF JOHNNIE EISEN, © EGO FILM ARTS

newsprint on canvas back in 1912. Just as cinema was finding its popular voice, Picasso began sticking newspapers to the gesso surface to create his famed *"papiers collés"* — breaking the frame of art for the first time. Picasso set the art world on its ear because he brought the present day horrors of "the news" into the privileged and permanently pressed universe of timeless art. Critics were horrified to see a headline only days old hanging in respected salons. They chilled at the thought of the paper yellowing and the whole thing falling apart. The whole thing seemed like such a violation of the rules and expectations.

In Picasso's world, the conflict comes down to different notions of time and art: the modern world where newspapers are the popular artifact of life, and high art, where anything current or disposable is pooh-poohed on principle. The *papiers collés* stuck them both together, or as art critic Anne Baldassari writes in her book *Picasso Working on Paper*: "... tension [is generated] between the discordant modalities of representation: fragment of the real object, facsimile, printed sign or image, drawing. By materially situating these objects on the same plane, these modes belonging to distinct semantic families, the *papiers collés* mimes the work of psychic recognition that the subject, in his apprehension of a world strewn with heterogeneous signs, must work to accomplish for himself."[9]

The very same words could describe what Egoyan does in *Speaking Parts*. He says:

When the screen image contains something more immediate to the viewer (a loved one for example) a true surface can be developed if the viewer breaks the impassive nature of the screen identification process with a degree of involvement. This involvement may be internalized —

the image may trigger an event or a conversation — or it may find more overt manifestations ...

Can people live through imagistic representations of life? If they can, do they then need to gain control of how those representations are made? And if the answer is yes and yes, then at what point do the people fall in love with their own ability to conjure up that image. Does the loved one then become narcissistic?... *[In]* Speaking Parts *the repeating theme is people's relationship to each other in a world obsessed by representation.*[10]

The whole idea is to crack open the film surface, create gaps in time and logic to force the viewer into a synthetic stance – or, as Lisa in *Speaking Parts* says, "See things I hadn't seen before." From a life and death perspective, representation becomes a way of holding on to the dead loved one, but it is also — by the mere fact of being a two-dimensional image without context — a complete distortion of the person, and a potential psychic trap in the mind of the surviving loved one.

Egoyan expects the audience is smart enough to connect the dots and get involved in the narrative, becoming a part of the process itself. But as we know by now, more people know his name than know his oeuvre. Apparently we aren't as excited by the intellectual challenge as he might like — but that hasn't stopped Egoyan, and several other filmmakers, from shattering film convention in a bold attempt to reorient our eyes vis à vis the frame. Instead of merely looking at it passively, people like Egoyan, Lepage, Cronenberg, Natali, McKellar and others want us to get past the frame, past cinematic device, and into the metaphysical fabric of the narrative.

Getting it on With the Grim Reaper

Taking us a step further, Lynne Stopkewich's *Kissed* (1996) urges us to get past the social frame and into the fabric of coffin quilting. On the surface, *Kissed* seems to be a sex story, which is why I included it in the inventory of sexual dysfunction, but at its heart this movie is concerned primarily with death, which serves to define our central character, the corpse-loving embalmer's apprentice, Sandra Larson (Molly Parker). Sandra seems like a nice girl and she has a string of male suitors who'd love to take her out, but Sandra is not attracted to the boys she meets outside the funeral parlour. She is only interested in the dead flesh that arrives daily from the morgue. Sandra is keenly aware of the fact that it's not "normal" to be sexually attracted

to dead people, but she can't help herself — and so she makes furtive, late-night visits to the funeral home where she trips the light fantastic with every stiff in sight.

It's clearly odd, and rather jarring, to watch an attractive, vital, young woman climb aboard a dead body to achieve sexual satisfaction, which is why *Kissed* created such a furor when it was first released in 1996. Beyond the sensationalist imagery, though, Stopkewich's film (based on the story by Barbara Gowdy) touches on some very profound and perfectly Canadian points — namely, negative space, as it is symbolized in the lifeless bodies on the slab. Consider the film's opening sequence: The screen is black and we hear Sandra's voice-over telling us that "When you die, your earthly self turns into your disintegrated self

Kissed (1996): Young Sandra Larson (Natasha Morley, left) prepares for her love affair with death by staging an elaborate funeral for a dead animal with her childhood friend (Jessie Winter Mudie) in Lynne Stopkewich's debut feature that ruffled feathers as a result of its necrophilic themes. KHAREN HILL AND BONEYARD FILMS

and you radiate energy." The screen flashes white, then we see the funeral parlour's prep room. Sandra's voice-over continues: "When a thing turns into its opposite, when love turns into hate, life into death, there are always sparks ... I've seen bodies shining like stars. I'm the only person I've ever heard of who has."

Sandra isn't talking about sex, per se, she's actually talking about seeing the "other" side. Every time Sandra mounts one of the dead men, she is filling her internal void (her vagina) with death. Yes, it seems repulsive, but there is nothing all that graphic in the film to make us squirm, because the voyage is symbolic. By filling herself with death, Sandra could not be more alive — or more present. Returning to the doughnut hole analogy for just a second, we could say that Sandra affirms herself in "positive" space because she now has a hole — with "nothing" in it. Or, as Sandra says: "Energy is transformation, it is the craving and the desire. And all transformation — all movement, all process — happens because life turns into death."

Death and Acceptance

In the "Survivors and Surviving" chapter, I opened up the film discussion with a comparative analysis of *Surfacing* and *Deliverance*. Now, as we approach the end of the Canadian film odyssey, we'll return to the concept of survival and the land of us-and-them to see how our exploration of death and the great beyond stands in stark contrast to the Hollywood tradition. To do this, we'll look at a more recent set of movie bookends: Don McKellar's *Last Night* (1998) and the spate of end-of-the-world movies out of Hollywood that preceded the millennium, such as *Armageddon*, *Independence Day* and *Deep Impact*.

All these movies pivot on a doomsday premise. In *Deep Impact* and *Armageddon*, the Earth is threatened by a giant asteroid that could easily collide with our little blue marble and take it out of the game. In *Independence Day*, the threat hearkens back to the gloriously propagandist days of the Cold War, when aliens threaten all human life on Earth. It's up to mankind to pull off a miracle and save the day, which adds up to astronauts landing on the asteroid and blowing it up with nuclear weapons, or else a few brave fighter pilots soaring into space and taking out the alien mother ship. And guess what? In all three far-fetched cases, the American male heroes succeed.

Leave it to us sincere Canadians to not even make the attempt to stop whatever it is from happening. In *Last Night*, the end of the world is presented as an inescapable fact. When the movie opens, humanity has been aware of its impending doom for months. Now, people are counting down the final six hours, looking for a moment of meaning against the surreal backdrop of a city (an anonymous Toronto) in the grips of complete anarchy.

Last Night, then, is not an action-adventure movie about trying to survive a cataclysmic event, but a cerebral and yes, heartfelt investigation into what makes life worth living.

On screen, this translates into two entirely different visions of the Apocalypse.

The American movies are doused with special effects to keep our eyes riveted to the potential pyre, while McKellar simply relies on human dialogue and behaviour as he brings us into the lives of several people on the last day on Earth.

In other words, in the Canadian vision there is a quiet acceptance of the inevitable: We will all die, one day or another. In the Hollywood vision, death is something that must — and can — be conquered. Sheer lunacy, of course, but this is crucial to under-standing the American ethos as packaged by Tinseltown: Deny reality at all costs, and if you can't straight-out deny it, then at least reinvent it to suit your own agenda.

Personally speaking, I preferred McKellar's vision to that of Mimi Leder, Michael Bay or Roland Emmerich, and I'll explain why.

While the characters in the American movies spend the duration of the film focused on the impending outside force that's about to kill them, the characters in *Last Night* focus on themselves as they try to find meaning in their short — and getting shorter — lives.

For Patrick (played by McKellar), the day revolves around going home to sit and eat din-ner with his oblivious family, who treat doomsday like Christmas dinner, pulling out the special napkins and tablecloths while the mother dumps guilt on the children. Once the dinner is over, Patrick simply wants to go home to his apartment, sip champagne on the roof and watch the world end — by himself. "Alone?" asks Sandra (Sandra Oh), a stranger who finds herself accidentally sharing her last moments with Patrick. "Yes," he replies, frus-trated. "If that's not so hard to understand."

For Duncan (David Cronenberg), an over-achieving executive with the gas company, the last day is spent calling customers to thank them for the business and assure them that Petrolia (the fictional gas company) will make an effort to keep "the gas flowing — right until the end."

For Craig (Callum Keith Rennie), self-realization is equated with sex. Craig tries to

Last Night (1998): Not even consumer culture can save the world in Don McKellar's end-of-the-world movie where we watch a group of human beings live out the remaining six hours of their lives. In this scene, Sandra (Sandra Oh), shuffles through a near-empty, looted market looking for something to cook up for her last supper. ODEON AND RHOMBUS MEDIA

cross as many sexual fantasies off his list as possible: sex with a virgin, sex with two women, sex with a man, and sex with his favourite French teacher, Madame Carlton (played by who else but the Canadian screen icon, Geneviève Bujold).

Sandra just wants to get home to her husband, Duncan, so they can have one last dinner together and die in each other's arms as part of their suicide pact.

Not one of these people is running around looking for spaceships and rockets and nuclear armaments. They are looking inward, into the deepest recesses of themselves, so that when they die — as we all will — they can do so with a better understanding of what life was all about.

In the context of survival, this presents us with a difficult equation to reconcile. The American movies show us a battle for human survival at its most basic. But McKellar shows us a group of people who have quietly accepted their fate. So how can they be survivors if they all die?

I've reconciled it this way: First, even though they die, they are "creative non-victims" because they continue an intellectual quest. And second, there's more to survival than staying alive, which we all know is a time-limited occupation. Survival, in the broadest sense, means continuity. It can be continuity of the species from a purely biological point of view, but it can also mean continuity of an idea from a purely spiritual point of view.

In the American films, we see that really it's all about the American way and the perpetuation of American values. For instance, when Morgan Freeman appears on television at the end of *Deep Impact* to tell the people they will rebuild their nation, we see shots of the Statue of Liberty underwater. But it doesn't matter:

the American belief system is still alive and well and providing a sense of meaning for those who are still alive.

In the Canadian imagination, the individual — not the larger social order and the shared mythology — is the locus of meaning. For instance, in *Last Night*, not once do we see a character emerge wrapped in the flag with a hand over his or her heart, as we see several times in the other three movies. The closest McKellar comes to flag-waving jingoism is on the soundtrack, where he plays a perfect mix of Canadiana, highlighted by the climactic moment in the countdown of all-time greatest hits which he gives to the Edward Bear Canadian classic, *Last Song* — and even there, it's clearly an individual choice. As the DJ introduces the tune to his listeners he says: "This one is my choice ... so don't bother calling the station ..." There are a few other beautifully Canadian details, such as the final sequence, which once again discards guns as tools for problem solving. There are also dialogue fragments such as Patrick's reply to his sister (Sarah Polley) on the subject of the public rioting and manslaughter in the streets. "Let's not forget that we have this old tradition in our family of not killing people." Also, keep an eye on what Craig and Patrick are drinking in their final moments together: Molson Canadian.

In the big picture, each person in *Last Night* comes to an understanding of self before moving on into the great wide open. While such small, personal revelations may not seem to carry a whole lot of emotional force (and therefore have little propagandist value), I think they are meaningful to viewers who can look at these people finding unbelievable amounts of personal strength at the eleventh hour and imagine themselves in their shoes. These are ordinary people, and

The world is not saved, but since it's everyone's last night on Earth, the occasion merited a parade in Don McKellar's *Last Night*. Try and spot Sarah Polley in the crowd of revellers. ODEON AND RHOMBUS MEDIA

yet, because they have chosen to investigate their own souls instead of blowing up an asteroid, they realize what life is all about. They come to understand the true beauty of being alive and being able to love each other. Their physical lives may come to an end, but their humanity survives. For me, that translates into a far larger type of hero: a hero who needn't destroy something to affirm himself, but someone who can quietly move into the next plane with a reservoir of courage, embracing it as the last chapter in a beautifully human existence.

From these examinations of our relationship with death, we can see that death is the ultimate empty hole. Where other filmic traditions attempt to hide its presence behind nubile starlets and collagen injections, the Canadian film tradition stares it straight in the face — it even kisses it on the lips. What we get out of this close relationship to the absolute emptiness is nothing less than a more complete understanding of who we are, as we come to feel, and explore, all dimensions of what we are not. It's a bit of a backward affirmation, but it suits our "negative" psyche. For a doughnut without a hole is just a pastry, and life without death has no meaning.

PROFILE

David Cronenberg

Born 1943 — Toronto, Ontario

He is prolific, profitable and perhaps one of the most "commercial" directors in Canada. Not surprisingly, he is also one of the most misunderstood. He is a thinker and a sensationalist, a survivor and a nihilist, a humble outsider and a self-absorbed snob, a proud Canadian and a disciple of Hollywood genre. Fortunately, David Cronenberg loves a good dichotomy. In his godless universe, meaning must be self-derived through a process of personal investigation — and no mental tools can chisel away at the subconscious like conflict and a good intellectual challenge.

For this reason, Cronenberg movies inevitably deal with a character in the midst of a transformation. In most cases, the transformative agent is something tangible and hostile from the outside, but inevitably born from within — either mentally or physically. For instance, in *Shivers*, his early feature film shot in Montreal, Cronenberg subjected an entire apartment building to the transformative sexual powers of a sewer-bred parasite. "Normal" people living private lives in secluded dwellings became sexual omnivores, cavorting with perfect strangers. Similarly, in *eXistenZ*, Cronenberg showed two sane employees of a software manufacturer completely lose themselves in a preprogrammed maze after plugging directly into the biomechanical hardware through a "bioport" at the base of their spines. Even his biggest "Hollywood" film to date, *The Fly*, dealt with similar transformative issues as a scientist (Jeff Goldblum) accidentally splices his genetic material with that of a housefly, with horrific results. In almost every case, Cronenberg shows us uptight or emotionally repressed people altered by acts of their own imagination, or else symbolically altered by grotesque creatures of Cronenberg's own imagination. In this way, Cronenberg is able to deconstruct the "creative" moment from inside out: he shows us people digging away at their insides, desperate to get something out of them — desperate to express themselves in some way ... or other.

The son of a journalist-philatelist father, Milton, and a mother, Esther, who played the piano for the National Ballet, Cronenberg grew up surrounded by books and the wide open spaces of an as-yet untamed Toronto. He has a sister, Denise, who currently works as a costume designer, and does many of her brothers' movies. He remembers riding his bike through the remaining wooded areas and catching butterflies, then going home and analyzing his catch. His house was packed with books.

"I remember row upon row of them and thinking it was a giant treasure trove of information. I loved the books, but I also read comics. I read early *Donald Duck* and *Superman* comics. I haven't thought about those in years, but you know, they all have a creepy tone to them. Even Donald ... ducks really shouldn't be wearing suits."

Young David tried his hand at writing his own stories. Most were science fiction tales and fantasy-laden romps into the prepubescent male imagination. Cronenberg sent some of these early manuscripts to publishers, and while none were published, he did receive encouraging letters, urging him to continue.

Originally registered as a University of Toronto science student, Cronenberg switched to English, where he developed a fascination with film. While he was still a student, he began experimenting with a 16mm Bolex and made a few shorts, including *Transfer* and *From the Drain* — a story that offered filmdom a glimpse of what was to come as scary things emerge from the bathroom sink.

The first film that captured the attention of critics was a film called *Stereo*, the story of a crazy Dr. Luther Stringfellow who heads up the Canadian Academy of Erotic Inquiry. Within this highly institutional setting, seven young people volunteer for a sort of lobotomy that removes their speech centre but gives them telepathic abilities. As they begin to master their new brain waves, the doctor introduces new stimuli and new drugs, exposing an inbred "polymorphous perversity" within the subjects. Eventually they all freak out and two of them self-destruct. His second feature, *Crimes of the Future*, follows a similarly dark arc. As one scientist comes up with a new disease, called "rouge's malady," which makes people engage in homosexual fantasy and other acts of so-called sexual deviance, another man of medicine regenerates human organs by using venereal diseases. Not much in the Cronenberg formula has changed over the years. He's still obsessed by the limitations of "the flesh" contrasted against the vast wilderness of the mind that just loves playing tricks on us gullible humans.

Cronenberg, good Canadian that he is, survived. He made *Rabid* starring porn star Marilyn Chambers, which proved to be another smash success, raking in $7 million on a $500,000 budget. He then went on to make *Fast Company* (a racing car movie) and *The Brood*, a story about a couple on the skids that is supposedly inspired by his real-life divorce from his first wife, Margaret, and a subsequent custody battle. In 1981, he made *Scanners* — the movie where a bunch of talking heads explode like so much pus between a pair of tweezers. The film gained more critical attention and *Newsweek* even called him the next heir to the horror throne. Two years later, he made *Videodrome* — the last film he wrote and directed until 1999's *eXistenZ*. *Videodrome* tells the story of a greedy and slimy television executive who finds a strange TV signal off a satellite, and gradually becomes unable to separate reality from fantasy. Woods' character is a sex-obsessed sleaze who has a giant hole in his abdomen which plays (what else?) videotapes, the tool of his seduction and inevitable destruction.

Success bred more of the same, and in the same year, Cronenberg came out with *The Dead Zone*, starring Christopher Walken. Filmed with American cash, Cronenberg considers *The Dead Zone* one of his most commercial movies because the characters follow a classic arc — right into the pointy end of a pair of scissors in the bathtub. *The Dead Zone* was another critical success, and Cronenberg earned seven Edgar Allan Poe nominations for his work.

In the heirarchy of fears, Cronenberg's obsessive quirk would be classified under "body envelope disgust." According to a University of Pennsylvania researcher, Paul Rozin, "body envelope violation disgust" relates to our fear of seeing things that are supposed to be inside the body, outside the skin, and vice versa. For instance, the scene in *Videodrome* where Woods feels his chest and pulls out a videocassette, or the scene in *Alien* where John Hurt's belly explodes with a baby creature are examples of body-envelope violation and they related back to a primal phobia of being entered by a force or a thing beyond our control.

Because Cronenberg can conjure more body envelope openers than most, he is considered a master of horror. But he is probably much deeper than simply a horror king in the tradition of Wes Craven or Stephen King, who prefer to "show" rather than "suggest" psychological terror. Because Cronenberg is an intellectual with a penchant for drilling right into the bone of a given issue, his films operate on several levels. This not only gives him plenty of room to play with form and expectation, but it provides a platform for his own distinct brand of humour. His humour works best when it is in the same frame as one of his grotesque concoctions, because that way he gets the shock of the disgust reaction and a recognition of the familiar — the two main ingredients needed to prompt a laugh reflex. For instance, there is a sequence in *eXistenZ* where the publicist Pikul (Jude Law) and the developer Allegra Geller (Jennifer Jason Leigh) find themselves in a hotel room on the lam. The conversation drips with innuendo:

ALLEGRA: *Don't tell me you were never fitted [with a bioport]?*
PIKUL: *... Look, I've been dying to play your games. But I have a phobia about having my body penetrated — surgically.*

All sex in Cronenberg movies is transformative, and usually in a bad way. "I talked about it endlessly when *Crash* came out, the relationship between sex and death. My God, I'd love to take the credit for being the first to put those two together! But, you know, I think we've got 5,000 years of human history doing it first," he says. "I'm always amazed when people ask me why I would link sex and death. And it's like, 'Hello, don't you read?' I believe the body is the central fact and everything in my movies reflects that — the imagery, the props, everything. I mean this is not Carol's [Spier] inner life you are seeing, it is mine."

Despite the bizarre, bent or perverted nature of sex in Cronenberg films, racy scenes have a habit of selling tickets at the box office, and that phenomenon has given Cronenberg an international profile. At first, he was seen as a Canadian Roger Corman — a hip schlock artist who put pop idols like Debbie Harry of Blondie in the same frame as weird sex and corporeal mutilation, thus paving the way for the likes of latter-day scenesters like Quentin Tarantino and Guy Ritchie. When *The Fly* came out in 1986, starring Geena Davis and Jeff Goldblum (as well as Cronenberg himself, featured in a cameo as Davis' gynecologist), Cronenberg's reputation in Hollywood soared even higher. He was smart and marketable, and the film even picked up an Oscar nomination for best make-up effects, but the Toronto son had no intention of leaving Canada. He was still firmly rooted in Canadian soil, and with his newly discovered commercial pull, he set out to make *Dead Ringers* — a story about twin gynecologists (both played by the ever-creepy Jeremy Irons) who trade places to feed their strange, sexual habits. The film was disturbing, decidedly smart and rather successful. At a time when people were getting rich on junk bonds, snorting cocaine off toilet seats and sipping Beaujolais Nouveau at downtown bistros, Cronenberg's landscapes laced with weird sex and psychological addictions seemed to capture the essence of the era. As the crazy eighties drew to a close, Cronenberg attempted one of his most ambitious projects to date: a filmed version of William S. Burroughs' *Naked Lunch*. Long considered "unfilmable," *Naked Lunch* starred Peter Weller as William Lee, a haunted artist who kills his own wife (by mistake), turns to hallucinogens for escape, and realizes through a fog of mugwumps that he is actually a homosexual. *Naked Lunch* won the best director and best screenplay awards from the U.S. National Society of Film Critics. It was also awarded a string of Genies and earned a best screenplay prize from the Boston Society of Film Critics.

With *Naked Lunch* classified as a success, Cronenberg — who was long considered too nonlinear by Hollywood's straight-line-loving production community — was given the cash to adapt David Henry Hwang's hit, the Tony-award winning sex tragedy, *M. Butterfly*. Based on the true story of a French diplomat who falls in love with a Beijing Opera diva only to discover his true love is a man — and funded in part by Warner Brothers and David Geffen — *M. Butterfly* opened the 1993 Toronto Festival of Festivals (as it was then called) with much ado. But even as one floated around the harbourside party where Cronenberg flapped around under a big black cape, it was clear the film didn't have the magic. At that moment, people didn't want to talk about the film that starred John Lone as the diva and Jeremy Irons as his hapless French embassy wooer — and in most cases, people still don't.

Crash, on the other hand, is a movie that generally inspires long, drawn-out conversations about sex, death, cars and whether or not Cronenberg is just a shlock artist scamming himself off as an auteur, or the real thing. The 1996 movie that starred Holly Hunter, James Spader and Rosanna Arquette had its international premiere at Cannes, where it was the sole Canadian film in competition for the coveted Palme d'Or. It didn't win, but it did cause a big commotion. As journalist Craig McInnis reported from Cannes: "During the screening of the film, peals of laughter had rung through the auditorium as the film's characters engaged in a variety of kinky sex acts, including a back-seat tryst in a car wash and a chest-licking encounter between two men." By the end of the festival, Cronenberg was either a genius or a brain-addled deviant — depending on who one spoke to — leaving the jury no other option but to create a prize just for *Crash*: a special jury prize for "audacity and innovation." A few years later, Cronenberg was asked to take on the prestigious post of chief juror at Cannes, becoming the first Canadian to ever do so.

By 1997, Cronenberg was interested in returning to the typewriter, and he began playing with a story idea about a writer being trapped by one of his own creations. When he was asked to interview Salman Rushdie for the Canadian tech-culture magazine, *Shift*, he used the opportunity to take his idea a bit further. Because Cronenberg was also playing *Myst* (a popular fantasy-oriented video game) at the time, he decided to use the "author" idea against the backdrop of the $8-billion world of video game publishing — thus allowing him to explore the Frankenstein syndrome, as well as his personal, ontological interest in the nature of reality and the function of free will. The project was originally in development with MGM, but when he told the head of the studio he wanted to cast Jennifer Jason Leigh in the role of Allegra Geller in *eXistenZ*, the executive shriveled in his swivel chair. "He said, 'When I think of Jennifer Jason Leigh, I think of dark, depressing little movies that don't make any money.' And I said, 'Yes, that's what I want to do,'" said Cronenberg, who was clearly frustrated by MGM's withdrawal from the project at the eleventh hour.

While some critics, including myself, saw *eXistenZ* as an astute statement on the massively popular brand of self-willed brainwashing at the hands of video games, audiences were far more reluctant to embrace this highly challenging piece of work. For some, it was too disjointed to be satisfying, while others were simply too depressed by this mental landscape — especially after seeing the similarly-themed action-packed thriller *The Matrix*, which opened just a few weeks before *eXistenZ*. Cronenberg hasn't said much about the critical reaction to his most ambitious film to date, but there's no doubt he takes what some critics say to heart. "I remember Jay Scott had written some fairly negative things about my first couple of movies," Cronenberg said in 1999. "But then he told me this story ... He was telling me his mother was dying and he'd gone to New Mexico to be with her and she had seen, weirdly enough, *Shivers*. She told him how much I understood about death. After that, he promised he'd go back and look at the films again and write something from a different perspective, but he never did ... He passed away before he had the chance."

Once again, Cronenberg is haunted by the spectre of things that never came to pass, but as always, entertaining ghosts of his own creation is something that pleases the bespectacled filmmaker.

"If you live in Hollywood, you can't really believe in yourself as an artist," says Cronenberg. "I remember doing an interview with John Landis and John Carpenter and me — I was just talking about art and the responsibility of the artist, and the artist does this, and the artist does that. Then I stopped talking. And then I looked at them — and their mouths were hanging open. And I said, 'What? What?' And they said, 'You called yourself an artist.' And I said, 'Yeah.' And they said, 'We would never do that. At least, not in public,'" he says. "You know, it's interesting and kind of sad, but the ultimate taboo in Hollywood has nothing to do with all those usual taboos, it has to do with thinking of yourself as an artist. You can't be an artist. You have to be an entertainer — keep the folks all up and perky ... I don't really get that. Given the choice between that or art, I'd rather be an artist."

FILMOGRAPHY: *Transfer* (1966) | *From the Drain* (1967) | *Stereo* (1969) | *Crimes of the Future* (1970); *Jim Ritchie Sculptor* (1971) | *Shivers* (AKA *The Parasite Murders, They Came from Within*) (1975) | *The Victim* (1975) | *The Lie Chair* (1975) | *The Italian Machine* (1976) | *Rabid* (1976) | *Fast Company* (1979) | *The Brood* (1979) | *Scanners* (1980) | *Videodrome* (1982) | *The Dead Zone* (1983) | *The Fly* (1986) | *Dead Ringers* (1988) | *Hydro* (1989) | *Naked Lunch* (1991) | *M. Butterfly* (1993) | *Crash* (1996) | *eXistenZ* (1999)

PROFILE

Don McKellar

Born 1963 — Toronto, Ontario

ODEON AND RHOMBUS MEDIA

Happy to be low profile but unmistakably self-assured, Don McKellar is the epitome of a Canadian film hero. He'd be embarassed by such a description — no doubt — but that only makes the case for his latter-day cinematic sainthood that much stronger. In fact, McKellar never even craved a career in film, preferring to make his dramatic mark as a playwright and actor before he was seduced into the world of two-dimensional shadows by then-editor Bruce McDonald, who asked him to write some scenes for a dead-end road movie called *Roadkill* in the late 1980s.

"Bruce had heard of me through the Toronto theatre community. I had founded the Augusta Company because there was a group of us who were disillusioned with the local theatre scene. The shows we did were collective efforts, meaning there was no accredited author or director. We all shared the credit, which we thought was the right thing to do. We did pretty well and got some good reviews and that's how Bruce heard of me," says McKellar. "I knew who Bruce was because he was Ron Mann's [*Grass, Twist, Comic Book Confidential*] editor and Egoyan's, so when he asked me to write some scenes for a few hundred bucks I did it. I remember he invited me over to his place to talk about it and he had all these maps and album covers and told me about this idea he had for a movie, which would turn into *Highway 61*.

"Bruce liked the pages I'd written and I guess that's how I got into film, but I was never one of those guys who always wanted to be in movies. I kind of liked movies too much to go to film school or to consider a career in film," he says.

McKellar's first love was writing — or at least a girl who loved writing. He had a girlfriend who was into poetry and the two of them applied for a special literature program taught by Margaret Atwood. They were both successful and McKellar's love for the written word continued to evolve. Around the same time, McKellar began experimenting with his skills as a performer — first as a failed gymnast, then later as a magician.

McKellar took the advice of the sage gym teacher to heart and, like so many other famed Canadian heroes (well, at least one: Paul in Robertson Davies' *Fifth Business*), dedicated himself to the art of prestidigitation. McKellar was so successful at sleight of hand, he financed his way through school by making things disappear, then reappear, then disappear. Clearly, the idea of creating gaps in perception appealed to McKellar, who revels in the art of subtle subversion:

"People these days, or at least executives in Hollywood, want to have all the answers played out straight before you. Executives in Hollywood read those books by Sid Field and all that. They are craft books designed to elicit a certain response ... they are rigged to lead you some specific place and when you watch those movies, you can feel where it is they are trying to take you, and this is symptomatic of American film in general: they've distilled everything down to a certain formula. Hollywood screenwriting has degraded into this perverse game that is played with the audience, and the audience knows exactly what's going to happen — except for a few minor variations. You know someone is going to die, but you don't know which one goes first. And then when the person you didn't expect to die first dies, you say, oh, never saw that coming ... There's nothing wrong with a craft book. They are mostly common sense. But no other art form would think of such a thing. Like, who on earth would swallow a craft book on how to write a poem?"

McKellar's own first film project was a short, titled *Blue*. Made in 1992 at the Canadian Film Centre, the Toronto film school opened by Norman Jewison in 1988 to nurture and train up-and-coming Canadian film talent, *Blue* featured a split narrative. One plotline involved a woman reminiscing about her days as an early porn star, the other focused on an anal-retentive wall-to-wall carpet vendor (played by David Cronenberg) with an addiction to hardcore smut. The two stories interweave until the final frame, when we realize the porn star is actually the supposedly straight-laced aunt of the supposedly straight-laced carpet vendor.

"That was the first time I directed and I was hoping to transfer some of the ideas I had worked on in theatre company to film. We were doing a lot of juxtaposition between documentary and drama. I was really interested in exploring the subtext of the scenes and thanks to Tracy Wright [who played the unrequited lover of Cronenberg in *Blue*, as well as in *Last Night*, not to mention the role of Vivian Klitorsky in Cynthia Roberts' *Bubbles Galore*] I think we got it. In fact, I'm happy to say that *Blue* is used as part of the curriculum at Boston University because of Tracy's deft handling of the subtext ..."

McKellar continued on the same subversive tangent after he was asked to write a film about Glenn Gould. Here, he broke narrative expectation again by transforming the classic dramatic arc into a less obvious curve that moves through 32 vignettes instead of one seamless narrative script.

"I was a little apprehensive to write a movie about Glenn Gould because I was familiar with his work and his life — and I mean, the man removed himself from society, which isn't all that dramatic. I was also intent on not reducing the artistic experience to an act of mimicry. You know I have a huge problem with these films about the artist because they lead up to this moment of enlightenment where you see the actor playing the instrument or painting the picture. I think that takes away from the real artistic moment because all you're doing is paying attention to the actor to see how well he or she approximates the action. You aren't thinking of the music, or the art. So one of the first rules François [Girard, the director of *Thirty Two Short Films About Glenn Gould*] and I set down was that we would never see him play the piano. Then François' whole notion of the 32 short films was very liberating, because I'm always trying to find a way to fragment the story. It's my natural impulse because it lets me get around that sort of three-act structure, and the whole Hollywood formula. With that, I could create a subliminal narrative beneath the 32 short films. I was excited by that because it let me explore other scenes that wouldn't necessarily be a part of an artist biopic," says McKellar.

McKellar says each of the short films was as an entity unto itself, but the meaning in each was reliant on its context within the larger film structure.

"I've always believed that if a scene can be moved around, it shouldn't be there. In *Thirty Two Short Films*, all the films work in juxtaposition. I still followed a chronological structure, so in a sense, the classical arc is still there, it's just hidden. That sounds like a subversive impulse and I recognize that, but that's what I do. If a craft book tells you to do one thing, I'm always going to try and do the opposite."

McKellar says the subversive impulse is part of what he loves about the Canadian experience in general. "There is a reluctance to believe in certain constructs in this country. We have no superheroes, and our more skeptical tradition overall, as well as our cinema, reflects that. The best Canadian cinema validates skepticism as a real option."

After *Thirty Two Short Films About Glenn Gould* was released to rave reviews and established director François Girard as a leading Canadian talent, he and McKellar began working on *The Red Violin*, a convoluted story that broke linear structure again by breaking time and using an inanimate object — the title violin — as the main "protagonist." Once again, McKellar's subversive sensibilities were noted, only this time, with a slew of financial backers from five corners of the globe, he was asked to defend his decisions. He relates one

story of an American studio bringing in their "art film specialist" who was, of course, British. At issue was the American character played by Samuel L. Jackson. The Americans didn't think he was sympathetic enough, so they asked McKellar to write a scene about the man spending some time in a park with his family. "People will like him because he goes to parks?!" was McKellar's reply. After that, they didn't ask for changes.

As the millennium was drawing to a close, McKellar was asked to take part in an international series of films about the historic occasion called *2000 as seen by* ... The films were supposed to revolve around the idea of the new date, but McKellar — ever the subliminal rebel — figured a millennium movie would be dated within a few months of New Year's 2000, so he looked for a broader picture and made his movie about the end of the world. Without knowing there were at least two other megaprojects in the works in Hollywood — *Deep Impact* and *Armageddon* — McKellar began writing a story about people who know the end of the world is upon them, but they can't do a thing about it.

"But I was also thinking about what makes a Canadian movie Canadian, and what would the Canadian response be? The movies Americans make on that subject are all about the man who is going to stop it — Bruce Willis or someone. I've always felt excluded from those films because no one I know has a nuclear arsenal ... Most of us would have to accept it. That last bunch of armageddon movies hadn't come out yet, but *Independence Day* had come out and I remember thinking of that scene where the aliens destroy France. You see this shot of a man with a baguette standing by the Eiffel Tower and poof — there goes France. But at the end of the movie, you see all these people dancing around because the world was saved, even though this was like the worst disaster that had ever befallen humanity. The Earth is almost completely destroyed, but it's all okay now. No one was even sad. Canada wasn't even in that movie, we're gone, so what would the Canadian reaction have been? We would have had to deal with it, which is far more difficult. There's also a satiric side to that, where you have people carrying on sangfroid about the whole thing, but for me I found there was something very moving about being forced to deal with tragedy. So I asked the people I knew how they would deal with it and sex was clearly one of the ways, and not just from my pervert friends, but from a lot of people. The other way people would have tried to cope was through the creation of something, you know try and do something they never had the courage or time to try before. Others said they would just retreat into a personal space. So that's how *Last Night* came together," he says.

"As for the set design in the film, I was thinking of not just the millennium, but wrapping up the century, so I was gravitated to those instances of optimistic modernism. Like the gas company is International Style and the scenes in Craig's apartment are in that Jetson sixties mode, the family suburban house is 1970s. To me, they all shared a certain innocence in design as they looked toward the future. Once again, I found that more moving because here there is no future." McKellar says his fascination with emptiness and alienation is not a morose obsession or a self-apologetic approach. He is simply trying to show another side of human experience — one that rings a little truer in his own era.

"I believe in morality and trying to be better, but I just find American movies are so preachy about it. I hate the moralizing that goes on in Hollywood film because it feels so fake," he says. "Right from the beginning, I thought I would write from my own experience and write what I wanted to see. I had so little faith in cinema as a career that I didn't have a lot at stake, so I did what I wanted. I thought no one will see it anyway so I will write what I want to write. I've always thought that I'm not so abnormal and idiosyncratic that no one will understand. I always think at least a few people will get it, but I'm constantly surprised by just how many people do understand. And from what I can see of the things that work in Canadian film, it seems to be the more idiosyncratic films are the ones that do the best."

McKellar says it's Canada's willingness to embrace the offbeat and idiosyncratic that will always keep him here, even though he now regularly receives invitations for work in the United States. "The thing about making movies in the United States is that you start making compromises in the hopes that it'll help you make the film, that one personal film burning in your heart. So you make that one compromise, and then another, and sooner or later you can't tell which was the compromise film and which one wasn't. Here, there isn't that pressure to reduce everything to the lowest common denominator, and that's why I love it here. We operate outside the system. We are rebels, I guess. And as a skeptical intellectual, I gravitate to change."

McKellar's next project is an adaptation of Nobel Prize-winning Portuguese author José Saramago's *Blindness*, a story of a man who is hit by a car and plunged into an empty whiteness. While the story has nothing to do with snow-blindness, or any other Canadian phenomenon, McKellar says he felt a certain affinity with Saramago's ironic tone and optioned the rights, proving that no matter how patriotic McKellar may be — his vision is global.

"I'm very proud to be Canadian. I've even seen the change in Cronenberg and Jewison. I see how proud they are to be Canadian. I hope it continues. The film industry seems to lurch from one crisis to the next, and in a lot of ways it's pretty bad, but we still make movies because we can problem-solve and think of new, creative solutions like cofinancing. We aren't trapped into a single model industry — even though some people can't get their heads out of the box and think of a different way. It's like the Canadian identity question and all the hand-wringing that used to go on because it wasn't an overt presence. We were floundering. Well, I'm comfortable with the floundering. I don't feel we have to define ourselves as much as we used to. We are more confident, so why all the hand-wringing? I don't think it's necessary. We are who we are, we just don't have to scream it every five seconds by waving a flag."

SELECTED FILMOGRAPHY: *Roadkill* (writer, actor, 1989) | *Highway 61* (writer, actor, 1991) | *The Adjuster* (actor, 1991) | *Blue* (director, short film, 1992) | *The Bloody Nose* (director, short film, 1992) | *Thirty Two Short Films About Glenn Gould* (actor, writer, 1993) | *Exotica* (actor, 1994) | *Dance Me Outside* (writer, 1994) | *When Night is Falling* (actor, 1995) | *Camilla* (actor, 1995) | *Last Night,* director (actor, 1998) | *The Red Violin* (actor, writer, 1998) | *Elimination Dance* (actor, 1998) | *The Herd* (, actor, 1998) | *eXistenZ* (actor, 1999) | *The Passion of Ayn Rand* (actor, 1999) | *A Word From the Management* (2000) | *waydowntown* (actor, 2000) | *Vinyl* (interviewee, 2000)

CHAPTER TEN

The Leap of Faith

SELLING CANADIAN FILM

RUSSELL: *Usually people in my line of work have to drive long distances by themselves.*
RAMONA: *What is your line of work?*
RUSSELL: *I'm a serial killer.*
RAMONA: *A what?*
RUSSELL: *A serial killer ... A person who commits a series of fairly unmotivated murders based on certain compulsions. It's more of an American thing traditionally, but it doesn't have to be. It's like everything else: There's this colonial attitude that if you want to make it, you have to go down to California ...*
RAMONA: *Are you really a serial killer?*
RUSSELL: *Well, I've never killed anyone before, but that's my ambition ... I know it's getting tougher every year. These days you have to kill about 20 people before anyone takes you seriously ... But what other options do I have?*

A scene from **Roadkill**[1]

In the fall of 2000, the Canadian Academy of Cinema and Television hosted a book release party for Maria Topolovich's *And the Genie Goes To ...* a highly readable coffee-table tome that outlines the history of film awards in Canada. Topolovich, who is also the president of the Academy, was in Vancouver to talk about the book over wine and cheese. I asked her if there was anything that really surprised her in the course of her research, and her answer was immediate: "I had no idea how successful we were ... even then. We had the beginnings of a very strong and very viable private industry, but for some reason, it's not something that most people in the industry — or the public — are even aware of I wasn't."

As the past nine chapters have shown, when we talk about the history of Canadian film, we generally find ourselves thinking about its institutional roots: John Grierson, the National Film Board and the CBC. But there was a film industry in this country before it became a government concern — before we developed an internal cynicism about Canadian film and its earnest, propagandist tendencies in the name of Canadian unity.

Those who predated government film policy, as well as those who choose to live outside the institutional community, are mavericks, by definition. I mean, think of the forward-thinking leap of faith demonstrated by Manitoba farmer James Simmons Freer (1855–1933), Canada's very first filmmaker, who picked up a camera and turned the lens toward the wide-open prairie in 1897. Collectively titled *Ten Years in Manitoba*, Freer's work was picked up by the Canadian Pacific Railway corporation, which sponsored Freer and his films on a tour of Europe to promote immigration. Freer's images of empty landscapes and simple agrarian life set the claustrophobic European imagination aflame, proving so popular that the Canadian government decided to get involved, sponsoring a second European tour in 1902. Freer moved on to become staff editor at the *Winnipeg Free Press*, but he never made movies again. Even without him, immigration films became Canada's first film commodity. In order to meet the demand, the CPR commissioned films from Bioscope and Edison Co. to sell the national sizzle to new Canadians.

The experiment was working. Films were making money and attracting new bodies to fill the vacant landscape — people who believed in the nation called Canada. The indigenous film industry was moving in synch with the rest of the world's and there was no hint of self-loathing in those halcyon days. We even prompted some American brain drain as Ontario's Trenton Studios and Halifax's Bioscope Co. became a mecca for young American directors and actors looking for a career in motion pictures. And so it was that the first Canadian narrative feature, *Evangeline* (Bioscope, 1913) — based on a Longfellow poem about the expulsion of the Acadians in 1775 — was directed by and starred Americans. Locals were only cast in minor, supporting roles. Nearly 100 years later, things don't look all that different. Despite spikes in post-war nationalism and short runs on large, privately financed films such as *Carry On, Sergeant!* (1927), Canada was having a hard time competing with the Americans, who were beginning to buy up the competition. They were consolidating their efforts in California — where there was sun and where everything from island, jungle and desert-scapes to urban spaces could be found within a few miles of Hollywood. And so it was there, in this new Eden, that a community of outsiders fashioned the modern golem of blockbusters from the desert dust with dreams of reshaping the world order.

While it was mostly New Yorkers who moved west in an effort to escape the stranglehold of the Motion Picture Patents Company (which attempted to control who could make films by controlling who could use the equipment), some of those original film founders were Canadian.

Mack Sennett was 17 when he left Canada for the States. He worked as an actor for Biograph, and was even featured in films by legendary American director D. W. Griffiths. Sennett set out to learn as much as he could from the master of the day, and eventually turned his attention to directing, as well. Without the autonomy to carry out his own vision, Sennett left Biograph to found the original Keystone Studios in Hollywood in 1912.[2] Sennett is usually credited with the creation of the silent slapstick genre and the term "Keystone cops." His interest in building franchise farce hardly seems to fit the Canadian psyche, but when you think of how those silly movies were really the first to mock authority and subvert the nascent formula, his Canuck sensibilities begin to emerge. They only grow stronger when you consider that his favourite object of satire was none other than D. W. Griffith, his former colleague at Biograph and the very father of film patriotism (as creator of *Birth of a Nation*). Many Keystone movies mocked Griffith's earnest tone and hero-worship — as his list of one-time employees suggests: Charlie Chaplin, Fatty Arbuckle, Buster Keaton, Gloria Swanson, Carole Lombard and Frank Capra. For all of his success, Sennett's studio died with the introduction of sound. The whole surrealism of the slapstick comedy was undermined by the naturalistic device that allowed the audience to hear "Stop, Thief!" instead of reading it, and Keystone died.

After the First World War essentially eliminated the competition in France and Italy, the emerging Hollywood titans were people such as Karl Laemmle (Universal), Adolph Zucker (Famous Players), Samuel Goldfish (later Goldwyn), William Fox (Fox Film), Harry, Abe,

Jack and Sam Warner (Warner Brothers) and the former Canadian, Louis B. Mayer (who left Saint John when he was eight). Mayer formed the Metro Picture Corporation (which evolved into Metro-Golwyn-Mayer, or MGM).

These early fathers succeeded beyond their wildest dreams, and they fashioned a film tradition that forms the very foundation of "The American Way." For the past century, the American identity has been shaped by Hollywood's portrayal of American values — and we can see it every time the likes of Michael Bay or Jerry Bruckheimer shows us a universe-saving hero such as Will Smith or Bruce Willis draped in the Stars and Stripes.

Even John Grierson recognized the complete mind-control of movie-making, the only difference was the agenda. Ours started out as a tool of social change and empowerment, while theirs began as a business with excellent social spin-off potential.

As we've already seen, there were a few anomalies along the evolutionary road of Canadian film. There were freethinking entrepreneurs like farmer Freer; George Brownridge, who set up the studios in Trenton, Ontario; Ernest Shipman, husband of proto-feminist Nell; and Gordon Sparling, one of the last "independent directors" working on Canadian productions at Associated Screen News in Montreal. Even after the Depression reduced the film industry in Canada to what Peter Morris described as a "branch plant of Hollywood,"[3] a few stray seeds took root in the cracks of the Canadian Shield and managed to survive. One of those mavericks was Budge Crawley, a man who loathed the institutional production system and created his own brand of commercial documentary, but others followed. Garth Drabinsky managed to create one of the largest theatre chains in North America with Cineplex, a company that dared tackle the Americans head-on on their own home turf. Robert Lantos and Victor Loewy helmed the rise of Alliance, and Frank Giustra, a junior mining mogul and securities specialist, gave birth to Lions Gate Entertainment Corp. Giustra hoped the Vancouver-based Lions Gate would become Canada's first full-fledged "studio" — and he even bought out Stephen J. Cannell's North Shore Studios to make sure he had all the pieces. He looked to the United States. for financial help and found a willing partner in Peter Guber, one of the most notorious producers in Hollywood. Giustra was soon relegated to playing a supporting role in the company he created — but his dream lives on and grows more successful every year, having picked up two Oscar-winning movies, *Gods and Monsters* and *Affliction*.

Another high roller who went toe-to-toe with Hollywood was Edgar Bronfman, Jr., who leveraged his family's liquor-built empire, Seagram, to purchase Universal and a host of other entertainment properties. Seagram no longer exists, having been bought out by European media giant Vivendi. Edgar Jr.'s decision to focus on film instead of the booze business may seem unprecedented in the family dynasty, but it's worth noting that Edgar Sr., older brother to Charles and father of Edgar Jr., once made a $40-million play for MGM in 1969 and acquired a 15 percent stake in the studio. The family is said to have lost $10 million in the deal.

While each one of these aspiring Canadian film moguls set their sights on the United States, the entrepreneurial spirit is alive and well in Canada. It is possible to "go big" and "stay home" — it's just not all that common an occurance as most people with "big picture" ambition tend to head south in search of greener paycheques, while the Americans continue to use Canada as a backlot.

Ever since the days of *Evangeline*, Americans saw Canada as either an ideal place to shoot or an ideal source of "exotic content," with our red-serged Royal Canadian Mounted Police, abundance of First Nations people and wide-open frontier. In the early years, Hollywood loved making movies about Canada — the only problem was, they were entirely American in nature as they reaffirmed the same hackneyed hero myths and flag-waving inanities as their own efforts. Pierre Berton wrote an entire book on the subject called *Hollywood's Canada* (1975), which points out such things as historically incorrect totem poles and the wrong type of Canadian fur hats. *Vancouver Sun* reviewer Marke Andrews said the book was "disappointing"[4] in its serious approach, while another *Sun* writer, Trevor Lautens, astutely remarked: "Does anyone think Hollywood accurately depicts the United States?"[5]

With the odd exception — such as *South Park, Bigger, Longer and Uncut*, which featured the tune "Blame Canada" and showed us to be a bloodthirsty group of warmongers — Hollywood stopped making films about the Candian experience long ago. But they haven't stopped making films in this country. Ninety years ago, Canada was hidden under a blanket of Stars and Stripes and today, nothing much has changed. I live in Vancouver and I see American post office signs, American flags, American licence plates and American police cars almost every single day as big-rigs, C-stands and trailers have become an inherent part of the Vancouver landscape. More than $1 billion worth of production takes place in Vancouver annually, and of that, more than 80 percent is American. The same holds true in other production centres such as Toronto, Montreal, Calgary and Winnipeg.

Using Canadian locations, crews and equipment to make an American movie is what's commonly referred to as the "service industry" in film circles, and it represents the lion's share of people gainfully employed by movie-making in this country. From a critical perspective, the service industry presents something of a conundrum when analyzing Canadian film because it falls between the cracks of the identity question. On one side, we have to be happy about the employment and the huge cash injection American productions bring with them; on the other side, we have to lament the fact that all those young people with so much talent are generally making second-rate cultural products for the American market.

For some, like director Sturla Gunnarsson (*Such a Long Journey, After the Axe, Rare Birds, Scorn*) the wasted talent is just a heartbreaker. "When I was a kid growing up in B.C., we used to cut trees and strip-mine the landscape to send off to the States. Now, we're strip-mining our culture and shipping it off to the same place," Gunnarsson said when I last saw him at the 2000 Victoria Independent Film and Video Festival (one of the coolest festivals in the country). Gunnarsson had just wrapped his last film, *Rare Birds*, a comedy starring Molly Parker (set in Newfoundland), which was produced, in part, by Janet York at Vancouver's S. L. Feldman and Associates. He was bagged from the shoot in Cape Spear, but in that post-stress, fatigue-induced euphoria, he was unloading some baggage about how he was feeling about the biz in general:

The problem isn't that Canadians are not interested in Canadian culture — it's the unfortunate fact that we speak English that really hurts us. We have no language barrier separating us from the flood of

American content. Even Mexico has an easier time maintaining its identity than we do as Canadians. It's like people don't think anything exciting ever happens here — they think it's all happening down in the States. I work for Americans all the time, but I don't feel it's where all the excitement is. I direct American episodics in Toronto to make money because it's the only way I can make a living as a filmmaker in this country. If I didn't have to do it, I wouldn't. But if it lets me make the movies I want to at the end of the day, then it's all worth it, because I love making movies. I love wrestling all that amorphous creativity to the ground and coming up with something that people can watch. I find that very satisfying.

The Medium is the Message

The compromised position of the filmmaker in Canada — as a person who may crave to make movies in this country, but finds it financially difficult, if not impossible to do so — has not gone unnoticed by legislators and cultural watchdogs. Ever since the Grierson years at the Film Board, almost anyone who cared to look could see there were problems in film production in Canada. By 1965, things moved forward when then-Secretary of State Maurice Lamontagne asked Gordon Sheppard, an independent film producer, to do some research and suggest some solutions to the nagging cultural dilemma. What Sheppard came up with is the kernel of the current bureaucratic noodle called "Feature Film Policy." Depending on who you talk to, this was either the best thing that ever happened to Canadian film or the very worst, as it spearheaded the way for the gradual dismantling of the NFB and the CBC in an effort to give the private sector a more active

role. It took several years, and countless nasty exchanges, to take shape, but the government's Feature Film Policy is now the backbone of domestic production. It essentially puts a chuck of change on the table (at last count it was about $100 million a year, as of October 2000) — then asks producers to prove why the money should go toward making their dreams, instead of someone else's, come true.

If it's any comfort to any bitter, underfunded producers who may be reading, it's not like the government develops these policies out of thin air, regardless of what Opposition MPs and your beer-drinking buds may say. Prior to the release of the latest policy by Heritage Minister Copps, a private consulting firm in Toronto interviewed hundreds of people — including me — in order to prepare a report. Perfectly flattered by the attention from the number-cruncher (and one from the big city at the centre of the universe, at that!) I blabbed and blabbed about everything from theatre ownership and the overall excellence of contemporary Canadian film, to the tough conditions for B.C. filmmakers who can barely afford to shoot in their own towns as a result of deep-pocketed American competition for locations and crews. It was another one of those talks about Canadian film that ends on an ambiguous note: we're doing well, but we could always be doing better.

The last question the interviewer asked was something about the service industry and whether or not it was a good thing. I pointed out the "cultural export" problem mentioned above, but there was another side to the issue that wasn't readily apparent: the overall look — or what's called the "production values" — of Canadian movies has improved by leaps and bounds in the space of a few short years. From cringing at the sight of sound booms dropping into frame, awkward compositions without artistic purpose, unmatched sight lines, bumpy dolly shots and laborious editing (I don't talk about any of those films in this book), I found myself saying things like: "The movie was good, it didn't even look Canadian." Shame on me, I know, but anyone who's lived through a student film festival knows what I'm talking about. We love looking at pretty pictures and well-crafted films. It lets us fall into the story without effort. If a film is constantly reminding you of the filmmaker's lack of technical skill, it's a real slog. I hadn't slogged in a long time, and if I was going to give credit to anyone for our sudden bump into the big leagues of "film look," it was the Americans. Thanks to the service industry, local film crews were learning every trick in Hollywood's book. If Americans were exploiting our cheap-loonie labour force to make studio dreck, we got the gold of experience in return. And when the Americans pack up and head back to that sprawling parking lot called LaLaLand for the winter, the crews stick around at home — working on deferral (no pay) to make movies for their friends.

I remember talking to Reg Harkema (Vancouver-based director of *A Girl is a Girl* and editor of McKellar's *Last Night*, Guy Maddin's *Twilight of the Ice Nymphs* and Bruce McDonald's *Hard Core Logo*) who told me he got the best people in the city to work on his movie for nearly nothing (well, on deferral). "A section of the community is really cool about helping out. So as long as you shoot, like, in the middle of February, they're happy to be there because they wouldn't necessarily be doing anything else."

If Harkema idolized Jean-Luc Godard for his idiosyncratic, non-formulaic style and openness to spontaneity, then how would the presence and participation of American-trained crew affect the outcome of the film? If

Marshall McLuhan suggested the "medium is the message," would Reg's subtextual and "subformal" message be transformed by these speakers of slick American film grammar? Would his low-key story of a naive 20-something nice guy fruitlessly searching for the perfect mate suddenly turn into a sappy teen romance aching for the presence of Josh Hartnett and Jennifer Love Hewitt?

The answer was a resounding "No" — at least as far as Reg's film was concerned. When it screened at the 1999 Vancouver International Film Festival I wrote the following notes in the paper: "The film arrives at its very valid points without much fuss, eschewing formal narrative structure and using improvisation-based performances. Harkema's believable characterizations of ordinary people make this the rough little gem it is ... "[6] Harkema had a clear vision of what he was trying to do artistically, and as a result, there was no visible influence of an American model. But that doesn't mean it doesn't happen, particularly if the director him or herself happens to make a lot of American episodic television. After all, film is a language and the more you speak a certain dialect, the more it sinks into your subconscious to cause subtle changes in the neural network, and the harder it is to shake.

When Anne Wheeler's film *Marine Life* was released in 2001, some people felt it was steeped in a TV style and, as a result, lacked the depth needed for a movie. The host of CBC radio's *Definitely Not the Opera*, the fabulously talented broadcaster Nora Young, mentioned it during our weekly chat and I had to agree — at least on some level. However, I couldn't decide if it was the actual look of the film that made me feel that way, as it relied a lot on close-ups, two-shots and other "TV-safe" compositions instead of the typically filmic, broad landscape shots we've come to know and love-hate. Wheeler certainly directs a lot of TV. But she's also one of the most respected film directors in the country for her grounded approach to storytelling and subtle human touch. Was it the framing that was telling me "TV" or the fact that Cybill Shepherd (a familiar TV presence) happened to be the star of this movie? Or was it none of the above? Was *Marine Life*'s small-screen feel the result of its small scale story of a burnt-out, twice-divorced middle-aged lounge singer? Nothing epically dramatic happens in *Marine Life*. It probes the everyday problems of life in a very intimate way, refuses cinematic contrivance, and simply lets the story tell itself. This is part of its strength, but I guess we've come to expect something much larger in scale when it comes to the big screen, thanks to Hollywood — where pretty much everything comes down to size.

Mr. Big

"I have no doubt in my mind that the people who left Canada for the United States [to pursue a filmmaking career] would be very sad, bitter people if they had stayed here," says Don McKellar. McKellar also suggests the best way to deal with Americans in Hollywood: "Honesty ... It always disarms people down there if you give them a really honest answer ... We must be honest. I'm serious about that. Play the integrity card ... and they will be at your feet. When you do a meeting in Hollywood, people always ask you, 'How did it go?' and, 'Who did you see?' and, 'So and so is moving up?' but I always say, 'Well I don't know, I'm from Canada, I don't know.' They're always very impressed because you aren't following to see who's who and what's happening. You stand apart, and somehow, that's really glamorous to them."

An unflagging supporter of Canadian film, McKellar says he had no desire to pursue a career in flag-waving Hollywood because he didn't think he'd be allowed the same creative freedom he gets up here, where the dollars may be smaller, but the leash on the creative spirit is almost infinite. "I don't think I've made any compromises [in past work]. I've made changes at the suggestion of people I know, but only because I believed they were true. I can't think of a time when I said, 'Well, okay, this is what I have to do to get this film made. Otherwise, I would like to think that if I really had impulses I was suppressing, I would follow those — even if it made me an art filmmaker with my little digital camera ... I like to think that if I felt something was a compromise, I'd abandon it," McKellar said, pointing out the obvious differences between our system and Hollywood's. For McKellar, our system was preferable, but for others, being stuck in Canada would be a prison sentence because they need a different type of personal affirmation to give their lives meaning.

There are thousands of Canadians in Hollywood at the moment, and most — like James Cameron, Norman Jewison, Arthur Hiller, Ivan Reitman, Lorne Michaels, Jim Carrey, Mike Myers, Michael J. Fox and Keanu Reeves (to name but a few) — left Canada in order to pursue their dreams of making a living, if not fame and fortune, in the entertainment industry. Like the expatriate Conrad Black, who wanted to abandon his Canadian passport when it blocked his admittance into the British House of Lords, some Canadians have different needs. For others, especially those who left prior to the mideighties — before we began to free ourselves from the chrysalis of institutional thinking — they simply ran out of room to grow. *Saturday*

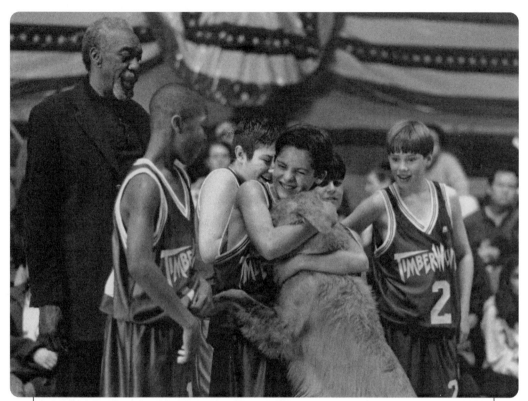

Air Bud (1997): He loves the smell of dog-breath in the morning, for Josh Framm (Kevin Zegers), it smells like victory. Based on Kevin DiCicco's real life pet, *Air Bud* starred a talented golden retriever named Buddy an animal that could actually score a basket by bouncing it off his nose. There is now an *Air Bud* franchise, though Buddy died of cancer after the first film was completed. KEYSTONE, RED SKY ENTERTAINMENT

Night Live creator Lorne Michaels talked about why he left Canada, in a *Saturday Night* magazine interview. He was trying to get a Canadian variety show off the ground with the CBC. He demanded creative control and was told: "If you're that good, why are you here?"[7] That was in 1973, when Canadian film was equated with crappy films created through the Canadian Film Development Commission (CFDC — progenitor to Telefilm), which set out to make films with commercial appeal, but instead created the substandard movies that came to define the period known as "the tax-shelter era" (including films such as *Explosion, The Reincarnate, Face-Off* — a hockey movie, not John Woo's martial arts

thriller — and the suitably titled *It Seemed Like a Good Idea at the Time,* starring the Canadian actress Yvonne De Carlo). There wasn't much of a future for the filmmaker who craved to tell stories to a world audience, perhaps because the flipside of our "marked preference for the negative" is that we deny self-starters who believe in themselves obsessively. The self-created style of person has a hard time making it in this country because, good socialists that we apparently are, we are quick to pull everyone back down to street level. Then again, some people's egos are just too big for us mild-mannered Canadians to really handle.

Telefilm Tension

Robert Vince is the Vancouver-born producer who made *Air Bud* — one of the most profitable movies ever made in Canada, winner of the Golden Reel award for the biggest money-maker in 1997 — and the first in a series of animal-sport movies including *Air Bud 2* and *Most Valuable Primate*, in which furry little creatures become all-star athletes. Vince moved to Los Angeles after the first movie, which was picked up by Disney, established him as part of "the scene." Vince says he hangs out "regularly" with other ex-pat Canucks such as Ivan Reitman and he says he hasn't lost a shred of his Canadian identity since he's been in the lap of LaLaland. He is a proud Canadian, he says. His move to Malibu was more for business purposes than personal needs, but it's clear from his films that he's in no rush to make art movies, and in that regard, he speaks for a number of people. In the decade I've covered Canadian film for different media, I've encountered enough people who can't stand Canadian film because they find it "pretentious" or "incomprehensible" or "boring."

Vince puts it this way: "We have a system that rewards people who make movies that no one wants to see. I made a movie that made money because it was fun and it spoke to people in a way they could understand. I believe in a free market. I trust the people. That's why I will never be a Telefilm whore and take money from the taxpayer to make a movie. If someone in the private sector won't invest in it, then maybe it's not worth making, you know? I hate it that we have this aversion to making money in this country. I remember getting into a [scrap] with Atom Egoyan at the Genies. He won for best picture and we won for the Golden Reel. I told him that if he'd made a movie that people had wanted to see, he could have won the Golden Reel instead of me," said Vince during a stop-over in Vancouver to promote *Most Valuable Primate*, a movie he directed as well as produced. *MVP* was about an orphaned chimpanzee who heads off in search of his lost family at a game reserve, but gets off the train in the wrong town. Lost and confused, the chimp befriends another dislocated outsider — a young man who craves to be a part of his small-town community, but lacking any hockey skills, he is completely lost. Enter the simian Paul Henderson to save the day. *MVP* garnered respectable box-office receipts, though nothing that compared to *Air Bud*. "Some people don't think a popular movie could be any good — just like I don't think a movie that bores people with its self-importance is any good. It's all how you look at it, I guess," Vince said.

Certainly Vince is not alone in the way he places the priority on cash instead of compelling social content or a Canadian message, and he's not the only one who has problems with government bureaucrats assuming such an important role in the creation of our cultural artifacts.

As filmmaker Penelope Buitenhuis observed: "The tragedy in Canadian film is that the bureaucrats have far too much power. It's always a problem in a government-dividend culture: the government controls the industry. My biggest sadness is that we get money to make movies, but no money to go out and distribute them. Even in Europe, there is no money to advertise. All this energy and time goes into making the film, but without ads or marketing and promotion, it's all for nothing. No previews. Really hard to be seen and heard when there's always this assumption that if you don't have stars, you'll never be able to make it successful ... How do you break through? Every director in Canada still fantasizes about being on David Letterman."[8]

Buitenhuis works on both sides of the institutional fence, as a commercial TV director and a documentary filmmaker at the NFB (*Tokyo Girls*). She is interested in making art as well as making money, echoing the sentiments of early maverick Budge Crawley, who hated the idea of a socially supported film system and rebelled against it by making his own commercially successful documentaries such as *The Man Who Skied Down Everest*. Other Canadian commercial winners include *The Changeling*, the Peter Medak-directed horror thriller starring George C. Scott as a haunted composer; *Porky's*, the Bob Clark teen sex-comedy set in 1954 Florida, and most recently, *The Art of War*, Christian Duguay's espionage action movie that starred Wesley Snipes and featured plenty of great shots of Montreal posing as every city in the world (look for the religious statuary dotting the skyline).

Star-spangled Social Justice

While some Canadians are happy to leave what they see as a small, stagnant pond ruled by petty bureaucrats, some Canadians have a harder time reconciling their national identity with the apparent compromise in the name of commerce — and work very hard to balance box-office appeal with a sense of social justice. The legendary Norman Jewison is one of those people. Born in Toronto in 1926, Jewison left for the United States after working as an actor, writer and director in television in the United Kingdom and Canada. While Jewison has turned out such commercial juggernauts as *Moonstruck*, *Fiddler on the Roof* and *The Cincinnati Kid*, he's also taken on movies that pack a powerful social statement such as *In the Heat of the Night* (best picture Oscar-winner that starred Sidney Poitier as a cop dealing with white racists in the

South), *A Soldier's Story* (a story about racism in the United States Army) and *Hurricane* (the story of Rubin Hurricane Carter, a black boxer wrongfully imprisoned for murder). Jewison is a classic example of a Canadian transposing his decidedly pluralistic, socially aware Canadian perspective onto his art and coming up with a strange hybrid that features a Tinseltown look and feel with a subversive social message. You won't find Jewison stranding his viewers in empty space, breaking narrative frame with photographic devices or warping linear time, but his Canadianess is hard to miss as he questions authority, subverts the mainstream opinion and gives the hero stance to the underdog.

Even Reitman, the man who rose to fame cresting on the wave of *The Cannibal Girls* and then made a mint with *Meatballs*, has clearly not lost touch with the core of his Canadian worldview. When Southam reporter Jamie Portman interviewed him about his 1993 comic smash, *Dave*, Reitman was caught up in the "family values" war that was raging in the United States in the wake of Candace Bergen's feminist triumph as a single working mother in *Murphy Brown*. "I like making family movies and I like watching them, but this whole 'family values' discussion is a lot of crap," said the man who produced David Cronenberg's *Shivers* and *Rabid*. Reitman said he may personally prefer light comedy to dark, sexual horrors but he defends the right of all filmmakers to express themselves. "We are in a pluralistic society that should allow all kinds of fare," he said. Reitman was no doubt articulating a perspective formed in part as a result of being the first man convicted under Canadian decency laws when he, and McMaster University classmate Dan Goldberg, were arrested for making the film *Columbus of Sex* in 1970. Despite support from the Canadian arts community at large, Reitman and Goldberg were fined $300 and given a year's probabation. Another sign of Reitman's Canadian roots can be seen in his choice of heroes and heroines. Like his fellow Angeleno transplant, James Cameron, Reitman shows us generally passive, but nonetheless heroic, men (think of Rick Moranis in *Ghostbusters*) and incredibly potent — often Amazonian — women, many of whom are played by Sigourney Weaver. Weaver not only played the alpha human in Cameron's *Aliens*, but she's also been featured in two key Reitman films, *Dave* and *Ghostbusters*.

No Stars in This Solar System

Speaking of big stars like Sigourney Weaver — who is not Canadian, but is certainly cool enough to be — there are a great many people in this country who wonder why we don't have that giant personality-splitting machine called the "star system." America has "stars." We have "actors." The rest of the world has a strange mix of something in between: a domestic star system that may be huge within a given country or culture, but relatively meaningless once removed from the natural habitat. It's not that we haven't done anything worldly or important, or that we lack talent. Canada has given rise to hundreds of "stars" — from Jim Carrey, Dan Ackroyd, Bruce Greenwood, Mary Pickford, Mike Myers, Celine Dion, Bryan Adams, Keanu Reeves, Carrie-Anne Moss, Pamela Anderson, Alanis Morissette, Shania Twain, Neve Campbell, Christopher Plummer, William Shatner, Paul Schaeffer, Donald Sutherland, Kiefer Sutherland, Campbell Scott, Geneviève Bujold, and many more — but for the most part, these stars had to leave native soil to be seen as celebrities instead of mere screen or stage talents.

If celebrity is defined by the sheer number of times an individual's image appears in the media, in turn creating a sense of mass awareness, then the biggest celebrities in Canada are bankers, businessmen, hockey players and American celebrities making movies in Canadian cities. It's kind of pathetic to pay so much attention to people who are, in the end, just people. But in a world without gods, I guess we need to create beings larger than ourselves, and so we have this artificial construct called the star system.

Created in the early days of film by Carl Laemmle, a rival producer to the powerful Patents Company, the star system was created with the express purpose of making money — and nothing else. It was a way of sucking loyalty from a naive public who began identifying with the people they saw on screen. According to Hollywood lore, Laemmle noticed that Florence Lawrence (a Canadian actress) had a huge following and lured her away from the Patents Company with the promise of better pay and real fame (up to that point, in order to keep the actors under the studio's thumb, they did not reveal the players' real names). After he signed her, he circulated anonymous rumours of her death to the media. Once they swallowed the hook, Laemmle issued counter-statements asserting Lawrence was still alive and well and working with his Independent Motion Picture Company. There was a public outcry over the misunderstanding, which Laemmle hooked on the Patents Co. as a bitter lie in the wake of losing their number one attraction. The media ate it all up without asking a single question and presto, the star system was born. To this day, it remains a sleazy little slime factory, pumping out innuendo and fabricated personal stories to keep celebrities on the front page, in the public eye and high on the must-see list.

In recent years, some Canadian entertainment types such as the broadcast baron Moses

Znaimer — the self-made success who turned a small TV station, CityTV, into an international multimedia force that includes MuchMusic, MuchMore Music, Bravo and other specialty channels around the world — have tried to create a star system for Canadian talent. While they do so with the highest cultural aims, I've always wondered if it really was such a good idea to transpose a mainstream American movie concept into the pluralistic and decidedly more socialist model of Canadian film. We're already bitter and jealous of other people's success as it is, and somehow I just don't think the two entities are copacetic. I'm not alone in that opinion, either.

I had a long talk with de facto Canadian celebrity Sarah Polley a while back when she was doing a slate of rare one-on-one interviews for the movie *Guinevere*, an Audrey Wells film about a shy young woman from the social elite who hooks up with a middle-aged and atrophying alcoholic art photographer played by Stephen Rea. "I'm happy we don't have a star system — the best thing about this country is that we don't have one," Polley said. "I'm ruthless about protecting myself as it is. If I went to parties all the time and read about myself I'd be pretty lost. I don't know how people do it — or why they would want to do it. It's their decision, but it's not my choice." Polley barely even does publicity for the movies she makes for the same reason, which made this appearance in her maple leaf Fluvogs even more impressive. Polley is profoundly patriotic about Canada and whenever possible — at least at that point in time in 1999 — she will make a Canadian film over most of the American projects she is offered. And in the wake of her performance in *The Sweet Hereafter*, there are many. Shortly before we spoke, she was featured on the cover of *Vanity Fair* as one of several young faces to watch for, but the only thing Polley walked away with, outside of the opportunity to meet so many other interesting young people, was how shallow the exercise was. "It's all about whose clothes you wear," she said. "I've never equated attention with success. I always believed success is being able to do what you love while maintaining a life. I like the fact that no one bugs me when I walk down the street here [in Toronto] ... We're cool about giving people their space, except during the film festival, when we all pretend to be American." Polley admits she wasn't always so proud to be Canadian. "It's the result of making four movies back to back in the States ... nothing turns you into a nationalist like spending time in there. The attitude can be overwhelming, so now, I'd have to say I love how self-deprecating we are."

Don McKellar agrees, saying a star system probably wouldn't sit right with the Canadian public, which has a built-in rejection button for perfection. Peter Outerbridge also echoed Polley's feelings: "There's a lot of animosity about [the star system] right now in Canada ... People see it as setting up a club mentality. I don't know if that's such a good thing ... it creates a clique within the industry. Some actors want the acknowledgement. Some don't. To me, the whole tragedy of the 'respect' argument is that it's all tinsel. There's nothing to it. It's not respect — it's merchandizing power, and I see a difference there. Some don't — and if they want to be a product, I say more power to them, just go to the States to do it because we need the difference if we want the industry to survive. We'll never get ahead by being the same."[9]

The Future

So how is the Canadian industry poised to meet the future? With more experience, talent and funding than ever before, suggesting we've finally emerged from the Dark Ages into the light of small-scale industry independence.

Alliance-Atlantis, under the chairmanship of Michael McMillan, is the largest Canadian entertainment company in history — and while it still receives a healthy amount of government funding despite being a publicly traded corporation that once had a share price in excess of $28, Alliance-Atlantis consistently makes profitable films. It's also evolving into a vertically integrated entertainment company with activities in production, distribution and exhibition. Alliance-Atlantis Cinemas was created when Famous Players and Alliance-Atlantis acquired Leonard Schein's (one-time director of the Toronto Festival of Festivals) Vancouver-based art-house chain, Festival Cinemas in June 1999. The move was significant because for the first time,

Canadian films — at least the ones produced by Alliance-Atlantis — were almost guaranteed to see the light of a projector bulb.

Alliance-Atlantis isn't the only company to make strides in the commercial arena. There are several small to medium-sized Canadian independent producers and distributors out there, and many of them are thriving in the wake of specialty channels and other content-hungry media.

Moving in tandem with this new dawn in Canadian film industry is Canada's budding reputation abroad as a vibrant film culture — in the wake of successful directors such as Denys Arcand, David Cronenberg and Atom Egoyan winning prestigious international awards. These Canadian directors have blazed a trail through the hostile wilderness of the film business and given others hope for success. Egoyan won the Grand Jury Prize,

Les Boys in black ties: David Cronenberg, Atom Egoyan, Istvàn Szabo and Robert Lantos — the man who's produced movies for them all – stand together for a perfect team Canada photo-op. Though Szabo is Hungarian, he directed *Sunshine*, a story he brought to the screen with collaborator and friend, Lantos. SERENDIPITY POINT FILMS

FIPRESCI prize and Ecumenical Prize for *The Sweet Hereafter* at Cannes, but it was his Oscar nominations for the same film that made him a household name to most Canadians. Certainly, as Egoyan himself observed, more people know his name than know his movies, but the fact that so many Canadians are familiar with Egoyan's name must be seen as encouraging because it's a lot better than nothing. But the importance of gaining the American stamp of approval remains a bitter pill for almost any Canadian in the entertainment industry — not because you have to prove yourself to Americans, but because you have to prove yourself to Americans before you become a success back home.

Canada is turning out some excellent motion pictures, but people still ask the same question: "Why can't we be more like Australia? They make good movies and they aren't a big country." I hate hearing this. It still happens — even after a movie like *The Sweet Hereafter* — because Canadians still have this blind spot about self. When was the last time you saw a really good Australian film? I've seen at least 20 recent movies out of Australia and New Zealand in the past five years, and most of them — with the exception of *The Piano* — are weaker than anything I've seen unspool up here. *Oscar and Lucinda* and *In a Savage Land* were two of the stronger efforts, and they were only half-realized efforts about the same subject: the colonial experience. And we think we're the ones who are stuck in the same groove? Every tradition has good films and bad films to show for its efforts, and Canada's success rate is as high as any other nation's. The only difference is that we don't see the crappy foreign films here because no distributor would spend money promoting a flop in a new territory.

Where we are finding the greatest degree of success in financing is through co-productions and joint ventures. Canada and several provinces have excellent tax incentives to stimulate production, which makes us an attractive creative partner on the international scene — even if it may mean setting at least part of the film in Canada. *The Red Violin*, for instance, had financial support from several nations involved in the production with the majority of the $14-million (CDN) budget coming from the United States. It was set partially in Montreal to maintain an element of Canadian content, and to meet eligibility requirements for Canadian tax credits and grants, but its scope is truly international. Not only was the film financing pulled together from companies and broadcasters in Canada, the United Kingdom, France and the United States, but the movie features an international cast including Samuel L. Jackson, Greta Scacchi, Jason Flemyng, Sandra Oh, Colm Feore, Sylvia Chang, Monique Mercure and Rémy Girard. It was also shot in five countries: Italy, Austria, England, China and Canada.

Comfortingly, just as we begin to look outward for financial help and creative partners, we are also looking inward with as much apparent confidence. Over the past 20 years, we have built an infrastructure from the ground up through film schools, cooperatives, cinematheques, art groups, salons, Norman Jewison's Canadian Film Centre in Toronto, film camps, elementary and secondary school film programs and film festivals — as well as an increasing array of professional organizations.

Better still, the films we've made in recent years prove we can be be distinctly Canadian, and perfectly hip all at the same time. We are making excellent movies and best of all, Canadians are beginning to take notice.

Much like little Kaspar (Christoph Koncz) in François Girard's *The Red Violin*, the Canadian film tradition is bursting with creative power, but continues to be weak when it comes to fiscal physique. Whether or not Canadian film manages to win the internal and external battle against institutional forces, one thing is certain: the art will survive.
ODEON AND RHOMBUS MEDIA

More Canadians than ever are watching domestic work. It's certainly tough, if not impossible, to break even in this country alone, but all the logistical problems in the world have yet to quash the vital Canadian spirit of creation.

Canadians are incredibly resourceful people, and when it comes to making movies, they can stretch a dollar further than most. "Canadians make garage band movies," says Peter Outerbridge. "We can shoot a film in 22 days. Our actors are reknowned for being able to shoot 12 pages a day and we have directors who can think on their toes." We can see examples of this type of resourcefulness straight across the Canadian film landscape, from director Scott Smith renting a

theatre and "four-walling" his own film *rollercoaster* to get it in front of audiences, to Blaine Thurier, who never made a movie in his life before but picked up a digital video camera and just started shooting *Low Self-Esteem Girl*. It looks as if we're finally getting over the wall of self-loathing and self-sabotage, and optimistically — if not naively — pushing ahead with our dreams. Like anyone stepping out on their own, away from the protective but stultifying force of the institution, we may get scared along the way and crave the familiarity of the protective box. But if we can love ourselves enough to be true to who we are, and not worry if people like us or not, or how much money we can make, we stand to build an entirely new cinematic tradition — one born in the shadow of Hollywood, but secure enough to be itself.

Fade to Black, Roll Credits

Over the course of this voyage into the dark heart of Canadian film, we've seen how the Canadian condition is generally defined by what it is not: We are not American. We are not idealists. We are not jingoistic flag-wavers and we are not heroes in the classical sense of the word. In the past, people assumed this made us passive, weak and introverted, but as Tom McCamus said, there's a difference between being weak and being vulnerable. The weak person is simply crushed, but the vulnerable person is open-minded enough to remain open to possibilities and different interpretations of the world.

Canada is a country that has always been able to see both sides of a given equation, which is why we have become the world's most celebrated peacekeepers. Where other cultures may worship the "action hero," we offer the pensive man who tolerates difference and embraces the ambiguous nature of the universe itself. I think it takes a strong man to be open-minded, and a stronger man still who can accept a woman on her own terms. Canadian screen heroes can do all of the above. No, they don't carry guns and conquer the enemy — they wait to find common ground, map the best route, and as a result, have a much better chance at seeing the next day. As far as nation-building goes, such a low-key, internal and silent approach has been seen as a failure of identity.

As a woman, I see it differently. I see Canada as having a highly evolved sense of self, it's just that we choose to stay in the background, far from the front line and the flag-waving theatrics. This does not mean we've failed to achieve nationhood, it just means we've arrived at identity from a feminine perspective. Living next to the muscle-bound neighbour next door, we've learned to stay quiet, to become good mediators, to problem-solve instead of shoot and to celebrate diversity instead of looking for sameness. This is why we see so many strong women in Canadian film, and it also explains why there's a remarkable lack of progeny — Canada is still uncertain of its future.

Things are changing, though, and from what I can see they are changing for the better. When I look at movies like *Maelström* (Bibi makes peace with the son of the man she killed) or *Les Muses orphelines* (the young sister Isabelle takes off on her own to have a baby) or *Suspicious River* (Leila reconciles the ghosts of her past), I see women coming to grips with their internal demons and moving forward with full control over their own destinies. This shift from "crone" to young woman in control is an important sea change in the Canadian psyche, and I believe it's reflected in a palpable sense of nascent Canadian pride. I believe I am part of a generation of proud Canadians, possibly the proudest ever. All we have to do now is translate that love of the Canadian self into a love of Canadian screen, and sooner or later, we won't have to begin conversations about Canadian film with "the problem is ..." Instead, we can start fresh and reimagine ourselves, and the nation, as a limitless set of possibilities just waiting to be explored.

Norman Jewison

Born 1926 — Toronto, Ontario

© VILIAM

He was one of many young, talented Canadians who wandered south to fulfill his dreams — but he never abandoned his Canadian identity, and when it came time to reinvest in his cultural heritage, Norman Jewison didn't just give something back, he created a legacy in the form of the Canadian Film Centre (or The Norman Jewison Centre for Advanced Film Studies). Located in an old mansion on the outskirts of metro Toronto, the centre opened its doors in 1986 and has since pumped out some of the best screen talents the country has to offer — many of whom are included in this book. So if you're wondering why Jewison gets extra everything for free in this spotlight section — while other Canadian-born genre-spinners such as James Cameron, Ivan Reitman and Arthur Hiller get nothing, it's because Jewison has never truly been co-opted by the studio system. Though his films tend to follow certain studio conventions, he makes movies that explore themes of social justice and tolerance, and sticks to his guns regardless of the potential backlash.

For instance, when Jewison's most recent film, *The Hurricane* (about the wrongful conviction and eventual release of boxer Rubin "Hurricane" Carter), was criticized for whitewashing facts and downplaying the contributions of the prize-fighter's legal team in favour of glorifying a group of Canadian social activists, Jewison never buckled and eventually enlisted the support of none other than Jack Valenti.

The Toronto son is used to controversy. After ending his tour of duty with the Royal Canadian Navy at the close of the Second World War, Jewison toured the American South where he got on a bus, sat in the back, and was given an impromptu lesson on segregation by the fuming bus driver who pointed at the sign COLORED PEOPLE IN THE REAR. It struck a chord in Jewison's Canadian psyche and set him on a mission. "It was my first exposure to apartheid in America, and it made a tremendous impression on me that people could go and serve their country in war and give their lives to a society and to a government that didn't allow them to have a cup of coffee in a department store or drink out of a public fountain. I found that inconceivable," Jewison told Southam reporter Jamie Portman during the publicity rounds for *The Hurricane* in 2000.

When Jewison returned to Toronto — where he actually attended the same high school as Glenn Gould — after a stint at the BBC in London (1950-1952), the University of Toronto grad began directing TV shows for the CBC. With network experience under his belt, he moved to the United States and began working for CBS, where he became a variety show king — producing such efforts as the "Legendary Judy Garland Show" in 1963 and '64. Having gained a reputation for comedy, Jewison's first film was the 1963 *Forty Pounds of Trouble*, which feaured Tony Curtis taking care of an abandoned six-year-old and climaxed with a chase through Disneyland. The film proved he could spin a comic tale, prompting a slew of other light entertainments such as

The Cincinnati Kid (1965), a Steve McQueen card-shark movie, and *The Russians Are Coming! The Russians Are Coming!* (1966), a spoof of Cold War paranoia that earned him the title of "Canadian pinko" in the trade magazine, *The Hollywood Reporter*. The criticism seemed a little severe for a puff piece, but in 1967, Jewison really did step away from the cult of conformity with the release of *In the Heat of the Night*. Revered to this day as a pivotal moment in American film for its blunt portrayal of racism and hate, *In the Heat of the Night* won the best picture Oscar of the year, in addition to four other statuettes. Jewison himself, however, was shut out.

His next few projects highlighted entertainment over social justice — *The Thomas Crown Affair* (1968) and *Gaily, Gaily* (1969) — but after watching the race issue continue to fester, Jewison picked up sticks and headed back to Britain, where he could continue his film career without compromising his morality. While there, he adapted the famed stage play *Fiddler on the Roof* to much critical acclaim, and hooked up with Andrew Lloyd Webber and Tim Rice for the screen version of *Jesus Christ Superstar*. He hit a low point with the roller derby movie *Rollerball* in 1975, but he returned to the front line in the fight for social justice with a vengeance in 1979 with the courtroom drama, *And Justice For All*, and in 1984 with *A Soldier's Story* — another murder mystery with a pointed race angle as it explores a black man's place in a white man's army. The film introduced Denzel Washington to the masses and featured a standout supporting performance from diva Patti LaBelle. It was even nominated for an Academy Award, but once again, Jewison was not a winner. Even the universally lauded *Moonstruck*, which earned Oscars for Cher and screenwriter John Patrick Shanley, failed to earn Jewison the stamp of peer approval. It was only in 1998 that Jewison

earned the recognition of Tinseltown when he was awarded the Irving G. Thalberg memorial award for his outstanding contribution to the cinema. I still remember watching him accept the prize with the utmost humility: he reminded the blockbuster-manic audience that storytelling was the essence of film. His speech was so elegant and simple that it was hard to disagree with anything he said, let alone take offense. Like I said, the man may make a living in the United States — but his heart remains 100 percent Canuck.

In a recent *Life and Times* documentary produced for CBC Television, which features Bruce McDonald interviewing Jewison on a train chugging across the Canadian landscape, Jewison talks a lot about his roots and how being Canadian shaped his world vision. He talks about the landscape and the quality of the light and the smell of the trees. He pushes the private sector to invest in Canadian talent and says "If you want to play, you have to step up to bat."

We know he did. But whether or not Jewison becomes the founding father of a whole new tradition of financially and dramtically viable English Canadian filmmakers — or just a proud, patriotic anomaly in the so-called "self-loathing" Canadian wilderness — remains to be seen.

FILMOGRAPHY: *Forty Pounds of Trouble* (1963) | *The Thrill of It All* (1963) | *Send Me No Flowers* (1964) | *The Art of Love* (1965) | *The Cincinnati Kid* (1965) | *The Russians Are Coming! The Russians Are Coming!* (1966) | *In the Heat of the Night* (1967) | *The Thomas Crown Affair* (1968) | *Gaily, Gaily* (1969) | *Fiddler on the Roof* (1971) | *Jesus Christ Superstar* (1973) | *Rollerball* (1975) | *F.I.S.T.* (1978) | *... And Justice For All* (1979) | *Best Friends* (1982) | *A Soldier's Story* (1984) | *Agnes of God* (1985) | *Moonstruck* (1987) | *In Country* (1989) | *Other People's Money* (1991) | *Only You* (1994) | *Bogus* (1996) | *The Hurricane* (1999)

Garth Drabinsky

Born 1948 — Toronto, Ontario

TORONTO FILM LIBRARY

Few Canadians have simultaneously inspired as much awe, admiration, skepticism, sycophancy and disgust as Garth Drabinsky, the high-flying entrepreneur behind the joystick of such dazzling, daredevil crashes as Cineplex and Livent.

Love him or hate him, you have to hand it to the man for not only building an empire from the ground up, but doing it twice — if not more (surely, the man will make another return to the limelight he loves so much) — and flying the Maple Leaf in the face of star-spangled suits at every turn.

Determined to play the same game of self-creation cemented into American consciousness via Hollywood's marketing of the "American Dream" — to the point where he even took it upon himself to produce the American classic, E. L. Doctorow's *Ragtime*, on Broadway — Drabinsky fell victim to a variety of things, not least among them hubris.

The history of the entertainment industry is littered with the corpses of high flyers. It's just that so few of them have been Canadian — and fiercely, rationalistically Canadian — that Drabinsky's story not only stands out as a colourful aberration in our typically staid, and relatively small-stakes film history, but it made a dent in the Hollywood consciousness when a loud, and not-so-polite, citizen of a country that typically says "sorry" first nearly wrestled control of a premier movie chain away from its American partners.

Born in Toronto on October 27, 1948, Drabinsky was the eldest of three sons born to one-time farmboy and air-conditioning king Philip Drabinsky and his wife Ethel. A self-proclaimed entrepreneur since he left high school, Drabinsky sought positions of influence. He ran for president of student council promising his classmates wholesale school supplies. He won. He brokered power with grace, and even acted as a go-between between the rebellious sixties student body and the administration. No doubt, his proclivity in the arena of public speaking and the art of a pitch attracted him to law school and earned him a law degree, but entertainment was always his preoccupation and in 1972, he approached Toronto film exhibitor, and local legend, Nat Taylor to see if he would invest in an entertainment magazine he was publishing called *Impact* (a freebie listings paper).

Taylor was a bit of an innovator in the business: he was one of the first theatre owners to realize the benefits of a small house and a big house when he split Ottawa's Elgin theatre in two: the Big Elgin and the Little Elgin. He'd put the big, new splashy release in the big theatre and pull the longer-running film into the more efficient little Elgin.

While Drabinsky was busy soaking up the lessons of Nat Taylor, he was also building a production partnership with Joel Michaels. In 1977, the duo was shooting *Silent Partner* in the bowels of the newly opened eyesore called the Eaton Centre in downtown Toronto. Drabinsky and Michaels also made *The Changeling*, the film directed by Peter Medak and starring George C. Scott and Melvyn Douglas, as well as *Tribute*, the Oscar-nominated film starring Jack Lemmon.

Taylor and Drabinsky expanded all across Canada and the United States, following a similar business plan of erecting multiple screen theatres, or else refurbishing grand old movie palaces in decadent detail. In 1982, they opened the Beverly Center Cineplex in Beverly Hills. The 14-screen theatre was glamorous and costly. While Drabinsky didn't hold on to the Beverly Center very long — eventually ceding control to Alfred Taubman (a developer and head of Sotheby's) — he did get something important out of his foray into the heartland of moving-picturedom: by taking advantage of the U.S. antitrust laws, Drabinsky was able to get a shot at showing major releases that the studios denied him at home. If he could show them in the United States, then why not Canada? It was this logic that he hoped would push Canadian officials into investigating what Drabinsky saw as preferential booking policies among the majors.

On July 1, 1983, Drabinsky had his victory when the majors were forced to sign an agreement that allowed all exhibitors to bid on product, an event that essentially changed the exhibition and distribution business in Canada, at least on paper. Before he achieved his most lasting legacy, Cineplex began to buckle under the weight of its huge debt-load from capital expenditures. The solution to their cash flow problems came in the form of an IPO. Engineered by Myron Gottlieb (head of

Merit Investments, and a business partner), the IPO raised about $4 million, but when interest rates moved up in the teetering days of Trudeau's time in office, the stock crashed to the point where the Ontario Securities Commission put a halt to trading. The miracle of self-creation appeared to be over.

Drabinsky was sinking in a Red Sea of ink. He looked to Norman Levy, a Hollywood producer he met while shooting *The Changeling*. Levy worked at 20th Century Fox as vice-chairman, and together with his billionaire boss Martin Davis, the two bailed Cineplex and Drabinsky out of a cash bind. For reasons that aren't all that clear — some have speculated it was an anti-Canadian bias — Davis wanted to get out of the deal with Drabinsky and the relationship dissolved after nine months.

Without a major cash infusion, Cineplex was vulnerable again. This time, it was the Bronfmans (Canada's one-time liquor barons who recently sold their legacy to Vivendi after Edgar Jr. tried to make it big as a movie dude himself with the leveraged purchase of Universal-MCA), via Leo Kolber, who bailed him out when CEMP (named after heirs Charles, Edgar, Minda and Phyllis) bought the majority share interest in the company — an alternative they thought preferable to putting Drabinsky out of business for not paying his rent to Cadillac Fairview, a subsidiary of CEMP.

The other good news was that in December 1982, the Combines Investigation branch brought the studios to the mat. Six months later, the studio chiefs signed a letter of intent guaranteeing everyone access to their product through a bidding system. Garth won the proverbial battle, but war was brewing. Before it had time to wage in earnest, however, Drabinsky — flush with Bronfman capital — bought out Odeon from the Zahorchak family for $22 million. He also purchased a string of U.S. theatres called the Plitt circuit (1985). He was now a real presence in the United States.

By 1986, Drabinsky had formed a relationship with MCA and then-president Sid Sheinberg to keep the acquisitions coming and the debt-load guaranteed by deeper pockets.

MCA was a fully integrated entertainment corporation with fingers in music, publishing, television and movies. But it was top heavy and bottom poor. It needed an exhibition partner to achieve — as all companies desire to achieve — vertical integration. Sheinberg and Drabinsky had lunch. Not long after, they had a deal, too. MCA would take a 49 percent interest in the company for an initial $159 million U.S. In return, Cineplex would give MCA a foothold in exhibition. It looked good, but it would have looked better in hindsight had Drabinsky told the Bronfmans (who bailed him out) that he was going to sell half of what was now called Cineplex-Odeon to MCA. With more money in the company coffers, Drabinsky bought more. And more. And more. He bought Sterling Recreation, Walter Reade and Circle theatre chains. The acquisitions earned him the name of Darth Grabinsky in the industry, Garth Vader to his own employees — but that wasn't necessarily a bad thing in a business where fear goes a long way toward getting the desired result.

Most people in the industry figured their wholesale acquisition agenda boosted theatre prices far beyond their worth — but since it was Drabinsky who caused the inflation and in turn paid the inflated prices, no one was all that eager to stop him. Drabinsky justified the gushes of cash leaving Cineplex coffers with plans of closing in on key markets. He was right ... up to a point.

Debt continued to mount. He sold some theatres throughout rural Ontario to Carena

Bancorp Inc. in an effort to show some bottom-line good news. But the deal was bad for two reasons: it was too rich and posed no risk to Carena, and second, it ticked off the Bronfmans for a second time. Carena was owned by Hees International Bancorp Inc. — controlled by Peter and Edward Bronfman, the Toronto cousins of the Montreal Bronfmans who were bought out of the Seagram inheritance for $20 million.

Undeterred from his dreams of building something really, really big — at this point, it's hard to know if even Drabinsky had a clear idea as to what he was really shooting for — Cineplex had accumulated a $664-million debt. Drabinsky sold off assets, such as a post-production facility, but it didn't inspire investor confidence. Besides, by this point there were people betting on Drabinsky to fail — stock market traders who stood to win big if Cineplex stock tumbled. Rumours flew on both sides of the border about the long-term future of the upscale theatre chain.

Tension erupted between MCA and Cineplex, or more precisely, between Drabinsky and Sheinberg. According to producer David Puttnam, the problem may, in part, have been the result of lingering nationalist distrust between the two. Tensions between the two large, confident and self-made men came to a head after MCA got wind of Drabinsky's clandestine plan to buy out the Claridge shares (part of the Bronfman family holdings), and gain controlling interest of the company.

After weeks of backroom brokering, there was an almost legendary shareholder shakedown that pushed Drabinsky (and his partner Myron Gottlieb) out of Cineplex, the company he had created. Part of his separation agreement with Cineplex included taking with him the live entertainment concerns of Cineplex and the Pantages Theatre in Toronto, a property that Drabinsky treated as a labour of love, refurbishing its gold-leaf ceiling and every other ornate detail in the aging entertainment palace.

Drabinsky was by then in the process of staging *Phantom of the Opera* at the Pantages, and had already pulled in $20 million in advance ticket sales. When the lights went up on the production, he found himself at the helm of a whole new entertainment company that would make just as many headlines, and cause just as much shareholder fury: Livent.

Livent's history shares so much in common with that of Cineplex — particularly on the charge of inventive bookkeeping — that it's hard to imagine why people didn't run away when they saw him coming. But according to all accounts, Drabinsky is a great cheerleader and an even better salesman. With a whole new venture under his command, the empire builder wasted no time in expanding the Livent premise into other markets.

By 1995, it had opened a brand new theatre in Vancouver and had plans of creating a circuit with six theatres in four cities, including Toronto, Vancouver, New York and Chicago. By 1996, the business pages were full of stories about Drabinsky's personal million-dollar bonuses and declining Livent revenues. The stock was once again on thin ice.

In New York, where Drabinsky occupied the offices of legendary Great White Way producer J. J. Schubert, he hoped to avenge the movie business for his rush from the seat of power, and to avenge legitimate theatres as well. The kings of 42nd Street fell in the wake of Edison's popularization of motion pictures. When Drabinsky opened his theatre on January 18, 1998 with an impressive production of *Ragtime*, he truly believed theatre was in for a large-scale comeback.

He bet big on his hunch. He created the largest producer of live entertainment in North America, but the returns didn't pour in as expected — particularly in Vancouver, where Drabinsky had projected that half a million people would see *Sunset Boulevard* and only 190,000 did. Profits tumbled. They recorded a loss of $44.1 million for 1997, compared to a profit of $11 million in 1996. The cumulative debt in the company was estimated at somewhere around $220 million.

No more than five months after opening the Ford Centre in New York, Drabinsky abdicated as chairman and CEO of Livent to U.S. interests headed by New York financier Roy Furman and L. A. super agent Michael Ovitz (founder of Creative Artists Agency).

He said the move was personally motivated. "Nobody on my board was asking me or telling me to do it. This was something I took on my own initiative, using several relationships I had in the business ... The thing I know about myself right now is clearly that the passion I have for producing theatre is unbridled. I'm not in Livent for the job. I don't need to work any more ... but I want to stay working hard for what I am passionate about — the creative process," Drabinsky told Southam News reporter Jamie Portman after he switched posts.

While the new American bosses, Ovitz and Furman, went to great lengths to calm any fears of a malevolent U.S. presence in the Northern fortress, it was hard to ignore the optics of the takeover, which looked like Canada was surrendering its hard-won clout on the cultural scene to yet more deep-pocketed Yankees — who seem to win at absolutely everything because to them (if the Nike ads are correct), winning is more important than playing the game.

The team assured the Canadian media

that Drabinsky's creative vision would be honoured, and as for personal relationships, Furman said, "Garth likes me, I like Garth, Garth likes Michael, Michael likes Garth ... He (Ovitz) has great admiration and affection for Garth. He always thought that Garth was a big thinker and a big doer, that he left everybody else in the dust."

In June, Drabinsky found a supporter in business buddy, Livent board member and fellow "think-big" entrepreneur, publishing mogul Conrad Black. Southam, which happened to be one of Livent's biggest creditors in the wake of Drabinsky's massive marketing campaigns that purchased — or at least booked — hundreds of pricey, full-page newspaper ads, agreed to purchase a five percent stake in Livent, a deal worth $12.2 million U.S. ($18.1 million CDN), or $8 U.S. a share ($12 CDN), for 1.5 million shares.

By August of 1998, Drabinsky must have been having big-time déjà vu. After the Ovitz-Furman takeover, he was suspended as vice-chair of the company and escorted from the Toronto headquarters when the new management team uncovered "serious irregularities" in the Livent books.

The day after Drabinsky was shown the door, shareholders launched a class action lawsuit against the company in a New York district court, alleging they had been "misled" into buying "artificially inflated stock." As the investigation continued, there were reports of double books and other financial wizardry. Out-of-pocket shareholders started looking to lynch the financial auditors who prepared the year-end statements, and there were calls across the Canadian investment community to change the way reports are compiled and checked in order to assure investor confidence.

Drabinsky did not take all this sitting down. He tried to protect his name by launching a lawsuit of his own against accounting firm KPMG for breach of confidence and conflict of interest. KPMG was investigating him for Livent after being his own accountants for many years, thereby examining books that they themselves had prepared.

For all the pain and misery, Drabinsky was asking for $26 million in damages.

In court documents, Drabinsky claimed the weeks that followed his removal from the Livent offices "were the worst two weeks of my life," a roller-coaster ride that left him feeling "completely besieged, violated, humiliated and distraught."

Drabinsky won the first volley. The court ordered a halt to the KPMG investigation because of conflict of interest complaints. "This is clearly a mortal blow to management and clearly a statement to [Michael] Ovitz that when you come to Canada you play fair or you suffer the consequences," Edward Greenspan, one of Drabinsky's lawyers, said after the decision.

He had a day of victory in court, but soon the RCMP were on the trail. So was the FBI and a host of agents from securities commissions on both sides of the border. When revised financial statements were released, Livent was in debt to the tune of $230 million. The company's credit rating was downrated by two bond points. On November 18, 1998, the company filed for protection from its U.S. creditors. Gottlieb and Drabinsky were fired. The company also launched suit against the two, seeking to recover $225 million in damages from alleged fraud and accounting irregularities.

On the upside, the company's productions of *Fosse* and *Parade* earned 17 Tony nominations and SFX, the world's largest producer of live entertainment, offered to purchase three of Livent's theatres (in New York, Chicago and

Toronto — not Vancouver) and a slate of productions for upwards of $100-million U.S. In November of 1999, the formal ending of Livent took place with the auction of several Livent furnishings, including the "one-of-a-kind" slate boardroom table.

In March of 2000, Drabinsky was named marketing consultant to Conrad Black's *National Post* — the newest Canadian daily in the country. But that's not all. Drabinsky settled out of court with KPMG for $11 million and in June 2000, Drabinsky announced his imminent return to theatre production with *The Island*, by South African playwright Athol Fugard, to the Bluma Appel Theatre in Toronto's St. Lawrence Centre beginning May 1, 2001. The play is a critically lauded anti-apartheid piece, and is a co-production with Britain's Royal National Theatre and the Market Theatre of Johannesburg.

For the moment, Drabinsky remains in the shadows, but there is little doubt the big dreamer with the obsessive passion for drama and a dramatic passion for Canada will be a presence — for better or worse — on the Canadian entertainment scene for a long time to come.

FILMOGRAPHY (as producer): *The Disappearance* (1977) | *The Changeling* (1980) | *Tribute* (1980) | *The Amateur* (1981) | *Losin' It* (1983)

PROFILE

Robert Lantos
Born 1949 — Budapest, Hungary

SERENDIPITY POINT FILMS

It is interesting to note that throughout Garth Drabinsky's reign as the leading Canadian entertainment figure in the trumped-up days of the early eighties, there is only one footnote to Robert Lantos — the man who co-founded and nurtured the largest production and distribution company in the history of Canada. The footnote appeared in April, 1988, when it was announced that Cineplex, already in deep financial straits, had signed a deal with Alliance that was supposed to give Alliance the much-needed production cash while giving Cineplex a product pipeline to fill its screens.

No one paid too much attention to the deal save a few producers who predictably sounded the doomsday alarm about consolidation of the independent scene, and worried that the independents would no longer be "independent" if publicly traded companies like Cineplex continued to dominate the fragile market.

For all the huffing and puffing, no one's house blew down, and at this point, few looked to Lantos as the likely lumberjack saviour of

Canadian film. Sure, people had certainly heard of him. He was the long-haired producer behind one of Canada's most scandalous outings in the seventies, *In Praise of Older Women* (1978). The Ontario Censor Board deemed the film too hot for mild-mannered Torontonians, and it demanded that two entire minutes be removed from the film before its world premiere at the Toronto Festival of Festivals. The ensuing scandal pushed Lantos into the public eye, and he knew exactly what to do with the attention: create himself as a larger-than-life persona in the peanut-sized Canadian film industry.

The son of a Jewish family that attempted to assimilate into the anti-Semitic Austro-Hungarian state, Lantos and his family left Hungary for Uruguay in 1958 (after the 1956 uprising), then migrated north to Canada in 1963. After earning a bachelor's degree from McGill, he spent two years pursuing post-graduate studies in communications and briefly flirted with the idea of becoming an academic. His life course changed after a trip to New York, where, out of innocent curiosity, the young Continental took in some screenings at the New York Erotic Film Festival. When he returned to Montreal a fortnight later, Lantos was in the film business: with borrowed money, he'd purchased the Canadian rights to the festival and was already thinking about his next move. He was 22. The next year, in 1972, he launched a modest, Montreal-based distribution company called Vivafilm, with Victor Loewy, to deal with the business of distributing the festival wares, and before long, the two men were heading into the unknown of Canadian private enterprise. Knowing little about the business, but full of confidence, the duo picked up the lease on a small art-house cinema in Vancouver called The Rembrandt. Loewy later said the move was "naive," but

they made it work by booking John Waters' *Pink Flamingoes* for months, raking in enough money to pay the rent and create seed money for their real dream: making movies.

With that end in mind, in 1975 Lantos also started (in partnership with Stephen Roth) RSL, a movie production company set up in tandem with Vivafilm. The next year, Lantos produced his first feature, *L'Ange et la femme*, the spiritual and simultaneously sex-laden story about the archangel Gabriel who saves a young woman after she is gunned down by terrorist thugs. The film starred Carole Laure, and was directed by her famous husband Gilles Carle (*Un Air de famille, La Mort d'un bûcheron, Maria Chapdelaine, Le Crime d'Ovide Plouffe*), but attracted little attention. What attention it did get was the sole result of the sex scenes between Laure and co-star Lewis Furey, where Furey revives the dead woman with his magic touch. Ooohlahlah.

Quick to learn from his experience — a trait that never seemed to define Drabinsky — Lantos' second feature would capitalize on sex, the one sure thing that could bring people into the theatres in droves. For Lantos, *In Praise of Older Women* was about a lot more than just sex and making a reputation for himself: he says he cared a lot about the film because it mirrored some of his own, personal experience.

Based on Hungarian-born author Stephen Vizinczey's (note: Vizinczey would later play stepfather to another filmmaker with Canadian roots named Mary Harron, who made *I Shot Andy Warhol* and *American Psycho*) novel about a young man who services the sexual needs of several mature females, *In Praise of Older Women* easily became the most notorious — if not the most critically lauded — film to ever emerge from the lily-white, and sexually lily-livered, Canadian landscape.

People were so desperate to catch the movie, that in Brian D. Johnson's book celebrating the 25th anniversary of the Toronto festival, *Brave Films Wild Nights*, he dedicates most of the chapter for 1978 on the ill-behaved crowds pressing to get in to The Elgin Theatre while conspiring festival staff pulled off the old switcheroo, changing the censored reel for the uncut one — all beneath the censor's watchful eye. It's a good story, and one made even better when you insert Lantos into the equation. Lantos, whom Johnson refers to as the "ebullient arriviste from Montreal," requested that he, director George Kaczender, and stars Karen Black and Helen Shaver be delivered to the Elgin in horse-drawn carriages. Remember, it was Lantos' first premiere. He had soaked up the atmosphere and star-appeal of Cannes from a distance. This was his chance to take a lap around the glam pool.

With a hit film under his belt and a better understanding of how the distribution system worked, Lantos was given the chance to work in the United States, but he declined — knowing that he'd have to make too many compromises just to get a film off the ground.

When Lantos started, it was also a relatively low-risk enterprise, thanks to the famed tax-shelter funding formula — or the "Capital Cost Allowance" — that granted complete tax write-offs for movies that met Canadian content regulations. Buckets of cash poured into the Canadian film industry and annual production surged from three to 37 features in the space of four years (1974-1978). But without a critical mass of experienced talent to bring these stories to the screen with any integrity or passion, the tax-shelter experiment proved to be a pathetic waste of time

and money that deflated the image of Canadian film domestically and abroad.

"We've come such a long way since the tax-shelter years. Back then, there was no Canadian company with a worldwide infrastructure for marketing films. Yes, I made *Agency* and a bunch of other movies with American stars in various states of stupor [check out the somnabulent Robert Mitchum]. But I steadfastly refused to latch onto any of the Canadianized American "packages" dressed up with has-been stars, which hoards of Hollywood producers and agents were shopping to Canadian partners. For better or for worse, I made my mistakes — and occasional successes — with my own projects," says Lantos. "After the international success of *In Praise of Older Women*, I produced several failures. Through them I realized how hard it was to make a hit movie — and how hard it was for a film to find an audience. We needed to find a way to get movies into the marketplace."

The 1985 merger of RSL, Vivafilm and ICC (International Cinema Corp.) to create Canada's first major distribution company was a ballsy move, but Lantos had partners (Stephen Roth, Denis Heroux and John Kemeny — the producer of *The Apprenticeship of Duddy Kravitz*, *Atlantic City* and *Quest for Fire*). He also knew it was the only way to kick-start the Canadian film scene: "We needed to stockpile a library that would attract financial backers in order to build a strong corporate entity that would not be exposed to the vagaries of film financing. With a strong enough balance sheet, we could raise our own capital and make the movies we chose to," says Lantos.

In 1998, after 13 years of building Alliance Communications into the largest production/distribution company in Canada, as well as a specialty broadcaster and movie exhibitor,

Lantos sold his controlling interest in Alliance to TV production house Atlantis, run by the former projectionist and Queen's film studies grad, Michael MacMillan. According to the exit deal, Lantos would hand over the reins of the company to MacMillan and sell his stock in exchange for an output deal whereby the newly formed Alliance-Atlantis would distribute the movies that Lantos made through his new company, Serendipity Point Films. With this new company, Lantos is looking to make — are you ready? — marketable Canadian movies. Movies that he cares for. And so far, so good. *Sunshine*'s box-office fortunes set Serendipity in the black, and now Lantos is putting together projects like *Men with Brooms*, a Paul Gross comedy about curling, starring Leslie Neilsen and Molly Parker, *Picture Claire*, the new Bruce McDonald movie starring Gina Gershon and Juliette Lewis, and *Ararat*, Atom Egoyan's new film about the Armenian genocide, starring Bruce Greenwood, Elias Koteas, and Marie Josee Croze. These movies may feature some American stars, says Lantos, but he insists he's not interested in Hollywood genres.

"Canada has a great tradition of storytelling. We make films that play all over the world ... films that are sold internationally. We are sought after by prestigious festivals. Just look at the achievements of the last few years: Grand Prix in Cannes for *The Sweet Hereafter*, Academy nominations for *The Sweet Hereafter*, Golden Globe nominations for *Sunshine*, to list a few. We are part of an alternate economy — along with indigenous cinema of many other countries. We now have a nucleus of filmmakers who have elected to stay in this country and who can attract international distribution. Directors like Egoyan, Cronenberg, Girard, Rozema and Arcand. They are respected names the world over." He says the future of Canadian film has never looked brighter, but there's no room to get cocky when you're in the shadow of Hollywood.

Lantos says the American control of the entertainment industry is no conspiracy, it's just economies of scale. "The studios' goal is to make 'franchise' blockbusters that will gross hundreds of millions of dollars and spawn sequels, merchandising opportunities to sell everything from lunch boxes to video games, theme park rides, animated spin-offs, records and so on. They need the whole globe to make this economic model work. The stakes get higher and higher, which is why they have abandoned the business of storytelling. Their model leaves no room for artistry and vision. Decisions are made by marketing teams, not by filmmakers. Their goal is to design a winning formula and keep duplicating it until it is milked dry.

"The studios have vacated the field when it comes to making serious (and not so serious) films for discriminating adult audiences. So, opportunistically speaking, this is our best battleground."

FILMOGRAPHY (as producer, feature films only): *L'Ange et la femme* (1976) | *In Praise of Older Women* (1977) | *Agency* (1978) | *Suzanne* (1979) | *Your Ticket Is No Longer Valid* (1980) | *Heavenly Bodies* (1983) | *Bedroom Eyes* (1983) | *Separate Vacations* (1984) | *Joshua Then and Now* (1985) | *Black Robe* (1991) | *Whale Music* (1993) | *Johnny Mnemonic* (1994) | *Never Talk To Strangers* (1995) | *Crash* (1996) | *The Sweet Hereafter* (1997) | *Strike* (1998) | *eXistenZ* (1998) | *Felicia's Journey* (1999) | *Sunshine* (1999) | *Stardom* (2000) | *Picture Claire* (forthcoming, 2001) | *Men With Brooms* (forthcoming, 2001) | *Ararat* (forthcoming, 2001)

Reviews

Okay, there are so many noteworthy Canadian films out there — certainly more than one hundred. So, what's included in this section is, by no means, a complete list. I just couldn't resist the lure of one hundred — such a nice, round number. Here, I've compiled movies that, to me, illustrate relevant Canadian themes, and movies that may have been passed over — or perhaps misunderstood — on first reading. It's about time for a little revisionism, so, I felt free to indulge in my own interpretations. What can I say? I loved *In Praise of Older Women* and I positively adored *Shivers* — a classic that was trashed in its day as a waste of taxpayer dollars.

You'll notice that I've used maple leaves (instead of stars) for my rating system. Films are rated out of five maple leaves — with a five-maple leaf rating as "classic" status, and a single maple leaf as "poor."

The Adjuster (1991)

Directed by Atom Egoyan
Starring Elias Koteas, Arsinée Khanjian, Maury Chaykin, Don McKellar
Running time: 102 minutes
🍁🍁🍁 ½

Noah (Koteas) is an insurance adjuster whose entire personal identity is based in his job. Regularly showing up at house fires to comfort the victims, Noah ushers them all aboard his own ark of salvation: a cheesy motel on the outskirts of town, where he doles out his own brand of solace. This can be sex, or simply nice words, depending on what he believes the client needs, because Noah genuinely cares. Constantly uttering the phrase "You're in shock — even if it doesn't feel like it," Noah seems to find a sense of personal meaning as he helps the victims navigate the depth of their loss — to the point where he approaches the "schedule of missing items" with near religious zeal. No wonder many of his clients call him an "angel."

As Noah floats around in the void of lost personal effects and lifestyles, his wife (Khanjian) exists in a different type of void as a film classifier. Watching endless scenes of sex and violence, she is forced to navigate the moral and personal emptiness of modern culture and make decisions about what is appropriate and what is not from a completely detached perspective. She finds no meaning in the monitoring exercise itself, but she does find satisfaction in taping the material that will be cut — and showing it to her sister, who speaks no English.

While Noah and his wife may seem to be a very alienated couple, a feeling that is only exaggerated by the location of their home — a lone house in the middle of an unfinished subdivision

— Bubba (Chaykin) and his wife are a rich couple who are so bored by life they play voyeuristic games on unsuspecting strangers. In one sequence, Bubba plays a bum on a subway while his wife, dressed in Chanel and pearls, sits down next to him. As everyone watches, the wife takes Bubba's grimy hand and places it up her skirt.

For the viewer, *The Adjuster* presents some challenges as it uses layers instead of straight narrative events to create the dramatic tension. Surreal, and yet strangely funny, *The Adjuster* is a tale of several maladjusted people just trying to find a little pleasure in a cold and hostile environment.

CANADIAN CHECKLIST: Weird sex | Empty landscape | Language barriers | Voyeurism | Internal demons | Dysfunctional marriage | Missing items (in this case from fires) | Personal alienation | Humour is based in irony | Symbolic references to "colonies" and "freezing" (at the wart doctor's)

Agnes of God (1985)
Directed by Norman Jewison
Starring Jane Fonda, Anne Bancroft, Meg Tilly, Gratien Gélinas
Running time: 98 minutes
❦ ❦ ❦

How can you not get a thrill watching Jane Fonda scoot around Montreal smoking cigarettes? Sure, that's a pretty lame excuse for liking a movie, but I can still conjure the image of Fonda under muted blue Canadian skies, and the rush of recognition that came along with it. The movie isn't much of a standout, considering the man behind the camera is Canada's superdude director, Norman Jewison — but it's one of the few films he actually shot in this country, which is why it's included here.

Based on a play by John Pielmeier, *Agnes of God* opens with a nun, Sister Agnes (Tilly) giving birth to a child. The child is stillborn and soon the police are brought in to investigate the case as a possible murder. Because the young nun seems entirely off her rocker, the authorities also bring in a psychiatrist, Dr. Livingston (Fonda), to assess the situation. Agnes tells the doctor the baby was conceived immaculately, but being a woman of science, Livingston looks for a menacing earthly presence to explain the conception. Standing in her way is Mother Superior, Miriam Ruth (Bancroft), who wants to protect Sister Agnes from the doctor's prodding.

While the film puts all the pieces together in linear fashion, there's something missing in this mix and it's a believable spiritual presence. The whole movie pivots on the question of faith, and poses the doctor against the dorm mother to bring it home to the viewer. The faith question is a theme that plays to the very heart of the Canadian film tradition because it's an intangible. When you're talking about a belief in God, we have to get a sense of what's not visible, but perhaps present all the same. This is a film that begged for a typically Canadian treatment where the viewer, with the narrative fragments, is left to pull the pieces together according to his or her own personal beliefs. Jewison's American-influenced storytelling can't really accommodate negative space, and so the main theme of the film — faith, which is purely internal — is pushed up to the surface where Jewison can frame it for his audience with awkward speeches about God and circular debates between Livingston and Mother Superior. It's still a decent piece of entertainment, but when you're talking about the meaning of life, and the nature of the universe, it could have — should have — been a whole lot more.

CANADIAN CHECKLIST: Dead baby | Potent women | Identity issues | Orphans | Cerebral-spiritual split | Questions institutional notions of spirituality

Air Bud (1997)
Directed by Charles Martin Smith
Starring Michael Jeter, Kevin Zegers, Wendy Makkena, Bill Cobbs, Jay Brazeau, Nicola Cavendish, Brendan Fletcher
Running time: 98 minutes
🍁🍁🍁

Mourning the death of his father, Josh Framm (Zegers) moves to a small town where he's a complete outsider. Feeling sad and alone, Josh spends his days shooting hoops and remembering the good times with his dearly departed dad. One day, he shows up at his scenic haunt and discovers he's not so alone after all: he meets a stray dog. The golden retriever is a runaway entertainer who can do amazing tricks — and one of them is shooting hoops. The two exiles find comfort in each other's company, and soon, Josh and Buddy are trying out for the school basketball team.

Fame makes Josh a popular kid, but it also brings a few demons in its wake when the evil clown who once owned Buddy decides the dog is worth big bucks, and sets off to repossess the pooch.

Your classic boy-and-his-dog story with a new, athletic twist, *Air Bud* began as a feel-good movie for kids and became another top-grossing Canadian effort. Now, *Air Bud* has evolved into an entire film franchise — only now it's called *MVP* and it features hockey-playing chimps. Watch the first one, and you'll see a sweet little movie with a lot of heart — but don't make the American mistake of looking for "more," because you'll only end up disappointed.

CANADIAN CHECKLIST: Missing parent/orphan (father) | Identity issues | Outsider stance
Bonding with "other" — in this case the dog, Buddy | Internalized demons

The Apprenticeship of Duddy Kravitz (1974)

Directed by Ted Kotcheff
Starring Richard Dreyfuss, Micheline Lanctôt, Denholm Elliot, Jack Warden, Randy Quaid, Joe Silver
Running time: 121 minutes
🍁🍁🍁 ½

One of the first movies I can remember that actually showed me where I lived, *The Apprenticeship of Duddy Kravitz* somehow legitimized the Canadian experience to Canadians — and somewhat ironically, made a bona fide star out of its American lead in the process.

Richard Dreyfuss plays Duddy Kravitz, a character born from the imagination of Montreal-based author Mordecai Richler. Duddy is part weasel, part brass-balled hero, which means we have a love-hate relationship with him throughout the film. We want him to "do the right thing," but as a member of an oppressed minority, Duddy's idea of the "right thing" doesn't always mesh with that of the WASPy mainstream.

When we first meet Duddy, he's a wide-eyed teenager living in Montreal's Jewish ghetto in the forties. His mother is dead, leaving Duddy to define himself in opposition to his under-achieving father (Warden), a taxi driver with small dreams. Duddy has big dreams: he wants to be a somebody, and following the advice of his grandfather — who works the postage-stamp size plot of dirt in his backyard — he focuses his life on becoming a big-time landowner.

While working as a waiter at a Laurentian resort, he meets Yvette (Lanctôt — who married Kotcheff before she turned her own talents to directing) and the two opposites enter a romantic relationship. With all this added pressure on Duddy's masculine identity, he looks for shortcuts to financial success. He turns to filmmaking, recording weddings and bar mitzvahs, and eventually falls in with a two-bit gangster named Dingleman. Duddy becomes a drug smuggler, a pinball king and a scam artist — but we still like him because he's so focused on his dream. It's when he takes advantage of a young epileptic that he falls out of favour, not just with the audience, but with his sweetie, Yvette.

A Canadian film in an American mould, *The Apprenticeship of Duddy Kravitz* was hailed as a milestone in Canadian film by outsiders — winning the Golden Bear at the Berlin Film Festival — but once again, halfheartedly embraced by Canadian critics who felt the film was either too Canadian, or not Canadian enough. Kvetch. Kvetch. It's not a brilliant movie and it's not as good as the book, either, but it's a solid piece of filmmaking with some standout performances, some good scenes and best of all, a real Canadian story.

CANADIAN CHECKLIST: Outsider stance | Missing parent (mother) | Film on film images (we get to see one of Duddy's movies) | Mixed romance | Love-hate relationship with hero

Black Robe (1991)

Directed by Bruce Beresford
Starring Lothaire Bluteau, Tantoo Cardinal, Aden Young,
Sandrine Holt, August Schellenberg, Billy Two Rivers
Running time: 100 minutes
❦❦❦❦

Set against the backdrop of an as yet uncolonized Canada, *Black Robe* tells the story of the first Jesuit missionaries to set foot in the New World with hopes of converting the Aboriginal peoples to Christianity.

Lothaire Bluteau (Daniel in *Jesus of Montreal*) reprises his role of the saintly martyr as he plays Father Laforgue, a man of God who fears nothing — even when he should. Believing he is on a mission from the Almighty himself, Laforgue heads upriver with his Algonquin guide in search of his brothers, who have built a mission in the midst of this vast, empty landscape. Realizing too late that he was leading his Algonquin friends into hostile territory, Laforgue is forced to watch as the Iroquois close in with deadly consequences.

Australian director Beresford handles the subject matter without drawing judgements, and as a result, gives us a film that leaves us with an empty pit in our stomachs as we search for some larger sense of meaning that simply isn't there.

Tragic, bloody and surreal, the film offers valuable insight into the Canadian condition as it shows us our ugly colonial beginnings without any desire to decorate the truth with pretty lies.

CANADIAN CHECKLIST: Other meets other/twin imagery | Questions faith | Road to nowhere | Empty landscape | Death, disease, destruction | Outsider stance

Blockade (1993)

Directed by Nettie Wild
Documentary
Running time: 90 minutes
❦❦❦ ½

While Vancouver-based filmmaker Nettie Wild generally turns her lens on issues outside Canada (*A Rustling of Leaves: Inside the Philippine Revolution, A Place Called Chiapas*), *Blockade* focuses on the events that led to the December 1991 Gitksan blockade of the Hobenshield family mill in Hazelton, British Columbia — when a group of Native and non-Native protesters put their bodies between the trees and the loggers.

For the majority of the protesters, the issue goes deeper than mere logging. It's about 270 years of oppression and land appropriation at the hands of white Europeans. As we watch band members walk through one clearcut after another, talking about the spiritual significance of the earth and nature, it's hard not to feel the pang of white guilt and shake your head at the shortsightedness of these completely white "resource-management" strategies.

What makes Wild's documentary more enlightening than a news report, and more satisfying than plain propaganda, is the balance she brings to the issue — and Roy Forbes' excellent guitar soundtrack. Wild never falls into the trap of spinning a lopsided film for the sake of entertainment (*Roger and Me*, anyone?). Instead, she photographs the issue from all sides, capturing the nuances — and best of all, the humanity — behind each perspective.

You can't hate anyone in this movie; nor for that matter, can you agree with any one argument. It's complicated, and while Wild breaks it down into a picture we can understand, she refuses to simplify matters to make it easier on the viewer. In the process, she forces us to think about what we might do if we ran the zoo — and in the end, personal responsibility and communication is the only solution to these fundamental Canadian problems.

CANADIAN CHECKLIST: Open-ended documentary | Focus on the land | Pluralist perspective | Female point of view | White vs. Aboriginal tensions

Les Boys (1997)
Directed by Louis Saïa
Starring Marc Messier, Rémy Girard, Serge Thériault, Michel Barrette, Paul Houde, Luc Guérin, Yvan Ponton, Roc Lafortune, Michel Charette
Running time: 107 minutes
❋ ❋ ❋ ½

When Bob, Stan, Ti-Guy and the boys get together for their weekly hockey game, it's the closest thing you can find to a religious experience in increasingly secular Quebec. The boys are fanatics, and when their sponsor — and favourite bar owner (played by the ubiquitous Girard — is forced to put his entire net worth on the line in the name of hockey, they approach the big match as though it were a holy war.

One of the most successful Canadian films ever, and the only film in the world that probably outgrossed *Titanic* in certain territories, *Les Boys* pulled in an amazing $6.8 million at the box office, winning it the Golden Reel award in 1998.

Part of the success can be attributed to the film's subject matter: everyone knows Canadians — and specifically Montrealers — have puck-shaped hearts. The rest can be explained by the film's tongue-in-cheek treatment of the buddy-bonding cliché. The boys in *Les Boys* are all complete knobs — from the nerdy real estate agent and the nice, but knobby, gay lawyer to the nose-candied guitarist — but that doesn't mean we don't like them. Eager to be macho superstars, they end up looking like complete idiots and essentially undo all the Hollywood sports clichés about athletic manliness. They bicker and fight and finally, when it comes down to the crunch, they get it together.

A fun, often hilarious study of the male ego and its many flaws, *Les Boys* shows even the losers can find hero status with a hockey stick in hand.

CANADIAN CHECKLIST: Hockey | Subversion of Hollywood hero | Hockey | Diversity within team | Hockey | Outsider stance | Hockey

Bye Bye Blues (1989)

Directed by Anne Wheeler
Starring Rebecca Jenkins, Michael Ontkean, Chad Krowchuk, Jyoti Dhembre, Tom Alter
Running time: 110 minutes
✦✦✦✦

Rebecca Jenkins plays Daisy Cooper, a mother on the lone prairie trying to raise her kids while her husband is held as a POW during the Second World War. At first, this traditional mom is frightened and depressed without her man, but as the story progresses, Daisy begins to bloom.

Looking for a way to keep food on the table, Daisy turns to her love of music and her piano skills and hooks up with a kicking swing band. As Daisy's quiet life turns into a series of gigs and a blur of bandstands, she develops a romantic relationship with one of the boys in the band. When her long lost hubby finally returns home, he finds a changed woman. Daisy is now a self-supporting, self-realized human being who can't go back to being a mousy creature of the hot-house. She must be free, but whether or not her husband can handle her newfound strength is the big question.

Reminiscent of golden age classics like the *Best Years of Our Lives*, Wheeler mingles bits and pieces of Hollywood with a modern Canadian sensibility to come up with a film that is steeped in the romantic side of wartime nostalgia without being pat or predictable. Accented by gorgeous shots of the rolling Alberta landscape, you can feel Wheeler's love for the land through the lens. A real beauty with good tunes, *Bye Bye Blues* is an important part of the Canadian film canon.

CANADIAN CHECKLIST: Potent women | Empty landscape | Missing person (husband) | Outsider stance | Creativity as liberation | Realistic treatment of potentially oversentimental subject matter

Café Olé (2000)

Directed by Richard Roy
Starring Andrew Tarbet, Laia Marull, Stephanie Morgenstern, Dino Tavarone
Running time: 94 minutes
✦✦✦

Punching a hole through the wall that separates us, *Café Olé* is a romantic comedy built on linguistic difference. Written by Montrealer Emil Sher and directed by Québécois director Richard Roy, *Café Olé* explores two veritable Canadian taboos: the flowery notion of romantic love and the normally lethal linguistic abyss that separates one Canadian from the next.

If that weren't enough novelty, *Café Olé* is also a comedy that features — are you ready for it? — well-adjusted sexual intercourse. I know it sounds too incredible to believe, but Sher and Roy pull it off with flying colours without sacrificing any Canadian angst in the process.

Malcolm is a nice guy that women adore. Tall, caring, funny and sensitive, this video store clerk never wants for female attention, but he's too picky to commit. Malcolm's entire notion of romantic love has been shaped by Hollywood, and so naturally, nothing he finds in real life can compare to the greasy-lensed brand of studio romance he sees in the movies. His friend, Sal (Tavarone) tries to help, as does his brother and his abused downstairs neighbour, Sharon (Morgenstern), who lives in the underbelly of romantic love: domestic terrorism.

There's plenty of linguistic symbolism in this Sher script to chew on, and because it does not focus on English-French tensions, we can step back a little and laugh at the things that normally make us cry. A bold entry into the unknown of Canadian romantic comedy, Roy plays on the subtleties of Sher's witty script and avoids cliché in the process.

CANADIAN CHECKLIST: Outsider stance | Language barrier | Synonym/twin imagery | Pluralist perspective | Montreal landscape (look for the famed Schwarz's deli in the background)

Calendar (1993)

Directed by Atom Egoyan
Starring Arsinée Khanjian, Atom Egoyan, Ashot Adamian
Running time: 74 minutes
♣ ♣ ♣ ½

The big reflecting mirror comes out in this one as Atom Egoyan directs, shoots, writes and stars in his own movie about a photographer/filmmaker who ends up being the victim of his own drama. Hired to shoot images of Armenian churches for a calendar, the photographer heads to Armenia with his wife, and returns home to Canada a single man.

As the film peels back layer after layer like so many pages of the calendar — a motif Egoyan uses literally as he offers us flashbacks photo by photo — we piece together the scenario that led to the end of the relationship: the photographer hired a translator, and as his wife gets closer to the land and the language, the photographer pulls back to the point where she becomes part of the scenery.

It could have been a pretentious nightmare, but because Egoyan brings an absurd sense of humour to the film, it sidesteps self-importance to step smack in the middle of a steaming mound of self-parody.

When the photographer returns home without his wife, he brings home a series of different women, serves them the same wine, has the same stilted conversation, and then points them in the direction of the phone — where we learn all of them speak a different language. He seems to want a replacement for the wife he lost, but even when she calls, he can't bring himself to pick up the phone because it might just compromise his control over the situation.

Smart, funny and complete, *Calendar* remains one of my favourite Egoyan movies. He proves you can make a great film about navel-gazing — just as long as you don't take yourself too seriously.

CANADIAN CHECKLIST: Outsider stance | Film-on-film images | Language barrier | Potent woman | Voyeurism | Non-linear structure | Landscape defines emotional tone

Careful (1992)

Directed by Guy Maddin

Starring Kyle McCulloch, Gosia Dobrowalska, Sarah Neville, Brent Neale

Running time: 100 minutes

🍁🍁🍁 ½

A perfect mixture of weird sex, snow and Oedipal tragedy, *Careful* digests almost every single Canadian archetype (except hockey) and spews them out in swatches of stylized colour and old-time technique to make for a strange and entirely surreal voyage into the deepest crevasses of the Canadian psyche.

Clearly inspired, in part, by the early mountain films of Dr. Arnold Fanck and Leni Riefenstahl (that showed various types of heroes and heroines boldly climbing towards the bosom of the Lord), Maddin's story is set in the fictional European berg of Tolzbad. Everything looks exactly as it should in this faux-homage to the triumph of heroism, but Maddin subverts it down to the last frame as he shows a community of people who fall victim to the "hero" formula. Set high in the mountains (but filmed on soundstages) people are very "careful" not to speak too loudly, lest they trigger an avalanche that would bury the town under a blanket of snow. But for all the silence, things still go terribly wrong.

A widowed mother keeps one son in the attic because she can't deal with the memory of the boy's father. Meanwhile, her favourite son wants to sleep with her and her other boy is haunted by the ghost of the dead father. Once again, the women are in charge of the men — in perfect Canadian fashion — but this time, there is no salvation. There is no room for heroism in Maddin's quirky universe, but there's plenty of room for witty spoofs on victimhood.

Sumptuous to look at and altogether inspired in its reconstitution of Canadian themes, *Careful* is a true Canadian cult classic.

CANADIAN CHECKLIST: Watch for the Canadian flag to appear in a crucial "victim" scene | The landscape is nothing but snow | Oedipal and Electra fantasy | Failed heroes and hauntings | Orphans | Internal demons | Family dysfunction | Fragmented narrative | Humour is irony-based | Overriding themes of repression

The Changeling (1980)

Directed by Peter Medak

Starring George C. Scott, Trish Van Devere, Melvyn Douglas, Jean Marsh

Running time: 115 minutes

🍁🍁🍁🍁

When I saw this movie for the first time, I was 14 years old and it was the scariest thing I had ever seen — after *The Brady Bunch* Hawaiian special. The film opens with an idyllic shot of beautiful snowy mountains (which is supposed to be in the States, but is actually on Vancouver's North Shore) and a happy family outing. Seconds later, tragedy strikes: John Russell (George C. Scott) watches as his wife and daughter are killed by a runaway truck.

Months later, he takes a teaching job on the West Coast to leave the ghosts behind, but finds himself haunted anew when he moves into an old mansion with bad plumbing. He hears banging at certain hours of the day — and it's getting louder. Inevitably he climbs into the furthest recesses of his attic with little more than a flashlight, and discovers the horrific truth.

Full of thrills, chills and solid performances from its veteran cast, the movie manages to conjure an incredible amount of suspense with little more than two-dollar props. A veritable how-to book on how to shoot and edit a scary movie without numbing your audience with quick cuts.

CANADIAN CHECKLIST: Dislocated father figure | Dead children | Internalized demons | Identity issues

Cinéma Vérité: Defining the Moment (1999)
Directed by Peter Wintonick
Running time: 102 minutes
♣ ♣ ♣ ½

A documentary about the pivotal shift in documentary film, *Cinéma Vérité* follows the evolution of static, institutional non-fiction film into a flowing — and often shaky — vehicle of artistic expression.

Montreal-based filmmaker Wintonick includes a shot of Terrence Macartney-Filgate — regarded as one of the pioneers of the *Candid Eye* series — sitting on a Toronto streetcar with a digital camera, filming Wintonick's crew as they are filming him. It's a wonderfully reflective image that captures the essence of the movement and sets up the history lesson that follows, as Wintonick examines Canada's part in a filmmaking revolution.

Along the way, we get samples of the movies that gave rise to the movement known as *cinéma vérité*, Cinema Direct, Kino Pravda, Free Cinema and for those who aren't afraid of compound words, auteur-driven non-fiction. From Michel Brault talking about *Pour la suite du monde* to Jean Rouch's recollections of the era, we get a full tour of the era and see how it paved the way for the rise of such documentary perversions as "Reality TV" and *The Blair Witch Project.*

Featuring clips of *Lonely Boy, Les Raquetteurs, Canary Island Bananas, La Lutte, The Days Before Christmas* and *Chronique d'un été,* the viewer gets a full view of the films and the people that pulled the camera off the tripod and put it back in human hands.

CANADIAN CHECKLIST:
It's a documentary about documentary film. How much more introspective can you get?

Cold Comfort (1989)

Directed by Vic Sarin
Starring Margaret Langrick, Maury Chaykin, Paul Gross
Running time: 88 minutes
🍁🍁🍁 ½

Paul Gross plays Steven, a travelling salesman who nearly dies when he falls asleep in his car in the middle of a blizzard. Half-entombed in snow, the handsome man is rescued by Floyd, an odd tow-truck driver played by the perfectly (professionally) odd Chaykin, who takes him home to his funky lair: an old gas station where he and his daughter Dolores (Langrick) live a rather strange domestic life. Before you know it, the stranger is turned into a caged pet for the nubile young woman, and Floyd begins to grow jealous of his daughter's new love.

Predating *Misery*, *Cold Comfort* nails the same horror — only with a lot more humour. Chaykin is so good at being funny and creepy at the same time that we always get the feeling nothing too awful could ever happen, and in some ways, we're right.

A quirky voyage into the dark heart of the desolate Canadian landscape, *Cold Comfort* is a veritable treasure trove of Canadian themes — and a pretty good movie, to boot.

CANADIAN CHECKLIST: Weird sex | Snow | Family dysfunction | Outsider stance | Passive man | Potent woman | Identity issues | Missing people | Characters defined by landscape | Fragmented narrative

Company of Strangers AKA Strangers in Good Company (1990)

Directed by Cynthia Scott
Starring Alice Diabo, Winifred Holden, Cissy Meddings, Mary Meigs, Catherine Roche, Michelle Sweeney, Beth Webber
Running time: 101 minutes
🍁🍁🍁🍁

When a tour bus breaks down in the middle of a verdant Canadian landscape, eight post-menopausal women are forced to return to the land — and do a remarkably good job of it as they turn their nylons into fishnets and forage on frogs legs.

In the midst of this emptiness, they are left to fill each other's world with images of their own past as they share their unique lives and experiences. Largely based on improvisational performances from the cast of non-actors, former documentary director Scott (with co-writers Gloria Demers and Sally Bochner) fashions a palpably human story that plows beneath the surface and finds the rich warmth of sincere relationships.

According to true Canadian form, most of the action is emotional instead of plot-driven, which gives the film a slow, but perfectly real, pace. Adding steam to the lazy locomotive is a sense of suspense, which flows from the fact that all these women are in their twilight years. We feel they may not have all that much time left, but where a Hollywood story would have turned that urgency into a race against the clock, Scott sits back and shows us the natural rhythm of life in all its relaxed, timeless beauty.

A marvel of a movie that will stick with you long after the final credits roll.

CANADIAN CHECKLIST Female protagonists | Characters poised against the landscape | Outsider stance | Steeped in realism (improvisational style) | Creative non-victims

Le Confessionnal (1995)

Directed by Robert Lepage
Starring Lothaire Bluteau, Patrick Goyette, Jean-Louis Millette, Kristin Scott Thomas, Ron Burrage, Richard Frechette, Francois Papineau, Marie Gignac, Normand Daneau, Anne-Marie Cadieux.
Running time: 100 minutes
❧❧❧❧

Pierre (Bluteau) is an art student and prodigal son who returns to Quebec City from a three-year tour in China for the funeral of his father. As he walks around the empty house he grew up in, Pierre notices the outlines of family pictures that once hung on the wall. He paints everything over, but the outlines reappear throughout the film, regardless of how many coats — or colours — Pierre applies. The image is important and foreshadows the rest of the film as the missing pieces of the family's past begin to bubble up beneath layers of lies.

The victim of the deception is Marc, Pierre's so-called brother. The son of Pierre's aunt, Marc was orphaned early on. His mother killed herself and his father's identity was never determined. Marc can't shake his feelings of abandonment and flirts with self-destruction in a variety of ways: drugs, anonymous gay sex, dysfunctional straight sex and straightforward suicidal urges. Pierre wants to help his "brother," but what Marc really needs is a sense of personal identity, and on that score, Pierre is almost as lost as Marc.

Eager to solve the mystery, Pierre begins to trace the story back to the beginning with the help of a creepy ex-priest who lives at the Hotel Frontenac. Through flashbacks, Lepage shows us Quebec City in 1952, the year it provided the backdrop for Alfred Hitchcock's *I Confess* — the movie where Montgomery Clift plays a guilt-ridden priest torn between his vows and bringing a murderer to justice. The intercut flashbacks mirror the modern-day story, and soon, we begin to isolate parallels between the Duplessis era and the democratic rebellion in Tiananmen Square, between *I Confess* and the ex-priest's story, and between Marc's missing father and the ghostly outlines bleeding through Pierre's red paint.

The layering works nicely and the whole film fuses in the final frames. The only real problem is Pierre's ignorance. With so many clues thrust in his face, he fails to put the puzzle together before it's too late. This was frustrating, because the viewer is wise to the real story by the midway point, and when you're screaming at the screen in the hopes of bringing the protagonist up to speed — it's hard to sit back and let the film chug towards its tragic end. All the same, *Le Confessional* is an emotionally and visually rich journey that unfolds with elegance, style and intelligence as it turns over the rock of patriarchal institutionalism to reveal a teeming mass of ugly lies.

CANADIAN CHECKLIST: Outsider stance | Identity issues | Missing people/father | Film within a film (*I Confess*) | Language barrier | Weird sex | Dysfunctional family | Twin imagery (the "brothers") | Empty landscape | Guilt

Cosmos (1997)

Directed by Jennifer Alleyn, Manon Briand, Marie-Julie Dallaire, Arto Paragamian, Andre Turpin, Denis Villeneuve
Starring Pascal Contamine, Igor Ovadis, Marie-Helen Monpetit, David La Haye, Marie-France Lambert, Alexis Martin, Elise Guilbault
Running time: 100 minutes
❦❦❦ ½

The brainchild of super-producer Roger Frappier, *Cosmos* features six separate stories — all directed by different Quebec-based directors — rolled into one feature film. Holding this layered narrative together is the mystical Greek taxi driver, *Cosmos*, who appears at just the right moment to offer different characters rides to different destinations, all of which lead to one central point in space: the one deep down inside called personal truth.

For one character, truth is telling a personal story on film instead of selling out to the forces of mindless commercialism. For another, truth is finding out the results of an AIDS test. For another, it's getting past the bullshit and feeling love for a partner.

Shot in grainy black-and-white by accomplished cinematographer André Turpin (who also directs one of the segments), *Cosmos* might seem to have more style than substance — at least on first glance. But as the stories gradually come together through Cosmos the cabbie, the "immigrant-other" who sees all, the narratives collapse into one big message about identity and truth, and that is: make "no deals," have the courage to be yourself and the world will likely accept you for who you are.

CANADIAN CHECKLIST: Missing people | Mistaken identity | Broken relationships | All-seeing immigrant-other as dramatic foil | Layered narrative | Linguistic fragmentation

Crash (1997)

Directed by David Cronenberg
Starring Elias Koteas, Holly Hunter, James Spader, Rosanna Arquette, Debra Unger
Running time: 100 minutes
🍁🍁

Without a doubt the most controversial film of David Cronenberg's career (thus far), *Crash* is based on the book by J. G. Ballard and tells the story of several people whose lives — and bodies — have been permanently altered by car crashes.

Spader plays a Toronto film producer whose life takes a creepy turn toward scar-obsession and sexual suicide after he's involved in a car accident that takes the life of another man — Holly Hunter's husband. He is compulsively drawn toward the moment of impact. Sex and car crashes become interchangeable in this perfectly grotesque effort that features everything from shots of hands covered in love juice to a medical researcher (Koteas) who stages elaborate recreations of famous car-deaths, particularly the accident that claimed James Dean.

Had the film been able to successfully communicate the survivor guilt — and resulting suicidal urges — of its characters without resorting to cheap sexual tricks, the movie certainly would have lived up to its billing as a masterpiece of psychological horror. As it is, it feels more like a badly acted porn movie than anything all that revolutionary. All the same, the film stands as a watermark (high or low — depending on how you look at it) in the Canadian film annals as a movie that ruffled everyone's feathers.

Banned in London, alternately jeered and cheered in Cannes, few of Cronenberg's films have prompted such a strong reaction from critics and audiences alike. Personally speaking, I hated this movie — but I still appreciated Cronenberg's examination of the deep suicidal tendencies that tempt all of us to just drive off the road into oblivion.

CANADIAN CHECKLIST: Conspicuous absence of children | Sexually ambiguous characters (bisexuality, homosexuality) | Weird sex | Death, disease | Outsider stance | Landscape defines character | Survivor guilt | Internal demons | Mind-body split | Missing people

C't'à ton tour, Laura Cadieux (1998)

Directed by Denise Filiatrault
Starring Ginette Reno, Mireille Thibault, Sophie Lorain, Sonia Vachon, Renée Claude
Running time: 91 minutes
🍁🍁🍁🍁

Steeped in quiet, humorous pathos, this film from the pen of Michel Tremblay and the lens of actor-director Denise Filiatrault is a beautiful meditation on life, love and the nagging human insecurities that keep us contained in a mental chrysalis.

Ginette Reno, the pop star who blew everyone away in *Léolo*, plays the title character: an overweight mother who makes regular visits to Dr. Sansfacon (Dr. Noway) — a quack of a gynecologist who gives women shots that he sells as slimming treatments. It might as well be snake oil, because the women who inhabit his waiting room day in and day out are as heavy as they ever were. Not that they care, because after years of treatment, their visits to the doctor have become a kind of therapy. They laugh, they cry, they share each other's lives and stab each other in the back. It's all part of life, and it's also the backbone of this plotless film.

It's a difficult movie to pull off, but Filiatrault (a veteran actor in her own right) understands the value of performance and subtly pulls out all the dramatic stops — without any jarring moments of melodrama or absolute boredom. Reno is perfect in the lead role, and she seems capable of telling us everything there is to know about motherhood with one self-effacing glance. It's a remarkable performance that makes this quiet film a true emotional standout.

CANADIAN CHECKLIST: Female-oriented | Outsider stance | Internal demons | Guilt | Silence over melodrama | Built on human interaction | Ambiguous ending

Cube (1997)
Directed by Vincenzo Natali
Starring David Hewlett, Nicole deBoer, Nicky Guadagni, Andrew Miller, Wayne Robson, Maurice Dean Wint
Running time: 90 minutes
❧ ❧ ❧ ❧

Another one of those Canadian movies that does gangbuster business in Europe but dies a quick death at home, *Cube* marks the feature debut from Canadian Film Centre graduate Vincenzo Natali.

The story of six complete strangers who find themselves marooned in the middle of a giant, booby-trapped maze, *Cube* starts off like a sci-fi action-adventure movie and ends on an ambiguous and altogether existentialist note. When we first enter the revolving Cube — which looks like a giant Rubik's puzzle — Natali and screenwriters Graeme Manson and André Bijelic establish the suspense factor by showing us one of the Cube's victims, a man sliced up into bloody little bits with razor wire as he attempts to escape. It's an arresting start, and one that carries a lot of symbolic weight as disintegration becomes the keyword on all scores. The six strangers try and hold themselves together. They help and support each other, hoping to maximize the skills of each prisoner in a bid to escape the maze. One is good at math, another is good at physical tasks, another is good at logic and design, et cetera. Cooperation gets them far, but not far enough — and that's when the group begins to disintegrate, with disastrous results.

While the suspense and sci-fi elements are well done, *Cube*'s main strength is the intellectual brainteaser it presents the viewer as it pushes us to ask ourselves what we might do in the same situation. A great study in human behaviour — with the performances to back it up — *Cube* is a smart, funny and deeply disturbing effort that signals a new, fantasy-oriented leaf on the geneological tree of Canadian film.

CANADIAN CHECKLIST: Outsider stance | Existential bent | Subversion of sci-fi genre (no laser blasters or spaceships) | Stranded in middle of nowhere | Death, disease, destruction

Dead Ringers (1988)

Directed by David Cronenberg
Starring Jeremy Irons, Geneviève Bujold, Heidi von Palleske, Barbara Gordon, Shirley Douglas
Running time: 115 minutes
🍁 🍁 🍁

What could be creepier than a double helping of Jeremy Irons holding gynecological instruments? A double helping of Jeremy Irons holding gynecological instruments in a David Cronenberg movie, that's what.

The story of Beverly and Elliot Mantle (Irons and Irons), identical twins who have an obsessive interest in the female reproductive organs, *Dead Ringers* could have been called the *Vagina Dialogues* — if it weren't for the highly disturbing, misogynist content that is guaranteed to make every woman squirm.

Why any woman would be interested in the hollow-eyed, drug dependent boys is beyond me, but without fail, the younger brother is a master seducer. When he grows bored with one woman, he simply passes her on to big brother. The arrangement works until the big brother falls in love with an actress (Bujold) who arrives in their office with a curious medical problem: she has two vaginas. For obvious reasons, both boys become transfixed with this medical anomaly that would appear to have the equipment to satisfy them both.

Pointy speculums, claw-shaped finger-tools and a whole tray of twisted surgical instruments make for a skin-crawling look at the stirrup experience, but one that articulates more than a few crucial Canadian themes.

CANADIAN CHECKLIST: Twin imagery | Internal demons | Outsider stance | Identity issues | Fear of female power | Ambiguous ending | Fractured narrative

Le Déclin de l'empire américain (1987)

Directed by Denys Arcand
Starring Dominique Michel, Dorothée Berryman, Louise Portal, Geneviève Rioux,
Pierre Curzi, Rémy Girard, Yves Jacques, Gabriel Arcand
Running time: 101 minutes
🍁 🍁 🍁 🍁 🍁

A veritable classic, and the first film to truly establish Canada on the populist film map, *Le Déclin de l'empire américain* is a satirical, and undeniably poignant, look at a group of self-absorbed university professors who have analyzed their world and themselves into a state of emotional numbness.

Over the course of the movie, which opens with one history professor (Dominique Michel) expounding her theory about the decline of the American empire, cracks begin to appear in their near-impeccable intellectual facades. We discover that one woman is addicted to a potentially dangerous sadomasochistic relationship, another woman is screwing her friend's husband, and yet another character is dying of AIDS. Juxtaposed against the timeless, natural beauty of Quebec's Eastern Townships, all the yapping and hypocrisy within the country house forms a beatifully flawed counterpoint to the world outside, suggesting that all the brainpower in the world may actually be a liability when it comes to enjoying the small pleasures life has to offer.

Funny and moving all at the same time, thanks to director Arcand's ability to find beauty in the flaws, *Le Déclin de l'empire américain* remains a high watermark on the Canadian filmscape and one of the best comments on the materialistic 1980s ever put to film.

CANADIAN CHECKLIST: Internalized tensions | Tendency for characters to overanalyze | Weird sex, dysfunctional romance | Layered narrative with different points of view | Contains a gap: between the beauty of the world and the characters' ability to see it | Natural landscape contrasts internal landscape | Ambiguous ending

Deep Inside Clint Star (1999)
Directed by Clint Alberta
Running time: 88 minutes
❧ ❧ ❧

A strangely surreal documentary that goes well beyond the box, this film takes us deep inside rez life to reveal a diverse group of young Canadians. Posing as a hipster camera jockey, Clint takes on the moniker of Clint Star — bon vivant filmmaker and self-appointed sex symbol — who turns the lens on his friends and neighbours like some latter-day Robin Leach.

Through his eyes, we see people like Tawny Maine, a woman struggling to reconcile her Egyptian-Swedish-Aboriginal identity, and Harvey, a kid coming to grips with his homosexual identity. From dark, sexy secrets to all-out despair and finally redemption, *Deep Inside Clint Star* strikes so many human notes that the movie feels like some symphonic celebration of being young, Native and alive.

Because Star trains the camera on his own navel for the duration, the film slides off the documentary workbench and into the land of self-expression, where the thrill of self-recreation mingles with tell-all confessions for a potent and highly unique take on the Aboriginal experience in Canada.

CANADIAN CHECKLIST: Outsider stance | Identity issues | Personal subversion of form | Finds diversity within group

Dirty (1998)

Directed by Bruce Sweeney
Starring Babz Chula, Tom Scholte, Benjamin Ratner, Nancy Sivak
Running time: 94 minutes
🍁🍁🍁

You've got your *Dirty Dancing*, and then, crawling like a slug up Patrick Swayze's leg, you've got your *Dirty*. The second feature from Ontario-born, Vancouver-based director Bruce Sweeney, *Dirty* is an example of the type of movie that makes people think Canadian film is all about smoking dope and screwing your mother.

Not that David (Scholte) wants to screw his mother, he just wants to screw Angie, a middle-aged dope dealer with a talent for making David feel like a bad little boy. A queen of sexual humiliation and cold, hard encounters, Angie doles out a unique brand of assertive, robocopulation that David cannot stop thinking about. He's obsessed, like all the other characters crawling around in this subbasement of an emotional space. Self-indulgent, self-absorbed and entirely unnable to grow up and take responsibility, the characters in *Dirty* are not the kind of people you'd want to hang out with on a long weekend. They are people you turn your back on in a bar because they already owe you money and they're bound to ask for more.

Chula provides the high point in the film as the ass-kicking Angie. The rest seem to bob along in her wake, half-submerged, making for an uneven but memorable film that will surely make you want to shower.

CANADIAN CHECKLIST: Potent women | Passive men | Sexual obsession/weird sex | Nonlinear narrative | Realistic treatment | Characters are all missing something | Outsider stance

Double Happiness (1994)

Directed by Mina Shum
Starring Sandra Oh, Stephen Chang, Alannah Ong, Donald Fong, Callum Keith Rennie.
Running time: 87 minutes
🍁🍁🍁 ½

On one side, Jade (Oh) is a nice girl desperate to make her traditional, Chinese mom and dad proud, but on the other, she's a young, liberated Canadian woman who wants to break out of the box she grew up in and express her inner truth.

Thinking she can pull off both identities simultaneously, she dates the Chinese boys her parents want her to see — including a cute, clean-cut lawyer who faces the same internal dilemma. Faking her way through one situation to the next, Jade appears to be pulling it off — but when she meets Mark (Rennie), a white university student with a roguish charm, she's forced to make a decision about whose life she's living: is it the one her parents want, or the one that will make her happy?

A simple story that handles complicated themes with skill, this movie succeeds artistically as well as emotionally. The real gravy are the performances from this stellar cast, particularly Oh in the lead as she captures the humour and pathos of Jade's experience without emotional excess. A great beginning to what I hope is a long and brilliant career.

CANADIAN CHECKLIST: Pluralist perspective | Outsider stance | Identity issues | Potent women | Passive men | Internalized twin

Earth (1998)
Directed by Deepa Mehta
Starring Aamir Khan, Nandita Das, Rahul Khanna, Maia Sethna
Running time: 102 minutes
🍁🍁🍁🍁

Based on Bapsi Sidhwa's autobiographical novel *Cracking India*, *Earth* exhumes one of the ugliest chapters in Indian history: the 1947 Partition that separated India from Pakistan. Told through the eyes of a young Parsee girl, Lenny, who watches her entire world fall apart, the movie is fragmented into different strata. On one level, we see things as Lenny might: on the surface, where things are all about balloons and ice cream cones and hanging out with Ayah, the beautiful nanny pursued by a wide array of suitors from different backgrounds. On another, we see the deep roots of racism as the adults begin to splinter off into different religious groups.

At the beginning, Mehta pulls back from elaborating on difference and simply shows us the beauty of life in pre-Partition Lahore, where people lived peacefully side by side. But as the British proceed with the political separation, society begins to fracture along with the land, ending in senseless violence and bloodshed on all sides. Friends are suddenly enemies and lovers are torn apart by politics.

What makes *Earth* work is the subtle dynamic that Mehta works into each layer, and her commitment to tell a huge story through one set of eyes. Through Lenny, we understand the sense of loss and betrayal as she is forced to watch her perfect life slip through her tiny little fingers. A very powerful and moving film, *Earth* is one of Mehta's true triumphs.

CANADIAN CHECKLIST: Fragmented narrative | Outsider stance | Landscape shapes the people | An unspoken message of the benefits of pluralism | Political subtext played out on interpersonal level | What's missing? A place to call home

Emporte-moi (1999)

Directed by Léa Pool

Starring Karine Vanasse, Miki Manojlovic, Pascale Bussières, Niki Huston

Running time: 94 minutes

🍁🍁🍁🍁

Filmmaker Léa Pool turns the lens on her inner child in this coming-of-age story of an emotionally, sexually and ancestrally confused 13-year-old girl living in Montreal. Hanna (Vanasse) is the child of a mixed Catholic-Jewish marriage and has — *quel surprise!* — a nagging identity problem. Her dysfunctional poet father sits around the house all day and stews about injustice, while her spunky martyr of a mother works in a sweatshop, comes home, cooks the dinner, then types up her husband's masterworks into the wee hours of the morning. Of course, that's when she has time to work between all the fighting.

Set adrift in this river Styx, Hanna has only one island of refuge: movies. In the womby darkness, she watches Godard's *Vivre sa vie* (a film Jean-Luc described as the story of a woman who sells her body to keep her soul). Within frames, Hanna is on the verge of selling her body to emulate her hero (and they say kids aren't affected by what they see ...). Fortunately for her, with the help of her older brother and a kind teacher, Hanna takes an exit off the autoroute to auto-destruction and manages to find herself.

A heavy but highly entertaining film that seems to mark the end of Pool's personal baggage chapter — at least for the moment.

CANADIAN CHECKLIST: Internal demons | Identity crisis; split self | Fragmented narrative | Potent women | Lesbian themes | Weird sex/ prostitution | Landscape mirrors alienation | Outsider stance

eXistenZ (1999)

Directed by David Cronenberg

Starring Jude Law, Jennifer Jason Leigh, Don McKellar, Ian Holm, Sarah Polley, Willem Dafoe

Running time: 97 minutes

🍁🍁🍁🍁

Set in the not-too-distant future, *eXistenZ* takes its cues from our modern-day reality where entertainment is a chief economic tent pole, and electronic games are the closest thing to an interactive art form. In this world, people like software designer Allegra Geller (Leigh) are gods, and those who play her games are the brainwashed flock — a religious subtext that Cronenberg installs in the opening sequence, where he shows us a focus group of gamers sitting around in a church. They are all waiting to try a new game from Antenna Research called *eXistenZ*, a game that feels so real, you can't tell the difference between artifice and reality. Just as the gamers begin, however, there's an attempt on Allegra's life by an anti-gaming terrorist group that believes in realism — not the false escapism that Allegra fashions so seamlessly through her software.

Where other Cronenberg movies often push gore over a good idea, *eXistenZ* finds a perfect balance between tumours of the flesh and health of the human spirit, which forces the viewer to make his or her own decision about what's "healthy" and what's "sick." Is ramming an organic coaxial cable up your spine a good thing — or a bad thing? Is thinking for yourself a good thing? Or a bad thing? Is reality a good thing, a bad thing, or something that may not exist at all?

These are the questions that rattled around in my head as I watched this movie in open-mouthed amazement at how well Cronenberg nailed the gamer's addictive high. As detailed as your worst nightmare and just as surreal, *eXistenZ* is a fully realized film that completes its intellectual argument on every level and proves Cronenberg is a true Canadian subversive — despite his apparent attraction to American genre.

CANADIAN CHECKLIST: Fragmented narrative | Ambiguous ending | Potent female | Passive male | Guilt | Realism questioned | Existential bent | Outsider stance/alienation

Exotica (1994)

Directed by Atom Egoyan.
Starring Bruce Greenwood, Mia Kirshner, Elias Koteas, Arsinée Khanjian.
Running time: 104 minutes.
❧ ❧ ❧ ❧

A perfectly Canadian film about sex, *Exotica* is steeped in sexual obsession, desire and longing — but it's not really about sex at all. Taking its name from the peeler bar that provides the dramatic backdrop for the film, *Exotica* offers plenty of hip-shaking, lap-smacking dance sequences, but love is finally what brings everyone together under the same roof to frolic, fret and fall in this pimped-up paradise.

For Francis (Greenwood), a tax auditor investigating an eccentric pet store owner (McKellar), the Exotica is his way of connecting to a severed emotional limb that continues to haunt him. For Christina (Kirshner), Francis' favourite dancer, who wears a schoolgirl's uniform, the Exotica provides the sense of family she was denied. For the DJ Eric (Koteas), the bar is his soul connection to his lost soulmate, and for the club owner, Zoe (Khanjian), Exotica is symbolic skeletal remains of her own mother.

As the dancers peel off their silken threads, Egoyan strips the characters of secrets to unveil truth. An intricately told tale with many inviting folds, *Exotica* ultimately finds quiet beauty in the naked soul.

CANADIAN CHECKLIST: Fragmented narrative | Outsider stance | Weird sex | Missing people | Potent women | Broken men | Landscape is beautiful and threatening

Felicia's Journey (1999)

Directed by Atom Egoyan
Starring Bob Hoskins, Elaine Cassidy, Arsinée Khanjian.
Running time: 116 minutes.
❦ ❦ ❦ ❦

Based on William Trevor's novel, *Felicia's Journey* follows the lovesick travels of a young pregnant woman who is disowned by her family and leaves home to look for Johnny, the father of her unborn child. Travelling from Ireland to Birmingham, Felicia (Cassidy) becomes an outsider in the midst of hostile industrial landscape. Sensing her alienation, another loner named Hilditch (Hoskins) offers to take her under his wing. Hilditch is a creepy man with a nagging Oedipal complex, but he seems perfectly harmless as we watch him cook himself into another world every night. The child of a TV chef, Hilditch has a career as a caterer, but he's forever comparing himself to his dear old mom, Gala (Khanjian). Every night he watches old tapes of his mother's show, and every night he reverts back to being a chubby little kid who desperately wants to make his mother proud.

The obsessive routine takes on greater significance as the movie unravels, but Egoyan resists revealing all the pieces of his puzzle off the bat and pushes us into the darkest recesses of Hilditch's mind while intercutting dreamy images of the young, innocent Felicia. The two characters become a study in sympathetic contrast. Hilditch longs to return to the bosom of his mother as a pure, untainted boy while Felicia, the young lover with the saintly face, is on the verge of losing her innocence about love. Hilditch represents the ordered adult world that keeps everything in check with machinery and routine, while Felicia embodies the soulful, but chaotic, human experience. The two are on a collision course and Egoyan cranks up the suspense level through juxtaposition and silence.

What makes the movie work is the way Egoyan pulls us into this virtually static movie on an emotional level. We want Felicia to find Johnny. We also want Hilditch to find happiness. Even if we think it's a lost cause, we can't help but hope. Egoyan plays with these expectations, taunting us into playing the same game of denial that bonds Hilditch and Felicia together.

It's another complicated story, full of gaps and negative space, but it comes together through the mirror image of the two lost souls. The film left me with a quiet ache, but a better appreciation for all the little things that make life worth living.

CANADIAN CHECKLIST: Identity issues | Outsider stance | Potent women | Passive men | Twin dynamic | Dead babies | Dislocation

Five Senses (1999)

Directed by Jeremy Podeswa
Starring Mary-Louise Parker, Pascale Bussieres, Richard Clarkin, Brendan Fletcher, Marco Leonardi, Nadia Litz, Daniel MacIvor, Molly Parker, Gabrielle Rose, Tara Rosling
Running time: 96 minutes
❦❦❦ ½

Jeremy Podeswa puts everything he ever learned from his years working with Atom Egoyan to good use in this movie that picked up the Genie for best direction in 1999. The story of several people who are missing something deep in their soul, *The Five Senses* takes on an allegorical structure where each character represents a specific sensory problem.

Gabrielle Rose plays a massage therapist awash in guilt because her daughter was babysitting a small child who is now missing. To cope with her internal demons, she offers her services free to the fretting mother (Molly Parker). Another character is slowly going deaf (Volter), one spies on people (Fletcher), one is dating a man she cannot understand (Mary-Louise Parker), and another (MacIvor) cleans houses smelling for messes.

A good idea told with absolute tidiness, this film is fashioned from the fibre of the Canadian film tradition as it pushes us into empty space — that place that transcends sensory input and challenges us to look within for answers.

CANADIAN CHECKLIST: Non-linear format | Interwoven vignettes | Negative space | Sympathetic landscape | Outsider stance | Language issues | Missing children

4 Days (1999)

Directed by Curtis Wehrfritz
Starring Kevin Zegers, Colm Meaney, Lolita Davidovich
Running time: 90 minutes
❦❦

While the movie itself is a failure, *4 Days* is a good example of some key Canadian themes — hence, its inclusion here. A coming-of-age/road movie/crime thriller based on the novel by John Buell, *4 Days* features *Air Bud*'s Kevin Zegers as the son of a bank robber named Milt. Milt has just pulled off a bank job when he's gunned down, leaving young Simon — who's pretty much called "the kid" throughout — holding the loot. Knowing his dad's old buds will be sniffing around for the kill, the kid heads into the scenic Quebec landscape to disappear.

Within hours, a heavy by the name of Fury (Meaney) is on his trail, with Milt's cleft-palate gal pal Feather, (Lepage regular Anne-Marie Cadieux) to guide the way. Meanwhile, the kid hooks up with a redhead loner named Chrystal (Davidovich) on the run from her hubby. The two hole up together in a remote motel, and sooner than later, the kid is shedding his innocence along with his briefs.

The whole plot comes to a head at this abandoned summer retreat, where Fury, Milt's gal pal and Chrystal's beau, surround their prey, leaving the kid no chance of escape — save the ultimate exit plan.

Exactly what happens at the end is unclear, but it's a downer all the same. In fact, it's such a contrived downer that it proves just how much the Canadian psyche craves the dark side, often without any redeeming artistic purpose. Still, it's an interesting Canadian mix, full of stunning Quebec landscapes in the midst of scenic autumn.

CANADIAN CHECKLIST: Father/son baggage | Identity issues | Weird sex | Classic Canadian landscape shots | Road to nowhere | Drowning | Layered narrative | Shot in Shawinigan (home of Jean Chrétien)

Ginger Snaps (2000)
Directed by John Fawcett
Starring Katharine Isabelle, Emily Perkins, Mimi Rogers, Kris Lemche
Running time: 108 minutes
✤ ✤ ✤

This subversive teen horror movie starts out with so much promise, it almost bears no resemblance to its final frames that simply rehash slasher cliché. The story of two sisters who are high school outsiders, *Ginger Snaps* begins as a clever and witty coming-of-age metaphor, but gradually spirals into the cold, hard ground as just another coulda, woulda, shoulda been a contender. When we are introduced to Brigitte (Perkins) and Ginger Fitzgerald (Isabelle), they are Goth disciples of their very own personalized religion. Late bloomers who have yet to menstruate or engage in pubescent sex games, Brigitte and Ginger amuse themselves by staging their own gory deaths and taking pictures — which only strengthens their position outside the high school universe, which is all about "belonging" to the right clique. Not that Brigitte and Ginger care about the other kids. Sworn friends until the end, the two are empowered by mutual refusal to conform to the suburban reality that surrounds them in subdivision hell, where their chipper Mom (Mimi Rogers) tries to hide her marital dissatisfaction with a bright smile and a wardrobe of embroidered gingham dresses.

When Ginger gets her period, however, things begin to change. She grows hair and her hormones overflow. On the surface, she becomes a classic teenager, but in this script by Karen Walton, she becomes a whole lot more: she turns into a werewolf.

The coming-of-age metaphor works perfectly as the two sisters begin to drift apart, separated by a sea of blood and hair and sexual desire. If Walton and director Fawcett had been able to keep their eyes on the metaphorical implications instead of the blood and guts rigours of the genre, *Ginger Snaps* would have been a truly subversive — and often hilarious — feast for a cynical age. As it is, you kind of wish they'd just lopped off the last third of the movie and let this thing wriggle in ambiguity instead of laboriously bludgeoning the whole thing to death.

CANADIAN CHECKLIST: Subversion of genre — watch for the line: "Let's forget the Hollywood rules ..." | Powerful women | Passive men | Nature the monster | Weird sex | Personal alienation | Oppressive landscape | Nonconformity

A Girl is a Girl (1999)

Directed by Reg Harkema
Starring Andrew McIntyre, Paige Morrison, Laurie Baranyay, Aeryn Twidle, Jo-Ann MacDonald
Running time: 88 minutes
❦❦❦ ½

The first feature film from Vancouver-based filmmaker Reg Harkema (editor of *Hard Core Logo*, *Twilight of the Ice Nymphs, Last Night*), *A Girl is a Girl* is a kinder, gentler meditation on Canadian alienation as it tells the story of Trevor (McIntyre), a really nice guy looking for a that one perfect girl.

Little does Trevor know he's a victim of mass-media marketing campaigns, and really, there is no such thing as the smart, funny, *Sports Illustrated* swimsuit model who lives and breathes to make Trevor feel good about himself. Instead, women are just people — or, as the title suggests: a girl is really just a girl.

For the bulk of this offbeat charmer, we watch Trevor make an ass of himself in a variety of ways, with a variety of different women as he slowly comes to accept the lack of feminine perfection — not to mention his own shortcomings. Good dialogue, strong performances and Harkema's loose, Godard-inspired approach make *A Girl is a Girl* a witty and stylish outing into the netherworld of twenty-something romance.

CANADIAN CHECKLIST: Potent women | Passive men | Relationship dysfunction | Weird sex | Outsider stance

Goin' Down the Road (1970)

Directed by Don Shebib
Starring Doug McGrath, Paul Bradley, Jayne Eastwood, Cayle Chernin, Nicole Morin, Pierre La Roche, Ted Sugar, Don Steinhouse, Ron Martin
Running time: 87 minutes
❦❦❦❦❦

They've had it with life in boring, dead-end Cape Breton. Pete (McGrath) and Joey (Bradley) want a taste of the good life. They want to date beautiful women, eat gourmet food and work at well-paying white collar jobs. They want the proverbial pot o' gold, and so they pack up their rusted-out Chevy and head on down the road to that Canadian Shangri-La on the shores of Lake Ontario: Toronto.

When they arrive, the two boys are completely high from the simple act of moving. They are full of hope and dreams, but this ain't no American movie where the underdog always wins and the plum life falls from a tree. This is Canada, where truth stings and Anne Murray sings. Despite their best efforts — well, at least they try to get good jobs — the boys end up in a depressing apartment, with depressing jobs, dating depressed women.

It's a depressing movie, but what makes the voyage worthwhile is the way Shebib captures the essence of what Toronto critic Geoff Pevere described as "hoser culture" — an experience defined by beer, hockey, pogie and low self-esteem.

What I like about the movie is the way it refuses to apologize for these Canadianisms. In fact, *Goin' Down the Road* lacks any identity crisis to speak of — which still makes it something of an anomaly in the identity-seeking Canadian tradition. *Goin' Down the Road* marked the beginning of English-Canadian self-reflection and while a lot has changed over the years, there's still a hint of Pete and Joey in every Canadian as we continue to search for something better on the outside, instead of embracing the beauty within.

CANADIAN CHECKLIST: Road to nowhere | Passive men | Rooted in realism | Refusal of American Dream | Stubbies | Outsider stance

The Grey Fox (1982)
Directed by Phillip Borsos
Starring Richard Farnsworth, Jackie Burroughs, Ken Pogue, Wayne Robson, Timothy Webber
Running time: 92 minutes
🍁 🍁 🍁 🍁

Set against the surreal beauty of the Canadian west, *The Grey Fox* stars Richard Farnsworth as the great stagecoach robber, Bill Miner. It picked up almost every Genie Award on offer in 1983.

The film opens with Miner's release from jail, where he's spent the past 30 years of his life. Now a free man in a changed time, the aging thief tries to rebuild the fragments of his broken life and heads up to Canada — Kamloops way, where he hooks up with a lady photographer, played by Burroughs. With few resources and few skills, Miner returns to his old ways in a sad, but strangely amusing, comeback bid.

The story of a loner in a strange new world, this film gives us a feel for the times through Borsos' relaxed pacing, expansive wilderness shots and contrasting encounters with new machinery that herald the arrival of the industrial age — such as the automatic apple peeler that Miner holds in the opening sequence.

A slow, but visually rich journey into the stunning heartland of the Canadian frontier, *The Grey Fox* feels like a Western on Valium, so just lie back and enjoy the ride. Farnsworth nails the part, and hands in a warm, human and, well — altogether Canadian — performance as the politest criminal to ever say "Stick 'em up."

CANADIAN CHECKLIST: Sympathetic landscape | Outsider stance | Photographic imagery | Internal demons/tension | Subversion of western genre (no shoot-outs or horse stunts)

The Grocer's Wife (1991)
Directed by John Pozer
Starring Simon Webb, Susinn McFarlen, Jay Brazeau, Nicola Cavendish, Andrea Rankin
Running time: 100 minutes
❦ ❦ ❦ ½

Set against the backdrop of Trail, British Columbia, a smelter town and home to the two-time world champion Trail Smoke Eaters hockey club, John Pozer's debut feature is a timeless look at small-town paranoia and romantic dysfunction.

Tim Midley (Webb) is a waif of a man who fears the world and remains under the control of his domineering mother, Mildred (Rankin). Things change, somewhat drastically, when Tim — a smokestack specialist — tells his dear old mum to close the window on the night they start up the new stack. She doesn't listen, and winds up dead the next day. Without his mother standing in the way, Tim befriends a stripper (McFarlen) who moves in to the house without so much as an invitation. Suddenly, things look a lot like they used to around the old Midley home, with Tim skulking around between bouts of abuse from the psycho peeler. You wouldn't think such a nebbish would be considered a romantic prize, but in the eyes of the grocer's wife, Mrs. Friendly (Cavendish), Tim is a little boy in need of some love and attention.

Excellent performances from the mousy Webb and the ball-busting females bring a lot of humour into this grainy, black-and-white world where the big, black cloud of doom is more than a metaphor — it's part of the landscape. A wee bit too long and a bit on the slow side, *The Grocer's Wife* shares a lot of ground with *Mon Oncle Antoine* without being a slave to realism. Surreal, strange and funny, *The Grocer's Wife* marked the beginning of a new Canadian vision in British Columbia.

CANADIAN CHECKLIST: Potent women | Passive men | Landscape defines character | Missing people | Ambiguous ending | Fragmented narrative | Death, disease | Twin imagery (mother, stripper) | Oedipal baggage | Identity issues

The Hanging Garden (1997)
Directed by Thom Fitzgerald
Starring Chris Leavins, Kerry Fox, Christine Dunsworth
Running time: 90 minutes
❦ ❦ ❦ ½

A talking statue of the Virgin Mary, an obese ghost of a childhood past, and a horticulturally obsessed parent make for a strange mix of the sick and surreal in this debut feature from Maritimer Thom Fitzgerald.

Told from the point of view of William (Leavins), *The Hanging Garden* focuses on William's return to his old hometown for his sister Rosemary's wedding. Now an attractive young man, William was once a very introverted, weight-challenged kid. As the story unfolds, the abscess of William's pain emerges to the surface: his sister is marrying the boy Willy had a crush on as a teenager. Yes, William is gay, and now that he's out, he can deal with his self-loathing past, which Fitzgerald personifies in the form of a chubby kid hanging from an apple tree.

The Biblical overtones don't stop there: Granny has a statue of the Virgin Mary that provides her with plenty of spiritual, and in an odd way sexual, pleasure. Guilt and sex, sex and guilt: in Fitzgerald's universe, the two go together like two buff jocks in the same shower. Maybe that's why *The Hanging Garden* is so much fun to watch: because for all the shame and melodrama that fires up this family's furnace, Fitzgerald pulls back to show these people in a wider frame — where we can see them for the nutbars they are.

Wacky Canucks are always a blast, and Fitzgerald sets them off like so many firecrackers under the teacher's chair. Clever, sassy and surreal, *The Hanging Garden* brings a little light into the typically dark Canadian family room.

CANADIAN CHECKLIST: Guilt | Weird sex | Religious questioning | Internal demons | Twin imagery | Thematic use of nature | Family dysfunction

Highway 61 (1991)
Directed by Bruce McDonald
Starring Valerie Buhagiar, Don McKellar, Earl Pastko, Peter Breck, Jello Biafra, Johnny Askwith, Tracy Wright, Hadley Obodiac
Running time: 102 minutes
🍁🍁🍁🍁

The second instalment in Bruce McDonald's road trilogy (the first being *Roadkill*, the last *Hard Core Logo*), *Highway 61* features Buhagiar as a rock 'n' roll femme fatale named Jackie Bangs and Don McKellar as nice guy barber, Pokey Jones. The film opens with a bar brawl that leaves Jackie with a valuable chunk of narcotics that she wants to sell in the United States. Her only problem is she lacks a car and a mule — who miraculously appear in the form of a dead body (the mule) and the barber, Pokey (patsy with a car), who finds the body frozen in a bathtub at the beginning of the motion picture.

With little time to spare before she makes the drug deal, Jackie convinces Pokey that the dead body is that of her brother. Feeling pity, Pokey agrees to take the precious car that was left to him by his parents (who died when he was just a kid) and drive her down to New Orleans. The two set off on a surreal rock 'n' roll road adventure with a coffin strapped to the roof, with Pokey acting as pop culture tour guide. Along the way, they meet a variety of people — including a bingo-addicted devil who buys souls faster than he can claim them, and an untalented family of pint-sized performers.

Co-written by McDonald, McKellar and Allan Magee, *Highway 61* follows the real Highway 61, which goes from Thunder Bay to New Orleans, and the movie features plenty of comparisons between Americans and Canadians. We generally get the better deal, as we come off as slightly naive, but good-hearted people, while the Americans are portrayed as borderline psychotics with guns. While the swipes at the Stars and Stripes are gentle, there's no mistaking the film's criticism of America's fascination with guns, strip malls and celebrity.

CANADIAN CHECKLIST: Frozen dead people | Coffin as baggage (see Mon Oncle Antoine) | Road movie that leads nowhere | Canadians know more about American pop culture than Americans (Pokey) | Sex and death mingle | Potent woman protagonist | Passive, but heroic, male protagonist | Juxtaposition of American landscape and Canadian perspective

I Love a Man in Uniform (1993)
Directed by David Wellington
Starring Tom McCamus, Brigitte Bako, Kevin Tighe, David Hemblen
Running time: 97 minutes
🍁 🍁 🍁

Few people can communicate "creepy" quite like Tom McCamus, and in this minimalist thriller from David Wellington, McCamus lets his creep factor fly as he plays a bank clerk in the midst of an identity crisis. Henry Adler is a quiet loner — a victim just waiting to happen, but all that changes when the part-time actor gets a bit part in a reality-TV cop show called *Crimewave*.

Once Henry puts on the costume, his whole personality begins to change. From mild-mannered bank clerk living in a Kafka-esque reality, Henry metamorphoses into an uber-cool cop who walks, talks and acts like a swaggering force of fascism. Soon, he's so addicted to the power trip that he steals the costume and plays cop in real life. Crossing the line always involves risk, and sooner than later, Henry's potent alter ego is confronted by the real thing — a real cop who manipulates Henry to his own advantage. Unable to distinguish one reality from another, Henry begins to lose his mind and the film implodes, leaving bits and pieces of self all over the screen.

Heady, cool and hard-edged, *I Love a Man in Uniform* is a thriller for anal-retentive types who prefer to keep everything clenched up inside — just like Henry. And while Wellington uses his brain more than his heart amid this sterile urban landscape, McCamus' sad eyes and soft voice bring a human side to an altogether inhuman universe. Uneven, but nonetheless complete, this film proves Wellington is a filmmaker with incredible intensity and commitment to his own vision.

CANADIAN CHECKLIST: Identity issues | Father issues | Twin imagery | Internalized sense of self | Drama in silence | Outsider stance | Passive male | Subversion of Hollywood convention

I've Heard the Mermaids Singing (1987)
Directed by Patricia Rozema
Starring Sheila McCarthy, Paule Baillargeon, Anne-Marie Macdonald
Running time: 81 minutes
✦ ✦ ✦ ✦

Polly Vandersma (McCarthy) is a thirty-something outsider/orphan who escapes her dead-end reality by taking photographs of the things that catch her fancy. From urban landscapes to voyeuristic shots of lovers kissing, Polly's pictures are snapshots from her own special little world that give her a great deal of pleasure, as well as a sense of purpose. When she gets a job working for a gallery owner in downtown Toronto as a gal Friday, Polly's world begins to change. Impressed by the cool and sexy gallery owner, Gabrielle (Baillargeon), Polly makes an extra — but futile — effort to fit in. She thinks the gallery world is full of well-educated, open-minded intellectuals who know everything, only to discover it's just a big scam populated by big egos.

While the external plot is relatively thin — little more than a story about Polly, her pictures and her crush on the gallery owner — Rozema paints a rich internal landscape that McCarthy brings to the screen with juicy brush strokes, and Rozema shoots in grainy black-and-white to mirror Polly's art. Baillargeon is absolutely stunning as the sexed-up mother/lover type and writer-actor Anne-Marie Macdonald does a convincing job playing the chiclet-toothed, square-jawed artist in shining armour.

Sexy, stylish and steeped in a Canadian melancholy, *I've Heard the Mermaids Singing* was part of the initial move toward magic realism that freed Canadian film from the tethers of realism — and let it fly into the ether of the imagination.

CANADIAN CHECKLIST: Gay sex | Outsider stance | Orphans | Emacipation of imagination through photography | Potent women | Passive men | Subversion of institutional mentality | Film on film images | Fear of self-expression | Internal landscape

In Praise of Older Women (1978)
Directed by George Kaczender
Starring Tom Berenger, Karen Black, Helen Shaver, Susan Strasberg
Running time: 110 minutes
✦ ✦ ✦

The first film to rip the bodice off the pasty white body of Canadian culture, this film adaptation of writer Stephen Vizinczey's novel was positively scandalous when it screened at the Toronto Festival of Festivals, and it became a sizable success as a result of the furor. *In Praise of Older Women* proved a few things to the puny Canadian industry that was still largely controlled by bureaucrats: it proved we, the Canadian public, had an appetite for more than back bacon, pork rinds and maple syrup. It also proved we could make movies about ourselves that weren't entombed in earnest intentions.

A coming-of-age romance, *In Praise of Older Women* focuses on Andras Vayda (Berenger), a young boy who apprentices in the art of love as a teenager in Hungary and then moves to Canada to escape. Vayda is a sweet young thing with a handsome face and a deep respect for women, which makes him the favourite boy-toy of a few older women — particularly Maya (Karen Black), a very lonely married woman who shows Andras the proverbial ropes. By the time he becomes a philosophy professor drinking espresso in Montreal, Andras is an accomplished sex-smith able to charm women from their culottes with little more than a mischievous grin.

A true Canadian milestone in the continuing excavation of our repressed psyche, *In Praise of Older Women* shows us a relatively functional entry into the boudoir. It was trashed by critics of the day for being a tad melodramatic and softly pornographic, but it survives well now that we've all acknowledged there is sex in the city.

CANADIAN CHECKLIST: Weird sex | Potent women | Passive men | Pluralist perspective | Frigidity | Missing parents | Dysfunctional romance

J. A. Martin photographe (1977)
Directed by Jean Beaudin
Starring Monique Mercure, Marcel Sabourin, Luce Guilbeault
Running time: 101 minutes
❀ ❀ ❀ ½

In 19th-century Quebec, a quiet, introverted photographer heads into the rural cantons once a year to chronicle life's big events. From weddings to family portraits, communions and industrial mills, J. A. Martin (Sabourin) moves from event to event with detached professionalism. It works just fine, until his wife, Rose-Aimée (Mercure, who won the acting prize at Cannes for this role) decides she wants to tag along on his next journey. Through clenched teeth, old J. A. agrees — no doubt realizing that any argument is futile once Rose-Aimée makes a decision.

The next scene shows them packing up the big black wagon and heading out of town on a journey that ultimately changes their lives. A diametric opposite to Atom Egoyan's *Calendar*, where a couple falls apart on a photographic journey, *J. A. Martin photographe* shows an estranged couple slowly come together. Through images more than action, Beaudin captures the whirling eddies of emotion that suggest larger transformations just beneath the surface as these two different people fall in love for what we believe may be the very first time.

While there are darker elements such as miscarriage, child labour and abuse, the film refuses to indulge in any emotive moments — taking on the relaxed pace of real life, where bad things happen, but life always moves on. Set against the backdrop of a rich, green, Eastern summer, Beaudin also finds the Edenic side to the Canadian landscape, which makes the movie something of a novelty — even a quarter-century later.

Not exactly riveting entertainment, *J. A. Martin photographe* is a movie for all those people who preferred *The Thin Red Line* to *Saving Private Ryan*.

CANADIAN CHECKLIST: Outsider stance | Film on film imagery | Dead babies | Dysfunctional romance | Vast landscape | Rooted in realism | Denies closure | Resists conventional pacing

Jésus de Montréal AKA Jesus of Montreal (1989)
Directed by Denys Arcand
Starring Lothaire Bluteau, Catherine Wilkening, Johanne-Marie Tremblay, Remy Girard, Robert Lepage, Gilles Pelletier, Yves Jacques
Running time: 119 minutes
❦ ❦ ❦ ❦

Following on the heels of *Le Déclin de l'empire Americain* — which took a sidelong glance at the Ivory Tower mentality of the intelligentsia — *Jesus of Montreal* blows out the main institutional carbuncle in the Québécois psyche: the Catholic church.

At first, it almost looks as if Arcand may be offering us a hip new interpretation of the scriptures as he shows us a relatively liberal priest looking to perk up the old Passion Play at L'Oratoire St. Joseph — a church on Mont Royal whose many steps attract hundreds of martyr-hungry holy types each year.

The priest hires a troupe of young, hip actors to give the stations of the cross a new twist. Daniel (Bluteau), who plays Jesus, is recruited by Father Leclerc (Pelletier) to head up the thespian flock. From there, Daniel brings others into the fold: Constance (Tremblay) is a Mary character who's sleeping with the Padre; Martin (Girard) dubs porn films into French; René (Lepage) works at the planetarium describing the origin of the universe in scientific terms, and Mireille is a beautiful young actress whose virtue is compromised by starring in sleazy ads.

Cynical and secular, the actors are hesitant, but paycheques speak louder than principles and they step up to the challenge, rewriting and reinterpreting the scripture to play up the importance of personal spirituality instead of blind faith in the institutional, cross-topped box. The play proves to be an overwhelming success with the critics and the public alike (one of my favourite scenes has a TV reviewer declaring *"Emouvante!"* — Moving! — several times over with lachrymose indulgence). When the big-hats hear about it, though, all hell breaks loose — symbolically speaking, at any rate. The actors are asked to tone the play down, or else risk being booted off the site altogether — but they can't bring themselves to submit to the authority. They've been transformed by the experience: they feel their pimped-out, whored-up actor souls have been redeemed by their play and they refuse to comply.

CANADIAN CHECKLIST: Outsider stance | Subversion of institutional mentality | Identity issues | Send-up of commercialism | Beer jokes: The average IQ of a beer drinker is described as "10 points lower, and he'd be a geranium." | Awareness of medium (internal commentary on filmmaking and the role of theatre to recreate the world, highlighted by the fact that Arcand himself plays the Pilate figure) | Fragmented narrative | Emotionally ambiguous ending

Just Watch Me (1999)

Directed by Catherine Annau
Starring Doug Garson, Evan Adams, John Duffy, Jocelyne Perrier, Sylvain Marois, Susanne Hilton, André Gobeil, Meg McDonald
Running time: 76 minutes
🍁 🍁 🍁 🍁

An atypical documentary about the children of the Trudeau era, *Just Watch Me* turns the spotlight on eight Canadians who grew up during the sixties and seventies as part of the great bilingual experiment. Without an overt agenda or sentimental plea for "national unity," Annau simply lets her subjects tell their stories — which turn out to be funny, enlightening and altogether moving as they talk about their feelings about Canada, and in turn, how they feel about themselves as Canadians.

Evan Adams (who we saw in *Smoke Signals*), is a First Nations actor and medical student who says Trudeau's dream made room for everyone, including Aboriginal peoples, which is why he continues to hope for bilingualism — even in the redneck West. For Doug Garson, a kid who was sent to the Catholic school in Winnipeg so he could be bilingual, the idea had a lot of merit, but he's not sure if it will ever work. For André Gobeil, a separatist who grew up in a Liberal household, Trudeau's dream of a unified Canada doesn't leave enough room for his Québécois identity. He fears his kids could end up with anglicized names, or speak French with English intonation — things that Gobeil feels would hurt his personal identity and bleed the Québécois cause of vital lifeblood. For Gobeil, Trudeau was an idol who "left a bitter taste in my mouth." Suzanne Hilton is a bilingual Montrealer, canoe-enthusiast and Trudeau fan who had eggs thrown at her door after the last referendum. John Duffy is a Torontonian who once felt Anglo guilt for the long suffering of the French-Canadians. He dreamed of unity and tried hard to be the perfect self-apologizing Canadian — but now feels cynical, and "defines himself, in part, against that [notion of the perfect Canadian]." Jocelyne Perrier was a lot like André Gobeil, and believed her identity as a Quebecker was the only thing that really gave her meaning — until she moved outside Quebec, and suddenly, "my identity became Canada."

The most moving story comes from Sylvain Marois and Meg McDonald, who fell in love in Quebec City, nearly broke up over the referendum, and now live on the West Coast — where they both teach French.

There is nothing more moving that real human drama, and that's exactly what Annau captures in this crafty outing that maps the post-Trudeau Canadian experience, and finds a self-possession against a backdrop of national doubt.

CANADIAN CHECKLIST: Documentary that is not a standard documentary | Ambiguous ending | Internalized identities | Language as means of personal identification | Great landscape shots | Canadian tunes

Kanehsatake: 270 Years of Resistance (1993)

Directed by Alanis Obomsawin
Documentary
Running time: 119 minutes
❦ ❦ ❦ ❦

When land developers began mowing down trees on a sacred Mohawk site to build a golf course expansion, the Mohawks protested by erecting a blockade. Shortly thereafter, the police were called in, and the famous 1990 armed standoff between the Mohawk Nation and the Sûreté du Quebec and the Canadian Armed Forces began.

Obomsawin was the only filmmaker given access to the drama behind the lines, and as a result, she's the only one to document the other side of what became the most acrimonious land battle in modern Canadian history, which lasted a gut-clenching 78 days.

Where the police attempted to spin a story of Native terrorists and gun-toting warriors, Obomsawin shows us a decidedly different image of these "masked marauders." Through her lens, this rag-tag group of ironworkers and family men emerge as heroes fighting in the name of justice, truth and honour. These men were willing to die for the land. After years of watching their territories erode at the hands of white governments who expropriated in the name of the "public good," we can understand why these people finally put their foot down and said enough is enough. Besides, how can you justify the development of ancestral lands for a golf course?

A powerful look at the lesser-seen face of the Aboriginal experience in Canada, *Kanehsatake* shows us the spark that ignited a new sense of Aboriginal pride and self-determination that continues to shape the Canadian condition.

Obomsawin returned to Oka several years later for *Rocks at Whiskey Trench*, a film that looks at what happened when the women and children were convoyed off the reserve in case things turned violent: they were pelted with rocks by swarms of white hooligans.

A must-see chapter of Canadian history, *Kanehsatake* is a documentary one can't — and shouldn't — forget.

CANADIAN CHECKLIST: Outsider stance | Landscape defines character | Identity issues | Colonial baggage | Personal documentary

Kanada (1993)

Directed by Mike Hoolboom
Starring Babz Chula, Gabrielle Rose, Sky Gilbert, Andrew Scorer, Mike Hoolboom, Kika Thorne
Running time: 65 minutes
❦ ❦ ❦ ½

Kanada brings Gabrielle Rose and Babz Chula together as lovers in a desperate time: war is brewing and Prime Minister Wayne Gretzky could suspend the Charter of Rights to keep Lucien Bouchard in his place (this film prognosticated Bouchard's arrival).

Can these two women hold their relationship together or will they split apart like the nation around them? A clever metaphor for the codependent Canadian condition, *Kanada* finds experimental filmmaker Mike Hoolboom at his most intense — and most inspired. The film is as fragmented as the subject matter, complete with ultra-polarized images, and Hoolboom puts the political banter of the day into the mouths of these babes for a complete, and refreshing, Canadian apocalypse. Funny, moving, well written and well acted, the movie is one of the few overtly political films to ever emerge from English Canada.

Kanada is sadly not available on video or DVD, but if you live in a city with a cinematheque, a museum or a cool art-house cinema, you may be able to harass a programmer to bring in a print. If you're a fan of the truly bizarre, this is definitely one worth whining for.

CANADIAN CHECKLIST: | Experimental subversion of genre | Dysfunctional relationship | Dysfunctional politics | Weird sex | Hockey | Outsider stance | Fragmentation | Twin imagery | Potent women

Kissed (1996)

Directed by Lynne Stopkewich
Starring Molly Parker, Peter Outerbridge, Jay Brazeau, Natasha Morley, Jessie Winter Mudie
Running time: 80 minutes
❦ ❦ ❦ ❦

Based on the short story by Barbara Gowdy and brought to the screen by Stopkewich and co-writer Angus Fraser, *Kissed* rivals *In Praise of Older Women* as the most sensationalized Canadian love story to ever hit the screen.

Where the latter caused a sensation for its relatively well-adjusted graphic sexual content, *Kissed* caused a fracas because it focuses on necrophilia. Sandra Larson (Molly Parker) is a nice gal with a big secret: she is sexually aroused by the sight of a dead man's corpse, and she gradually consummates her passion with a stream of stiffs that floats through the funeral parlour where she works.

Jealous of her romantic attraction to dead men, her would-be boyfriend (Peter Outerbridge) attempts to woo her away from the slab in several different ways, but all his efforts prove futile because Sandra is looking for a sense of negative affirmation, or communion with the other side. By climbing aboard dead bodies, Sandra's hole is filled with dead flesh — which, in turn, makes her completely alive.

A perfect example of finding something positive in the negative, *Kissed* clearly touched a nerve in the Canadian psyche and cemented our national image as sexual deviants abroad — which, let's face it, is the best thing that happened to our Canadian identity since Paul Henderson scored the winning goal against the Red Army.

CANADIAN CHECKLIST: Weird sex | Potent woman | Passive man | Hole in the soul | Outsider stance | Fractured narrative | Magic realism

Last Night (1999)

Directed by Don McKellar
Starring Sandra Oh, David Cronenberg, Sarah Polley, Don McKellar, Callum Keith Rennie, Geneviève Bujold
Running time: 96 minutes

🍁 🍁 🍁

While America was busy blowing its star-studded prosthestic wad at asteroids in movies like *Deep Impact* and *Armageddon* at the turn of the millennium, Canadian director/writer/actor Don McKellar was busy thinking about the human drama that might accompany the end of the world.

Beginning his film at 6 p.m. on the last night on Earth, McKellar begins his human tapestry with Sandra (Oh), who goes "shopping" at a looted-out grocery store to find something special for her last meal with her husband, Duncan (Cronenberg), an uptight executive for the gas company. She finds food, but her car is trashed by roaming thugs, leaving her marooned on the wrong side of town. As all this unfolds outside his window, Patrick (McKellar) lies on the floor getting ready for his last family dinner at his parents suburban home. When he arrives, denial hangs in the air like so much cooking grease as his mother wears her Christmas outfit and hands her grown children stockings full of old toys. Even the house seems to be in denial: it's furnished in immaculate late sixties, early seventies decor. When Patrick gets home, he runs into Sandra, and the two begin a brief but incredibly profound friendship.

Meanwhile, Patrick's friend Craig (Rennie) is out to satisfy his remaining moments of sexual curiosity with several bedmates — including his elementary school French teacher (Bujold).

At first, all the characters are separated from one another by fear and paranoia, but as the stories dovetail, we realize each one of them is connected to the other: we are all one giant "fraternity of man." What makes McKellar's film truly magical is the way he slips beneath the characters' calloused skin and finds a warm, human heart aching for companionship. As a result, McKellar's apocalypse has far more meaning, and far more emotional impact, than any special-effects-laden effort to emerge from Hollywood. There is nothing fancy here, just a beautiful affirmation of simple truths: we never get enough time, but love makes the short time we have worth the pain of living.

CANADIAN CHECKLIST: Alienation | Survivor guilt | Dysfunctional romance | Weird sex | Oppressive landscape | An inability to express emotion

The Law of Enclosures (2000)

Directed by John Greyson
Starring Brendan Fletcher, Sarah Polley, Shirley Douglas, Diane Ladd, Sean McCann
Running time: 111 minutes
🍁 🍁 🍁

One of John Greyson's first attempts at — forgive me — straight narrative fiction, this adaptation of American writer Dale Peck's novel deals with the first and last day of a couple's relationship.

Brendan Fletcher and Sarah Polley play Hank and Bea, two young outsiders who form a deep bond when it looks as though Hank will die from a tennis-ball-size tumour at the base of his skull. Bea offers herself to the angst-ridden Hank so that he won't have to die chaste, but when the operation to cure his cancer is a success, the two young lovers are given a chance at lifelong happiness. But without looming tragedy, they lose focus — and drift apart.

Forty years later, we meet up with Hank and Bea as mature adults. Their flowing passion has turned into a stagnant pond of marital routine littered by senseless squabbles and petty disagreements. Still, they have one last chance to reignite the waning flame. But first, they must rediscover the people they once were. Only then can they retrace their steps and rediscover the place they once shared as young lovers.

A meditative story told with minimalist precision, *The Law of Enclosures* is a film that shows the tragedy of lost love by showing us the gaping hole it leaves behind.

CANADIAN CHECKLIST: Outsider bonding | Dysfunctional relationship | Landscape defines character (contrast between natural and urban worlds) | Missing love | Non-linear narrative | Death, disease

Léolo (1992)

Directed by Jean-Claude Lauzon
Starring Gilbert Sicotte, Maxime Collin, Ginette Reno, Yves Montmarquette, Julien Guiomar, Pierre Bourgault, Giuditta Del Vecchio, André Lachapelle, Denys Arcand, Lorne Brass
Running time: 115 minutes
🍁 🍁 🍁 🍁 🍁

One of the first Québécois films to embrace magic realism and the emancipation of the imagination, *Léolo* is nothing less than a revelation in the Canadian film tradition. The story of young Leo Lauzon, a kid who refuses to accept the working-class, Montreal reality in which he finds himself, *Léolo* opens the door to fantasy in the first frame.

"Everybody thinks I am French-Canadian, but that is not what I am," begins the narrator (Sicotte), leading us into this warped first-person universe. Leo would prefer to believe he is really the son of an Italian tomato-packer who masturbated into a shipment of Romas bound for North America and was conceived when his mother tripped into a fruit stand. For this reason, he insists on being called Léolo Lauzon. It gives him some distance from what he describes as "the black hole of his family," which, we discover, is prone to a certain type of mental illness that locks its victims into an internal world.

As the film progresses, we watch Leo get closer and closer to that world as the forces of adulthood become stronger and stronger. Leo's only form of release is writing, which he does compulsively — hoping, perhaps, that the "word-tamer" (a schoolteacher played by former politician and Lauzon's own mentor, Pierre Bourgault) will recognize Leo's self-alienation and rescue him with understanding. But ever since Nell Shipman left the Canadian tundra, rescue has not been a real Canadian option. Reality simply gets uglier every second, as we watch Léolo's friends rape a cat and his big, muscle-bound brother Fernand be humiliated at the hands of a cruel English punk. No wonder Leo wants to escape this real world, where not even love can overcome all the ambient pain.

An amazing feat of visual style that moves fearlessly through time and space without losing us along the way, *Léolo* is a masterpiece of movie-making and a milestone achievement in its ability to show us the internalized landscape of the Canadian condition.

CANADIAN CHECKLIST: Leo defines himself in negative terms: "Because I dream, I am not." | Missing "father" imagery | Internal narrative | Missing babies | Weird sex | Family dysfunction

Lilies (1996)

Directed by John Greyson
Starring Marcel Sabourin, Jason Cadieux, Aubert Pallascio, Matthew Ferguson, Danny Gilmore, Brent Carver, Gary Farmer
Running time: 96 minutes
❦ ❦ ❦ ❦

Based on Quebec playwright Michel Marc Bouchard's play, *Les Fleurettes*, *Lilies* revolves around a homosexual love affair and its tragic consequences. Set in the midst of the Duplessis era, 1952, an aging Bishop makes his way to a penitentiary in rural Quebec to administer what he believes to be last rites to a dying prisoner. When he enters the confessional, he recognizes the prisoner as a childhood friend and is promptly locked in. The confession was a trap. Now the Bishop (Sabourin) is forced to watch a reenactment of the entire homoerotic tragedy played out by the inmates. For this reason, Greyson's entire cast of characters — male and female — is played by men, lending the film an entirely surreal edge that is, in turn, exaggerated through intercutting beautiful outdoor tableaux with the oppressive prison interior.

The whole point of the exercise is to exact a confession from the Bishop (Sabourin) so that Simon, the prisoner, can find a sense of peace with the past.

Full of nifty visual tricks and some two-tissue performances from the talented cast, *Lilies* is a seamless mesh of Greek tragedy, Catholic baggage and the colonial experience — one memorable motion picture.

CANADIAN CHECKLIST: Internalized twin imagery (the two male lovers) | Colonial baggage | Missing "father" figure | Religious guilt | Outsider stance

Live Bait (1995)

Directed by Bruce Sweeney
Starring Tom Scholte, Kevin McNulty, Babz Chula, David Lovgren, Micki Maunsell, Jay Brazeau
Running time: 84 minutes
♣♣♣ ½

Trevor MacIntosh (Scholte) is a nice guy who just can't seem to have a good time having sex. There's something missing, and as he scans his mother's face looking for understanding, his longing only grows stronger. Enter Charlotte Peacock, a wacky iron-working sculptress played by Vancouver's grand dame of the stage, Micki Maunsell. Looking like a cross between Louise Nevelson and little orphan Annie, Charlotte seems to understand exactly what uptight Trevor needs. "We need to open it up a little," she says, staring into an egg of steel with her blowtorch. With the same artistic touch, Charlotte takes the jaws of life to Trevor's clenched sphincter — opening a hole big enough for Trevor's Oedipal baggage to come tumbling out.

Part *Harold and Maude*, part *Eraserhead*, Sweeney's black-and-white film has a timeless, surreal quality that makes it look as though the entire drama were unravelling in heaven — a heaven where God is a woman. There's a quiet charm to *Live Bait* that makes this funny and absurd film impossible to resist.

CANADIAN CHECKLIST: Potent women | Passive men | Weird sex | Oedipal themes | Outsider stance

Love Come Down (2000)

Directed by Clement Virgo
Starring Larenz Tate, Martin Cummings, Deborah Cox
Running time: 99 minutes
♣♣♣ ½

Replete with all the familiar Canadian themes — familial dysfunction, addiction, paternal abandonment and self-loathing — *Love Come Down* may seem like yet another trip down the tangled garden path, but it's not. This fourth feature from Jamaican-born, Toronto-based director Clement Virgo is actually a comedy.

A story of two brothers who have packed the violent death of one parent into their as-yet unchecked emotional baggage, the film stars American Larenz Tate as Neville, a substance-abusing goof who dreams of doing stand-up. Vancouver's Martin Cummins (who has his own substance-addiction story in *We All Fall Down*) stars as Matthew, a pro boxer who appears to love getting the crap punched out of him. When the movie begins, both brothers are stuck in their respective ruts, but when Neville finds himself attracted to Nico, a beautiful lounge singer played by pop diva Deborah Cox, forces of nature eventually derail routine. As Virgo begins unravelling the source of their pain through flashbacks and voice-overs, we begin to identify with these two misfits — because even though their traumatic life events are unique, they are universal screw-ups and we recognize them.

As the film progresses, Virgo begins taking us back in time to the crucial life event that holds both brothers down: the death of their father, and the guilt that came with it. They need to forgive each other, and forgive themselves. Where guilt has typically proven to be something of a problem in Canadian film, Virgo finds the ultimate solution: faith, and in this case, faith in God. Not to be confused with any formaly "institutional" concept of the Almighty, this god takes the shape of a former junkie nun named Sister Sarah, played by Sarah Polley. "God loves you," she tells the struggling Neville. "God loves you ... "

They may be three little words, but they are three little words that — to the best of my recollection — I've never heard before in the entire history of Canadian film.

CANADIAN CHECKLIST: Missing father | Confused parental identity | Pluralism | Outsider stance

Lulu (1996)
Directed by Srinivas Krishna
Starring Kim Lieu, Michael Rhoades
Running time: 96 minutes
❧ ❧ ❧

One of the darkest immigrant stories to hit the fan of the Canadian experience, *Lulu* tells the story of a mail-order bride from Vietnam (played by the untrained actress Kim Lieu) who finds nothing but pain, alienation and heartache in downtown Toronto. A sort of *Goin' Down the Road* from a pluralist perspective, *Lulu* quietly shows us how expectations for a better life collapse in the face of the cold urban reality.

There are many disappointments in Lulu's life — such as losing the man she really loved, dealing with her bitter parents and discovering her new Canadian husband is impotent — but she hides them all behind a flawless mask that betrays no emotional connection to the world whatsoever. The only moment of real emotion comes via a documentary filmmaker's lens as he records Lulu's story.

Lulu pulls away from the elements of fantasy that Krishna explored in *Masala*, and steers toward gritty, quiet Canadian realism where dramatic strength is often communicated with perfect silence. With little more than stone-faced glances into the lens, Lieu communicates a sense of internal female rage that she cannot express, lest she bruise the fragile male egos that surround her.

A portrait of Asian restraint in the face of the alienating Canadian wilderness, *Lulu* is a memorable exploration of the immigrant experience in the Great White North.

CANADIAN CHECKLIST: Pluralist perspective | Outsider stance | Potent women | Impotent men | Alienating landscape (watch for landscape painting in the hospital) | Fragmented narrative | Dramatic moments come through silence, not the spoken word | Dislocation

Maelström (2000)

Directed by Denis Villeneuve
Starring Marie Josée Croze, Jean-Nicolas Verreault, Stephanie Morgenstern, Pierre Lebeau
Running time: 88 minutes
❦❦❦❦

Laced with love, guilt and a desire for self-destruction, *Maelström* fits right in to the Canadian tradition of near-fatalistic realism — until you realize the narrator is an ancient fish about to have its head cut off by some large, sweaty, hairy Norseman. After that, you never really know what to expect from Denis Villeneuve's film, which centres on a few crucial days in the life of Bibiane (Croze), a beautiful young entrepreneur who seems to have it all — at least on the outside.

The film opens with Bibiane having an abortion. Awash in guilt from the procedure, Bibi tries to numb herself with drugs and alcohol, but only succeeds in making things worse when she gets behind the wheel of her black BMW and hits a man while driving home drunk from a party. As the guilt crests in Bibi's mind, Villeneuve's camera moves become almost claustrophobic, but thanks to the fish's presence (which Villeneuve uses as a type of moral chorus echoing the surface action), the film never feels oppressive because just as it ties us down to reality by showing us the nasty consequences of irresponsibility, it pushes us to free our minds with fish-inspired fantasy.

In this way, the film knocks us off our moral pedestal in the first fifteen minutes because even though Bibiane has done terrible things, Marie Josée Croze's interpretation of the part is so sympathetic that it's hard to write her off as unworthy of forgiveness. Not even the son of the man she hit with her car can find it in his heart to loathe her.

As a result, everything here is disemboweled, messy and undeniably non-linear. Fortunately, this was Villeneuve's intent. After all, the narrator in *Maelström* is an ancient fish lured up from the safe dark depths by a Norweigian fisherman who infused the waters with the music of Grieg.

An altogether original tale, replete with humour, fantasy and palpable emotion, *Maelström* succeeds where many other Canadian films have failed, and it ushers in a new generation of innovative auteurs.

CANADIAN CHECKLIST: Moral ambiguity | Abortion | Missing people (dead father) | Orphans | Potent women | Family dysfunction | Pluralist perspective | Language barrier | Water/flood imagery

Map of the Human Heart (1993)

Directed by Vincent Ward

Starring Anne Parillaud, Jason Scott Lee, Annie Gallipeau, Robert Joamie

Running time: 109 minutes

❦❦❦❦

The story of two Métis children who meet and fall in love as children, *Map of the Human Heart* deals with two lost people on a personal quest for identity. Opening in the Arctic in the 1930s, Avik (Robert Joamie/ Jason Scott Lee) is a young Inuit boy who stumbles into a goggled man from another place: a mapmaker and aviator (Patrick Bergin). When the cartographer realizes Avik has tuberculosis, he brings him back to Montreal, where he first meets Albertine, another orphan who teaches him the ways of the white world. The two form a deep bond, which director Ward shows us through Avik's connection to Albertine's chest X-ray, which he keeps with him throughout the film.

Separated after their stay in the sanitorium, the two miraculously meet again during the Second World War. Avik is a pilot and Albertine (Annie Gallipeau/Anne Parillaud) works at bomber command examining surveillance films.

Packed with stunning cinematography, some incredibly original love scenes and moving performances from the stellar cast, *Map of the Human Heart* proves there is a warm, loving heart beneath our cool exteriors — it just took a New Zealand director to show it to us on the surface. Canadian filmmakers generally hide it between layers of narrative plot and cinematic device.

CANADIAN CHECKLIST: Landscape shots | Indigenous central characters | Symbolic use of the photographic image | Orphans | Doomed romantic love

Margaret's Museum (1995)

Directed by Mort Ransen

Starring Helena Bonham Carter, Clive Russell, Kate Nelligan, Kenneth Welsh

Running time: 114 minutes

❦❦❦ ½

When a movie contains an image of a duplex that half-disappears into a sinkhole, it kinda screams "Canadian!" — and that's exactly what *Margaret's Museum* is: a truly Canadian experience about coal mining in Cape Breton. Can you say "depressing times two"?

The story of Margaret (Helena Bonham Carter, who picked up a Genie for her part), a potty-mouthed wingnut who watches over the town of Glace Bay from her very own private little happy place, the film does a good job distracting us — but we all know something bad is going to happen. Mining towns are built on the buried corpses of miners — it's part of the landscape when you make a living underground.

Ransen introduces death early, but he doesn't push it in our faces until the final frames. In the meantime, we watch the loner Margaret fall in love with a strapping coal worker (Clive Russell) while the rest of her wacky family goes about its daily craziness.

After seeing Lars Von Trier's *Breaking the Waves* — which deals with similar themes, characters and images — *Margaret's Museum* looks a tad unsophisticated, but then again, that's the crux of its charm.

CANADIAN CHECKLIST: Internal demons | Mind/body split | House split | Outsider stance | Landscape defines character | Family dysfunction | Death, disease | Missing people

Marine Life (2000)
Directed by Anne Wheeler
Starring Cybill Shepherd, Peter Outerbridge, Alexandra Purvis, Gabrielle Miller
❦❦ ½

Based on the work of Vancouver writer Linda Svendsen and brought to the screen by the West's own Anne Wheeler, *Marine Life* has an undeniable "wet coast" feel as it navigates the life of an aging lounge singer and her dysfunctional family.

Like many female characters cast in the same mould as Mary Tyler Moore, Ally McBeal and Bridget Jones, June (Shepherd) feels she has failed as a woman. She has not lived up to her socially ascribed gender roles, and so she moves from one crisis to the next learning bit by bit, fit by fit. She does a good job trying to hold things together, but while her youngest daughter craves quality time with her disinterested ex, her eldest seeks refuge from an abusive partner. Meanwhile, her married son is a screw-up and her current boyfriend, the marine biologist Robert (Peter Outerbridge), is feeling needy — which causes even more tension in the already overburdened family unit.

The look and feel of waterlogged Vancouver adds to the emotional undertone of stagnation, but as many people remarked when the film first screened at the 2000 Toronto International Film Festival, the whole thing feels more like a TV show than a feature film. Whether or not this is a function of Svendsen's story or Wheeler's direction is hard to say, but there's no doubt the film avoids steep dramatic arcs in favour of shallow, somewhat banal, and perfectly everyday events. Because TV shows deal with the same character week in and week out, they can get away with minimal plot development and marginal character transformation, but we generally expect more from a feature film. We expect life or death decisions and enlightenment — none of which is present in the muted tones of *Marine Life*. A benevolent take would be to see this as a subversion of Hollywood expectation and a return to a brand of storytelling on a human scale. Personally, I took the benevolent view because I enjoyed the experience of watching the film, even though at times it felt a lot like watching an aquarium: slow, but strangely soothing.

CANADIAN CHECKLIST: Stronger females than males | Dysfunctional family | Human drama on a human scale | Miscommunication | Feelings of personal failure based on gender role expectations | Stagnation

Mob Story (1990)

Directed by Gabriel Markiw, Jancarlo Markiw
Starring Margot Kidder, Robert Morelli, Brian Paul, Kate Vernon, John Vernon, Al Waxman
Running time: 98 minutes
❧ ❧

It's not a great movie, but I caught this one after seeing *Ishtar* — and it was downright brilliant by comparison. The story of a mob boss forced to flee the United States after a rival clan tries to rub him out, *Mob Story* unfolds against the frozen backdrop of Winnipeg, where the old Don spent his salad days.

The weather accounts for a lot of the humour in this stupid little gem: every time someone opens a door to the outside, a cloud of dry ice fills the screen. No, it's not much to hang a movie on, but there are other high points, such as Kidder dancing on tables, snappy dialogue and powerful women who make the men with guns look small and stupid.

A good example of what happens to American genre in Canadian hands, *Mob Story* is no classic — it's not even a must-see, but it is a decent rental that shows us where we live.

CANADIAN CHECKLIST: Potent women | Passive men | Landscape/cold weather as running gag | Subversion of American genre

La Moitié guache du frigo (2000)

Directed by Philippe Falardeau
Starring Paul Ahmarani, Stéphane Demers, Geneviève Néron
Running time: 90 minutes
❧ ❧ ❧ ½

Christophe is a young engineer who finds himself unemployed and on the job hunt. Hoping to unearth the core of the young professional's experience, Christophe's theatre-savvy roommate Stéphane decides to videotape his buddy's descent into personal hell. Following Christophe from one interview to the next with a camcorder, Stéphane becomes the objective voyeur — poking his lens into Christophe's inner space.

Inspired by the pathos of his subject matter, Stéphane gets funding for his project and the whole film assumes almost Frankensteinian proportions with an increasingly parasitic relationship to the drained host, Christophe. No longer a buddy in need, Christophe has become a rich source of exploitation. Ironically, the more Stéphane takes advantage of his ill-fated friend, the more he assumes a self-righteous pose about the whole deal, believing his film will somehow emancipate the masses by exposing corporate corruption.

After months of fruitless effort, Christophe is still unemployed and now completely demoralized. Sucked dry by his former pal, he heads off in search of a brighter tomorrow in Vancouver.

CANADIAN CHECKLIST: Self-aware camera | Subversion of documentary form | Steeped in "realism" | Outsider stance | Linguistic tensions | Passive hero

Mon Oncle Antoine (1971)

Directed by Claude Jutra

Starring Jean Duceppe, Jacques Gagnon, Lyne Champagne, Olivette Thibault, Claude Jutra, Hélène Loiselle, Lionel Villeneuve, Monique Mercure

Running time: 104 minutes

✤✤✤✤✤

Still referred to as one of the greatest Canadian films of all time, *Mon Oncle Antoine* marked the beginning of narrative feature film in Canada (right alongside Don Shebib's *Goin' Down the Road*) and set up much of the cinematic grammar we use in this country to this day with its use of natural light, blue hues, lack of narrative artifice and abundance of snow-covered landscapes.

The story focuses on Benoit (Gagnon), a kid living with his Uncle Antoine and Aunt Cecile, who run the general store in Black Lake, Quebec. On the brink of adulthood, Benoit embodies a manly sense of duty with a boyish flare for mischief — and Jutra revels in the ambiguity. He shows us Benoit playing pranks on his foster sister, Carmen, one minute and stumbling into sexual awareness the next.

As Benoit and the family get the store ready for Christmas, Uncle Antoine (Duceppe) is summoned to a house a few miles away, where a young man close to Benoit's age dies from a fever. Antoine obliges and trudges through a blizzard to pick up the body with Benoit in tow. They unceremoniously place the dead teen in a plain casket, then head back out into the cold night. Antoine, tired and depressed, gets sloshed. The sleigh bounces out of control and the coffin falls off the buggy, leaving Benoit to pick up the body — which has now tumbled out of the coffin. Absurd, grotesque and yet oddly funny, the scene shows Benoit wrestling with the corpse in the cold, empty night as Antoine, the incarnation of the old generation, numbs himself to the harsh reality around him. The image is almost a definitive one in Canadian film as it incorporates the landscape, death, a mirror image of self, and an undeniable sense of loneliness and outsiderism into one single frame. This melancholic progression into awareness is an intrinsic element in almost all Canadian cinema that followed.

As Ferdinand, the store clerk, Jutra takes part in his own drama and assigns himself the most ambiguous role of the film. Ferdinand seems to be the sole responsible figure. We see him balancing the books and playing first lieutenant to Aunt Cecile (Olivette Thibault) in the opening sequence, but Ferdinand is not to be trusted. He's sleeping with Antoine's wife under his roof, challenging the insititution of marriage as well as the Church. As a result, Ferdinand seems to stand apart from the rest of the townsfolk. He is an outsider who watches, semi-detached, as the life and death events of the town unfold around him. This could be seen as a commentary on the act of making a motion picture: he is central to the drama, but somehow always behind the scenes — shaping events emotionally, while letting fate and free will deal with the rest. Because the movie is built on a human scale, even the most depressing moments are comforting as they outline the geography of the human condition without false drama or misguided attempts at larger meaning.

CANADIAN CHECKLIST: Landscape covered in snow | Coming of age | Subversion of institutions | English/French relationship unbalanced and festering | Ironic sense of humour | Semi-detached, outsider perspective

Les muses orphelines AKA The Orphan Muses (2000)

Directed by Robert Favreau

Starring Marina Orsini, Céline Bonnier, Fanny Mallette, Stéphane Demers, Louise Portal, Patrick Labbé

Running time: 107 minutes

❋ ❋ ❋ ❋

Based on the play by Michel Marc Bouchard (who also wrote *Lilies*), *Les muses orphelines* is a dark story with a surprisingly upbeat finish that focuses on the Tanguay family, who live in a pimple of a small town on the backside of Quebec called St. Ludger-de-Milot. "Orphaned" by their mother and father at a young age, the Tanguay kids carry a lot of heavy bags that weigh them down to the point of near-complete mental, physical and spiritual inertia.

Spinning around the nucleus of her family like an electron is the youngest, Isabelle (Mallette), who works at the local mill opening and closing the barricade. Her older sister, and de facto mother figure, is Catherine (Orsini), who has a job teaching at the local elementary school.

When the film opens, we see Isabelle and Catherine fighting with each other in the car, which has the giant bust of a firefighter strapped to the roof. When the car veers off the road, we cut to the city, where their brother Luc (Demers) is having extremely bad sex with someone as the phone rings. Hearing about the accident, Luc steals a taxi and heads back home to St. Ludger-de-Milot — a place he swore he'd never set foot in after the cops ran him out of town for being a big shit disturber. He thought there was a tragedy, but when he learns it was all just a ruse cooked up by Isabelle, he decides to hang out for a bit and get reaquainted with his two sisters. Little does he know that Isabelle has more plans for Luc and her siblings. She spreads a rumour that Luc is dead, which brings the last sibling, Martine (Bonnier), home to the old house.

Once all four "orphans" are reunited, we learn that their mother isn't really dead — as Isabelle had been told all these years. She actually ran off with a swarthy Spanish dude and left her kids in the care of their father — who disappeared into a raging forest fire and never returned.

Shot against the vast landscape of northern Quebec, where aluminum plants and lumber mills are the sole industries, *Les muses orphelines* brings a rich visual sense to Bouchard's play in this winning effort by Favreau.

CANADIAN CHECKLIST: Outsider stance | Language barrier | Imagination as escape | Landscape defines character | Missing people (father, mother) | Potent women | Passive men | Family dysfunction | Nonlinear narrative

My American Cousin (1985)

Directed by Sandy Wilson
Starring Margaret Langrick, John Wildman, Richard Donat, Jane Mortifee
Runnng time: 95 minutes
❦❦❦❦

Sandy Wilcox (Langrick) is your average pre-teen growing up in British Columbia's Okanagan Valley in the late fifties — where the fruit is juicy but pubescent romance is a tad stale. Everything changes in Sandy's dull little life, however, when Butch (Wildman) — her handsome American cousin — comes to town in his hot red convertible. The girls are all atwitter at Butch's rugged physique and matinee idol good looks, and for one magic summer, Sandy feels like she's at the centre of the world. But all fantasies must end with a real thud, and Wilson's film captures the sense of lost innocence with all the sweet, melancholic longing that goes along with young love.

Based on Wilson's own coming-of-age experience, the film resonates with simple human truths — things we forget about in adulthood after the novelty of sex and kissing wears off like so much cheap make-up.

Perfectly detailed and rippling with subtle thespian muscle, *My American Cousin* captures a time and a place with astounding success, and takes us back to a time when everything American was considered superior on principle.

CANADIAN CHECKLIST: Canadian landscape | Worship of all things made in United States | Outsider stance | The romantic ideal fails to materialize

My Father's Angel (2000)

Directed by Davor Marjanovic
Starring Tony Nardi, Timothy Webber, Tygh Runyan, Brendan Fletcher, Asja Pavlovic
Running time: 86 minutes
❦❦❦ ½

The story of a Muslim family who escape Sarajevo and ethnic cleansing with their lives and little else, *My Father's Angel* takes place against the scenic backdrop of Vancouver — but focuses on the mental baggage this family of refugees can't leave behind.

The mother, Sayma, is catatonic, the result of being locked up and raped for six months by Bosnian Serbs. The father, Ahmed (Tony Nardi), prays on the bathroom floor every morning for an angel to end his wife's suffering. And Tygh Runyan plays son Enes, an old cynic in a teenager's body who can't adjust to life on the somnabulent West Coast.

They have their fair share of troubles, but life only gets more surreal when Ahmed is hit by a car driven by a famous Serb soccer star, which he deliriously mistakes for the angel of his prayers. When he comes to, he recognizes Djordje (Webber) and his brain is immediately transported back to war-torn Sarajevo. Ahmed calls Djordje the devil and runs away, hoping to erase the memories of his past. Meanwhile Djordje begins to process the hate crimes that took place back home. His wife hides every newspaper, but he's still determined to find out if his Serbian friends and relatives could have carried out such crimes against humanity.

While certain scenes might feel melodramatic out of context, I bought every single second of this movie, which was more than a testament to Marjanovic's success, I found it was ample proof that immigrant stories resonate deep in the Canadian psyche.

CANADIAN CHECKLIST: Outsider stance | Dislocation | Potent women | Passive men | Language barrier | Internal demons | Family dysfunction | Pluralist perspective | Survivor guilt | Natural landscape contrasts horrific internal landscape

New Waterford Girl (2000)
Directed by Allan Moyle
Starring Liane Balaban, Tara Spencer-Nairn, Cathy Moriarty, Mary Walsh, Nicholas Campbell
Running time: 97 minutes
❦ ❦ ❦ ❦

Mooney Pottie (Balaban) is a 15-year-old Cape Breton teen who sits in the bathtub and dreams of becoming an artist. But stuck in a dead-end mining town without money, Mooney's chances of leaving New Waterford are slim — until a mother and daughter from cosmopolitan New York move in next door.

Seeing her small town for the first time through someone else's eyes, Mooney suddenly realizes that her best chance for escape lies in getting pregnant, as all the deflowered young girls are transported out by train to the big city where they can mingle with the other sinners.

As Mooney puts her plan into action, her new best friend, Lou (Spencer-Nairn), begins avenging all the "bad girls" in town by punching out the countless no-good New Waterford Lotharios. While the plot synopsis makes this Tricia Fish screenplay sound like yet another weepy Canadian drama from the frontier, this is one of the first Canadian movies to ditch earnestness in the name of fun.

CANADIAN CHECKLIST: Empty and oppressive landscape | Abortion/empty attempt at creation | Opens with a marriage, and a funeral | Potent women | Passive men | Hole in the soul | Hockey | Frequent use of "eh?" | Soundtrack features all-Canadian tracks from the likes of April Wine and The Stampeders.

Night Zoo AKA Un Zoo la nuit (1987)

Directed by Jean-Claude Lauzon
Starring Gilles Maheu, Roger Lebel, Anna-Maria Giannotti, Corrado Mastropasqua, Lorne Brass, Jerry Snell
Running time: 115 minutes

🍁🍁🍁

A complete subversion of the Hollywood action flick, Jean-Claude Lauzon's first feature film borrows bits and pieces from thriller cliché — such as high-octane action sequences, guns, dirty cops and buddy bonding — but it pulverizes them into something completely different, and unmistakably hellish.

Lauzon's focus on the ugly side makes sense considering the story revolves around an ex-con who tries to reintegrate into society. What's harder to grasp is the idea that outside prison is often just as nasty as it is inside. Inside — outside. Internal demons — external demons — it's all familiar territory for the Canadian film buff. For Marcel (Maheu), however, it's all about his love-hate relationship with his aging and terminally ill father.

Having just been released from the big house, Marcel returns to his life outside in the hopes of rekindling his romance with Julie (Giannotti) while skirting the malevolent attention of a corrupt and sexually abusive cop — played by everyone's favourite Anglo asshole, Lorne Brass (who reappears in a similar role in Lauzon's second, and stellar effort, *Léolo*.)

As Marcel comes to grips with his criminal baggage, he also comes to embrace his father. As a symbol of their newfound bond, the two talk about trying to shoot a moose, but they are in the city. Out of touch with the landscape, these two broken men break into a zoo and shoot an elephant in the final frames — which makes for a nice bookend of the opening shot, which shows Marcel getting raped behind bars.

In effect, Lauzon spins two contradictory narrative lines — the thriller and the family drama — and juxtaposes them to maximize the sense of dislocation. It's a tough mix to pull off, but Lauzon finds just enough humour in the never-ending anguish to keep the complex weave of longing and love from unravelling.

CANADIAN CHECKLIST: Identity crises | Internalized demons | Weird/ violent sex | Natural landscape violated | Dysfunctional family | Silence instead of communication

Nô (1998)

Directed by Robert Lepage
Starring Anne-Marie Cadieux, Alexis Martin, Marie Brassard, Richard Fréchette, Marie Gignac, Eric Bernier
Running time: 85 minutes
❦❦❦❦

As one of the first overtly political films to opt for comedy instead of morose tragedy, *Nô* is nothing short of a revelation in the Canadian film tradition. Set against the backdrop of the 1970 October Crisis (when then-Prime Minister Pierre Trudeau passed the War Measures Act and forever turned the Quebec sovereignist cause against him), *Nô* is loosely based on Lepage's play, *Seven Streams of the River Ota*, consisting of a series of stories that deal with politics, language, identity, sex and relationships.

The film opens in Osaka at the World's Fair, where a troupe of Québécois actors are putting on a production of an empty Feydeau farce as part of the Canadian delegation. Our heroine, Sophie (Cadieux), learns she is pregnant, but can't quite figure out what to do. She tries to tell her boyfriend, Michel, back home, but he seems so distant that she can't bring herself to tell him. This is just as well, because five seconds later, two FLQ buddies barge in and demand to use his apartment as a safe house while they prepare a bomb and a manifesto.

Meanwhile, back in Japan, Sophie and a blind Japanese-French translator debate the correct course of action. Should she have an abortion, or not? She is full of indecision, and this yes-no teeter-totter is, of course, a symbol of the yes-no battle going on back home in Quebec. Should Quebec separate, or not? Should Sophie and Michel stay together, even though both are clearly different people with distinct identities?

Because Lepage is a visual thinker first, the subtext never overshadows the bright, flat surfaces — and that seems to be his whole point: we process what's on the surface before we even attempt to find the next layer. For this reason, Lepage includes references to the rigid formalism of Japanese Noh theatre (where everything is predestimed according to centuries-old traditions), characters like a two-timing Canadian ambassador and his uptight snob of a wife, an argument between Michel and his buddies on the importance of using correct grammar in their manifesto and the soothsayer blind translator, who can no longer see the surface of anything. Lepage even separates his narrative into two distinct surfaces: the "happy and unified Canada" Osaka scenes are shot on colour stock, while the Quebec "news" elements are shot in black-and-white.

A comedy with some very dark undertones, *Nô* ends up blurring the edges that separate comedy from tragedy, English from French, colour from black-and-white and personal identity from cultural massif. The end result is highly ambiguous, but not without hope — sort of like the future of the nation itself.

CANADIAN CHECKLIST: Dislocation | Fragmented narrative; several stories unfolding at once | Fusion of dreams and reality | Dysfunctional relationship | Lost children | Passive males and potent females | Pluralism

Les Noces de papier (1989)

Directed by Michel Brault
Starring Geneviève Bujold, Manuel Aranguiz, Dorothée Berryman, Monique Lepage,
Jorge Fajardo, Gilbert Sicotte
Running time: 95 minutes
🍁🍁🍁 ½

The opening shot is a maple tree in the middle of autumnal transition, and it's a good visual metaphor for the rest of the film (originally made for TV), which deals with "immigration and naturalization." Claire Rocheleau (Bujold) is a college professor on the cusp of turning 40. Emotionally hard and analytical, Claire begins to long for a real relationship instead of playing mistress to the married man she loves, but without the social tools to go out and find someone, Claire has resigned herself to the possibility she may become a bitter academic spinster.

At least that's what she thought before her sister set her up with a political refugee who's about to be deported. Pablo Torres (Aranguiz) is a strong, silent type who survived torture and death squads to come to Canada in the hopes of starting a new life, but the one-time journalist is now little more than a faceless dishwasher.

With little reason to say no, Claire eventually caves in and goes along with her sister's plan to save Pablo by marrying him — even though immigration authorities see Pablo's case as something of a pet project. Over the space of a weekend, Pablo and Claire are forced to learn everything they can about each other so they can pass the interview test, get married, and then promptly go their own ways. As the hours bring them closer together, the two loners come to realize they have feelings for each other — but neither one has the courage to say it out loud.

Rendered with detail and finesse by veteran director and cinematographer Michel Brault (who shot *Mon Oncle Antoine*), *Les Noces de papier* reaffirms the idea that pluralism — as embodied in the spiritual or physical embrace of another culture — is one way of dealing with internalized stress as it introduces a third vector into the Canadian tug-of-war.

CANADIAN CHECKLIST: Outsider stance | Pluralism | Natural light | Rooted in realism | Language | Ambiguous ending | Missing partner; search for other half | Identity issues

Parsley Days (2000)

Directed by Andrea Dorfman
Starring Megan Dunlop, Mike LeBlanc, Marla MacLean, Kenneth Harrington, Marcia Connolly
Running time: 76 minutes
🍁🍁🍁 ½

While most movies aimed at young adults would make you believe sex is nothing less than a breathless and sweaty moment of rousing spiritual epiphany, *Parsley Days* deals with the messy reality of copulation and the flipside to romantic love.

Kate (Dunlop) is a bike mechanic who has been with Ollie (LeBlanc), the condom king and birth control counsellor, for five years. To all their friends — both gay and straight — they are the ideal couple, but something is rotten in the state of Hallmark romance. Kate is restless and confused, but she's having a hard time expressing her feelings to Ollie because she's feeling guilty. Kate is pregnant, and she's not sure if the baby is Ollie's or that of her "slow student." Not that it really matters. Kate doesn't want to keep the baby, which introduces a whole new set of complications.

It may sound like the stuff of a mascara-smudging *Junior Miss* feature, but in the hands of Halifax director Dorfman, *Parsley Days* has more humour than heartbreak. The story chugs along with all the energy of a first-time feature, but Dorfman has the emotional finesse of an accomplished veteran, allowing her characters to remain accessible, honest and "authentic" for the duration.

CANADIAN CHECKLIST: Canoes | Dysfunctional romance | Abortion | Potent women | Passive men | Ironic sense of humour | Fragmented point of view | Outsider stance

Perfectly Normal (1991)
Directed by Yves Simoneau
Starring Robbie Coltrane, Michael Riley, Kenneth Walsh, Deborah Duchene
Running time: 104 minutes
🍁🍁🍁 ½

A microcosmic study of the Canadian psyche itself, this movie from Yves Simoneau pivots on the contradictory relationship between Renzo Parachi (Riley), a workaday beer bottle inspector, and Alonzo (Coltrane), a drifter with big dreams.

When the two meet in a cab one night after Renzo's mother has passed away, the film clicks into gear as Simoneau sets up the two men on opposite ends of the emotional spectrum, then introduces a dramatic catalyst: Renzo's parents have left him a small fortune in the sleeves of their record collection.

The discovery makes Alonzo dream bigger than ever. He concocts a scheme to open a restaurant with an operatic theme called La Traviatta. Renzo, however, would like nothing more than to build a small, humble house on the outskirts of town.

Simoneau never seems to tip his own hat in either direction, roaming around on the outside of the frame, depicting both men as somehow less than perfect — and clearly less than whole. This gives the viewer a chance to see both characters from a distance, where we can make decisions for ourselves about the "correct" course of action. The detachment gives the movie an almost melancholic tone, as though it were telling its jokes from the back of an empty room. This melancholy is enhanced by the cool, blue shots of Toronto in winter and the gritty, matte look of the mise en scene.

At one point, after Alonzo gets cold feet about his restaurant idea, Renzo convinces his buddy to keep going because "everyone needs a Traviatta" — everyone needs to dream and fantasize, especially people as grounded as Renzo.

CANADIAN CHECKLIST: Hockey | Beer | Snow | Outsider stance | Potent women | Passive men | Pluralist perspective | Orphans | Emancipatory power of the imagination

The Planet of Junior Brown (1997)
Directed by Clement Virgo
Starring Lynn Whitfield, Martin Villafana, Sarah Polley, Rainbow Francks, Clark Johnson, Margot Kidder
Running time: 91 minutes
❦ ❦ ❦ ½

A gifted kid, Junior Brown (Villafanna), creates a world within himself (almost literally) to escape his painful reality. His mother (Whitfield) is a control freak in deep denial about Junior's absentee father and Junior is an outcast at school because he is obese. The only escape route is his music, but without a piano, the gifted classical pianist is forced to haunt the piano store — where he hopes to one day play the prize grand piano that sits in the middle of the showroom. Making his life a little more bearable is a community of street kids who create wild contraptions in abandoned buildings and a weekly visit to his mentally ill piano teacher — Mrs. Peebs (Kidder) — who has horrifying visions, but still hears the imaginary notes that Junior plays with such finesse.

This is a world that is separated into dreamers and realists. Junior travels quite fluidly between both worlds, but we're never really too sure if he's simply playing along, or losing himself in his own world. Virgo makes the most of the ambiguity and keeps the viewer hanging in for the eventual catharsis.

The film doesn't exactly end on a high note, but it does leave room for hope.

CANADIAN CHECKLIST: Outsider stance | Fragmented narrative structure | Pluralist perspective | Missing father | Emancipatory power of the imagination | Survivor guilt (one character feels responsible for a fire that killed his family)

Le Polygraphe (1996)

Directed by Robert Lepage

Starring Marie Brassard, Josée Deschenes, Patrick Goyette, Serge Denoncourt, James Hyndman, Peter Stormare, Jean Deschênes, Richard Fréchette, Maria de Medeiros

Running time: 91 minutes

❧ ❧ ❧ ❧

Based on Robert Lepage's stage play, this self-aware murder mystery of a movie opens with a man, Francois Tremblay (Goyette), taking a lie-detector test after his girlfriend is found murdered. In the next sequence we see a woman, Lucie Champagne (Brassard), audition for a part in a movie based on a real-life murder case. Halfway through the film, we discover that it's the same case — and the two people are part of a larger web of characters who all have some connection to the dead woman.

For instance, there is the chief medical examiner, an East Bloc exile, who dates Lucie after she nearly collapses in the Metro station. And there's the film crew, which doesn't really care about the truth as long as they have a good ending for their movie.

Lepage has the patience of a needlepointer as he crafts an intricate story about truth and deception, internal demons and real murderers, identity and exile, walled cities in the free world, love and hate and several other contradictory elements. He constructs the film in interwoven layers, crafting a story where truth emerges between the cracks, in the negative, silent space that separates each character from each other. While a bit of a challenge to piece together, *Le Polygraphe* leaves enough of clues to keep us interested without relying on pat devices like perfectly sympathetic characters and linear form.

CANADIAN CHECKLIST: Internal demons (note the final image in the film, a Russian doll within a doll ...) | Guilt | Camera awareness/self-reflexive | Missing people | Fractured identity | Fractured place (references to Berlin) | Language | Potent women | Separation of mind and body | Ambiguous ending

Porky's (1981)

Directed by Bob Clark

Starring Dan Monahan, Mark Herrier, Roger Wilson, Cyril O'Reilly, Kim Cattrall

Running time: 90 minutes

❧ ❧

From the director of *Black Christmas* (the slasher sorority movie starring Margot Kidder and Andrea Martin) comes *Porky's*, the most profitable Canadian film ever spun, with more than $11 million in box office receipts. I was one of the teenagers who paid money to watch this piece of trash titillation when it first came out, and if you're scratching your head about why this film achieved such phenomenal success, I'll tell you: they saturated the airwaves with sexy advertising and released it in theatres everywhere. When Friday night rolled around and we were looking for something to do, we headed down to the multiplex looking for moronic fun, and *Porky's* fit the bill.

One of the first teenage sex comedies I'd ever seen, *Porky's* was like watching a porno version of *Happy Days* — where Richie and the Fonz were real boys looking to get laid.

Set in Florida in the late 1950s, the movie is about a bunch of horny high school kids who drill holes in the wall of the girls' shower and try to get into Porky's, a legendary dive where a man can lose his virginity overnight. Booted out on their first attempt, the kids go to great lengths to get back at the slimy bar owner and the rest of the heavies, with uneven comic results.

A low note as far as content goes, *Porky's* was nonetheless a turning point in Canadian film because of its relatively high production values. No one thought it looked "Canadian," and back then, that was high praise indeed.

CANADIAN CHECKLIST:

Um ... uh ... well it's a genre film made for the mass market, so there aren't any real Canadianisms — but because it's still king of the box office, it's a Canadian classic.

Possible Worlds (2000)
Directed by Robert Lepage
Starring Tilda Swinton, Tom McCamus, Sean McCann, Gabriel Gascon, Rick Miller
Running time: 93 minutes
🍁 🍁 🍁 🍁

Based on the stage play by John Mighton, this English-language debut from Quebec director Robert Lepage is a complex meditation on the nature of experience and Cartesian philosophy. This movie constantly asks you how you know what you know — and is there any way of knowing whether this world is real, or just a figment of your imagination?

Opening with a tip of the hat to Hitchcockian mystery convention, *Possible Worlds* begins with a murder: a man named George Barber (played by Tom McCamus) has been found dead in his home — minus his brain.

As the police investigate the concrete surfaces for things like fingerprints and other tangible clues, Lepage takes us on a series of surreal voyages into George's past in an effort to explain what's happened. He shows us George in a variety of greyish-blue, fluid worlds contained by windows, skylights and minimalist glass bricks.

For the viewer, the connection between these "possible worlds" seems hard to grasp at times — but when we realize George is just as confused as we are, we can let go of the collective, sensory-based assumption called reality, and simply float along beside him.

It's not easy to figure out what's going on, but Lepage's inspired visuals tell you all you need to know on an intuitive level. All you really have to do is watch. The images will inform your subconscious and the answers will come.

CANADIAN CHECKLIST: Landscape bathed in blue light | Rugged terrain | Passive protagonist | Potent woman | Ambiguity | Identity questions | Missing item: brain, and sense of self | Linguistic elements

Project Grizzly (1996)
Directed by Peter Lynch
Documentary
Running time: 72 minutes
❦ ❦ ❦ ❦

Troy Hurtubise is a self-described "close-quarter bear researcher," who has one dream: coming face-to-face with the king of Canada's jungle, the endangered species with the six-inch claws, the grizzly bear. There's only one real problem, and that's safety. Grizzlies could maul Troy to pieces in mere seconds, so he comes up with a plan: he will build a bear-proof suit that will keep his body safe.

With big dreams and some money he's managed to save, Troy begins to build his bear suit. Director Lynch shows Troy labouring over his man-shaped contraption from a distance so we get the full, eerie effect of watching a man powered by obsession.

The best part is the testing sequences, where we watch Troy lowered into the path of a pickup truck, then hit head-on. Perfectly absurd at every turn, the irony of Troy's dream of communing with nature while packed into a kevlar-laced can is not lost on the filmmakers, who turn this bizarre story of passion into a metaphor for the modern Canadian condition.

CANADIAN CHECKLIST: Outsider stance | Internal demons | Irony/absurdity | Rooted in realism/documentary | Man seeking harmony with nature

Les Raquetteurs (1958)
Directed by Michel Brault and Gilles Groulx
Documentary
Running time: 15 minutes
❦ ❦ ❦ ❦ ❦

Snow, snowshoes, snowshoe queens and a beat-challenged brass band blend together in this short, wild and positively hilarious short that captures the essence of the Québécois — and in many ways, Canadian — psyche, as it shows a group of warm-hearted people in the midst of a frigid landscape.

Considered to be the film that started the tradition of *cinéma direct* (AKA *cinéma vérité*) in Quebec, *Les Raquetteurs* can also be seen as the starting point in a continuing revolution against institutional film in Canada as it abandoned objective documentary distance and mingled with the people. When it was made in early 1958, the film was considered a bit too revolutionary by Grant McLean, the director of production at the NFB. He demanded *Les Raquetteurs* be dismembered into stock shots, but more creative minds prevailed (thanks to the efforts of Unit B director Tom Daly and producer Guy Glover). The film now stands as testament to the strength and courage of Canada's film pioneers.

There is no formal narrative to speak of, but the film does have a central ordering premise and that is to document an international snowshoers convention in the city of Sherbrooke, Quebec. In one of the earlier sequences, we see the mayor address the American delegation on the street in French. He offers the leader a key to the city — "the nicest city in the country" — but from his befuddled expression it's clear that he doesn't understand a word.

The language barrier isn't the only familiar Canadian theme, there are others to be found in a close reading of this brief masterpiece, such as a healthy skepticism regarding institutions (as illustrated in a shot of someone mocking the snowshoe queens), a sense of being the voyeur (the camera roams the crowd and lingers on certain faces like some form of visual eavesdropping), and all-out wackiness (snowshoe racers wiping out, false starts, dogs barking at the feet of fleet-footed raquetteurs and one shot of a woman left behind at the starting line, throwing her hands in the air as if to say "no fair.")

It's best not to get too pedantic about it, because the real beauty of *Les Raquetteurs* is the way it denies contrivance and conceit, and simply shows us images of real people doing a variety of goofy, human things with a lot of heart.

CANADIAN CHECKLIST: Non-fiction/Realism | Language barrier | Snow-bound landscape | Division | Non-heroic (we see a lot of showshoers fall flat on their fannies)

The Red Violin (1998)

Directed by François Girard
Starring Samuel L. Jackson, Greta Scacchi, Jason Flemyng, Colm Feore, Don McKellar
Running time: 130 minutes
❧❧❧❧

Like Jane Campion's *The Piano* — which featured an aging Victorian keyboard as the voice box for a mute Holly Hunter — François Girard's *The Red Violin* features a musical instrument as the main protagonist. It's not easy to make an inanimate object the main plot vehicle, but Girard and McKellar invest so much love in the little wooden frame that we begin to feel for it as it makes its way through three centuries of history.

Crafted by a 17th-century Italian master as a loving tribute to his wife and unborn child, the red violin is a "perfect acoustic instrument" with an almost empathic ability to articulate feelings buried deep within us.

The film opens at a Montreal auction house where several interested parties are vying to take the instrument home. Intercutting the repeated scenes at the auction house with scenes from the violin's long journey, Girard connects the people in the room to the violin's past. One group of hopeful buyers represents a monastery where a small orphan boy forged a relationship with the instrument; another shows us a libidinous Victorian violinist whose passion for playing isn't limited to music, while another takes us to Revolutionary China, where all Western instruments and luxury items were condemned to the bonfires.

While almost all the chapters are moving short films, one in particular (the Pope chapter) is a jarring disaster that would have been somewhat funny if it hadn't been handled so earnestly. However, the fact that it leaves a black hole in the centre of the film didn't bug me too much. Every Canadian hero has a tragic flaw, just as every Canadian film seems to have a hole in its centre — even *The Red Violin*.

CANADIAN CHECKLIST: Multilingual (contains dialogue in Mandarin, English, French, German and Italian) | Ambiguous ending | Orphans | Missing mentors | Weird sex with metaphorical meaning | Mistaken identity | Dead babies

Roadkill AKA **Move or Die** (1989)
Directed by Bruce McDonald
Starring Valerie Buhagiar, Gerry Quigley, Larry Hudson, Bruce McDonald, Don McKellar, Shaun Bowring, Joey Ramone
Running time: 80 minutes
✤ ✤ ✤ ✤

Shot in grainy black-and-white, this satirical look at all things Canadian opens with a spoof of the Canadian Wildlife Service's ubiquitous "Hinterland Who's Who" film reels that featured 60-second vignettes on different animal species and a very melancholy flute line. The first thing we see is the furry face of a northern cottontail rabbit twitching his cute little bunny nose, followed by the ominous sound of screeching tires and the roar of a huge internal-combustion engine.

Valerie Buhagiar stars as Ramona, a lowly intern for a slimy, pony-tailed rock promoter. When the booker can't reach his band, *The Children of Paradise*, he sends Ramona out to find them in the wilds of northern Ontario. As Ramona begins her adventure along the Canadian Shield, she notes that the "trees are getting smaller and rocks are cropping up everywhere ... I have the feeling a different set of rules apply up here." The words prove prophetic.

Ramona ends up at a gas station and discovers the wayward band in their Winnebago. She befriends the director (played by McDonald himself), who says "I want to make a movie about real life." Soon, non-driver Ramona turns into a wild woman behind the wheel as she and a cast of kooky Canadians tear up the highway. The object of the band's quest is to find the missing lead singer, Matthew, who disappeared without a trace, but like all road movies — and trips into hearts of darkness — there is something much larger going on beneath the surface. All these characters are in the process of self-realization.

For Ramona, it's all about self-empowerment and learning to speak up for herself while for someone like Russell (McKellar), a wannabe serial killer, it's all about realizing his "American Dream" of being a wanted criminal.

Roadkill was the first film to flush the institutional mentality out of English-Canadian cinema and became the starting point in a continuing revelation of Canadian self.

CANADIAN CHECKLIST: There is something missing: Matthew, the lead singer | Canadian landscape — look for the Sudbury Nickel | Road movie to nowhere | Roadkill (dead animals are a favoured Canadian motif) | Potent woman protagonist | Comment about realism — "I want to make a movie about real life" | Canoe

rollercoaster (1999)

Directed by Scott Smith
Starring Brendan Fletcher, Kett Turton, Crystal Bublé, Sean Amsing, Brent Glenen, David Lovgren
Running time: 85 minutes
❦❦❦ ½

More than a visual metaphor for the stomach-churning adventure called "coming of age," *rollercoaster* is a film that constantly defies expectation — and in some of the most courageous ways.

The story begins as a bunch of teenagers break into an amusement park off-season. Some just want to get away from the group home. Others are looking to make the biggest statement of their short lives by killing themselves. Without resorting to earnest speeches about the depth of their personal despair, Smith lets us see the pain of pubescent alienation through the lens. He shows us a small group of kids returning to a barren playground, crawling around on aching bones of an aging roller coaster, all set against the bruised skies of a Vancouver winter. Everything feels claustrophonic. The looming North Shore mountains are black walls against the horizon, and even the amusement park itself is fenced in. No wonder these young people feel trapped.

However, we can't forget these young rebels climbed over the fence themselves. They have to take some responsibility for their actions, and that's what Smith's larger story is all about as the teens gradually come to accept their roles in the larger drama called life.

Highlighted by dialogue that could have been taped outside the 7-Eleven on a Saturday night — and amazing performances from the ensemble cast, particularly Brendan Fletcher's portrayal of the sexually confused Stick — *rollercoaster* unveils the insecurities of budding adulthood with enough tenderness and confidence to make us care about people who have a hard time just caring about themselves.

CANADIAN CHECKLIST: Internal demons | Self-destruction | Outsider stance/alienation | Gender confusion | Hostile environment | Empty landscape | Unwanted pregnancy | Missing people

Rude (1995)

Directed by Clement Virgo
Starring Maurice Dean Wint, Rachael Crawford, Clark Johnson, Richard Chevolleau, Melanie Nicholls-King
Running time: 89 minutes
Rating: ❦❦❦

Director Clement Virgo's debut feature uses frames with light and shadow to render a dramatic picture of life on the urban streets of Toronto. Several stories unfold at once in this highly stylized film that weaves life, death and rebirth into the same strand of celluloid. There is one voice that holds it all together, and it belongs to Rude, an all-night deejay who broadcasts over the city like a mother lion watching over her cubs.

Rude's voice filters through one urban "project" in particular, and Virgo sails past the front door with his camera to take us into the personal lives of different people. The main story focuses on a grafitti artist and former dealer who returns home from prison hoping to start a new life with his wife and son. Standing in the way are his old drug-dealing buddies, who appeal to his sense of community — and finally threaten his son in a bid to bring him back into the fold. Other plots deal with the diseases of the urban landscape: drugaddiction, child abandonment and relationships in crisis.

Though the subject matter is dark, Virgo finds beauty in every frame thanks to his deft hand behind the camera — as well as his faith in God. Finally, it is faith that turns *Rude* into an inspiring tale of perseverance and commitment. It is also faith that makes Virgo one of the few Canadian filmmakers able to embrace rebirth, as well as ambiguity, as part of the Canadian experience.

CANADIAN CHECKLIST: Potent women | Missing father | Wilderness in urban landscape | Fragmented narrative

Rupert's Land (1998)
Directed by Jonathan Tammuz
Starring Samuel West, Ian Tracey, George Wendt
Running time: 94 minutes
❧ ❧ ❧

In this collage of popular Canadian motifs, Vancouver-based filmmaker Jonathan Tammuz creates a wall of kitsch decoupage in this movie that features bits and pieces of road-to-nowhere themes, paternal identity crises, and requisite amounts of B.C. bud.

Rupert (West) is the Canadian-born outsider who returns home from Britain for the funeral of his father, Carl. Rupert is a pleasant fellow, but he's got a problem. Whether it's a chip on his shoulder or a cricket bat up his ass is hard to tell, but Rupert has some serious identity issues that stem from his dad's absence, and they all pour out as he and his half brother Dale (Ian Tracey) make their way to the service in Prince Rupert.

Dale is a fisherman with a gruff demeanour and a habit of getting into trouble. Rupert is a lawyer with a goody-goody streak bigger than a Boy Scout jamboree. They are, of course, spiritual twins — two lost boys just looking for a sense of inner harmony.

While Tammuz's film doesn't really explore any novel territory — and relies a little too heavily on linear genre contrivance — the actors punch a little depth into the landscape with subtle performances and one or two moments of genuine inspiration. Aided by some great lines, the film finds a charming, offbeat sense of humour that carries it over the rough spots — like my favourite, uttered by a First Nations' bartender after Rupert mistakenly drinks some of his magic mushroom tea and panics, asking if he's going to see foreign gods. "No," says the bartender. "Local mushrooms, local gods."

A nice movie that's easy to watch, *Rupert's Land* is no masterpiece, but it's entertaining and absolutely beautiful.

CANADIAN CHECKLIST: Missing father figure | Outsider stance | Road to nowhere | Brotherly opposites, twin imagery | Vast landscape dwarfs characters | Death

Sam & Me (1991)

Directed by Deepa Mehta
Starring Ranjit Chowdry, Peter Boretski, Om Puri, Heath Lamberts
Running time: 94 minutes
🍁🍁🍁 ½

Two outsiders find mutual respect and understanding in Deepa Mehta's fiction debut. Nikhil (Chowdry, who also wrote the script) is a young man who just moved from India to Canada, where he lives under his uncle's thumb in a small Toronto rooming house. He feels untethered and entirely without purpose until his uncle Chetan (Om Puri) gets him a job taking care of his boss' father, Sam (Boretski). The two clash at first glance. Sam is desperate to return to Israel and Nikhil is humiliated by his nursing duties.

When they realize they are both lonely, displaced and entirely misunderstood, they begin to form a deep friendship — an event that Mehta communicates with a shot of the two men standing naked in the rain. Sam's moments of delusion become fewer and soon, Nikhil doesn't even mind being called a "schwarze" (Yiddish for black boy).

For all their newfound friendship, however, things turn ugly when Sam's family begins to see Nikhil as an irresponsible immigrant, out to take advantage of their money and status. Things end on a down note, with Sam and Nikhil's frienship severed by circumstance, but somewhere in the deep recesses of Nikhil's personality, and his profound compassion, there is reason for hope — even if Mehta keeps it well below the surface.

CANADIAN CHECKLIST: Language differences | Immigrant as outsider | Outsider bonding with outsider | Resistance to assimilation | Ambiguous ending | Underdog; atypical heroes

Shivers AKA They Came From Within or The Parasite Murders (1975)

Directed by David Cronenberg
Starring Paul Hampton, Joe Silver, Lynn Lowry, Allan Migicovsky, Allan Migicovsky, Susan Petrie
Running time: 89 minutes
🍁🍁🍁🍁

Right up there with *Mon Oncle Antoine* and *Goin' Down the Road*, *Shivers* ranks among the first order of Canadian classics. While the movie caused a big rotten stink when it opened in the not-so sexually liberated 1970s, a quarter century later we can love it for the passionately rendered cerebral shlock it is without feeling any guilt. I saw this movie for the first time in film school — an institution for gosh sakes — so clearly, I'm not the only one who thinks *Shivers* has been validated as an important Canadian oeuvre now that we can get past the sexual content.

It's still cheese, but what a wonderful fromage! What creepy intensity! What a stupid-looking blob! And still, it works. Set against the cool, blue skies of Montreal in a sterile concrete apartment complex, *Shivers* shows us what happens to the alienated apartment dwellers when they are besieged by parasites that turn them into sex maniacs. Released after a scientist kills a woman and dissolves her organs down the drain, the parasite moves through the pipes — and crawls into whatever orifice it can find on the other side. Once penetrated, the victims become unstoppable sex machines. Now, how's that for sticking it to the uptight Canadian psyche?

A smart and well-thought-out metaphor on urban alienation and the modern denial of death, *Shivers* goes deeper than you'd think.

CANADIAN CHECKLIST: Outsider stance | Weird sex | Sex and death | Internalized demon | Focus on natural vs. human-made landscape/outside-inside | Missing connections | Ambiguous ending

The Silent Partner (1978)
Directed by Daryl Duke
Starring Elliot Gould, Christopher Plummer, Susannah York, Celine Lomez, Michael Kirby, Ken Pogue, John Candy
Running time: 103 minutes
🍁🍁🍁

Elliot Gould plays Miles, a mild-mannered bank teller who outsmarts a bank robber (Christopher Plummer) in this rare example of a successful Canadian genre film. Miles gets the cash, while the baddie gets the blame. But how long can Miles outmanoeuver the evil thief? Longer than you might think, as every character deviates from expectation.

The Silent Partner actually has more than a few tricks up its cheesy little tax-shelter sleeve. Plummer uses his steely eyes to maximum evil effect, and Susannah York settles into the role of the nice teller next door with frumpy aplomb. Even Gould manages to pump a little zest into the nerdy part of Miles by turning him into an unabashed egotist.

Few of the characters are all that likeable — not even York, whose Julie Andrews act begins to wear — but the suspense factor and the smart script make sure we can watch their misdeeds with giddy excitement. At the very least, you can see what Toronto looked like when everyone wore wide-lapel suits and smoked Players.

A genuine piece of Canadian kitsch that holds up to the test of time plotwise — if not fashion-wise — *The Silent Partner* is a fossil worth digging up.

CANADIAN CHECKLIST: Canadian place names | Canadian money! | John Candy

Speaking Parts (1989)

Directed by Atom Egoyan
Starring Gabrielle Rose, Michael McManus, Arsinée Khanjian
Running time: 93 minutes
🍁🍁🍁 ½

The film begins in two worlds: a sort of video mausoleum where Clara (Rose) pushes buttons to conjure the image of her dead brother, and the hotel where Lance (McManus) works as a chambermaid between acting jobs — and where his supervisor, Lisa (Khanjian), ogles his every move.

Androgynous Lance prefers to keep to himself, but when he hears one of the hotel guests, Clara, is a screenwriter looking to cast the male lead in a movie, Lance leaves his résumé in her room. Clara is intrigued, and she's somehow reminded of her dearly departed brother every time she looks Lance in the eye. The two begin a bizarre relationship as Lisa becomes increasingly obsessed with Lance — renting every movie he's ever appeared in, even if it was only for a split second. As the pieces of the story begin to fit together, we discover that Clara has written a story about the sacrifice her own brother made to keep her alive. It's clearly a heart-wrenching tale that has a lot of personal meaning for Clara, but it's not really her story anymore: it was bought by a group of talking-head producer-types, who have different ideas about how the story should unfold.

In a way, the viewer becomes an intricate part of this process because just as Clara, Lance and Lisa become spectators to each other's lives, so does the viewer become a spectator to theirs. An endless series of reflecting mirrors and photographic devices, *Speaking Parts* pulls us into the cool clicking gears of the film process where the only humanity to be found is what we choose to see.

CANADIAN CHECKLIST: Film on film imagery | Outsider stance | Negative space | Missing people | Twin imagery | Identity issues | Fragmented narrative | Commentary on American-style reality-TV

The Suburbanators (1995)

Directed by Gary Burns
Starring Joel McNichol, Stephen Spender, Stewart Burdett, Jacob Banigan, Rogy Masri, Jihad Traya, Ahmad Taha
Running time: 87 minutes
🍁🍁🍁

It's a road movie with nowhere to go. A perfectly Canadian take on the romantic highway genre, *The Suburbanators* takes place mostly in crappy cars and buses against the flat, generic and universally ugly strip malls of suburban Calgary. Different groups of men are on their own specific quests. Al and Bob are looking to score some pot in their wood-panelled K-car. Eric (Jacob Banigan) and Carl (Stewart Burdett) are also looking to score some pot, but they don't have a car — they bum rides and take the bus.

At the beginning of the film, Al and Bob are voyeurs to an incident between Eric, Carl and a woman who ends up with a burnt shoe after bumping into the belligerent Carl. For Al and Bob, this is the highlight of their day — and they recount it to others along the way. For Eric and Carl, it's the beginning of what turns out to be a pretty bad, but also very revealing, day. Carl admits to being incredibly jealous of other people's success, while Eric — the most empathetic guy in the movie — almost finds a new awareness of the world that might take him beyond the suburbs. Not that anything too dramatic happens in these banal encounters with the lowest common denominator. The movie is a statement about what doesn't happen, more than anything remotely affirmative.

While these two teams of buddies are doing their no-thing, another group of men — these ones Arabic — are on a quest of their own: to retrieve their musical equipment from an apartment. Forced to flee the snoopy neighbour every time they try to break in, the three are left to ride the bus and roam the city. We don't know what they are saying (unless you speak Arabic), but you get the distinct impression they are exchanging the same empty platitudes as the others.

What sets this effort apart from other films in the slacker genre is that here, there are no devices such as guns or violence (except a hilarious salvo of pebbles) to give the film a steep dramatic arc. Everything happens at baseline, and so it truly turns into a study of the pedestrian — in every possible sense. The dialogue rings true (we get great lines like "my car is my penis"), the acting is frighteningly seamless, and the characters are rendered as complete idiots. And yet, for all their foibles, they are likeable. Their passive approach to life is redeemed by their sincerity, and their shallowness of mind is offset by a gentleness of spirit.

CANADIAN CHECKLIST: Pluralism | Empty landscape | Road movie to nowhere | Passive heroes

Such a Long Journey (1999)
Directed by Sturla Gunnarsson
Starring Roshan Seth, Soni Razdan, Om Puri, Naseeruddin Shah
Running time: 113 minutes
❦❦❦ ½

Based on the novel by Rohinton Mistry, this film tells the story of a simple man who watches his life crash into a cascade of shards when he is asked to perform an extraordinary task. Gustad Noble (Roshan Seth) has worked hard all his life in an effort to send his son to a good college and crank up the family's caste standing. When his son refuses to go to college, Gustad becomes rigid and controlling, which only makes his loyal wife Dilnavaz recoil in disgust.

On the same bumpy track as his own family, Gustad's country is also on the verge of chaos as India prepares for war with Pakistan. With few places left to turn for stability, Gustad looks to the solace of his work routine — but even there, trouble awaits when an old friend asks Gustad to do him a favour. Suddenly, all the constants in Gustad's life have been turned into variables, forcing him to question his fundamental assumptions about life, love and country.

A complicated story that finds focus through Gustad's confused eyes, *Such a Long Journey* weaves several layers of plot into a rich, emotional tapestry that may be confusing at times, but comes together through Gustad's character, who never forgets the importance of love. Have the patience to pull it together, and the film will stick with you — regardless of how long, or how short, your journey may be.

CANADIAN CHECKLIST: Outsider stance | Fragmented narrative | Father-son tension | Identity issues | Passive protagonist | Potent women | Political tensions echoed in family drama

Sunshine (1999)

Directed by Istvàn Szabo
Starring Ralph Fiennes, Miriam Margolyes, Jennifer Ehle, Rosemary Harris, Rachel Weisz, Molly Parker, Deborah Kara Unger
Running time: 179 minutes
🍁🍁🍁🍁

A sprawling cautionary tale about the dangers of assimilation, this Robert Lantos-Istvan Szabo collaboration clocks in around the three-hour mark and covers an entire century of human history.

Centred on the Sonnenscheins, a proud family of Hungarian Jews, the film opens in 1900 with the story of Ignatz, an ambitious young lawyer who converts to Christianity in an attempt to ascend to the upper ranks of Austro-Hungarian society.

Of course, it seemed like a good idea at the time, but as we watch the lives of Ignatz' progeny unfold — all played by English actor Ralph Fiennes — we soon realize that the price for assimilation, at least mentally, is often higher than simple, straightforward oppression.

The Sonnenscheins are beautiful, proud people who have been pushed into a cage of their own creation, because even though they are now Christians on paper, the State still see them as Jews — a fact that has predictably tragic consequences with Hitler's rise to power.

CANADIAN CHECKLIST: Survivor guilt | Outsider stance | Pluralist perspective | Missing fathers | Identity crisis

Surfacing (1971)

Directed by Claude Jutra
Starring Kathleen Beller, Diane Bigelow, Joseph Bottoms, R. H. Thompson.
Running time: 89 minutes
🍁

Based on the Margaret Atwood novel of the same name, *Surfacing* is a prime example of a bad movie based on a good book. The movie was in trouble before the cameras even started rolling, when producer Beryl Fox was forced to hire Claude Jutra days before the production was about to begin filming because director Eric Till ditched the project at the last minute. The script was deemed problematic, but with no time to rewrite, Jutra had to work with what he was given: bad dialogue, bad scenes and bad acting.

The story itself managed to survive the ordeal, however, and for that reason, it's still an important piece of the Canadian film puzzle as it highlights the importance of women in the Canadian tradition and the subtle refusal of the hero myth in general.

Kathleen Beller plays Kate, a woman who travels to Ontario cottage country with three friends to look for her missing father. As time wears on, the movie devolves into a strange premonition of *Blair Witch 2*, as the young people go a little loopy and begin playing head games with each other. There are scenes of dancing around dead herons, filming humiliating sex games, and a nasty encounter with a few redneck hunters.

Long on melodrama, the movie features a lot of screaming without any redeeming quiet moments. Considering the book itself is written in first person as a stream-of-consciousness encounter with the dark, wild side of human nature, it's a testament to Jutra's skills as a director that he managed to pull the project off at all — and make a tangible motion picture from an internal landscape.

CANADIAN CHECKLIST: Impotent men and potent women | Survival guilt | Suggestion of Electra fantasy | Personal alienation | Sex and death are packaged together | Oppressive landscape | What's missing? Father

Suspicious River (2000)
Directed by Lynne Stopkewich
Starring Molly Parker, Callum Keith Rennie, Mary Kate Welsh, Joel Bissonnette, Deanna Milligan, Sarah Jane Redmond
Running time: 92 minutes
🍁 🍁 🍁

Lynne Stopkewich returns to the dark side of sexuality in her second feature, which explores a motel clerk's fascination with prostitution. Leila Murray (Parker) is just another gal in a small town. She has a boyfriend. She works at the local motel and she knows almost everyone within spitting distance. Is it any wonder she's drawn to the geeky salesmen and truck drivers who drift through town?

Addicted to the rush of her double life, Leila begins to lose control and finds herself facing increasingly dangerous situations. Eventually, the encounters turn violent, but she can't stop herself, and as the plot unfolds, we begin to understand why.

Stopkewich attempts to balance two narrative layers at the same time, disguising a complicated story of emotional longing disguised as complete detachment. This is not an easy challenge, because both layers work in opposition to each other and fragment the point of view.

Based on the story by Laura Kasischke, *Suspicious River* is the kind of work that would seem to defy a filmed approach. The fact that it works as well as it does is a testament to Stopkewich's talent for navigating the lumps beneath the carpet, and Parker's ability to look alive and dead in the same frame.

CANADIAN CHECKLIST: Outsider stance | Weird sex | Strong woman | Survivor guilt | Missing parent

The Sweet Hereafter (1997)

Directed by Atom Egoyan
Starring Ian Holm, Sarah Polley, Tom McCamus, Bruce Greenwood, Arsinée Khanjian, Gabrielle Rose, Earl Pastko, Stephanie Morgenstern, Maury Chaykin.
Running time: 112 minutes
❦❦❦❦❦

A film that touches on the essence of love by throwing us into the abyss of loss, *The Sweet Hereafter* marks the apex of the English-Canadian film tradition as it navigates the empty space left in the wake of tragedy with a gentle but unsentimental eye.

Based on the novel by Russell Banks, *The Sweet Hereafter* focuses on a school bus tragedy in a small town, and the big city lawyer who drives into town looking to point the finger of blame. Holm plays Mitchell Stephens, a slimy litigator who makes a living off other people's pain with his empty promise of justice. Heartbroken and eager to make sense of what's happened, the tightly knit community lets him in, but it is Mitchell — not some outside villain — who is finally pushed into an emotional confession.

As the parents and the survivors struggle to carry on in this changed world, Mitchell finds himself haunted by his own emotional baggage. His drug-addicted daughter is constantly calling him on his cell phone, asking him for money. At first, Mitchell is cool. Afraid to throw any more hope and love into the black hole of her addiction, but desperate to revisit the days when he would have done anything to save her life, Mitchell is trapped in a cage of his own creation — and the flood of emotion is beginning to seep through the walls.

Using images, music and landscape to articulate the things that words simply cannot express, Egoyan pushes the audience into a cool, quiet world where love bleeds into emptiness, and we, the viewer can do little but watch — and weep — for the broken souls left behind.

One of those rare movies where performance, place and story all come together without excessive directorial force or pretense, *The Sweet Hereafer* is quite simply my idea of a perfect film.

CANADIAN CHECKLIST: Internal demons | Outsider stance | Silence does all the talking | Empty landscape | Fractured narrative | Broken time | Missing people/dead children | Weird/dysfunctional sex

Tales From the Gimli Hospital (1988)

Directed by Guy Maddin
Starring Kyle McCulloch, Michael Gottli, Angela Heck
Running time: 72 minutes
❦ ❦ ❦ ❦

Set on the shores of Lake Winnipeg in the old Icelandic fishing village of Gimli, *Tales from the Gimli Hospital* is a story based on the actual tragedies that beset a group of 19th-century settlers in Manitoba. They left a life of starvation and plague back home for a new life in the New World, only to find themselves starving during a Canadian winter. Those who didn't die of starvation suffered an equally gruesome death from smallpox, making for a perfectly Canadian colonial experience.

The story of two men, the fisher Einnar and the ever-flirtatious Gunnar, Maddin's film takes us inside primitive hospital life where everyone competes for the attention of the pretty nursing staff. Since Einnar and Gunnar lie next to one another, they begin telling stories about their past lives — only to realize they share past baggage. The film climaxes in a butt-pinching fight, but offers a surreal sense of eternal peace at the end as clouds and angels fuse into grainy grey blobs.

While the story hardly suggests comic potential, in the hands of Winnipeg-based filmmaker Guy Maddin, the tragic becomes a gateway to another plane. Light bends, spaces shift, objects blur — reality as a whole fragments into a splatter of black-and-white grains. In this world, even the ugliest of physical events — death and disease — are somehow suspended to a point where we can almost laugh. I laughed a lot at this movie, and so have many other Maddin maniacs, which is why *Tales From Gimli Hospital* was one of Canada's first bona fide cult movies, spawning fans and websites the world over.

CANADIAN CHECKLIST: Outsider stance | Death, disease, victims | Survivor guilt | Fragmented narrative | Escape via imagination | Magic realism | Hostile landscape | Missing people | Twin imagery (Gunnar and Einnar) | Weird sex

Thirty Two Short Films About Glenn Gould (1993)

Directed by François Girard
Starring Colm Feore
Running time: 94 minutes
❦ ❦ ❦ ❦

Opening with a shot of Glenn Gould in the middle of pure white snowdrifts, this perfectly Canadian movie takes us through the life of the legendary Canadian pianist. Neither a straight biopic, nor a documentary, nor a dramatic recreation of his life, the film mirrors the subject: through a series of short films — or movements — with recurring themes and shifting emphases.

As a result, the movie has a truly impressionist feel as it captures the emergence of an artist from the wilds of Canada who went on to become a world famous musician for his interpretations of the work of Bach — recordings of which were sent into the far-reaches of outer space on the Voyager probes.

The non-linear design and fragmented narrative structure were inspired by Gould's interpretation of Bach's *Goldberg Variations*, but these elements also articulate the essence of Gould's creative gift for piecing together different, often contrapuntal, strains and finding a sense of harmony. The film also goes some way toward explaining why Gould left the concert stage at the height of his career.

One particularly memorable scene involves a shot of Gould, masterfully played by veteran thespian Colm Feore, sitting in a greasy truck stop listening to the many conversations around him and finding a sense of rhythm, counterpoint and structure in the cacophony. Also noteworthy is a fragment of Norman McLaren's NFB animated piece, *Spheres*, which visually echoes the same sense of dynamic tension as Gould's playing.

Only Woody Allen's *Sweet and Low Down* has been able to capture the musician's condition with as much conviction, but no other film has done a better job of articulating the mystery of the artistic experience. *Thirty Two Short Films About Glenn Gould* is a standout in Canadian film and a key piece in the puzzle of Canadian creativity.

CANADIAN CHECKLIST: Odd protagonist | Documentary bits | Non-heroic perspective | Shots of snow | The CBC | Norman McLaren animation | Non-linear design

Today is a Good Day: Remembering Chief Dan George (1999)
Directed by Loretta Todd
Documentary
Running time: 48 minutes
❦ ❦ ❦ ½

Loretta Todd takes a documentary look at the most famous First Nations, and in a way most famous Canadian, movie star of the 20th century: North Vancouver son, Chief Dan George. From his early beginnings as a performer doing variety shows across Western Canada to his career-defining role in *Little Big Man*, Todd shows us the real person behind Hollywood's Aboriginal mask.

In doing so, she subtly pulls apart the entire American hero myth that pitted "cowboys against Indians" by showing us a man who refused to fit the mould. Featuring interviews with Dan George's family and working peers, such as Arthur Penn and Dustin Hoffman, Todd mingles celebrity and family, showing us a man who could accommodate both without losing his balance.

CANADIAN CHECKLIST: First Nations' perspective | Split world | Human scale | Different take on hero myth

The Top of His Head (1989)

Directed by Peter Mettler
Starring Christie MacFadyen, Stephen Ouimette, Gary Reineke, John Paul Young
Running time: 110 minutes
🍁🍁🍁 ½

Opening the film with a surreal sequence of a woman giving birth to a monkey, who just happens to have a chip implanted in his head, Mettler makes it clear — right off the top — that this is not going to be your average dose of escapism. In fact, the whole story only filters through in retrospect, because there is no immediately apparent plot, just cryptic clues that suggest something deeper is taking place.

Gus Victor (Ouimette) is a satellite-dish salesman. One day, he experiences an ability to see things from a different perspective — "as though he were God looking down on us." He can't really make head nor tail of what he sees, and nor can we. There is no context, no continuity, no skeleton to hang it on. In a way, Gus has become a human satellite dish, picking up stray signals.

When Gus' visions begin to focus on just one woman, a performance artist named Lucy, he is forced to abandon his sense of reality, and open himself up. He must learn to listen and Lucy (perhaps an allusion to the early hominid life form discovered by Donald Johanson in Ethopia? Or maybe just the Lucy that everyone loves?), is there to help him along on this spiritual excavation.

However, the police derail his train of thought (note train images), when he is mistaken for a pirate-broadcasting terrorist. The latter section of the movie plays out like a classic chase sequence, but only in parts, because Gus continues to have these surreal encounters — including a rather moving one with a woman named Yolanda who is about to lose her sight and spends her last sighted days taking pictures of the things she loves.

Innovative and intellectually explorative, *Top of His Head* is a film that espouses the McLuhenesque idea that the medium is the message, and in this case, the message is to open your mind for the best reception.

CANADIAN CHECKLIST: Outsider stance | Internalized identity | Fractured narrative | Subversion of genre | Experimental threads | Film on film/photographic imagery | Potent women | Passive protagonist

Top of the Food Chain (1999)

Directed by John Paizs
Starring Campbell Scott, Fiona Loewi, Tom Everett Scott
Running time: 99 minutes
❦ ❦ ❦

A great example of how Canadians look at genre films, *The Top of the Food Chain* turns the foundation of action-adventure movies — Cold War sci-fi — into a slow, absurd odyssey into the depths of ignorance.

Campbell Scott plays a moronic atomic scientist named Dr. Karel Lamonte, who relocates to the remote town of Exceptional Vista around the same time as the townspeople begin to vanish. There is something rather odd about this pipe-smoking professor type, but Paizs paints everyone in this film with the same coat of kookiness, so it's hard to tell who's the real oddball in this nut town (well, it was a nut town before the nut factory closed).

When the citizens of Exceptional Vista begin to turn up like masticated props from *Jaws*, everyone turns to the mysterious Dr. Lamonte to put an end to the gruesome riddle. There's only one snag: Dr. Lamonte is an idiot, therefore throwing into question humanity's right to sit at the top of the food chain. Perhaps more intelligent life forms from outer space see planet Earth as little more than a drive-thru window in the strip mall of the universe? Could we be the galaxy's favourite meat patty? Who knows?

To find out, you'll have to watch this cute and completely inoffensive, send-up of the post-war B-movie from Winnipegger John Paizs (*Crime Wave*), which has cult film tattooed into its celluloid skin.

CANADIAN CHECKLIST: Subversion of American genre | Outsider stance | Internal demons | Mocks institution/academics | Potent women | Passive men | Weird sex

Videodrome (1982)

Directed by David Cronenberg
Starring James Woods, Sonja Smits, Debbie Harry, Peter Dvorsky
Running time: 88 minutes
❦ ❦ ❦ ❦

One of my favourite horror movies, *Videodrome* beams you to the dark side of television with prophetic zeal. Spun with the manic flare of a psychotic selling street sermons, *Videodrome* is a cautionary tale about a man who thought he controlled TV, when in the end, it controls him.

James Woods plays Max Renn, a cable programmer who regularly pirates airwaves looking for new ideas. While scanning the band, he spies a truly weird sex channel called *Videodrome* — a station that shoves sex and death into the same sentence. Sitting there in the shabby control room with his equally creepy technician, Max feels immune. But *Videodrome* is no regular TV station, it's a mind-and-body-altering broadcast signal which is a downright killer. Max is titil-lated by the snuff stuff, and when his girlfriend gets involved with the creators of the broadcasat, he's hooked — body and soul. Or, as the tagline tells us: "First it controlled her mind, then it destroyed her body ... Long live the new flesh!"

By the end of the film, Max's entire body has been transformed into a giant — oh dear mother of God! — VCR. Oozing magnetic tape and hard plastic cases, Max is forced to accept a different type of physical reality — and therefore a different worldview.

Surreal and seedy, *Videodrome* says everything you ever needed to hear about the supremely evil powers of the boob-tube. They say Cronenberg is a chauvenist, but just because the station has a female face and voice, and happens to be evil incarnate, doesn't mean the real villain couldn't be a man. Behind every Cronenberg femme fatale, one usually finds the face of a man (see Roy Scheider in *Naked Lunch*) — or two (see Jeremy Irons in *Dead Ringers*). If you take the horror with a sense of humour, Cronenberg will never fail to tickle — just watch out for the claws.

CANADIAN CHECKLIST: Horror and humour fuse | Voyeurism | Guilt | Outsider stance | Internalized demons | Potent women | Impotent men | Separation of mind and body | Subversive commentary on entertainment industry

waydowntown (2000)
Directed by Gary Burns.
Starring Fabrizio Filippo, Don McKellar, Marya Delver, Gordon Currie, Jennifer Clement, Tobias Godson
Running time: 82 minutes
❧ ❧ ❧ ❧

Set against the backdrop of Calgary's "plus 15" skyway system, *waydowntown* is the story of a group of young office workers who bet a month's salary on who can stay inside the longest. As the junior executives gradually find themselves becoming more and more paranoid as a result of their voluntary entrapment within the environment they find most oppressive, Tom (Fabrizio Filippo), our narrator, finds himself lost in daydreams. At times, he ponders how superheroes can pick up whole cities, then magically replace them in the same place without reconnecting the pipes. At other times, he watches passively as the world goes by — connecting only briefly, and with bad results, with other mall habitués.

Filmed on digital cameras, this third feature from Alberta director Gary Burns has a low-budget look, good tunes and a confident, slacker sensibility that lends it a genuine hip factor seldom seen in Canadian film outside the likes of Bruce McDonald movies and William Shatner's wardrobe.

CANADIAN CHECKLIST: Outsider stance | Thematic use of landscape | Internal/external demons | Passive protagonist | Fragmented narrative | Emancipatory power of the imagination | Potent women (check out that office manager ... yikes!) | Victimhood; lack of control (not even McKellar gets to kill himself properly)

Zero Patience (1993)

Directed by John Greyson

Starring John Robinson, Normand Fauteux, Dianne Heatherington, Richard Keens-Douglas, Bernard Behrens

Running time: 95 minutes

🍁🍁 ½

Focusing on what was referred to in the late 1980s and early 1990s as the "AIDS epidemic," this second feature from Toronto-based director John Greyson tells the fictionalized story of Zero, the mythical gay French-Canadian flight attendant who was dubbed "Patient Zero" for supposedly introducing AIDS to North America.

Moving through several socially quarantined areas to tackle taboos such as homosexuality and anal sex via the narrator, a character study of Victorian Sir Richard Burton, Greyson manages to make a strong point about our apparently natural reflex to lay blame for a problem instead of simply dealing with the reality of a given disease.

Because he keeps his tongue firmly planted in cheek by co-opting an old Hollywood musical format, Greyson's bold-type political statements thankfully steer clear of the sledgehammer, but the script isn't entirely strong enough to balance the heavy social baggage with the light, musical tone of the movie itself.

For all its inconsistencies, there's enough raw passion and creative courage (there are talking anuses and shower boys with boners in this movie) behind the lens to make *Zero Patience* one of the most memorable explorations of AIDS, and the whole "Typhoid Mary" mentality, to ever hit the screen.

CANADIAN CHECKLIST: Outsider stance | Fragmented narrative | Broken time | Alternative approach to an issue of the day | Subversion of an American genre — in this case, the Golden Age musical | Formal tension: videotaped interviews intercut with production numbers

Notes

Introduction

1. Michael J. Wolf, *The Entertainment Economy*, p. 4

Chapter 1: Rooted in Realism

1. Gary Evans, *In the National Interest*, p. 4
2. Ibid. p. 4
3. Ibid. p. 68
4. Peter Harcourt, *Sight and Sound*, p. 37
5. Bruce Elder, *Canadian Film Reader*, p. 139
6. Evans, p. 78
7. Evans, p. 73
8. Interview by author.
9. David Clandfield, *Take Two*, p. 113
10. Evans, xi

Chapter 2: Survivors & Surviving

1. Martin Knelman, *Toronto Life*, 1982

Chapter 3: First Takes

1. Lee Clark Mitchell, *Westerns*, p. 135
2. Carl Jung, *Man and His Symbols*, p. 112–113
3. Ibid. p. 112–113
4. Interview by author.
5. Interview by author.
6. Margaret Atwood, *Survival*, p. 102

Chapter 4: The Tangled Garden

1. Peter Harcourt, *The Canadian Encyclopedia*, p. 765
2. Anne Newlands, *The Group of Seven and Tom Thomson: An Introduction*, p. 34
3. Ibid. p. 32.
4. Bruce Grenville, "The People's Choice," Exhibition booklet.
5. I found a great website about Highway 61 that tells you what you can see on the way. For more information, visit http://www.frontiernet.net
6. Margaret Atwood, *Survival*, p. 49
7. Ibid. p. 54

Chapter 5: Probing the Negative

1. Review: "Profound Virtue in *Felicia*'s Silences," by the author. *Vancouver Sun*, November 19, 1999, p. C3.
2. The Glenn Gould liner notes to the 1956 Bach Goldberg, Columbia Masterworks ML 5060 (1956) Bach: *The Goldberg Variations* — Glenn Gould, Piano. Can be viewed at (http://www.rjgeib.com/music/Top-Ten/gould.html). "Passacaille." Music terminology. Consisting of slow (usually) variations over a ground bass line or a reiterated harmonic scheme. In rock 'n' roll, this would be called the bass line.
3. McKellar made these comments about *Thirty Two Short Films About Glenn Gould* as part of a Praxis Centre for Screenwriters event, sponsored by Simon Fraser University at the Chan Centre, hosted by the author. April 22, 2001.
4. Interview by author.
5. Interview by author.
6. Interview by author. (Fragments of this interview appeared in the *Vancouver Sun*, October 3, 1998, under the headline "Lepage Risks Humour in the October Crisis." p. D1.)
7. Interview by author.
8. Interview by author. (Fragments of this interview appeared in the *Vancouver Sun*, October 23, 1998, under the headline "Man of Mystery." p. C1)

Chapter 6: Sex & the Great Repression

1. Interview by author, 1999.
2. Vito Russo, *The Celluloid Closet*, pp. 5–6
3. Interview by author, 2000.
4. Interview by author, 1993.
5. Maheu, "L'oedipe coloniale," *Parti Pris*, 1964. This article is cited at length in Bill Marshall's book *Quebec National Cinema*. I heard about it for the first time as a result of reading Marshall's text, so for any readers with an academic bent, I highly recommend it as supplementary reading.
6. Carl Jung, *Man and His Symbols*, p. 168

7. Kay Armatage, *Gendering the Nation*, "Nell Shipman, A Case for Heroic Femininity," p. 17-38. (For those seeking a separate look at women in Canadian film, the book is a wonderful academic anthology on the subject.)
8. Ibid. p. 35
9. Interview by author.
10. Margaret Atwood, *Survival*. pp. 170-172
11. Interview by author.
12. Atom Egoyan, *Speaking Parts*, from the introduction to the screenplay.
13. Interview by author. Fragments of this interview appeared in the *Vancouver Sun*, in the article "Harkema's Girl Trouble Led to Insight," October 5, 1999, p. C5.
14. Jung, *Man and His Symbols*, p. 178
15. Ibid. p. 191
16. Ibid. p. 169

Chapter 7: Crashing Into the Language Barrier
1. Bill Marshall, *Quebec Nationalist Cinema*, p. 185
2. Northrop Frye, *The Bush Garden*, p. iii
3. Interview by author.
4. Odile Tremblay, *Le Devoir*, June 10, 2000.
5. Marshall, p. 290

Chapter 8: Pluralist Perspectives
1. Interview by author.
2. Interview by author. Elements appeared in the *Vancouver Sun*, September 4, 1998, p. C1.
3. Interview by author.

Chapter 9: The Incredible Weight of Being
1. Interview by author.
2. Voice-over clip from the film *Confederation Park*, by Bill Brown.
3. Ingmar Bergman, *The Magic Lantern*, p. 90
4. Ibid. p. 94
5. René Descartes, "Discourse on the Method of Rightly Conducting the Reason, and Seeking Truth in Sciences," from *The World's Great Thinkers*, p. 183.
6. Sean Scoffield, *David Cronenberg's eXistenZ: A Graphic Novel*, p. 95
7. Bruce Kirkland, *Toronto Sun*.
8. Atom Egoyan, *Speaking Parts*, p. 45
9. Anne Baldassari, *Picasso Working on Paper*, p. 97
10. Atom Egoyan, *Speaking Parts*, p. 47

Chapter 10: The Leap of faith
1. A scene fragment from Bruce McDonald and Don McKellar's *Roadkill*.
2. The name "Keystone" now refers to a completely different Canadian company, Keystone Pictures, which created the *Air Bud* and *Most Valuable Primate* franchise.
3. Peter Morris, *The Canadian Encyclopedia*.
4. Marke Andrews, *Vancouver Sun*, September 26, 1995, p. C4
5. Trevor Lautens, *Vancouver Sun*, September 22, 1990, p. D19
6. Author, *Vancouver Sun*, September 23, 1999, p. D19
7. *Saturday Night*, Nov. 18, 2000, p. 39
8. Interview by author.
9. Interview by author.

Bibliography

Abbott, Jennifer, ed. *Making Video "In:" The Contested Ground of Alternative Video on the West Coast.* Vancouver: Video In Studios, 2000.

Adams, Michael. *Sex in the Snow: Canadian Social Values at the End of the Millennium.* Toronto: Penguin, 1997.

Andrews, Marke. "Pierre Berton: Times of His Life." *Vancouver Sun,* Tuesday, September 26, 1995, p. C4

Arden, Roy. "After Photography." *Canadian Art,* 17.4 (2000): 48–56.

Arden, Roy. "Kennedy Bradshaw: Vernacular Photography and Realism." *Canadian Art,* 15.4 (1998): 38-42.

Armatage, Kay, Kass Banning, Brenda Longfellow and Janine Marchessault, eds. *Gendering the Nation: Canadian Women's Cinema.* Toronto: University of Toronto Press, 1999.

Atwood, Margaret. *Survival: A Thematic Guide to Canadian Literature.* Toronto: Anansi, 1972.

Baldassari, Anne. *Picasso Working on Paper.* Trans. George Collins. London: Merrell, 2000.

Beattie, Eleanor. *A Handbook of Canadian Film.* Toronto: Peter Martin Associates Ltd, 1973.

Bergman, Ingmar. *The Magic Lantern: An Autobiography.* Trans. Joan Tate. New York: Penguin Books, 1987.

Bleiler, David, ed. *TLA Film and Video Guide.* New York: St. Martin's Griffin, 1999.

Changing Focus: The Future for Women in the Canadian Film and Television Industry, Toronto Women in Film and Television. Toronto: University of Toronto Press, 1991.

Charest, Rémy. *Robert Lepage: Quelques zones de liberté.* Québec: L'instant même-Ex Machina, 1995

Charest, Rémy. *Robert Lepage: Connecting Flights.* Toronto: Knopf, 1998.

Chomsky, Noam. *Language and Politics.* C. P. Otero, ed. Montreal, Black Rose Books, 1988.

Clark, Andrew. "Mister Saturday Night." *Saturday Night Magazine,* Nov. 18, 2000, pp. 32-44.

Cole, Janis and Holly Dale. *Calling the Shots: Profiles of Women Filmmakers.* Kingston: Quarry Press, 1993.

Cook, David A. *A History of Narrative Film.* New York: W.W. Norton & Co, 1981.

Cronenberg, David.,*eXistenZ: A Graphic Novel.* Toronto: Key Porter, 1999.

Descartes, René. "Discourse on the Method," *The World's Great Thinkers,* New York: Random House, 1947.

Douglas, Ann. *The Complete Idiot's Guide to Canadian History.* Toronto: Prentice-Hall, 1997.

Egoyan, Atom. *Speaking Parts.* Toronto: Coach House Press, 1993.

Evans, Gary. *In the National Interest: A Chronicle of the National Film Board from 1949 to 1989.* Toronto: University of Toronto Press, 1991.

Falsetto, Mario. *Personal Visions: Conversations with Contemporary Film Directors.* Los Angeles: Silman-James Press, 2000.

Feldman, Seth, ed. *Take Two: A Tribute to Film in Canada.* Toronto: Irwin, 1984.

Feldman, Seth and Joyce Nelson. eds. *Canadian Film Reader.* Toronto: Peter Martin Associates, 1977.

Ferguson, Will. *Why I Hate Canadians.* Vancouver: Douglas and McIntyre Ltd, 1997.

Foster, Charles. *Stardust and Shadows: Canadians in Early Hollywood.* Toronto: Dundurn Press, 2000.

Frye, Northrop. *The Bush Garden: Essays on the Canadian Imagination.* Toronto: Anansi, 1971.

Frye, Northrop. *The Great Code.* New York: Harcourt Brace Jovanovich, 1982.

Griffin, Nancy and Kim Masters. *Hit & Run: How Jon Peters and Peter Guber Took Sony for a Ride in Hollywood.* New York: Touchstone, 1996.

Harcourt, Peter. "The Innocent Eye: An Aspect of the Work of the National Film Board of Canada." *Sight and Sound,* 34.1 (1964-65)

Hammond, Paul, ed. *The Shadow & Its Shadow: Surrealist Writings on the Cinema.* 3rd ed. San Francisco: City Lights Books, 2000.

Henighan, Tom. *The Maclean's Companion to Arts and Culture.* Vancouver: Raincoast Books, 2000.

Honour, Hugh. *Romanticism.* New York: Harper & Row, 1979.

Hubbard, Jaimie. *Public Screening: The Battle for Cineplex Odeon.* Toronto: Lester & Orpen Dennys Ltd, 1990.

Johnson, Brian D. *Brave Films, Wild Nights: 25 Years of Festival Fever.* Toronto: Random House, 2000.

Jones, Kent. "The Cinema of Atom Egoyan." *Film Comment*, 34.1 (1998) p. 32-39.

Jung, Carl G. *Man and His Symbols*. New York: Doubleday & Co., 1964.

Kirkland, Bruce. The Canadian Movie Guide @ http://www.sunmedia.ca/JamMovies

Knelman, Martin. *This is Where We Came In: The Career and Character of Canadian Film*. Toronto: McClelland and Stewart, 1977.

Kolomeychuk, Terry, ed. *Donald Brittain: Never the Ordinary Way*. Winnipeg: National Film Board, 1991.

Lammerlich, Yvonne. "Tracking Athabasca." *Canadian Art*, 18.1. (2001) pp. 48-53.

Lautens, Trevor. "Depressing Leftist Apologia From Berton." *The Vancouver Sun*, Saturday, September 22, 1990, p. D19

Lefevre, Karen Burke. *Invention as a Social Act*. Carbondale: Southern Illinois University Press, 1987.

Maheu, Pierre. "L'oedipe coloniale," *Parti Pris* 9-11(1964) pp. 19-29.

Marsh, James H. ed. *The Canadian Encyclopedia* 1988 ed. Edmonton: Hurtig.

Marshall, Bill. *Quebec Nationalist Cinema*. Montreal and Kingston: McGill-Queen's University Press, 2001.

Mitchell, Lee Clark. *Westerns: Making the Man in Fiction and in Film*. Chicago: The University of Chicago Press, 1996.

Monaco, James. *The Encyclopedia of Film*. New York: Perigee, 1991.

Monk, Katherine. "Profound Virtue in Felicia's Silences." *Vancouver Sun*. Friday, November 19, 1999, C3.

Morris, Peter. *The Film Companion*. Toronto: Irwin, 1984.

Murray, Joan. *The Best of Contemporary Canadian Art*. Edmonton: Hurtig, 1987.

Myers, Hugh Bingham. *The Quebec Revolution*. Montreal: Harvest House, 1964.

Newlands, Anne. *The Group of Seven and Tom Thomson: An Introduction*. Willowdale: Firefly Books, 1995.

Newman, Peter C. *The Canadian Revolution: From Deference to Defiance*. Toronto: Penguin Books, 1995.

Noble, Kimberley. "Why Gerry Schwartz Needs Air Canada." Maclean's, Oct. 11, 1999, 46-54.

Nowell-Smith, Geoffrey, ed. *The Oxford History of World Cinema*. Oxford: Oxford University Press, 1996.

Olive, David. *Canada Inside Out: How We See Ourselves, How Others See Us*. Toronto: Doubleday, 1996.

People's Choice, The: Komar and Melamid, Canada's Most Wanted and Unwanted Paintings. Exhibition pamphlet. The Dunlop Art Gallery, Regina Public Library, The Vancouver Art Gallery,. 2001.

Pevere, Geoff and Greig Dymond. *Mondo Canuck*. Scarborough: Prentice Hall, 1996.

Pevere, Geoff. "An Outsider's Aesthetic: Contemporary Independent Film in Canada." *The Independent*, June 1987, pp. 13-17.

Posner, Michael. *Canadian Dreams: The Making and Marketing of Independent Films*. Vancouver: Douglas & McIntyre, 1993.

Ranney, Austin. *Channels of Power: The Impact of Television on American Politics*. New York: Basic Books, 1983.

Reid, Dennis. *Krieghoff: Images of Canada*. Vancouver: Douglas & McIntyre with the Art Gallery of Ontario, 1999.

Rose, Barbara Wade. *Budge: The Story of Canada's Movie Maverick*. Toronto: ECW Press, 1998.

Ryan, Michael and Douglas Kellner. *Camera Politica: The Politics and Ideology of Contemporary Hollywood Film*. Bloomington: University of Indiana Press, 1988.

Salzman, Gregory. "Regarding Landscape." *Canadian Art*, 17.3. (2000) pp. 61-74.

Scott, Jay. *Great Scott! The Best of Jay Scott's Movie Reviews*. Toronto: McClelland & Stewart, 1994.

Smith, Denis. *Bleeding Hearts Bleeding Country; Canada and the Quebec Crisis*. Edmonton: M. G. Hurtig Ltd, 1971.

Russo, Vito. *The Celluloid Closet: Homosexuality in the Movies*, Rev. ed. New York: Harper & Row, 1987.

The Strange Objects of David Cronenberg's Desire. An Exhibition of Drawings, Objects and Creatures from the Films of David Cronenberg, catalogue. Tokyo: Seibu, 1993

Topolovich, Maria. *And the Genie Goes To ... Celebrating 50 Years of the Canadian Film Awards*. Toronto: Stoddart, 2000.

Tremblay, Odile. "Tourner en anglais au Québec." *Le Devoir*, June 10, 2000, p. B1.

Unterberger, Amy L., ed. *The St. James Women Filmmakers Encyclopedia*. Detroit: Visible Ink Press, 1999.

"We Are Canadian: Maclean's-Global Poll." *Maclean's*, Dec. 25, 2000, pp. 26-54.

White, Morton, ed. *The Age of Analysis*. New York: Penguin, 1983.

Wilson, Peter. "Michael Snow Pretty Pleased." *Vancouver Sun*. Thursday, November 17, 1994, p. C1.

Who's Who in Canadian Film and Television, 1999 ed. An annual guide published by the Academy of Candian Cinema and Television. Toronto: Global Press.

Wolf, Michael J. *The Entertainment Economy*. New York: Times Books, 1999.

Acknowledgements

Film critics tend to live in small, dark rooms with sticky floors and giant screens. We don't get out much. As a result, we don't often fraternize with the real people who actually go out and pay to watch films. We sit inside our own four walls and make judgements far from the madding crowd. I always thought this was the best way to be a critic — to be untainted by popular opinion — but I was wrong. I never knew just how out of touch I was until I met Derek Fairbridge, a Canadian film lover who, when standing in a long lineup outside Vancouver's Ridge Theatre to watch *Felicia's Journey*, had an epiphany. Derek saw hundreds of people just like him eagerly waiting to get in to watch a domestic movie and, being the book editor he is, pitched a book about Canadian film to his colleagues at Raincoast Books. They approved. Then he sent me an e-mail wondering if I'd be interested in authoring such a project. I get lots of e-mail. Mostly, it's people asking for something, pitching something, ranting about something — but never in my life has anyone ever asked me to share a dream. Derek asked me to turn his dream into words, and in doing so, reminded me that film resonates far beyond the four walls of a sticky-floored movie theatre. Film speaks to the soul in each of us, creates invisible bonds of common experience and helps us understand who we are. Without Derek, this book would not exist and I'd be just another alienated movie critic, closeting a deep — but tragically unhip — love for Canadian film.

Derek's passion and commitment to this project have been my beacon in times of creative chaos. His editing talent has made this book better, and his love of Canadian film has given me great hope that maybe, just maybe, there are thousands of others out there just like us: proud Canadians just waiting to revel in the tangled beauty of our own reflections. Thank you, Derek, for asking me to write this book, but thank you more for renewing my faith in this incredible, unique and fragile experiment in nationhood called Canada. I Believe. So you rock ... like totally, eh?

I'd also like to thank everyone else at Raincoast Books who showed faith in a nervous, first-time author and greeted me with warmth and respect: Lynn Henry, Michelle Benjamin and particularly Ana Torres, who had the tenacity to round up all the artwork contained herein. Without you, this would be little more than a big lump of grey pages. Thanks for helping me bring this monster to life.

To my editors at the *Vancouver Sun* — particularly Carol Toller — thank you for giving me the time and flexibility to make this project happen. I had no idea what was involved in writing anything quite so large, so thanks for saying "yes" every time I'd show up with a panicked glare in the office and ask for more time off on short notice. I could not have done this without your understanding. Also, I'd like to thank my colleagues at the *Vancouver Sun* for being supportive, particularly Marke Andrews, my fellow film critic, who patiently covered for me during my absence — and whose one-man dramatic recreation of the SCTV *Goin' Down the Road* sketch deserves a Genie. You're a total Gord, Marke.

Beyond the internal support network, I owe thanks to all the people I've met covering film in this country and abroad — from fellow writers, to the many filmmakers and actors. I feel very fortunate to have enjoyed such stimulating exchanges about Canadian film with so many well-spoken people. This book is essentially ten years of professional pop culture exposure compacted into a few hundred pages. Whether you are mentioned here by name or not (I wish I could have included everyone), your experiences have shaped this book because they have shaped me.

None of these dialogues could have taken place without the help of all the unsung publicists out there who bring people together for professional purposes. So thanks to Susan Smythe, Carrie Wolfe, Andrea Grau, Mark Slone, Bonne Smith, Stacey Holland, Anna Maria Muccilli, Mary-Catherine Snelgrove, Ken MacIntyre, John Bain, Sandy Silver, Brent Calvert, Moira Keigher, Virginia Kelly, Nancy Yu, Denny Alexander, Jennifer Otter, Cindy Gordon, Leri Davies, Ian Caddell, Angela Heck, Anita Wong, Helen Yagi, Alexa Deans, Hussein Amarshi, Joelle Medina, Bill Vigars, Maureen Verkaar, and every other person whose ever booked an interview for me over the years. You are the people who make it into a dialogue — you also make the job a lot easier. I'd especially like to thank Judy Holm, Mary-Pat Gleeson and Jennifer Rideout for being extra nice when I knew so little.

For all the festival fun, I'd like to thank the staffs of Toronto International Film Festival, the Vancouver International Film Festival, the Victoria Independent Film and Video Festival, the Seattle Film Festival and the Sundance Film Festival. For all the wine and cheese chat about Canadian film, let me say thanks to Judy Jackson-Rink, Brigitte Prochaska and Maria Topolovich at the Academy of Canadian Cinema and Television. Also, a nod of appreciation to the people at the Pacific Cinémathéque (and cinematheques around the country) who program the Canadian films the commercial houses don't. Without you, many of these films would not be seen at all.

Because my bio on the CBC website turned out to be one of the deciding factors in who got the call, I am forever indebted to *Definitely Not the Opera* producer Bill Smith for hiring me (and Mia Stainsby for recommending me), as well as all the people and techs who make it the best eight minutes of my week: Nora Young, Doug Holmes, John Wendells, Don Irvine and everyone else in the 'Peg, Toronto and Vancouver studios. Merci bien.

Thanks to my family and friends, for being patient and supportive while I floated off in my own spaceship for a year. I'd also like to thank my friend Leonard Schein for all of his personal support and professional assistance in helping me navigate the contractual world, as well as the wacky world of Canadian film distribution. I want to thank Susan Carroll, my first reader. To all the guys who let me play hockey with them. I know I'm no Hayley Wickenheiser, but thanks for letting me feel the fire of the ice — and be a part of the great Canadian game.

Last, but certainly not least, I'd like to extend a huge honkin' thank you to Atom Egoyan, who not only took the time out of a very busy schedule to write the foreword, but who's been something of a mentor to me and the Canadian film world at large for the past decade. Your continuing generosity of time and spirit is an inspiration — not to mention a beautiful reminder of what it means to be Canadian. Thank you for everything, especially for the art that inspires us all.

Index

About the Author

Born in Montreal in 1965, Katherine Monk moved to the Vancouver in 1984 to study English at the University of British Columbia. After completing her degree in 1988, she was elected city editor of *The Ubyssey* student newspaper and returned to academic life as a post-graduate film student at UBC. In 1990, she was hired at the *Vancouver Sun* as a summer staffer. After a few stints in the world of low-budget filmmaking, Monk returned to the *Sun*, where she has worked as a news writer, copy editor, production editor, political columnist and pop music critic. She has been nominated for a Western Magazine Award for arts reporting. She currently writes movie reviews and entertainment features for the *Sun*, in addition to being a contributor to CBC Radio One's *Definitely Not the Opera*.

NATASHA MORIC